Psychology of Sustainability and Sustainable Development in Organizations

This volume answers calls for improving sustainability and sustainable development in organizations from a psychological point of view. It offers a range of perspectives on the current research in the psychology of sustainability and sustainable development to highlight effective ways of improving well-being and healthy sustainable development in organizations.

Section 1 introduces the concept of the psychology of sustainability and sustainable development as well as macro topics of related issues in organizations. Section 2 focuses on themes traditionally recognized in organizational psychology literature, such as performance, negotiation, leadership, resistance to change, innovation, and digital transformation. Section 3 presents variables to enhance sustainability and sustainable development in organizations and considers levels of prevention. Topics include humor awareness as a primary prevention resource in organizations, intrapreneurial self-capital as an individual preventative strength, compassion within organizations, perfectionism as an inhibitor in organizational contexts, and job crafting from individual to collaborative to organizational, meaningfulness and sustainable careers.

With a clear psychological focus on the topic of leading sustainability efforts, this book will be of great interest to students and academics who want to learn more about corporate sustainability. It is also a useful resource for business executives, team leaders and managers.

Annamaria Di Fabio is Full Professor of Work and Organizational Psychology at The University of Florence, Italy, and an elected member of the Board of Directors of the International Association of Applied Psychology (IAAP).

Sir Cary L. Cooper is 50th Anniversary Professor of Organizational Psychology and Health at the ALLIANCE Manchester Business School, Manchester, UK, and Chair of the National Forum for Health & Wellbeing at Work. He was knighted by the Queen for contributions to the social science.

Current Issues in Work and Organizational Psychology

Series Editor: Cary L. Cooper

Current Issues in Work and Organizational Psychology is a series of edited books that reflect the state-of-the-art areas of current and emerging interest in the psychological study of employees, workplaces and organizations.

Each volume is tightly focused on a particular topic and consists of seven to ten chapters contributed by international experts. The editors of individual volumes are leading figures in their areas and provide an introductory overview.

Example topics include: digital media at work, work and the family, workaholism, modern job design, positive occupational health and individualised deals.

Psychology of Sustainability and Sustainable Development in Organizations
Edited by Annamaria Di Fabio and Cary L. Cooper

Burnout While Working: Lessons from Pandemic and Beyond
Edited by Michael P. Leiter and Cary L. Cooper

Occupational Health and Wellbeing: Challenges and Opportunities in Theory and Practice
Edited by Andrew Kinder, Rick Hughes and Cary L. Cooper

Flexible Work: Designing Our Healthier Future Lives
Edited by Sarah H. Norgate & Cary L. Cooper

Current Issues in Work and Organizational Psychology
Edited by Cary L. Cooper

Organizational Change: Psychological Effects and Strategies for Coping
Edited by Maria Vakola and Paraskevas Petrou

For more information about this series, please visit: https://www.routledge.com/Current-Issues-in-Work-and-Organizational-Psychology/book-series/CURRENTISSUES

Psychology of Sustainability and Sustainable Development in Organizations

Edited by
Annamaria Di Fabio and
Cary L. Cooper

LONDON AND NEW YORK

Designed cover image: © Colin Anderson Productions pty ltd/Getty Images

First published 2024
by Routledge
4 Park Square, Milton Park, Abingdon, Oxon OX14 4RN

and by Routledge
605 Third Avenue, New York, NY 10158

Routledge is an imprint of the Taylor & Francis Group, an informa business

British Library Cataloguing-in-Publication Data
A catalogue record for this book is available from the British Library

Library of Congress Cataloging-in-Publication Data
Names: Di Fabio, Annamaria, editor. | Cooper, Cary L., editor.
Title: Psychology of sustainability and sustainable development in organizations / edited by Annamaria Di Fabio and Cary L. Cooper.
Description: Abingdon, Oxon ; New York, NY : Routledge, 2024. | Series: Current issues in work and organizational psychology | Includes bibliographical references and index. |
Identifiers: LCCN 2023012437 (print) | LCCN 2023012438 (ebook) | ISBN 9781032079363 (paperback) | ISBN 9781032079387 (hardback) | ISBN 9781003212157 (ebook)
Subjects: LCSH: Organizational behavior. | Sustainability--Psychological aspects. | Sustainable development--Psychological aspects. | Organizational change.
Classification: LCC HD58.7 .P797 2024 (print) | LCC HD58.7 (ebook) | DDC 302.35--dc23/eng/20230322
LC record available at https://lccn.loc.gov/2023012437
LC ebook record available at https://lccn.loc.gov/2023012438

ISBN: 978-1-032-07938-7 (hbk)
ISBN: 978-1-032-07936-3 (pbk)
ISBN: 978-1-003-21215-7 (ebk)

DOI: 10.4324/9781003212157

Typeset in Times New Roman
by Taylor & Francis Books

Contents

Illustrations

Figures

Tables

Contributors

Neal M. Ashkanasy, UQ Business School, The University of Queensland, Australia.

Aneesh Banerjee, Bayes Business School, City, University of London, UK.

Marijana Baric, Anglia Ruskin University, UK.

Ajay Bhalla, Bayes Business School, City, University of London, UK.

Stuart C. Carr, UNESCO Chair on Sustainable Livelihoods, Massey University, New Zealand.

Cary L. Cooper, Alliance Manchester Business School, University of Manchester, UK.

Jo da Silva, Arup, UK.

Annamaria Di Fabio, University of Florence, Italy.

Adrian Furnham, University College London, UK.

James Graham, Norwich Business School, University of East Anglia, UK.

Viki Harvey, Norwich Business School, University of East Anglia, UK.

Darrin Hodgetts, Massey University, New Zealand.

Veronica Hopner, Massey University, New Zealand.

Maureen E. Kenny, Boston College, USA.

Pita King, Massey University, New Zealand.

Ana Laguía, Universidad Nacional de Educación a Distancia, UNED, Madrid, Spain.

Joseph Lampel, Manchester Business School, University of Manchester, UK.

Chloe Lau, University of Western Ontario, Canada.

Jona Leka, University College London, UK.

James H. Liu, Massey University, New Zealand.

Duncan Maguire, Norwich Business School, University of East Anglia, UK.

Molefe Maleka, Tshwane University of Technology, Pretoria, South Africa.

Georgia Marunic, University of Florence, Italy.

Ines Meyer, University of Cape Town, South Africa.

George Michaelides, Norwich Business School, University of East Anglia, UK.

Juan A. Moriano, Universidad Nacional de Educación a Distancia, UNED, Madrid, Spain.

Rachel Nayani, Norwich Business School, University of East Anglia, UK.

Minh Hieu Nguyen, School of Psychology, Massey University, New Zealand/ Hanoi University, Vietnam.

Thomas A. Norton, Arup, UK.

José María Peiró, University of Valencia, Spain.

Johan Potgieter, Massey University, New Zealand.

Marc A. Rosen, University of Ontario Institute of Technology, Canada.

Willibald Ruch, University of Zürich, Switzerland.

Donald H. Saklofske, University of Western Ontario, Canada.

Mahima Saxena, University of Nebraska at Omaha, USA.

Martin M. Smith, University of British Columbia, Vancouver, Canada.

Jean-François Stich, ICN Business School, France.

Andrea Svicher, University of Florence, Italy.

Charles L. Tchagnéno, Université Bourgogne Franche-Comté, Besancon, France.

Gabriela Topa, Universidad Nacional de Educación a Distancia, UNED, Madrid, Spain.

Olga Tregaskis, Norwich Business School, University of East Anglia, UK.

David Watson, Norwich Business School, University of East Anglia, UK.

Foreword

E. Kevin Kelloway, PhD

Notions of sustainability and sustainable development appear to be far removed from the topics typically considered in the psychology curriculum. I suspect that many of us see such ideas as being the purview of environmental science or government policy – and only tangentially related to the topics, issues and methods that are the focus of research psychologists. Indeed, the ultimate goal of sustainability – to "preserve the planet for the future and to promote human well-being" (Di Fabio & Rosen, 2018, p. 3) – may seem too lofty and "fuzzy" for researchers focused on more immediate practical problems that characterize much psychological research.

As this volume attests, nothing could be further from the truth. Di Fabio and Cooper have brought together an impressive list of authors who develop – and in many ways define – the psychology of sustainability and sustainable development. In doing so, they draw links between sustainability and traditional topics in organizational research (e.g., leadership) as well as point out new areas of inquiry.

Well-being at work – a burgeoning area of research in organizational psychology research – is positioned at the centre of this emerging field. As the sustainability goals of the United Nations (2018) illustrate, there is no sustainability without health. At the same time, a focus on sustainability requires a new focus on how employment structures (e.g., precarious employment) and the nature of work (e.g., decent work) contribute to individual well-being.

From this base, it is a comparatively small step to see how traditional areas of research in organizations can be applied to issues of sustainability. Leadership, employee ownership and changing cultures are all considered within the context of sustainability – building important bridges between "traditional" organizational behavior/psychology topics and sustainability. I hazard a guess that both our understanding of these topics as well as our understanding of sustainability benefit from this cross-fertilization across fields.

Finally, the chapter authors offer important insights into how psychology can be applied as a mechanism of primary prevention in organizations. In doing so, we are led to see how organizations can implement sustainability. Whether it is through building a supportive e-mail culture, focusing on humour in organizations, addressing issues of perfectionism or implementing job-crafting solutions, the various chapters offer practical and evidence-based strategies for enhancing organizations and implementing a culture of sustainability in organizations.

Di Fabio and Cooper have set themselves a challenging task – to define a psychology of sustainability and sustainable development that is both conceptually rich and theoretically grounded. Have they completed their task? Arguably, no. In effect, they set out to define a new field of inquiry within psychology. That task is not – and perhaps cannot be – completed. However, this volume makes important connections to existing research in psychology and sets the broad parameters within which psychological researchers can come to grips with issues of sustainability and sustainable development.

This is an important work. I have found it almost impossible to consider the contributions without asking "But, what about … ??" and "Have you thought about … ??". This is how a field develops – by stimulating researchers to ask new and more complex questions. In this sense Di Fabio and Cooper have succeeded in their task. Researchers will continue to expand on and develop the ideas presented in this volume and, in doing so, will develop a psychology of sustainability and sustainable development that builds on the work of this volume. As such, Di Fabio and Cooper have also introduced a new goal for psychological research – to preserve the planet for the future and to promote human well-being. A worthy goal indeed.

References

Di Fabio, A., & Rosen, M. A. (2018). Opening the Black Box of Psychological Processes in the Science of Sustainable Development: A New Frontier. *European Journal of Sustainable Development Research*, 2(4), 47. https://doi.org/10.20897/ejosdr/3933.

Harris, J. M. (2003). Sustainability and sustainable development. *International Society for Ecological Economics*, 1(1), 1–12.

United Nations. (2018). *About the Sustainable Development Goals.* https://www.un.org/sustainabledevelopment/sustainable-development-goals.

Section 1

Conceptual Frameworks and Themes

1 The Psychology of Sustainability and Sustainable Development and Wellbeing in Organizations

Annamaria Di Fabio and Cary L. Cooper

Wellbeing at Work: Promoting an Applicative Culture of Workplace Wellbeing

Wellbeing at work is important both for workforce wellbeing and health as well as for productivity and organizational health (Johnson et al., 2018; Robertson & Cooper, 2010).

Wellbeing at work deserves careful consideration (Hesketh & Cooper, 2019), even more so in the current post-COVID environment (Blustein, 2019). Distinguishing between hedonic and eudaimonic wellbeing (Ryan & Deci, 2001), hedonic wellbeing refers to happiness or pleasure, whereas eudaimonic wellbeing is considered the purposeful side of wellbeing. When studying wellbeing, it is also important to distinguish between psychological, physiological, societal, and financial wellbeing (Hesketh & Cooper, 2019). In the psychology of sustainability and sustainable development, psychological wellbeing is considered crucial, and it also emerges as the main theme of the work by Hesketh & Cooper (2019), where it is defined in terms of "how we think, process, behave and respond to others" (p. 28). In their work, a breadth of other aspects of wellbeing are also considered: physiological wellbeing, in terms of being free from harm or physical illnesses; societal wellbeing, in terms of societal wealth as well as friendships and relationships outside of the working environment; and financial wellbeing, which is a critical aspect that needs attention in the modern age of technology and consumerism, particularly since finances can be tied to other areas of wellbeing. The current era can be described through the acronym VUCA (volatility, uncertainty, complexity, and ambiguity), which refers to the characteristics of the contemporary environment (Casey, 2014), including adequate consideration of pay, the ageing workforce, the introduction of new technologies, and remote working in the workplace, with its both positive and negative effects.

In relation to wellbeing, the concept of discretionary effort introduced by Hesketh, Cooper, and Ivy (2017) turns out to be a key concept: discretionary effort is the amount of work people do beyond that for which they are paid, and it could be considered an expression of meaning and purpose at work. Hesketh and Cooper (2019), giving prominence to all these facets of

DOI: 10.4324/9781003212157-2

complexity, emphasized the value of planning an effective wellbeing strategy for business success. In particular, they suggest paying attention to leadership, resilience, and bullying to sustain a culture of wellbeing at work.

Leadership can make a fundamental contribution to enhancing the culture of wellbeing at work (Hesketh & Cooper, 2019). The focus is on transformational leadership (Bass, 1985; Burns, 1978) in relation to the promotion of wellbeing at work. Transformational leadership includes four components (Bass, 1985): idealized influence, inspirational motivation, intellectual stimulation, and individualized consideration. In the model by Bass (1985), transformational leadership exists side by side with transactional leadership, which is essentially characterised by an exchange between leader and followers. The transactional leadership style could lead to competitive workplace behaviours that do not contribute to generating a spirit of wellbeing and sustainability; therefore, this leadership style may be appropriate only in limited circumstances. Thus, a transformational leadership style seems more appropriate for sustaining wellbeing and sustainable development in organizations.

Leadership is a fundamental ingredient in organizations and should be carefully taken into consideration, including adequate training to equip and support this essential organizational role (Hesketh & Cooper, 2019). When the VUCA environment and discretionary effort are considered, the important contribution that leadership makes to organizational productivity and success is understandable. On the one hand, it is widely recognized that positive leadership behaviours make a positive contribution to wellbeing; and, on the other hand, wellbeing offers a lens through which it is possible to understand the complexity of leadership, which makes it a useful instrument for managing work in a way that favours workers and creates the right environment. A right environment includes both the physical environment and the psychological environment in which workers "can connect their own meaning and purpose in life to what they are doing in the workplace. An environment exists where employees feel connected; they identify with the company or brand and feel energized in their commitment towards it" (Hesketh & Cooper, 2019, p. 53). The authors, recognizing the great value of meaning and purpose at work, underline that meaning at work regards self-fulfilment through work and the perception that we can contribute to the wider good of the whole society through our working efforts; purpose at work involves the identity, values, beliefs, and ethics of workers, which push the passions, wants, and needs of workers.

In the described framework, another key aspect of wellbeing is personal resilience, the ability to cope with adversity that plays an essential role in dealing with stressful situations at work. Focusing on personal resilience, it is possible to underline two aspects: the first is the ability to cope with the challenges of everyday life; the second is having the reserves to face traumatic events that happen. Having "high levels of personal resilience can be a lifesaver" (Hesketh & Cooper, 2019, p. 85). Because resilience can be increased through training, it is fundamental to improve it to enhance wellbeing based on the authors' suggestions.

Another key facet of wellbeing involves paying attention to bullying (Hesketh & Cooper, 2019). On the one hand, leaders have the responsibility to ensure that they do not personally act in a bullying or threatening manner; and, on the other hand, leaders should guarantee that their employees do not engage in bullying acts in the workplace. Furthermore, they must also recognize and consider the subjectivity of bullying, which is often underestimated or unrecognized.

It is of great importance to promote an applicative culture of workplace wellbeing, which requires paying attention to problems and pitfalls that are an integral part of the complex environment (Hesketh & Cooper, 2019). Promoting an applicative culture of workplace wellbeing means having a strategy characterized by positivity, meaning, and purpose as well as setting goals that are realistic, realizable, and effectively communicated to workers to ensure they are aware of the goals to be reached. It is also suggested that workplaces implement training programmes focused on enhancing wellbeing, and they should give greater attention to the evaluation of training programmes' effectiveness. Training programmes need to consider all aspects of wellbeing (physiological, sociological, psychological, and financial), with a specific focus on increasing positive relationships between leaders and employees, which in turn could also favour worker engagement. Engagement is connected to wellbeing, and effective communication is a critical aspect of engagement. Improving communication as much as possible is an important ingredient for supporting wellbeing. Promoting resilience also promotes an applicative culture of workplace wellbeing. Since resilience can be increased through training, it is fundamental to implement resilience training in the workplace to enhance wellbeing at work.

Turning to problems and pitfalls, Hesketh and Cooper (2019) underline that it is not simple to implement a wellbeing strategy in the workplace, therefore it is essential to be centered on how to avoid errors during the implementation of approaches to promote wellbeing at work. First, it is fundamental to focus on the wellbeing strategy to be implemented and not get distracted by new ideas that might steal attention away. Second, mindset (Dweck, 2006) is critical, and maintaining an open mindset is important because the world is complex, uncertain, and ever changing. Third, it is important to use mistakes as learning and growth opportunities and not blame others if plans don't go as they should. An approach of managing by metric – that is, "if you can measure it, you can manage it" (Hesketh & Cooper, 2019, p. 107) – is not advised because it can be a source of stress and can threaten the wellbeing of workers. Making an analogy with sport, in sport activities you train to be the best you can be in the future when you compete, and this is perceived as right. However, when acting in a daily working reality, the definition of objectives can be important to have positive results, but these objectives must be realistic and sustainable (Hesketh & Cooper, 2019).

When facing the issue of problems and pitfalls, we have to deal with some concepts (Hesketh & Cooper, 2019): flow, culture, change readiness, and stigma. Flow (Csikszentmihalyi, 2013), in terms of having meaning and purpose at work, is considered a crucial aspect of wellbeing, while at the same time it refers to an optimal psychological experience that brings high productivity and performance at work. Organizational culture (Schein, 2010) is an essential element for wellbeing at work because a wellbeing approach needs to be situated within the context of a specific work environment. Hesketh and Cooper (2019) also remind us of the importance of change readiness, because change is one of the major stressors within working contexts, therefore it is essential to be prepared for changes and to be aware of the consequences that changes could have on workers. A final concept Hesketh and Cooper (2019) ask to be considered is stigma regarding mental health. It is essential to promote a culture that does not stigmatize mental health and that enhances kindness and compassion towards employees experiencing difficulties.

Particular attention should also be paid to monitoring and evaluating processes that are crucial aspects of organizational life (Hesketh & Cooper, 2019). First, it is necessary to establish clear and achievable goals, thus goal setting is a crucial element for evaluation and monitoring. Second, vision, mission, values, and ethics should be considered. Vision represents the dream of an organization – the aspirational plan. Mission is a more descriptive statement and includes how the organization wishes to realize its vision. Values need to be aligned with the vision and mission, and they are compromised if workers do not adhere to them. Ethics considers what is right and what is wrong, and it is important that organizations have strong ethics. It is essential that wellbeing is rooted in all these aspects, and all aspects need monitoring and evaluation to determine whether they are communicated to the workforce and whether the workforce is adhering to them.

Monitoring and evaluation draw attention to the issue of measurement. First, it is important to identify what we want to measure, having clarity about what it is we want to know. In this regard, key concepts in organizations are effectiveness, efficiency, productivity, and performance, but it is important not to lose sight of the fact that they need to be monitored and evaluated jointly with wellbeing. If workers perceive greater wellbeing, they are more likely to have higher productivity and performance. In terms of evaluation, it could be both external and internal. Evaluation needs to be carried out regularly, particularly when changes and innovations are implemented. Furthermore, it is obligatory to carry out evaluations, especially when new programmes of work are started, that include the wellbeing of workers.

Sustaining and fostering a workplace culture of wellbeing also involves consideration of useful tools and existing legislation. Hesketh and Cooper (2019) propose different tools. Wellbeing toolkits can be created for and adapted to every organizational context as well as different approaches to wellbeing. Wellbeing toolkits should not be too general, they should be based on good practice, and they should explain how they align with the specific organizational context. Other tools include exercises. Organizational exercises are useful for obtaining an overview of the organizational context under analysis in order to individuate resources and develop opportunities, future objectives, and exigencies in relation to wellbeing. Similarly, team exercises are useful for gathering quality feedback on wellbeing initiatives and other workplace projects included in the implemented wellbeing strategy. Finally, individual exercises can be used to look at workers' meaning and purpose in life, consider their unicity, and find common ground to implement the organization's overall wellbeing strategy. In addition, it is essential to identify and understand the legal framework in which a specific organization operates, which can depend on the organization's geographical location(s), pertinent jurisdiction(s), and the size of the organization. A variety of legislation needs to be considered in relation to wellbeing: for example, data collection and storage, health and safety legislation, and working-time directives. It is fundamental to consider both legal aspects and ethics within any wellbeing strategy. Paying attention to them will be helpful and productive since legal and ethical aspects in the workplace are connected to worker engagement, which can generate greater productivity and performance on the one hand, and can promote improved workplace wellbeing on the other.

Remote Workplace Culture

An important current challenge related to the construction of workplace wellbeing is being able to foster a remote workplace culture that is flexible, aligned with workplace wellbeing principles, and capable of generating wellbeing (O'Meara & Cooper, 2022). In relation to the post-COVID world of remote working, the phrase "the new normal" is an expression we probably shouldn't be using just yet because remote working is new, but it is far for being normal. In the current working environment, the concept of "normal" varies by team, department, organization, region, and country. There are only a few common themes that can be reconducted to this collective experience: an increased dependence on video, video's associated unique characteristics, and relative anxieties about them; a predominance of written communication; a lack of physical interaction; and an increase in professional and personal autonomy. In this context it is fundamental to promote a healthy remote culture. In fact, remoteness from the physical workplace can increase professional and personal autonomy, and this can lead to looking for new balances between work and other spheres of life, which also favors of the promotion of a greater wellbeing.

O'Meara and Cooper (2022) introduced the concept of "It's not just where we work, it's how we work" (p. 21). Remote work needs a culture shift. A first consideration relates to the time spent at work. Working a greater number of hours does not automatically mean having greater productivity. O'Meara and Cooper (2002), considering Frith (2016), pointed out that if workers remained at work late to finish their work, then there could be a problem of capability, productivity, or workload; whereas, if they remained at work to make a good impression on leaders or colleagues, then there is a problem of culture. There is a difference between being busy and being productive. Remote work culture can neutralize evaluation bias regarding rethinking traditional office hours or allowing employees with different working styles to produce results without being preoccupied about not being busy enough. Furthermore, working from home during the COVID-19 pandemic permitted workers to understand the positive aspects of working in their office as well as the negative aspects of working there, allowing them to realize how they can be more productive outside the office. However, remote working is not a recipe for changing a bad culture. The office is not a positive or negative concept in itself. There are offices where is a pleasure to work, and there are others that are terrible places. Enthusiasm relative to remote working is due to the fact that workers discovered the many possibilities derived from not having to work in a specific place for a specific number of hours. Unfortunately, it is not possible to solve all problems by leaving the office. For example,

issues relative to bullying, harassment, poor leadership, monotony, and lack of clear purpose remain in the case of remote working.

The establishment of a remote workplace culture also impacts recruitment, onboarding, and retention (O'Meara & Cooper, 2022). Recruitment can unquestionably be carried out remotely. Even before the pandemic, telephone and Skype interviews were alternatives to face-to-face interviews. Recruitment can be done remotely, even if it is not easy. It requires a change in the whole culture of recruitment. Interviews conducted remotely require special attention because they lack social cues, body language, and interactions between members of the hiring panel, and this could be more challenging, for example, when giving feedback to candidates. On the other hand, remote interviews have the advantage of minimizing peripherical stresses, for example, those connected with reaching the place of the interview (traffic, parking, etc.). However, there may be other peripheral stresses for candidates, for example, the internet connection not working properly. For organizations, planning to recruit remotely requires choosing and investing in a quality online platform because it can impact the quality of the interviews.

With regard to onboarding and retention, O'Meara and Cooper (2022) underlined that "geography is becoming less of a constraint on career choice" (p. 58). In this framework workers are required to adapt even more to remote recruitment and remote work. Sometimes it may be necessary to work without visual cues, but for good communication it is important that workers understand and adapt themselves to all changes necessary to communicate in an empathetic way. In relation to training and knowledge transfer, remoteness could be an opportunity to learn in comfort during formal trainings; however, there could be fewer possibilities for more informal learning opportunities, which can be offered in an office environment, particularly for young and new workers.

O'Meara and Cooper (2022) also reflect on the social impact of remote work. Remoteness at work has not only changed the way of working, but it has also had consequences beyond work, in commerce, the economy, and in whole communities. Working from home can have deep consequences for local and regional economies, transport, and culture. O'Meara and Cooper (2022) emphasize that "the community or the neighborhood or the city itself will take on more of the functions of an office" (Hoffower, 2021) (p. 63). Remote work has thus generated wide and deep changes in the world of work and societies (Blustein et al., 2019). It is fundamental to consider that not everyone can work remotely and not everyone want to (O'Meara & Cooper, 2022). There are some jobs that can never be done remotely, and there are some people who experience isolation during remote working and need to be supported. The COVID-19 lockdown led to the concept of "the stay-at-home commuter" (O'Meara & Cooper, 2022). Some commuters who switched to remote working retained the habits they had when they went to work in the office (for example, they cycled the route from home to work); however, for others, not having to go into the office gave them permission to do new activities they did not do before. The absence of the work commute gives individuals time for other activities. A shift in mindset emerges, which permits workers to evaluate alternative opportunities that are possible when it is not necessary to work in person. A new frontier in the "tedious culture war" opened, where some people are desperate to continue working from home, while others desire the opposite. It is important for managers to establish a healthy distributed culture based on cooperation and buy-in from both office-based and distributed team members. The risk is that remote work will become ideological, and organizations will take a position for or against it. It is fundamental to foster a sense of fairness to remove barriers to cooperation between those individuals who work remotely and those individuals who work in person in an office.

Another issue connected to remote work is work-life integration (O'Meara & Cooper, 2022). When individuals work at home, they bring their whole self to working remotely. The person's different roles all live together, and this facilitates greater authenticity. At the same time, the switch to working remotely can increase the risk of burnout and confusion regarding the borders between work life and home life. Moreover, the risk of burnout in remote workers can be aggravated by the fact that there are fewer visual and social cues signaling that it is time to stop working. Organizations need to carefully reflect on policies to prevent burnout when considering the introduction of more flexibility because different workers can have different needs. For organizations it is important to create the best environment for working both in the office and from home. An advantage of working from home is the opportunity for personalization that is not possible in an office. There is also the concept of "the third workplace", which refers to social settings that are different from the home or office, for example, cafes, bookstores, bars, or parks. Productivity can increase in unofficial workplaces. The concept of the third workplace adapts well to a hybrid way of working, where workers are permitted to dynamically choose a space to work, thus leaving selection of the best place to do the best work at the individual level.

According to O'Meara and Cooper (2022), when referring to organizational success, it is essential to pay attention to workers and their wellbeing. In relation to remote work and hybrid work, reflection is fundamental for the success of any new way of working. On the one hand, it is important to maintain productivity and the quality of work; however, on the other hand, remote work can enhance employee retention because it takes into account worker motivation and considers aspects of happiness. People who experienced remote working during the COVID-19 pandemic may have experienced valuable aspects of life while working remotely. Organizations should carefully consider the value of embracing a supportive, successful remote culture. Giving employees "the opportunity to finally move to the seaside, or get a dog, or spend more time with elderly relatives while they still can" (p. 97) could be a crucial ingredient for the success of the organization.

O'Meara and Cooper (2022) make wide-ranging suggestions for organizations exploring the possibilities of remote working, including considerations of wellbeing, environment, and incorporating aspects of inclusion and belonging. In this regard, wellbeing is connected to work environment, and it is important to reflect on work environment when planning for remote working. Remote working can be viewed as a possibility to eliminate obstacles, improve physical wellbeing, and sustain workers who desire to enhance their physical environment for both wellbeing and work effectiveness. One of the critical issues associated with remote working is the fact that workers away from the office can feel less of a sense of inclusion or belonging in relation to the organization. Poor digital skills and associated difficulties can aggravate weakened perceptions of inclusion and belonging. For this reason, digital literacy is important for protecting and enhancing workers' feelings of inclusion and belonging, and it is essential for the success of a distributed workforce. In some sectors, the absence of digital literacy could impede the progress of organizations trying to work remotely. Digital literacy permits people who work remotely to perceive that they are included in and belong to their organizations. In a remote context, digital problems can isolate workers and create anxieties or preoccupations.

Another issue connected to remote working is digital presenteeism. O'Meara and Cooper (2022), in line with Peel (2020), stated:

> Digital presenteeism is when you feel under pressure to always be available online, via video calls, phone, email or Slack. It's when you've done a full day's work, but feel pressure to log on or reply later than your normal or preferred working patterns, even if you feel exhausted or unwell.
>
> (O'Meara & Cooper, 2022, p. 107)

In relation to digital presenteeism, they pointed out as it is essential "to avoid at all cost[s] a blurring of the lines between 'too ill to come in' and 'too ill to work'" (p. 107). Remote working could possibly increase productivity, but it also presents great risk if employees continue to work from home even when they are sick. Presenteeism is damaging for workers, businesses, and economies. It is not only important to spread the idea of "agreeing to be absent" within work and hybrid cultures, but organizations should also promote an anti-presenteeism culture (O'Meara & Cooper, 2022).

At the same time, attention should be paid to identifying and responding to failure in remote working, because some workers who switch to remote working can present problems in terms of poor productivity and decreased wellbeing. In this regard, an organization should never adopt a dehumanized culture that only considers productivity. Workers who experience minor decreases in productivity or wellbeing when they work remotely are often those who add greater value to an organization when working in person in the office environment. In fact, they are often workers with certain soft skills and specific characteristics, such as those with gregarious personalities or a diplomatic nature. These soft skills and specific characteristics could be expressed less or go unused when working remotely. Taking care of workers with these soft skills and specific characteristics when working remotely is principally a question of wellbeing, rather than productivity, because they are valuable resources that contribute to the construction of an organization's remote workplace culture.

Remote work also permits the introduction of other concepts (O'Meara & Cooper, 2022), such as the modular workforce, which is a scenario where an individual works for an organization, but not exclusively. Measuring success in a distributed work force means considering only deliverables, not key performance indicators or return on investment. A distributed workforce needs to have more autonomy, compared to individuals who work in an office, because they do not wait for permission from a superior to take an action, and they have permission to work as effectively as possible. To establish a remote workplace culture and support communication in organizations, it is also important to have precise rules for call scheduling and to not make unscheduled calls. Embracing remoteness means that every policy, strategy, and process within the business is designed to work with a distributed workforce – it means that remoteness is not considered a compromise.

Furthermore, remote working can be an opportunity for some types of workers to thrive because it allows them to be more focused and avoid distracting elements in the office. It also important to remember that remote does have to mean from home. When creating a remote culture, workers' freedom to choose the best place to work for them is an element to be considered and valued (O'Meara & Cooper, 2022).

A hybrid future calls for balancing physical and virtual culture (O'Meara & Cooper, 2022). Organizations that would like to successfully transition from office-centric to hybrid need to make changes. It is necessary to improve workers' remote-work skillsets to reduce workplace anxieties. The hybrid model could be advantageous for both remote- and office-centric workers. However, this implies some challenges. First, organizations must find a solution that optimizes the advantages for both remote and office-based workers.

Second, the conception that a hybrid model permits the best of both working contexts can be challenging. A hybrid model brings with it a rise in worker autonomy, which was experienced by workers who experimented with working remotely. However, there are hidden obstacles that must be overcome in a hybrid working arrangement. For example, for workers with physical problems that create discomfort and who might struggle in the office, there may be the opportunity to remotely carry out work productively. Health matters or personal living situations may influence a worker's preference to work remotely or in the office. For this reason, organizations should consider hybrid work opportunities as well as the possibility of coming back to the office as needed. Third, organization should reflect upon the extent to which home can be a place of work. While working at home permits workers to have more freedom, there are two significant corporate and organizational risks: corporate surveillance and health and safety, which are difficult to control and enforce when an individual works from home. The greatest mistake an organization can make when transitioning to a hybrid model is trying to transfer the office culture into workers' homes. It is also hypothesized that there will be a decline in middle management in the algorithmically driven future with a distributed work-force and hybrid model of working (Kotkin, 2020).

"Establishing healthy remote cultures will be a balancing act" (O'Meara & Cooper, 2022, p. 189). There are many inherent, hidden inequalities in all working environments (offices, homes, third workplaces). The role of remote culture is to create workplace justice, attenuate the impact of these inequalities, and support organizations and their workers so that they are not overwhelmed by them.

Psychology of Sustainability and Sustainable Development

Within the domain of sustainability science (Rosen, 2017), the psychology of sustainability and sustainable development (Di Fabio, 2017a, 2017b; Di Fabio & Rosen, 2018, 2020) is a relatively new area of research. Sustainability science constitutes a transdisciplinary framework including various disciplines from applied and natural sciences to social and human sciences (Dincer & Rosen, 2013). This domain of sustainability science is focused on the study of factors that, at various levels, could damage different systems, including human, environmental, and engineered. Its aim is to preserve our planet and guarantee the health and wellbeing of human beings. Sustainability science aims to promote sustainable development anchored to the UN's sustainable development goals (SDGs; United Nations, 2020) thanks to the integrated contributions of different disciplines. In the sustainability science field, the psychology of sustainability and sustainable development offers a promising, innovative contribution for the safeguarding of the earth and the wellbeing of individuals. This research area enriches the transdisciplinary perspective of sustainability science, recognizing and integrating it with the value of the psychological approach and "opening the black box of psychological processes in support of the science of sustainable development[, which] is a new and exciting frontier" (Di Fabio & Rosen, 2018, p. 3). The psychology of sustainability and sustainable development was officially born as research area in 2016 in the scientific journal *Sustainability Science* (Springer), and the first dedicated section in the journal devoted to the subject was edited by Annamaria Di Fabio (University of Florence, Italy). Furthermore, in 2019 another section dedicated to the subject was created in the scientific journal *Sustainability* (MDPI), thereby accepting the challenge to open the black box of psychological processes in sustainability (Di Fabio & Rosen, 2018) for real improvements in sustainable development in the present and in the future. The current research area offers contributions for enhancing wellbeing "in relation to natural and other kinds of/in environments (natural, personal, social, organisational, community, digital, cross-cultural, and global environment[s])" (Di Fabio, 2021a, p. 1). At the core of this research area is the idea that internal psychological processes implicated in decision-making and behaviors related to sustainability and sustainable development deserve to be studied in depth, considering processes within individual(s), within environment(s), between individual(s), between environment(s), between individual(s) and environment(s), and between living being(s) and the natural world/universe, ranging from the past to the present and into the future (Di Fabio & Rosen, 2018). The psychology of sustainability and sustainable development introduces a change of perspective with respect to the framework of the "three E's" of environment, economy, and equity (Brundtland Report, 1987; Harris, 2003). It introduces new keywords for new narratives – promotion, enhancement, development, flexible change – while also taking into consideration the perspective of containment and reduction. The shift in focus is introduced to enrich the perspective, moving from the traditional, negative view that underlines pressures to a new course that emphasizes a positive view on opportunities/challenges for finding new solutions and renewing resources (Di Fabio, 2021a, 2021b).

Prevention, Psychology of Harmonization, and Decent Work

The psychology of sustainability and sustainable development framework emphasizes the worth of taking actions from a strengths-based prevention perspective (Di Fabio & Saklofske, 2021) while also considering a specific focus on primary prevention (Di Fabio & Kenny, 2015, 2016; Hage et al., 2007). The challenge is to not only remediate damages but to create and promote a culture for enhancing sustainability and sustainable development, with particular attention on individuals' interest, motivation, and self-efficacy for the realization of sustainable development goals (Di Fabio & Rosen, 2020).

In this preventive framework, the psychology of harmonisation is a "pillar for the research area of the psychology of sustainability and sustainable development" (Di Fabio & Tsuda, 2018, p. 1). The psychology of harmonisation (Di Fabio & Tsuda, 2018) refers to both "geographical and temporal perspectives, including meaningful construction processes from the past, to the present, and into the future using reflexivity processes at the individual, group, community, social, and national levels" (p. 1). The psychology of harmonisation emphasizes the relevance of a harmonic recomposition based on several internal and external complexities as well as from both geographical and temporal perspectives. Specifically, it involves consideration of the self (self, others, and nature/world) and others (near/far geographically as well as temporally) in diverse environments (e.g., natural, personal, social, organizational, virtual, cross-cultural, and global environments). Within strengths-based prevention perspectives (Di Fabio & Saklofske, 2021), the early enhancement of resources is important for each person, the system(s), and the environment(s), both throughout the world and in different cultural contexts. It is valuable to increase preventive resources through training to promote the "well-being of environment/s, individual/s and individual/s in the environment/s" (Di Fabio, 2021a, p. 1).

Decent work is also a relevant concept in relation to wellbeing in organizations. In a working environment characterized by precariousness and continuous transitions (Blustein et al., 2019), the issue of decent work is also relevant for vulnerable worker categories (Di Fabio & Svicher, 2021; Svicher & Di Fabio, 2021).

In the literature, the concept of decent work was improved through the introduction of psychological factors in addition to social and economic factors (Blustein et al., 2016). Within the psychology of working theory (PWT; Duffy et al., 2016), framed in the previously developed psychology of working framework (PWF; Blustein, 2006), the decent work concept includes five dimensions: "(a) physically and interpersonally safe working conditions, (b) access to health care, (c) adequate compensation, (d) hours that allow for free time and rest, and (e) organizational values that complement family and social values" (Duffy et al., 2017, p. 206). A study by Di Fabio and Kenny (2019), which analyzed the psychometric properties of the Italian version of the Decent Work Scale (DWS; Duffy et al., 2017) in the Italian context, deepens the study of decent work by employing both a quantitative and a qualitative approach. In particular, the qualitative approach offered interesting stimuli. A correspondence emerged between three qualitative categories and three of the five factors of the scale (adequate compensation, physically and interpersonally safe working conditions, and free time and rest). At the same time, the qualitative approach showed the value of relationship and meaning for decent work.

Decent work is one of the seventeen SDGs of the United Nations (2020) 2030 Agenda for Sustainable Development that is deeply connected with the psychology of sustainability and sustainable development. Furthermore, the framework of the psychology of sustainability and sustainable development creates a new axis of psychological reflection that includes the value of meaning (Di Fabio & Blustein, 2016) as a key ingredient for a sustainable construction (Di Fabio & Rosen, 2018), and results in relation to decent work confirm it. Aspects such as coherence, direction, significance, and belonging are essential for enhancing both the hedonic and eudaimonic wellbeing of individual(s) as well as environment(s) (Di Fabio & Rosen, 2018). From a psychological perspective, the psychology of sustainability and sustainable development calls for authentic meaning for individual(s) and organization(s) as well as for societies. Meaning, purpose, and connection (Di Fabio & Blustein, 2016) are seen as fundamental aspects, both from spatial and temporal perspectives. It is an approach that calls for harmonization of the complexity found in individuals, organizations, and environments, whether near or far in space and time (Di Fabio & Tsuda, 2018).

The Psychology of Sustainability and Sustainable Development and Wellbeing in Organizations

Wellbeing is a theme of great relevance and promise for the success of organizations (Johnson et al., 2018; Robertson & Cooper, 2010). "Good Health and Well-being" is also one of the UN's seventeen SDGs and aims to guarantee healthy lives and wellbeing for all.

In a healthy organizational framework (Di Fabio, 2017a; Di Fabio et al., 2020), there are two areas of emphasis. On the one hand, the focus is promoting the health, wellbeing, and safety of workers; on the other hand, the emphasis is on enhancing organizational effectiveness and productivity, including creating a healthy business (Di Fabio. 2017a). The healthy organizations framework emphasizes a strict association between workers' wellbeing and organizational wellbeing (Di Fabio, 2017a; Peiró, 2008; Peiró & Tetrick, 2011). It is also important to consider a positive organizational health psychology (Di Fabio, 2017a; Di Fabio & Peiró, 2018), which emphasizes a positive organizational approach with a focus on promoting "well-being of workers at different levels (individual, group, organization, and inter-organization) to promote healthy organizations" (Di Fabio, 2017a, p. 3). This perspective is in line with the wellbeing movement (Johnson et al., 2018; Robertson & Cooper, 2010) aimed at facilitating leaders' understanding of the value of improving working environments so that employees can feel trust, autonomy, valorization, and balance between work and life, which promotes wellbeing at work (Hart & Cooper, 2001).

The relevance of wellbeing in organizations is aligned with a sustainable perspective. The psychology of sustainability and sustainable development supports organizational wellbeing in a positive organizational health psychology framework, including strengths-based prevention perspectives (Di Fabio & Saklofske, 2021), primary prevention perspectives (Di Fabio & Kenny, 2015, 2016; Hage et al., 2007), and the promotion of organizational interventions to increase wellbeing at different levels and processes (workers, groups, organizations, and inter-organizations).

In relation to healthy organizations and within the framework of the psychology of sustainability and sustainable development, both hedonic and eudaimonic wellbeing are considered relevant, particularly the value of eudaimonic wellbeing and the aspect of meaning (Di Fabio, 2017a, 2017b; Di Fabio & Blustein, 2016). For sustainability and sustainable development, meaning is essential since the identification of personal meaning and the authentic self allows individuals to achieve complete work self-realization. Meaning nurtures workers' true sustainability and sustainable development, representing a deep, intrinsic motivation connected to the personal, authentic values of individuals.

In this framework of healthy organizations, the psychology of sustainability and sustainable development emphasizes the value of positive relationships to promote wellbeing in organizational contexts (Blustein, 2011; Di Fabio, 2016) starting from leadership processes (Di Fabio & Peiró, 2018). The psychology of sustainability and sustainable development highlights promising prospects in relationships and leadership, underlining the value of management and leadership styles that are deeply respectful of the essential role of relationships play in the wellbeing of workers, such as the construct of human capital sustainability leadership (Di Fabio & Peiró, 2018) centered on "healthy people as flourishing and resilient workers, [and] on healthy organizations as thriving and successful environments characterized by the positive circle of long-term well-being and performance" (Di Fabio & Peiró, 2018, p. 3). In particular, there is value in a leadership style that is aware of details of meaning and the relevance of relationships, that engages in the construction of positive narratives to mobilize energies and face the challenges of realizing sustainable development (Di Fabio, 2017b), and that builds organizational environments in compliance with the pillar principles of the wellbeing movement (Johnson et al., 2018; Robertson & Cooper, 2010).

References

Bass, B. (1985). *Leadership and performance beyond expectations.* Free Press.

Blustein, D. L. (2006). *The psychology of working: A new perspective for career development, counseling, and public policy.* New York: Routledge.

Blustein, D. L. (2011). A relational theory of working. *Journal of Vocational Behavior,* 79(1), 1–17. doi:10.1016/j.jvb.2010.10.004.

Blustein, D. L. (2019). *The importance of work in an age of uncertainty: The eroding work experience in America.* Oxford University Press.

Blustein, D. L., Kenny, M. E., Di Fabio, A., & Guichard, J. (2019). Expanding the impact of the psychology of working: Engaging psychology in the struggle for decent work and human rights. *Journal of Career Assessment,* 27, 3–28. doi:10.1177/1069072718774002.

Blustein, D. L., Olle, C., Connors-Kellgren, A., & Diamonti, A. J. (2016). Decent Work: A psychological perspective. *Frontiers in Psychology,* 7, 407. https://doi.org/10.3389/fpsyg.2016.00407.

Brundtland Report. (1987). *Our common future.* New York: Butterworth.

Burns, J. (1978). *Leadership.* Harper & Rowe.

Casey Jr, G. W. (2014). Leading in a 'VUCA' world. *Fortune*, 169(5), 75–76.

Csikszentmihalyi, M. (2013). *Flow: The psychology of happiness.* Random House.

Di Fabio, A. (2016). Positive Relational Management for healthy organizations: Psychometric properties of a new scale for prevention for workers. *Frontiers in Psychology: Organizational Psychology*, 7, 1523. doi:10.3389/fpsyg.2016.01523.

Di Fabio, A. (2017a). Positive Healthy Organizations: Promoting well-being, meaningfulness, and sustainability in organizations. *Frontiers in Psychology: Organizational Psychology*, 8, 1938. doi:10.3389/fpsyg.2017.01938.

Di Fabio, A. (2017b). The psychology of sustainability and sustainable development for well-being in organizations. *Frontiers in Psychology: Organizational Psychology*, 8, 1534. doi:10.3389/fpsyg.2017.01534.

Di Fabio, A. (2021a). The psychology of sustainability and sustainable development: Transdisciplinary perspectives. *Journal of Psychology in Africa*, 31(5), 441–445. doi:10.1080/14330237.2021.1978670.

Di Fabio, A. (2021b). Psychology of sustainability in organizations: The new scenario for healthy business, harmonization and decent work. In A. Di Fabio (Ed.), *Cross-cultural Perspectives on Well-Being and Sustainability in Organizations* (pp. 3–13). Switzerland: Springer.

Di Fabio, A., & Blustein, D. L. (2016). Editorial on the Research Topic "From Meaning of Working to Meaningful Lives: The Challenges of Expanding Decent Work". *Frontiers in Psychology: Organizational Psychology*, 7, 1119. doi:10.3389/fpsyg.2016.01119.

Di Fabio, A., Cheung, F., & Peiró, J.-M. (2020). Editorial to Special Issue "Personality and individual differences and healthy organizations". *Personality and Individual Differences*, 166. doi:10.1016/j.paid.2020.110196.

Di Fabio, A., & Kenny, M. E. (2015). The contributions of emotional intelligence and social support for adaptive career progress among Italian youth. *Journal of Career Development*, 42, 48–59. doi:10.1177/0894845314533420.

Di Fabio, A., & Kenny, M. E. (2016). From decent work to decent lives: Positive Self and Relational Management (PS&RM) in the twenty-first century. *Frontiers in Psychology. Section Organizational Psychology*, 7, 361. doi:10.3389/fpsyg.2016.00361.

Di Fabio, A., & Kenny, M. E. (2019). Decent work in Italy: Context, conceptualization, and assessment. *Journal of Vocational Behavior*, 110(Part A), 131–143. doi:10.1016/j.jvb.2018.10.014.

Di Fabio, A., & Peiró, J. M. (2018). Human Capital Sustainability Leadership to promote sustainable development and healthy organizations. *Sustainability MDPI*, 10(7), 2413. doi:10.3390/su10072413.

Di Fabio, A., & Rosen, M. A. (2018). Opening the Black Box of Psychological Processes in the Science of Sustainable Development: A New Frontier. *European Journal of Sustainable Development Research*, 2(4), 47. doi:10.20897/ejosdr/3933.

Di Fabio, A., & Rosen, M. A. (2020). An exploratory study of a new psychological instrument for evaluating sustainability: The Sustainable Development Goals Psychological Inventory. *Sustainability*, 12(18), 7617. doi:10.3390/su12187617.

Di Fabio, A., & Saklofske, D. H. (2021). The relationship of compassion and self-compassion with personality and emotional intelligence. *PAID 40th Anniversary Special Issue: Personality and Individual Differences*, 169, 110109. doi:10.1016/j.paid.2020.110109.

Di Fabio, A., & Svicher, A. (2021). The Psychology of Sustainability and Sustainable Development: Advancing Decent Work, Inclusivity, and Positive Strengths-based

Primary Preventive Interventions for Vulnerable Workers. *Frontiers in Psychology*, 12, 718354. doi:10.3389/fpsyg.2021.718354.

Di Fabio, A., & Tsuda, A. (2018). The psychology of harmony and harmonization: Advancing the perspectives for the psychology of sustainability and sustainable development. *Sustainability*, 10(12), 4726. doi:10.3390/su10124726.

Dincer, I., & Rosen, M. A. (2013). *Exergy energy, environment and sustainable development* (2nd ed.). Amsterdam: Elsevier Science Publishers.

Duffy, R. D., Allan, B. A., England, J. W., Blustein, D. L., Autin, K. L., Douglass, R. P., ... & Santos, E. J. (2017). The development and initial validation of the Decent Work Scale. *Journal of Counseling Psychology*, 64(2), 206–221. doi:10.1037/cou0000191.

Duffy, R. D., Blustein, D. L., Diemer, M. A., & Autin, K. L. (2016). The psychology of working theory. *Journal of Counseling Psychology*, 63, 127–148. doi:10.1037/cou0000140.

Dweck, C. S. (2006). *Mindset: The new psychology of success* (1st ed.). Random House.

Frith, B. (2016). Over-ambitious workers make other insecure. *HR Magazine*, 22. https://www.hrmagazine.co.uk/content/news/over-ambitious-workers-make-others-insecure.

Hage, S. M., Romano, J. L., Conyne, R. K., Kenny, M., Matthews, C., Schwartz, J. P., & Waldo, M. (2007). Best practice guidelines on prevention practice, research, training, and social advocacy for psychologists. *The Counseling Psychologist*, 35(4), 493–566. doi:10.1177/0011000006291411.

Harris, J. M. (2003). Sustainability and sustainable development. *International Society for Ecological Economics*, 1(1), 1–12.

Hart, P. M., & Cooper, C. L. (2001). Occupational stress: Towards a more integrated framework. In N. Anderson et al. (Eds.), *Handbook of Work, Industrial and Organizational Psychology*, Volume 2, London: Sage.

Hesketh, I., & Cooper, C. (2019). *Wellbeing at work: How to design, implement and evaluate an effective strategy*. Kogan Page.

Hesketh, I., Cooper, C. L., & Ivy, J. (2017). Wellbeing and engagement in policing: The key to unlocking discretionary effort? *Policing: A Journal of Policy and Practice*, 11(1), 62–73. doi:10.1093/police/paw021.

Hoffower, H. (2021). Remote work didn't wipe out big cities – it made them even bigger. *Business Insider*, 20. https://www.businessinsider.com/remote-work-made-cities-bigger-nyc-san-francisco-metro-areas-2021-9?ref=nodesk&.

Johnson, S., Robertson, I., & Cooper, C. L. (2018). *Wellbeing: Productivity and Happiness at Work* (2nd ed.). London: Palgrave Macmillan.

Kotkin, J. (2020). *The coming of neo-feudalism: A warning to the global middle class*. Encounter Books.

O'Meara, S., & Cooper, C. L. (2022). *Remote workplace culture*. Kogan Page.

Peel, A. (2020, 27 October). Digital presenteeism. *Digital People*. https://digitalpeople.blog.gov.uk/2020/10/27/digital-presenteeism.

Peiró, J. M. (2008). Stress and coping at work: New research trends and their implications for practice. In K. Näswall, J. Hellgren, & M. Sverke (Eds.), *The individual in the changing working life* (pp. 284–310). Cambridge: Cambridge University Press.

Peiró, J. M., & Tetrick, L. (2011). Occupational health psychology. In P. R. Martin, F. M. Cheung, M. C. Knowles, M. Kyrios, L. Littlefield, J. B. Overmier, & J. M. Prieto (Eds.), *Wiley-Blackwell IAAP handbooks of applied psychology: IAAP handbook of applied psychology* (pp. 292–315). Hoboken, NJ: Wiley-Blackwell.

Robertson, I., & Cooper, C. L. (2010). *Wellbeing: Productivity and Happiness at Work*. London: Palgrave Macmillan.

Rosen, M. A. (2017). Sustainable development: A vital quest. *European Journal of Sustainable Development Research*, 1(1), 2. doi:10.20897/ejosdr.201702.

Ryan, R. M., & Deci, E. L. (2001). To be happy or to be self-fulfilled: A review of research on hedonic and eudaimonic well-being. In S. Fiske (Ed.), *Annual Review of Psychology* (Vol. 52, pp. 141–166). Palo Alto, CA: Annual Reviews.

Schein, E. H. (2010). *Organizational culture and leadership* (4th ed.). Jossey-Bass.

Svicher, A., & Di Fabio, A. (2021). Job Crafting: A Challenge to Promote Decent Work for Vulnerable Workers. *Frontiers in Psychology*, 12, 681022. doi:10.3389/fpsyg.2021.681022.

United Nations. (2020). *Sustainable development: The 17 goals.* https://sdgs.un.org/goals. Accessed 11 July 2021.

2 Psychology of Sustainability and Sustainable Development in Organizations

Empirical Evidence from Environment to Safety to Innovation and Future Research

Marc A. Rosen and Annamaria Di Fabio

Opening the Black Box of the Psychology of Sustainability and Sustainable Development

The research area of the psychology of sustainability and sustainable development (Di Fabio & Rosen, 2018) acknowledges and incorporates the value of psychological approaches in the implementation of processes related to sustainability and sustainable development. It opens a new, promising path that permits future advancements in the field of psychology of sustainability and sustainable development.

Psychological processes have a role in relation to the natural environment, being involved in decisions and behaviors connected to environmental and sustainability issues. Psychology can also provide a worthy contribution to the establishment of a culture of sustainability and sustainable development in relation to the 17 sustainable development goals (SDGs) of Agenda 2030 of the United Nations.

Internal psychological processes involved in decision-making and behaviors, alone and in relation with external processes, deserve to be studied in depth, considering processes within individual(s), within environment(s), between/among individuals, between/among environments, between/among individuals and environments, and between/among living beings and the natural world/universe, from the past, in the present, and into the future (Di Fabio & Rosen, 2018, 2020).

The advanced and complex research framework involved in the psychology of sustainability and sustainable development is important in relation to these aspects. Using a psychological lens to offer new contributions towards sustainability and sustainable development is important in relation to the natural environment as well as the conventionally wider framework concerning ecological, economic, and social factors (Brundtland Report, 1987). It also allows us to introduce a complex approach and a positive narrative perspective on the great challenges to be faced. Furthermore, it ensures that quality of life and well-being are psychologically considered in connection with the environment(s), including the natural environment as well as

DOI: 10.4324/9781003212157-3

individual(s), communities, and organizations in the environment(s) (Di Fabio & Rosen, 2018). This current research area introduces a critical difference in addressing the broad theme by recognizing the need for integrating a positive approach. The mainstream perspective focused on the three "Es" – environment, economy, and equity (Harris, 2003) – is based on the verb "to avoid" (to exploit, to deplete, to irremediably alter), whereas the psychology of sustainability and sustainable development (Di Fabio, 2017a, 2017b; Di Fabio & Rosen, 2018) differs from this traditional framework by introducing a positive perspective centred on the importance of regenerating resources, not just progressively using fewer resources. In addition, new keywords and narratives are introduced (Di Fabio, 2017a). For example, different terms are used – promote, enrich, develop, and flexibility – to underline the value of concrete actions, instead of only avoidance; enriching/equipping, instead of not exploiting; developing, instead of not depleting; and flexibility in terms of change, instead of irreversibly. The shift changes the focus from using fewer resources (decreasing quantity), which is a non-positive view that emphasises harm/danger, to a focus on the opportunities and challenges of finding new solutions that emphasize different uses of resources, regenerating resources, positive incentives, and creative pathways that link the past with the present and the future (Di Fabio & Rosen, 2018; Di Fabio & Tsuda, 2018).

Psychology of Sustainability and Sustainable Development: Empirical Evidence

Empirical evidence has emerged regarding the necessity to implement this promising research area in upcoming years (Di Fabio & Rosen, 2018). This chapter presents empirical evidence for the research area based on the production of two international research and intervention laboratories at the University of Florence (Italy): (1) Cross-Cultural Positive Psychology, Prevention, and Sustainability; and (2) Work and Organizational Psychology for Vocational Guidance, Career Counseling, Career Development, Talents, and Healthy Organizations. The results are organized according to four kinds of environments: natural, personal, social, and organizational.

Natural Environment

Regarding the *natural environment*, the main focus is on research regarding connectedness to nature as a proxy variable for finding the implications of behaviors related to responsibility for and protection of the environment. Connectedness to nature was originally considered "the extent to which an individual includes nature within his/her cognitive representation of self" (Schultz, 2002, p. 67), but it has been extended to incorporate the affective and experiential aspects of the individual's connectedness to nature (Mayer & Frantz, 2004). Since connectedness to nature is considered a proxy for positive behaviors related to the environment, the research is particularly centred on the antecedents of connectedness to nature in terms of paying attention to positive, increasable resources for supporting and improving behaviors.

Di Fabio and Bucci (2016) analysed the relationship between empathy (Davis, 1980), which is a critical variable for human relationships that is increasable through specific training, and connectedness to nature in Italian high school students, for the first time also controlling for personality traits. Very few studies have examined the relationship between empathy and connectedness to nature in the literature, and, to the best of our knowledge, they have never controlled for personality traits. The results showed that empathy explained additional variance for connectedness to nature beyond that explained by personality traits, pointing out the possible crucial role of the perception of being able to put yourself in others' shoes (Davis, 1980) in perceiving greater connection to nature. Moreover, Di Fabio and Kenny (2018b) deepened this research by studying Italian workers. The results showed that empathy mediated the associations between the big five personality traits (in particular, agreeableness and openness) and connectedness to nature, emphasizing the value of empathy in relation to connectedness to nature, which is in line with a preventive perspective centred on the enhancement of individual strengths.

Individual differences in connectedness to nature have also been studied. Di Fabio and Rosen (2019) investigated the associations between the big five personality traits and connectedness to nature in Italian university students, while also trying to respond to the exploratory research question of whether gender differences exist in connectedness to nature. The results showed positive associations of agreeableness and extraversion with connectedness to nature in particular, and they also showed that there were no gender differences in relation to connectedness to nature. Intrapreneurial self-capital (Di Fabio, 2014) emerged as another promising resource in relation to connectedness to nature. In the study by Duradoni and Di Fabio (2019) of Italian workers, which examined the associations of personality traits, intrapreneurial self-capital, and connectedness to nature, intrapreneurial self-capital mediated the relationship between extraversion and connectedness to nature. These results pointed out the promising contribution of intrapreneurial self-capital in promoting workers' connectedness to nature. Furthermore, Di Fabio et al. (2019) analysed the relationships between connectedness to nature, intrapreneurial self-capital, and eudaimonic well-being in terms of meaningful work, as gauged by the Work as Meaning Inventory (WAMI; Steger et al., 2012) in Italian workers: intrapreneurial self-capital mediated the relationship between connectedness to nature and meaningful work, underlining promising perspectives for enhancing eudaimonic well-being at work, starting from connectedness to nature through intrapreneurial self-capital.

Personal Environment

Regarding the *personal environment*, research has considered psychological resources, also in strengths-based prevention perspectives (Di Fabio &

Saklofske, 2021), for the well-being – both hedonic and eudaimonic – of individuals as well as psychological resources for facilitating adaptive outcomes.

One study (Di Fabio & Kenny, 2018c), which extended the results of previous research (Di Fabio et al., 2017), analysed the associations between intrapreneurial self-capital (Di Fabio, 2014) and hedonic and eudaimonic well-being in Italian university students. Intrapreneurial self-capital was able to explain additional variance with respect to the big five personality traits for hedonic well-being, positive and negative affects (Watson et al., 1988), and life satisfaction (Diener et al., 1985) as well as for eudaimonic well-being, life meaning (Morgan & Farsides, 2009) and flourishing (Diener et al., 2010).

In addition to intrapreneurial self-capital, other personal psychological resources in relation to well-being emerged: acceptance of change, emotional intelligence, life project reflexivity, resilience, gratitude, and humour styles.

In Italian university students, acceptance of change (Di Fabio & Gori, 2016b) explained additional variance in both hedonic and eudaimonic well-being, controlling for personality traits (Di Fabio et al., 2023a).

Trait emotional intelligence (Petrides & Furnham, 2000) explained additional variance beyond the big five personality traits in hedonic well-being and eudaimonic well-being in both Italian high school students and university students (Di Fabio & Kenny, 2016b, 2019).

Life project reflexivity (Di Fabio et al., 2018) explained a percentage of incremental variance in both hedonic and eudaimonic well-being after controlling for personality traits in Italian university students (Di Fabio et al., 2022).

Di Fabio and Palazzeschi (2015) showed that resilience (Campbell-Sills & Stein, 2007) explained a percentage of incremental variance beyond the big five personality traits in relation to both hedonic and eudaimonic well-being in Italian high school students.

Gratitude (Watkins et al., 2003) explained a percentage of incremental variance in both hedonic and eudaimonic well-being after controlling for personality traits in Italian university students (Di Fabio & Palazzeschi, 2023).

In the personal environment, in relation to psychological resources able to facilitate adaptive outcomes, we can consider also the following results.

Emotional intelligence was studied in relation to resilience. Di Fabio and Saklofske (2014), in a study conducted on Italian high school students that used trait emotional intelligence (Petrides & Furnham, 2000), self-reported emotional intelligence (Bar-On, 1997), and ability-based emotional intelligence (Mayer et al., 2002), showed that trait emotional intelligence explained additional variance with respect to resilience in relation to self-reported emotional intelligence (Bar-On, 1997) after controlling for fluid intelligence and the big five personality traits. On the contrary, ability-based emotional intelligence did not offer a contribution to resilience. More recently, Di Fabio and Saklofske (2018) studied two different groups (Italian university students and

Italian workers) and showed that trait emotional intelligence explained incremental variance beyond personality traits in relation to resilience for both groups.

Trait emotional intelligence (Petrides & Furnham, 2000) was also able to explain additional variance in intrapreneurial self-capital (Di Fabio, 2014), controlling for personality traits in Italian university participants (Di Fabio & Saklofske, 2019b).

Resilience (Campbell-Sills & Stein, 2007) explained incremental variance beyond personality traits in relation to indecisiveness (Frost & Shows, 1993) in Italian high school students (Di Fabio et al, submitted a).

Gratitude (Watkins et al., 2003), a promising resource in strength-based prevention perspectives, was able to explain additional variance beyond personality trait with respect to hope (Snyder et al., 1991) in Italian university students (Di Fabio & Palazzeschi, in press a).

Humour styles (Martin et al., 2003) explained additional variance in perfectionism (rigid, self-critical, narcissistic), showing inverse relationships, when controlling for personality traits in Italian university students (Di Fabio, Smith, & Saklofske, 2020). Furthermore, in another study in Italian university students by Di Fabio and Duradoni (2020), humour styles were able to mediate the association between personality traits (extraversion, emotionality) of the Hexaco model (Ashton & Lee, 2009) and resistance to change (Oreg, 2003), showing inverse relationships between resistance to change and both self-enhancing humour and affiliative humour.

The results of these studies offer promising personal environment perspectives in terms of increasable psychological resources, both in relation to well-being and in the wider framework of facilitating adaptive outcomes.

Social Environment

Regarding the *social environment*, the research considered resources from strengths-based prevention perspectives (Di Fabio & Saklofske, 2021), such as emotional intelligence, positive relational management, and academic relational civility.

Trait emotional intelligence (Schutte et al., 1998) explained additional variance in social support (Zimet et al., 1988), after controlling for personality traits, in an Italian high school context (Di Fabio & Kenny, 2012). Ability-based emotional intelligence (Mayer et al., 2002) explained additional variance in social support (Zimet et al., 1988), after controlling for personality traits, in Italian high school participants (Di Fabio, 2015). These results underlined the value of emotional intelligence as a positive, preventive resource in the social context.

Positive relational management (Di Fabio, 2016) explained additional variance in both hedonic and eudaimonic well-being, after controlling for personality traits, in a study by Di Fabio and Kenny (2019b) carried out with Italian university students.

Academic relational civility (Di Fabio & Kenny, 2018a), a key resource for positive relationships in the academic context, explained incremental variance in hedonic well-being as well as eudaimonic well-being, after controlling for personality traits (Di Fabio & Kenny, 2018a), in Italian university students. These results highlighted the value of these increasable social-environment resources for enhancing both hedonic and eudaimonic well-being.

Organizational Environment

Regarding the *organizational environment*, empirical studies have focused on psychological resources amenable to training that can both enhance well-being and facilitate adaptive outcomes as well as the strengths-based prevention perspective framework (Di Fabio & Saklofske, 2021).

Promising resources include Human Capital Sustainability Leadership (Di Fabio & Peiró, 2018a) and Workplace Relational Civility (Di Fabio & Gori, 2016a). Human Capital Sustainability Leadership is a higher-order construct (including ethical, sustainable, mindful, and servant leadership) that aims to enhance flourishing, resilient workers and to promote healthy organizations, recognizing the positive, circular relationship between performance and long-term well-being (Di Fabio & Peiró, 2018a). Workplace Relational Civility is a relational style of work characterized by respect and concern for the self and others, interpersonal sensitivity, personal education, and kindness towards others (Di Fabio & Gori, 2016a), which is articulated in three dimensions (relational decency, relational culture, and relational readiness).

Human Capital Sustainability Leadership (Di Fabio & Peiró, 2018a) explained additional variance related to eudaimonic well-being, controlling for personality traits, in Italian workers (Di Fabio, & Peiró, 2018b). Furthermore, Human Capital Sustainability Leadership (Di Fabio & Peiró, 2018a) was able to explain additional variance, controlling for personality traits, in relation to decent work in Italian workers (Di Fabio, 2018a). Human Capital Sustainability Leadership is favoured by positive relational processes in organizations. A study by Di Fabio et al. (2023b) showed that positive relational management added a percentage of incremental variance beyond personality traits in relation to Human Capital Sustainability Leadership.

Workplace Relational Civility (Di Fabio & Gori, 2016a) explained additional variance in hedonic and eudaimonic well-being, after controlling for personality traits, in Italian workers (Di Fabio et al., 2016). Furthermore, Workplace Relational Civility (Di Fabio & Gori, 2016a) explained additional variance in acceptance of change, controlling for personality traits, in Italian workers (Di Fabio et al., 2016). A study by Di Fabio and Gori (2021) showed that Workplace Relational Civility explained additional variance in Human Capital Sustainability Leadership, controlling for personality traits, in Italian workers. Moreover, Workplace Relational Civility (Di Fabio & Gori, 2016a) offered a promising contribution to leadership styles in general. A study by Di Fabio and Pesce (2018), carried out with Italian workers, showed that

Workplace Relational Civility was able to explain additional variance with respect to both transactional leadership and transformational leadership, although particularly the latter.

Other promising resources in the organizational environment are the following: emotional intelligence, intrapreneurial self-capital, acceptance of change, insight, gratitude, job crafting, meaningful work, and the psychological focus in relation to decent work.

Regarding emotional intelligence and its promising associations, a study by Di Fabio & Svicher (2021) with Italian workers showed that trait emotional intelligence (Petrides & Furnham, 2000) explained incremental variance in Human Capital Sustainability Leadership (Di Fabio & Peiró, 2018a), controlling for personality traits. Trait emotional intelligence (Petrides & Furnham, 2000) also explained additional variance in positive relational management (Di Fabio, 2016) in Italian workers, controlling for personality traits (Di Fabio & Saklofske, 2019a). Furthermore, Di Fabio and Kenny (2021) showed that trait emotional intelligence (Petrides & Furnham, 2000) mediated the relationships between both positive affect and negative affect and meaningful work (Steger et al., 2012) in Italian workers. A recent study of Italian workers (Di Fabio & Saklofske, 2021) elucidated that trait emotional intelligence (Petrides & Furnham, 2000) was able to explain incremental variance with respect to the big five personality traits for compassion (Gu et al., 2017) as well as self-compassion (Neff, 2003), two promising variables in organizational contexts for promoting the well-being of workers and healthy organizations (Di Fabio, Cheung, & Peiró, 2020).

Another promising resource is intrapreneurial self-capital (Di Fabio, 2014). One study (Di Fabio et al., 2017) carried out on Italian workers showed that intrapreneurial self-capital explained additional variance with respect to big five personality traits for life satisfaction (Diener et al., 1985) and hedonic well-being as well as for flourishing (Diener et al., 2010) and eudaimonic well-being. In another study (Di Fabio & Gori, 2016c) of Italian workers, intrapreneurial self-capital was able to mediate the association between the big five personality traits (emotional stability) and flourishing (Diener et al., 2010).

Acceptance of change (Di Fabio & Gori, 2016b) is considered a promising preventive variable. In the study by Gori and Di Fabio (2015) in Italian workers, acceptance of chance mediated the relationship between extraversion and resilience of the big five personality traits. Furthermore, in a study by Di Fabio & Bucci (2015) in Italian workers, acceptance of change explained incremental variance beyond big five personality traits in relation to employability (Fugate & Knicki, 2008).

Insight (Gori et al., 2015) is another promising psychological increasable resource. A study by Gori et al., (2021) showed that insight mediated the relationship between trait emotional intelligence and acceptance of change in Italian workers. The study (Gori et al., 2021) showed that insight was able to mediate the association between the big five personality traits (in particular extraversion, agreeableness, and conscientiousness) and job crafting (Leana et al., 2009).

Gratitude (Watkins et al., 2003), a promising resource in strengths-based prevention perspectives, explained additional variance beyond the big five personality traits with respect to hedonic well-being, both in life in terms of life satisfaction (Diener et al., 1985) and job satisfaction (Judge et al., 1998), as well as eudaimonic well-being, both in terms of meaning in life (Morgan & Farsides, 2009) and meaning at work among Italian workers (Di Fabio et al., submitted b). Gratitude (Watkins et al., 2003) was also able to explain additional variance beyond the big five personality traits with respect to both acceptance of change and positive relational management in Italian workers (Di Fabio & Palazzeschi, in press b).

Other studies carried out regarding organizational environment identified meaningful work and decent work as promising variables. Meaningful work (Steger et al., 2012) was able to mediate the relationship between perceived work conditions and intention related to turnover in French workers (Arnoux-Nicolas et al., 2016). Meaningful work was also able to mediate the relationship between positive relational management (Di Fabio, 2016) and happiness (Lyubomirsky et al., 2005) in New Zealand managers (Haar et al., 2019b). A recent study (Svicher, Gori, & Di Fabio, 2022b) related to meaning at work proposed a network analysis of the Work as Meaning Inventory (WAMI; Steger et al., 2012) in Italian workers. The results showed that the most connected item within the overall network was the item related to the contribution of work to personal growth, which was able to link together the three dimensions of the instrument (positive meaning, meaning-making through work, and greater good motivations).

The Decent Work Scale (DWS; Duffy et al., 2017) offers new directions for research and interventions. A network analysis was conducted with Italian workers using the Decent Work Scale, which underlined the higher centrality in the network of the domain of organizational values that complement family and social values (Svicher et al., 2022). In relation to decent work, a study by Di Fabio, Svicher, and Gori (2021) showed that occupational fatigue, exhaustion, and recovery (OFER; Winwood et al., 2005) explained a percentage of incremental variance (inverse relationships and direct relationship) with respect to decent work in Italian workers, controlling for personality traits.

In this area some studies could be linked to sustainable development. Gori et al. (2020) showed that organizational justice (Colquitt, 2001) partially mediated the association between acceptance of change and job satisfaction in Italian workers. In another study, work-life balance mediated the association between Positive Relational Management and Organisational Trust in New Zealand managers (Haar et al., 2019a). Other interesting results emerged for work design-performance relationships (Peiró et al., 2020), where dispositions at the individual level mediated the association between work characteristics and job performance in Colombian workers.

Finally, in the organizational environment we also have a preventive research focus on positive psychological resources for career building and career development over the life-span of career decision-making self-efficacy and career adaptability. Examples include the following.

Svicher and Di Fabio (2021) showed that career decision-making self-efficacy (Betz & Taylor, 2000) explained a percentage of incremental variance beyond the big five personality traits in relation to hedonic and eudaimonic well-being in Italian university students.

A study by Gori, Topino, Svicher, and Di Fabio (2022) underlined that career adaptability (Savickas & Porfeli, 2012) was able to mediate the relationship between self-esteem and meaning in life (above all for the presence of meaning, but also for the search for meaning) in Italian workers. Furthermore, a significant and positive relationship between resilience and satisfaction with life, partially moderated by the chained effect of career adaptability and self-efficacy, controlling for education, was found in Italian workers (Topino et al., 2022). Furthermore, resilience (Campbell-Sills & Stein, 2007), as an implementable resource, explained incremental variance beyond personality traits in relation to the employability of Italian university students (Palazzeschi et al., 2021).

Sustainable Development Goals Psychological Inventory

Di Fabio and Rosen (2020) developed the Sustainable Development Goals Psychological Inventory (SDGPI), on the basis of the psychological literature, to explore critical dimensions that could promote realization of the 17 Sustainable Developmental Goals (SDGs) (United Nations, 2018). The inventory individuates interest, motivation, and self-efficacy as three psychological factors. Interests are related to an individual's likes and intentions for activities, enhancing the probability of the emergence of consequent practices (Lent et al., 1994). Motivation is distinguished (Deci & Ryan, 1985) as intrinsic motivation, which is the intrinsically natural search for opportunities and new possibilities; extrinsic motivation, which arises from external sources (e.g., rewards, money, or grades); and amotivation, which is a non-self-determined type of motivation that lacks extrinsic or intrinsic motivation. Finally, self-efficacy refers to the evaluation that people apply to their ability to achieve some actions that are needed for a specific level of activity or performance (Bandura, 1986). Regarding its structure, the SDGPI has 17 items for each of the 17 SDGs and takes into account each of the three factors. Participants are requested to indicate the extent "I am interested in" (interest), "I am motivated to act concretely for" (motivation), and "I feel able to act concretely for" (self-efficacy) on a 5-point scale (1 = not at all; 5 = very much). The SDGPI also permits qualitative analysis. Open-ended questions are included in the inventory to gain a more in-depth understanding of individuals' self-perceptions regarding the 17 SDGs. Individuals are asked: "Which of the 17 Sustainable Development Goals is the most important for me? Why?" and "Which of the 17 Sustainable Development Goals is the least important for me? Why?" Di Fabio and Rosen (2020) examined the qualitative answers of participants using conventional content-analysis procedures (Hsieh & Shannon, 2005). With regards to the question "Why is this the most important goal for me?", many categories arose: in first place "Prerequisite for reaching other goals" and in last place "Freedom". With regard to the question "Why is this the least important goal for me?", additional categories arose: in first place "Low priority and urgency" and in last place "Lack of emotional involvement".

A network analysis of the SDGPI was conducted in Italian university students (Svicher et al., 2022a), which highlighted that five SDGs had strong and statistically significant edges between interest, motivation, and self-efficacy: (1) SDG 4 – Quality education, (2) SDG 13 – Climate action, (3) SDG 15 – Life on land, (4) SDG 14 – Life below water, and (5) SDG 9 – Industry, innovation, and infrastructure. The study (Svicher et al., 2022a) also emphasized that the most central nodes were SDG 2 – Zero hunger and SDG 7 – Affordable and clean energy.

The SDGPI contributes to the objective of realising specific, tailored interventions that underline particular needs related to diverse targets and different realities and contexts, address the specificity of communities and countries, and maintain a cross-cultural perspective.

Analogies and Extensions to Safety and Innovation

The psychology of sustainability and sustainable development could also be a promising framework for the psychology of safety and the psychology of innovation.

The psychology of sustainability and sustainable development (Di Fabio & Rosen, 2018) mainly has two basic keywords – harmonization and generativity – related to the complexity of the difficult challenges that organizations must cope with in the 21st century. These challenges inherently include a three-sided configuration in the psychology of sustainability and sustainable development: (1) contextuality (the immediate problem in the context and its specific complexity), (2) globality (the problem in relation to global complexity), and (3) temporality (including the past, the present, and responsible consideration of the future world and future generations, both within and outside of the organization).

These considerations are informative in their own right in relation to the psychology of safety and the psychology of innovation. However, they can also help in better understanding the promising value of the psychology of sustainability and sustainable development framework.

Regarding the psychology of safety, it can be interesting to consider the manner in which safety is managed in industrial organizations. Of course, many safety technologies are employed, including personal protective equipment and safety automation, such as interlocks to keep people out of areas that are dangerous when equipment is operating. Also, a safety-oriented culture is often encouraged, which indicates to all personnel, from senior management down to workers, that safety is a priority in the organization. This very much involves a shift in psychological behavior to prioritizing safety, rather than productivity or profits or other measures.

But, it is interesting to note that, when devising safety procedures and technologies regarding what to do during an emergency, the emphasis is usually on automation, e.g., sensors to identify safety problems, automated alarms and warnings to alert everyone about a problem, and automated actuators to activate emergency devices, such as sprinklers, auto-shutdown equipment, and safety protection devices like high-volume ventilation systems that evacuate dangerous gases from a facility. Sometimes, safety procedures include actions for workers, such instructions to press the red emergency shut-down button on the equipment they use before exiting the premises in an orderly manner. But, given the psychological stresses and pressures on workers during an emergency situation, relying on workers to hit an emergency shut-down button during such a stressful event is not reliable and is often futile because, despite extensive education and training, people can become unpredictable in terms of behavior.

Others have also examined the psychology of safety in various fields. For instance, in the area of transportation, consider the case of self-driving electric vehicles. People often feel unsafe in such vehicles, compared to vehicles in which they drive, in part because they feel in control in the latter case and a loss of control in the former case. Yet, self-driving cars have the potential for much greater safety than human-driven cars due to their potential to communicate. This technology was examined by Viola (2021), who discusses the psychological aspects that affect the adoption of self-driving electric vehicles and indicates that the success of this technology is uncertain due to the many psychological factors that may hinder it, e.g., whether people are ready for fully automated driving and the absence of a human driver. The construction industry is another interesting example. The safety climate and safety performance in construction projects were examined by He et al. (2020), who concluded that, for improved safety performance, safety professionals need to invoke group-targeted safety interventions and focus more on supervisor psychological well-being. In the field of robotics, Zacharaki et al. (2020) describe the levels of safety needed during interactions between humans and robots, considering existing methods for psychological safety during human-robot collaboration as well as the psychological parameters relevant to integrating robots into social and industrial environments. In the field of healthcare, the manner in which inclusive leadership can mitigate psychological distress during a trauma or crisis was examined from the perspective of nursing, incorporating data from the COVID-19 pandemic (Ahmed et al., 2020). Finally, the way in which a psychosocial safety climate positively affects employee safety behavior through lowering psychological distress was examined (Mirza et al, 2022). The study showed that, to enhance safety participation and compliance, management should address psychosocial factors in the work environment, especially in dangerous or safety-sensitive industries.

Regarding the psychology of innovation, it is instructive to consider the manner in which technical innovation is dealt with by engineers and engineering firms. Often, engineers view their designs of new technologies, such as a new generation of smart phone that has significant improvements compared to existing technology, as obviously superior and, therefore, as the obvious choice consumers should and will make. But, often consumers make other purchase decisions that are clearly guided by factors other than technical superiority. This can lead to extreme frustration among engineers, who often cannot understand why consumers do not choose the obviously technically superior option. Anecdotes exist of engineers in such circumstances feeling like they want to 'tear their hair out'. Such frustration often stems from differences in the psychology of engineers and the psychology of consumers, suggesting that engineers – although often technically adept – often struggle in understanding the motivations and thoughts of the consumers of their products.

Others have also examined the psychology of innovation. For instance, for a high-tech firm, Mukerjee and Metiu (2022) examined the complex and recursive link between play and the psychological safety that is important to innovation. The study showed that, by recognizing the mechanisms and feedback loops linking psychological safety and play practices, the conditions that enable innovation in organizations today can be better understood. Also, Messmann et al. (2022) examined the importance of basic psychological needs satisfaction in the relationship between innovative work behavior and transformational leadership. They found that leaders should provide feedback on employee strategies for realizing innovative options as well as on their innovations to aid employees in becoming increasingly confident about what they can achieve and to improve their innovative contributions. In another investigation, Martinidis et al. (2022) demonstrated that, irrespective of continually improving infrastructure and technology, human-related facets of innovation are the most significant aspect of innovation, where the human factor in innovation has three main types of capital: human, social, and psychological, the latter of which encompasses the behaviors, attitudes, and values of people. The findings suggest that, to increase innovation, smart specialization policies that are more human in focus are needed. Furthermore, the effects of adaptive performance and person-group fit on innovation by employees were examined recently (Jena & Goyal, 2022) using a sequential mediation framework to understand the relation between employee innovation and emotional intelligence. The findings have particular value for human resources, especially for training teams and recruitment. Finally, the position of creative self-efficacy and mastery orientation in innovative work behavior and psychological capital was investigated by Kumar et al. (2022). The authors combined various perspectives in a framework and demonstrated that a partially mediated positive relationship between innovative work behavior and psychological capital is possible via mastery orientation.

Conclusions

The psychology of sustainability and sustainable development (Di Fabio, 2017a, 2017b; Di Fabio & Rosen, 2018) is a critical, innovative research and intervention area for sustainable development, sustainability, and related issues. Linking sustainability science (Rosen, 2009) to the study of psychological processes is an enriching step for understanding environmental decisions and behaviors as well as for establishing of a culture of sustainability. In this framework, the Sustainable Development Goals Psychological Inventory (Di Fabio & Rosen, 2020) is a concrete, specific, and useful tool. It represents a promising instrument for recognising critical psychological aspects of successful performance related to each of the UN's 17 SDGs (United Nations, 2018). The inventory permits individuals to acquire greater awareness of their self-perception of the SDGs, thus opening possibilities for realising specific, tailored interventions based on psychological factors connected to SDGs as well as the needs of specific targets/contexts. These interventions can be applied not only when critical issues have already emerged regarding people's self-perception of SDGs, but also, from a primary prevention perspective and strengths-based preventive perspective, to promote the early development of interest, motivation, and self-efficacy regarding SDGs.

In strengths-based prevention perspectives (Di Fabio & Saklofske, 2021), there is value in building resources for each person/people, for each system(s), for each environment(s), for person/people in the environment(s), and in different cultural contexts and throughout the world. According to these perspectives, the psychology of sustainability and sustainable development (Di Fabio, 2017a, 2017b; Di Fabio & Rosen, 2018) calls for the early building of improved awareness regarding preventive resources amenable to training and promoting the well-being of the environment(s), individual(s), and individual (s) in the environment(s).

From this perspective emerged the relevance of inclusivity, not only spatial but also temporal, which favours access to maturation processes and generativity for people near and far in space and time, including future generations, as well as an active mission at micro, meso, and macro levels to favour the construction of well-being (not only hedonic but also eudaimonic) and quality of life for environment(s), individual(s), and individual(s) in the environment(s). It is useful for this purpose to utilize the framework of the psychology of harmonization (Di Fabio & Tsuda, 2018). Harmonization includes both "geographical and temporal perspectives, including meaningful construction processes from the past, to the present, and into the future, using reflexivity processes at the individual, group, community, social, and national levels" (Di Fabio & Tsuda, 2018, p. 1). The psychology of harmonization highlights the importance of paying attention to a harmonic recomposition of many internal and external complexities, both temporally and geographically. In particular, this involves starting from the self (with parts of the self, others, nature, and the world) and starting from others who are near/far, geographically as well as temporally, in relation to different environments (natural, personal, social, organizational, and global). It also means paying attention to building positive narratives, details of meaning, purpose, and hope in order to carefully construct them in real and different contexts, taking care of their specificity and starting from approaches aligned with primary prevention (Di Fabio & Kenny, 2015, 2016a; Hage et al., 2007) and strengths-based prevention perspectives (Di Fabio & Saklofske, 2021).

All of these reflections also open future perspectives for research and intervention, including in terms of enhancing safety and innovation, considering contributions to the psychology of sustainability and sustainable development, continuing to open the black box of psychological processes through empirical research, and creating new opportunities for intervention.

References

Ahmed, F., Zhao, F., & Faraz, N. A. (2020). How and when does inclusive leadership curb psychological distress during a crisis? Evidence from the COVID-19 outbreak. *Frontiers in Psychology*, 11, 1898. doi:10.3389/fpsyg.2020.01898.

Arnoux-Nicolas, C., Sovet, L., Lhotellier, L., Di Fabio, A., & Bernaud, J.-L. (2016). Perceived work conditions and turnover intentions: The mediating role of meaning of life and meaning of work. *Frontiers in Psychology: Section Organizational Psychology*, 7, 704. doi:10.3389/fpsyg.2016.00704.

Ashton, M. C., & Lee, K. (2009). The HEXACO–60: A short measure of the major dimensions of personality. *Journal of Personality Assessment*, 91(4), 340–345. doi:10.1080/00223890902935878.

Bandura, A. (1986). *Social foundations of thought and action: A social cognitive theory.* Englewood Cliffs, NJ: Prentice Hall.

Bar-On, R. (1997). *The Emotional Intelligence Inventory (EQ-I): Technical manual.* Toronto, ON: Multi-Health Systems.

Betz, N. E., & Taylor, K. M. (2000). *Manual for the Career Decision Making Self-Efficacy Scale (CDMSES) and CDMSES – Short Form* (unpublished manuscript). Columbus, OH: Ohio State University.

Brundtland Report. (1987). *Our common future.* New York: Butterworth.

Campbell-Sills, L., & Stein, M. B. (2007). Psychometric analysis and refinement of the Connor–Davidson Resilience Scale (CD-RISC): Validation of a 10-item measure of resilience. *Journal of Traumatic Stress*, 20(6), 1019–1028. doi:10.1002/jts.20271.

Colquitt, J. A. (2001). On the dimensionality of organizational justice: A construct validation of a measure. *Journal of Applied Psychology*, 86(3), 386–400. doi:10.1037/0021-9010.86.3.386.

Davis, M. H. (1980). A multidimensional approach to individual differences in empathy. *JSAS: Catalog of Selected Documents in Psychology*, 10, 85.

Deci, E. L., & Ryan, R. M. (1985). The general causality orientations scale: Self-determination in personality. *Journal of Research in Personality*, 19(2), 109–134. doi:10.1016/0092-6566(85)90023-6.

Diener, E., Wirtz, D., Tov, W., Kim-Prieto, C., Choi, D. W., Oishi, S., & Biswas-Diener, R. (2010). New well-being measures: Short scales to assess flourishing and positive and negative feelings. *Social Indicators Research*, 97(2), 143–156. doi:10.1007/s11205-009-9493-y.

Diener, E. D., Emmons, R. A., Larsen, R. J., & Griffin, S. (1985). The satisfaction with life scale. *Journal of Personality Assessment*, 49(1), 71–75. doi:10.1207/s15327752jpa4901_13.

Di Fabio, A. (2014). Intrapreneurial Self-Capital: A new construct for the 21st century. *Journal of Employment Counseling*, 51, 98–111. doi:10.1002/j.2161-1920.2014.00045.x.

Di Fabio, A. (2015). Beyond fluid intelligence and personality traits in social support: The role of ability based emotional intelligence. *Frontiers in Psychology, Section Educational Psychology*, 6, 395. doi:10.3389/fpsyg.2015.00395.

Di Fabio, A. (2016). Positive Relational Management for healthy organizations: Psychometric properties of a new scale for prevention for workers. *Frontiers in Psychology: Organizational Psychology*, 7, 1523. doi:10.3389/fpsyg.2016.01523.

Di Fabio, A. (2017a). Positive Healthy Organizations: Promoting well-being, meaningfulness, and sustainability in organizations. *Frontiers in Psychology: Organizational Psychology*, 8, 1938. doi:10.3389/fpsyg.2017.01938.

Di Fabio, A. (2017b). The psychology of sustainability and sustainable development for well-being in organizations. *Frontiers in Psychology: Organizational Psychology*, 8, 1534. doi:10.3389/fpsyg.2017.01534.

Di Fabio, A. (2018a). *Human Capital Sustainability Leadership and Decent Work*. Poster presented at the second international cross-cultural conference "Healthier societies fostering healthy organizations: A cross-cultural perspective" organized by the Department of Education and Psychology, University of Florence, Florence, Italy, August 30–September 1, 2018.

Di Fabio, A., Bonfiglio, A., Palazzeschi, L., Gori, A., & Svicher, A. (2023b). Human capital sustainability leadership: From personality traits to positive relational management. *Frontiers in Psychology*, 14, 1110974. doi:10.3389/fpsyg.2023.1110974.

Di Fabio, A., & Bucci, O. (2015, September). *Dai tratti di personalità all'accettazione del cambiamento nell'employability [From personality traits to acceptance of change in employability]*. In P. Argentero (Chair), Thematic session on Cambiamento e gestione delle transizioni [Change and management of transitions] conducted at the Annual Conference of the Italian Association of Psychology (Organizational Psychology Section), University of Palermo, Palermo, Italy, 17–19 September 2015.

Di Fabio, A., & Bucci, O. (2016). Green positive guidance and green positive life counseling for decent work and decent lives: Some empirical results. *Frontiers in Psychology: Section Organizational Psychology*, 7, 261. doi:10.3389/fpsyg.2016.00261.

Di Fabio, A., Cheung, F., & Peiró, J.-M. (2020). Editorial to Special Issue "Personality and individual differences and healthy organizations". *Personality and Individual Differences*, 166, 110196. doi:10.1016/j.paid.2020.110196.

Di Fabio, A., & Duradoni, M. (2020). Humor Styles as New Resources in a Primary Preventive Perspective: Reducing Resistance to Change for Negotiation. *International Journal of Environmental Research and Public Health*, 17(7), 2485. doi:10.3390/ijerph17072485.

Di Fabio, A., *et al.* (submitted a). Resilience and Indecisiveness beyond personality traits in high school students. *Frontiers in Psychology: Organizational Psychology*.

Di Fabio, A., *et al.* (submitted b). Well-being of workers: gratitude as a positive resource beyond personality trait. *Frontiers in Psychology: Organizational Psychology*.

Di Fabio, A., Giannini, M., Loscalzo, Y., Palazzeschi, L., Bucci, O., Guazzini, A., & Gori, A. (2016). The challenge of fostering healthy organizations: An empirical study on the role of workplace relational civility in acceptance of change and well-being. *Frontiers in Psychology: Organizational Psychology*, 7, 1748. doi:10.3389/fpsyg.2016.01748.

Di Fabio, A., & Gori, A. (2016a). Assessing Workplace Relational Civility (WRC) with a new multidimensional "mirror" measure. *Frontiers in Psychology: Section Organizational Psychology*, 7, 890. doi:10.3389/fpsyg.2016.00890.

Di Fabio, A., & Gori, A. (2016b). Developing a new instrument for assessing Acceptance of Change. *Frontiers in Psychology: Section Organizational Psychology*, 7, 802. doi:10.3389/fpsyg.2016.00802.

Di Fabio, A., & Gori, A. (2016c). Neuroticism and flourishing in white collars workers: From Self-Esteem to Intrapreneurial Self-Capital for adaptive outcomes. In A. Di Fabio (Ed.), *Neuroticism: Characteristics, impact on job performance and health outcomes* (pp. 129–146). New York: Nova Science Publishers.

Di Fabio, A., & Gori, A. (2021). Workplace Relational Civility and Human Capital Sustainability Leadership for sustainable development in organizations: Empirical Evidence. *Counseling: Giornale Italiano di Ricerca e Applicazioni*, 14(2), 33–40. doi:10.14605/CS1422103.

Di Fabio, A., & Kenny, M. E. (2012). Emotional intelligence and perceived social support among Italian high school students. *Journal of Career Development*, 39, 461–475. doi:10.1177/0894845311421005.

Di Fabio, A., & Kenny, M. E. (2015). The contributions of emotional intelligence and social support for adaptive career progress among Italian youth. *Journal of Career Development*, 42, 48–59. doi:10.1177/0894845314533420.

Di Fabio, A., & Kenny, M. E. (2016a). From decent work to decent lives: Positive Self and Relational Management (PS&RM) in the twenty-first century. *Frontiers in Psychology: Section Organizational Psychology*, 7, 361. doi:10.3389/fpsyg.2016.00361.

Di Fabio, A., & Kenny, M. E. (2016b). Promoting well-being: The contribution of emotional intelligence. *Frontiers in Psychology: Organizational Psychology*, 7, 1182. doi:10.3389/fpsyg.2016.01182.

Di Fabio, A., & Kenny, M. E. (2018a). Academic relational civility as a key resource for sustaining well-being. *Sustainability*, 10(6), 1914. doi:10.3390/su10061914.

Di Fabio, A., & Kenny, M. E. (2018b). Connectedness to nature, personality traits and empathy from a sustainability perspective. *Current Psychology*, 40, 1–12. doi:10.1007/s12144-018-0031-4.

Di Fabio, A., & Kenny, M. E. (2018c). Intrapreneurial Self-Capital: A key resource for promoting well-being in a shifting work landscape. *Sustainability*, 10(9), 3035. doi:10.3390/su10093035.

Di Fabio, A., & Kenny, M. E. (2019). Resources for enhancing employee and organizational well-being beyond personality traits: The promise of Emotional Intelligence and Positive Relational Management. *Personality and Individual Differences* (Special Issue Personality, Individual Differences and Healthy Organizations), 151, 109278. doi:10.1016/j.paid.2019.02.022.

Di Fabio, A., & Kenny, M. E. (2021). Positive and negative affects and meaning at work: Trait emotional intelligence as a primary prevention resource in organizations for sustainable and positive human capital development. In A. Di Fabio (Ed.), *Cross-cultural Perspectives on Well-Being and Sustainability in Organizations* (pp. 139–152). Switzerland: Springer.

Di Fabio, A., Maree, J. G., & Kenny, M. E. (2018). Development of the Life Project Reflexivity Scale: A new career intervention inventory. *Journal of Career Assessment*, 27(2), 1–13. doi:10.1177/1069072718758065.

Di Fabio, A., & Palazzeschi, L. (2015). Hedonic and eudaimonic well-being: The role of resilience beyond fluid intelligence and personality traits. *Frontiers in Psychology: Section Developmental Psychology*, 6, 1367. doi:10.3389/fpsyg.2015.01367.

Di Fabio, A., & Palazzeschi, L. (2023). Gratitude: A promising resource for well-being beyond personality traits in university students. *Counseling. Giornale Italiano di Ricerca e Applicazioni*, 16(1). doi:10.14605/CS1612304.

Di Fabio, A., & Palazzeschi, L. (in press a). Hope: From personality trait to gratitude in university students. *Counseling: Giornale Italiano di Ricerca e Applicazioni*.

Di Fabio, A., & Palazzeschi, L. (in press b). Acceptance of change in workers: Personality traits or gratitude? *Counseling: Giornale Italiano di Ricerca e Applicazioni*.

Di Fabio, A., Palazzeschi, L., Bonfiglio, A., Gori, A., & Svicher, A. (2023a). Hedonic and eudaimonic well-being for sustainable development in university students: Personality traits or acceptance of change? *Frontiers in Psychology*, 14, 1180995. doi: 10.3389/fpsyg.2023.1180995.

Di Fabio, A., Palazzeschi, L., & Bucci, O. (2017). In an unpredictable and changing environment: Intrapreneurial Self-Capital as a key resource for life satisfaction and flourishing. *Frontiers in Psychology: Organizational Psychology*, 8, 1819. doi:10.3389/fpsyg.2017.01819.

Di Fabio, A., Palazzeschi, L., & Duradoni, M. (2019). Intrapreneurial self-capital mediates the connectedness to nature effect on well-being at work. *International Journal of Environmental Research and Public Health*, 16(22), 4359. doi:10.3390/ijerph16224359.

Di Fabio, A., Palazzeschi, L., Gori, A., & Svicher, A. (in press). Hedonic and eudaimonic well-being for sustainable development in university students: Personality traits or acceptance of change? *Frontiers in Psychology: Organizational Psychology*.

Di Fabio, A., & Peiró, J. M. (2018a). Human Capital Sustainability Leadership to promote sustainable development and healthy organizations: A new scale. *Sustainability*, 10(7), 2413. doi:10.3390/su10072413.

Di Fabio, A., & Peiró, J. M. (2018b). *Human Capital Sustainability Leadership and Eudaimonic Well-being*. Poster presented at the Second international cross-cultural conference "Healthier societies fostering healthy organizations: A cross-cultural perspective" organized by the Department of Education and Psychology, University of Florence, Florence, Italy, August 30–September 1, 2018.

Di Fabio, A., & Pesce, E. (2018). Workplace Relational Civility, leadership transazionale e leadership trasformazionale. *Counseling: Giornale Italiano di Ricerca e Applicazioni*, 11(2). doi:10.14605/CS1121805.

Di Fabio, A., & Rosen, M. A. (2018). Opening the black box of psychological processes in the science of sustainable development: A new frontier. *European Journal of Sustainable Development Research*, 2(4), 47. doi:10.20897/ejosdr/3933.

Di Fabio, A., & Rosen, M. A. (2019). Accounting for individual differences in connectedness to nature: Personality and gender differences. *Sustainability*, 11, 1693. doi:10.3390/su11061693.

Di Fabio, A., & Rosen, M. A. (2020). An exploratory study of a new psychological instrument for evaluating sustainability: The Sustainable Development Goals Psychological Inventory. *Sustainability*, 12, 7617. doi:10.3390/su12187617.

Di Fabio, A., & Saklofske, D. H. (2014). Promoting individual resources: The challenge of trait emotional intelligence. *Personality and Individual Differences*, 65, 19–23.

Di Fabio, A., & Saklofske, D. H. (2018). The contributions of personality and emotional intelligence to resiliency. *Personality and Individual Differences*, 123, 140–144. doi:10.1016/j.paid.2017.11.012.

Di Fabio, A., & Saklofske, D. H. (2019a). Positive relational management for sustainable development: Beyond personality traits – the contribution of emotional intelligence. *Sustainability*, 11(2), 330, doi:10.3390/su11020330.

Di Fabio, A., & Saklofske, D. H. (2019b). The contributions of personality traits and emotional intelligence to intrapreneurial self-capital: Key resources for sustainability and sustainable development. *Sustainability*, 11, 1240. doi:10.3390/su11051240.

Di Fabio, A., & Saklofske, D. H. (2021). The relationship of compassion and self-compassion with personality and emotional intelligence. *PAID 40th Anniversary Special Issue: Personality and Individual Differences*, 169. doi:10.1016/j.paid.2020.110109.

Di Fabio, A., Smith, M. M., & Saklofske, D. H. (2020). Perfectionism and a healthy attitude toward oneself: Could humor be a resource? *International Journal of Environmental Research and Public Health*, 17, 201. doi:10.3390/ijerph17010201.

Di Fabio, A., & Svicher, A. (2021). Emotional intelligence: A key for Human Capital Sustainability Leadership beyond personality traits. *Counseling. Giornale Italiano di Ricerca e Applicazioni*, 14(3). doi:10.14605/CS1432105Di.

Di Fabio, A., Svicher, A., & Gori, A. (2021). Occupational Fatigue: Relationship with Personality Traits and Decent Work. *Frontiers in Psychology*, 12, 3782. doi:10.3389/fpsyg.2021.742809.

Di Fabio, A., Svicher, A., Palazzeschi, L., & Gori, A. (2022). Revitalising Career Counseling for Sustainable Decent Work and Decent Lives: From Personality Traits to Life Project Reflexivity for Well-being. *Cypriot Journal of Educational Sciences*, 17(5), 1468–1476. doi:10.18844/cjes.v17i5.6675.

Di Fabio, A., & Tsuda, A. (2018). The psychology of harmony and harmonization: Advancing the perspectives for the psychology of sustainability and sustainable development. *Sustainability* 10(12), 4726. doi:10.3390/su10124726.

Duffy, R. D., Allan, B. A., England, J. W., Blustein, D. L., Autin, K. L., Douglass, R. P., ... & Santos, E. J. (2017). The development and initial validation of the Decent Work Scale. *Journal of Counseling Psychology*, 64(2), 206–221. doi:10.1037/cou0000191.

Duradoni, M., & Di Fabio, A. (2019). Intrapreneurial self-capital and connectedness to nature within organizations. *Sustainability*, 11, 3699. doi:10.3390/su11133699.

Frost, R. O., & Shows, D. L. (1993). The nature and measurement of compulsive indecisiveness. *Behaviour Research and Therapy*, 31(7), 683–692. doi:10.1016/0005-7967(93)90121-A.

Fugate, M., & Kinicki. A. J. (2008). A dispositional approach to employability: Development of a measure and test of implications for employee reactions to organizational change. *Journal of Occupational and Organizational Psychology*, 81, 503–527. doi:10.1348/096317907X241579.

Gori, A., Arcioni, A., Topino, E., Palazzeschi, L., & Di Fabio, A. (2021). Constructing well-being in organizations: First empirical results on job crafting, personality traits, and insight. *International Journal of Environmental Research and Public Health*, 18, 6661. doi:10.3390/ijerph18126661.

Gori, A., Craparo, G., Giannini, M., Loscalzo, Y., Caretti, V., La Barbera, D., ... & Schuldberg, D. (2015). Development of a new measure for assessing insight: Psychometric properties of the insight orientation scale (IOS). *Schizophrenia Research*, 169(1–3), 298–302. doi:10.1016/j.schres.2015.10.014.

Gori, A., & Di Fabio, A. (2015, September). *La resilienza nelle organizzazioni: accettazione del cambiamento come strategia positiva [Resilience in organization: acceptance of change as positive strategy]*. In P. Argentero (Chair), Thematic session on Cambiamento e gestione delle transizioni [*Change and management of transitions*] conducted at the Annual Conference of the Italian Association of Psychology (Organizational Psychology Section), University of Palermo, Palermo, Italy, 17–19 September 2015.

Gori, A., Topino, E., Palazzeschi, L., & Di Fabio, A. (2020). How can organizational justice contribute to job satisfaction? A chained mediation Model. *Sustainability*, 12, 7902. doi:10.3390/su12197902.

Gori, A., Topino, E., Svicher, A., & Di Fabio, A. (2022). Towards meaning in life: A path analysis exploring the mediation of career adaptability in the associations of self-esteem with presence of meaning and search for meaning. *International Journal of Environmental Research and Public Health*. 19(19), 11901. doi:10.3390/ijerph191911901.

Gu, J., Cavanagh, K., Baer, R., & Strauss, C. (2017). An empirical examination of the factor structure of compassion. *PLoS One*, 12(2), e0172471. doi:10.1371/journal.pone.0172471.

Haar, J., Di Fabio, A., & Daellenbach, U. (2019a). Does positive relational management benefit managers higher up the hierarchy? A moderated-mediation study of New Zealand Managers. *Sustainability*, 11, 4373. doi:10.3390/su11164373.

Haar, J., Schmitz, A., Di Fabio, A., & Daellenbach, U. (2019b). The role of relationships at work and happiness: A moderated mediation study of New Zealand managers. *Sustainability*, 11, 3443. doi:10.3390/su11123443.

Hage, S. M., Romano, J. L., Conyne, R. K., Kenny, M., Matthews, C., Schwartz, J. P., & Waldo, M. (2007). Best practice guidelines on prevention practice, research, training, and social advocacy for psychologists. *The Counseling Psychologist*, 35(4), 493–566. doi:10.1177/0011000006291411.

Harris, J. M. (2003). Sustainability and sustainable development. *International Society for Ecological Economics*, 1(1), 1–12.

He, C., McCabe, B., Jia, G., & Sun, J. (2020). Effects of Safety Climate and Safety Behavior on Safety Outcomes between Supervisors and Construction Workers, *Journal of Construction Engineering and Management*, 146(1), 04019092. doi:10.1061/(asce)co.1943-7862.0001735.

Hsieh, H. F., & Shannon, S. E. (2005). Three approaches to qualitative content analysis. *Qualitative Health Research*, 15(9), 1277–1288. doi:10.1177/1049732305276687.

Jena, L. K., & Goyal, S. (2022). Emotional intelligence and employee innovation: Sequential mediating effect of person-group fit and adaptive performance. *European Review of Applied Psychology*, 72(1), 100729. doi:10.1016/j.erap.2021.100729.

Judge, T. A., Locke, E. A., Durham, C. C., & Kluger, A. N. (1998). Dispositional effects on job and life satisfaction: The role of core evaluations. *Journal of Applied Psychology*, 83, 17–34. doi:10.1037/0021-9010.83.1.17.

Kumar, D., Upadhyay, Y., Yadav, R., & Goyal, A. K. (2022). Psychological capital and innovative work behaviour: The role of mastery orientation and creative self-efficacy. *International Journal of Hospitality Management*, 102, 103157. doi:10.1016/j.ijhm.2022.103157.

Leana, C., Appelbaum, E., & Shevchuk, I. (2009). Work process and quality of care in early childhood education: The role of job crafting. *Academy of Management Journal*, 52(6), 1169–1192. doi:10.5465/AMJ.2009.47084651.

Lent, R. W., Brown, S. D., & Hackett, G. (1994). Toward a unifying social cognitive theory of career and academic interest, choice, and performance. *Journal of Vocational Behavior*, 45(1), 79–122. doi:10.1006/jvbe.1994.1027.

Lyubomirsky, S., King, L., & Diener, E. (2005). The benefits of frequent positive affect: Does happiness lead to success? *Psychological Bulletin*, 131, 803–855. doi:10.1037/0033-2909.131.6.803.

Martin, R. A., Puhlik-Doris, P., Larsen, G., Gray, J., & Weir, K. (2003). Individual differences in uses of humor and their relation to psychological well-being: Development of the Humor Styles Questionnaire. *Journal of Research in Personality*, 37 (1), 48–75. doi:10.1016/S0092-6566(02)00534-2.

Martinidis, G., Komninos, N., & Carayannis, E. (2022). Taking into account the human factor in regional innovation systems and policies. *Journal of the Knowledge Economy*, 13, 849–879. https://doi.org/10.1007/s13132-021-00722-z.

Mayer, F. S., & Frantz, C. M. (2004). The connectedness to nature scale: A measure of individuals' feeling in community with nature. *Journal of Environmental Psychology*, 24(4), 503–515. doi:10.1016/j.jenvp.2004.10.001.

Mayer, J. D., Salovey, P., & Caruso, D. R. (2002). *Mayer-Salovey-Caruso emotional intelligence scale*. Toronto: MHI.

Messmann, G., Evers, A., & Kreijns, K. (2022). The role of basic psychological needs satisfaction in the relationship between transformational leadership and innovative work behavior. *Human Resource Development Quarterly*, 33(1), 29–45. https://doi.org/10.1002/hrdq.21451.

Mirza, M. Z., Isha, A. S. N., Memon, M. A., Azeem, S., & Zahid, M. (2022). Psychosocial safety climate, safety compliance and safety participation: The mediating role of psychological distress. *Journal of Management & Organization*, 28(2), 363–378. doi:10.1017/jmo.2019.35.

Morgan, J., & Farsides, T. (2009). Psychometric evaluation of the meaningful life measure. *Journal of Happiness Studies*, 10(3), 351–366. doi:10.1007/s10902-008-9093-6.

Mukerjee, J., & Metiu, A. (2022). Play and psychological safety: An ethnography of innovative work. *Journal of Product Innovation Management*, 39(3), 394–418. https://doi.org/10.1111/jpim.12598.

Neff, K. D. (2003). The development and validation of a scale to measure self-compassion. *Self and Identity*, 2(3), 223–250. doi:10.1080/15298860390209035.

Oreg, S. (2003). Resistance to change: Developing an individual differences measure. *Journal of Applied Psychology*, 88(4), 680–693. doi:10.1037/0021-9010.88.4.680.

Palazzeschi, L., Gori, A., Arcioni, A., Gazzaniga, M., & Di Fabio, A. (2021). Employability: dai tratti di personalità alla resilienza in studenti universitari [Employability: from personality traits to resilience in university students]. *Counseling: Giornale Italiano di Ricerca e Applicazioni*, 14(1). doi:10.14605/CS1412104.

Peiró, J. M., Bayona, J. A., Caballer, A., & Di Fabio, A. (2020). Importance of work characteristics affects job performance: The mediating role of individual dispositions on the work design-performance relationships. *PAID 40th Anniversary Special Issue: Personality and Individual Differences*, 157. doi:10.1016/j.paid.2019.109808.

Petrides, K. V., & Furnham, A. (2000). On the dimensional structure of emotional intelligence. *Personality and Individual Differences*, 29(2), 313–320. doi:10.1016/S0191-8869(99)00195-6.

Rosen, M. A. (2009). Energy sustainability: A pragmatic approach and illustrations. *Sustainability*, 1, 55–80. doi:10.3390/su1010055.

Savickas, M. L., & Porfeli, E. J. (2012). Career Adapt-Abilities Scale: Construction, reliability, and measurement equivalence across 13 countries. *Journal of Vocational Behavior*, 80(3), 661–673. doi:10.1016/j.jvb.2012.01.011.

Schultz, P. W. (2002). Inclusion with nature: The psychology of human-nature relations. In P. Schmuck & W. P. Schultz (Eds.), *Psychology of sustainable development* (pp. 61–78). Boston, MA: Springer.

Schutte, N. S., Malouff, J. M., Hall, L. E., Haggerty, D. J., Cooper, J. T., Golden, C. J., & Dornheim, L. (1998). Development and validation of a measure of emotional intelligence. *Personality and Individual Differences*, 25, 167–177. doi:10.1016/S0191-8869(98)00001-4.

Snyder, C. R., Harris, C., Anderson, J. R., Holleran, S. A., Irving, L. M., Sigmon, S. T., ... & Harney, P. (1991). The will and the ways: Development and validation of an individual-differences measure of hope. *Journal of Personality and Social Psychology*, 60(4), 570–585. doi:10.1037/0022-3514.60.4.570.

Steger, M. F., Dik, B. J., & Duffy, R. D. (2012). Measuring meaningful work: The work and meaning inventory (WAMI). *Journal of Career Assessment*, 20(3), 322–337. doi:10.1177/1069072711436160.

Svicher, A., & Di Fabio, A. (2021). Hedonic and eudaimonic well-being: Personality traits and career decision-making self-efficacy. *Counseling: Giornale Italiano di Ricerca e Applicazioni*, 14(3), 88–93. doi:10.14605/CS1432106.

Svicher, A., Di Fabio, A., & Gori, A. (2022). Decent work in Italy: A network analysis. *Australian Journal of Career Development*, 31(1), 42–56. doi:10.1177/10384162221089462.

Svicher, A., Gori, A., & Di Fabio, A. (2022a). The Sustainable Development Goals Psychological Inventory: A network analysis in Italian university students. *International Journal of Environmental Research and Public Health*. 19(17), 10675. doi:10.3390/ijerph191710675.

Svicher, A., Gori, A., & Di Fabio, A. (2022b). Work as Meaning Inventory: A network analysis in Italian workers and students. *Australian Journal of Career Development*. 31(2), 130–148. doi:10.1177/10384162221110361.

Topino, E., Svicher, A., Di Fabio, A., & Gori, A. (2022). Satisfaction with life in workers: A chained mediation model investigating the roles of resilience, career adaptability, self-efficacy, and years of education. *Frontiers in Psychology Organizational Psychology*, 13, 1011093. doi:10.3389/fpsyg.2022.1011093.

United Nations. (2018). *About the Sustainable Development Goals 2018*. Retrieved from https://www.un.org.

Viola, F. (2021). Electric vehicles and psychology. *Sustainability*, 13, 719. https://doi.org/10.3390/su13020719.

Watkins, P. C., Woodward, K., Stone, T., & Kolts, R. L. (2003). Gratitude and happiness: Development of a measure of gratitude and relationships with subjective well-being. *Social Behavior and Personality: An International Journal*, 31(5), 431–452. https://doi.org/10.2224/sbp.2003.31.5.431.

Watson, D., Clark, L. A., & Tellegen, A. (1988). Development and validation of brief measures of positive and negative affect: The PANAS scales. *Journal of Personality and Social Psychology*, 54(6), 1063–1070. doi:10.1037//0022-3514.54.6.1063.

Winwood, P. C., Winefield, A. H., Dawson, D., & Lushington, K. (2005). Development and validation of a scale to measure work-related fatigue and recovery: The Occupational Fatigue Exhaustion/Recovery Scale (OFER). *Journal of Occupational and Environmental Medicine,* 47(6), 594–606. doi:10.1097/01.jom.0000161740.71049.c4.

Zacharaki, A., Kostavelis, I., Gasteratos, A., & Dokas, I. (2020). Safety bounds in human robot interaction: A survey. *Safety Science,* 127(July), 104667. doi:10.1016/j.ssci.2020.104667.

Zimet, G. D., Dahlem, N. W., Zimet, S. G., & Farley, G. K. (1988). The Multidimensional Scale of Perceived Social Support. *Journal of Personality Assessment,* 52, 30–41. doi:10.1207/s15327752jpa5201_2.

3   Climate Change Denial

Causes, Consequences, and Cure

Jona Leka and Adrian Furnham

It is worse, much worse, than you think. The slowness of climate change is a fairy tale, perhaps as pernicious as the one that says it isn't happening at all, and comes to us bundled with several others in an anthology of comforting delusions: that global warming is an Arctic saga, unfolding remotely; that it is strictly a matter of sea level and coastlines, not an enveloping crisis sparing no place and leaving no life undeformed; that it is a crisis of the "natural" world, not the human one; that those two are distinct, and that we live today somehow outside or beyond or at the very least defended against nature, not inescapably within and literally overwhelmed by it; that wealth can be a shield against the ravages of warming; that the burning of fossil fuels is the price of continued economic growth; that growth, and the technology it produces, will allow us to engineer our way out of environmental disaster; that there is any analogue to the scale or scope of this threat, in the long span of human history, that might give us confidence in staring it down.

(Wallace-Wells, 2018, p. 5)

The Problem of Climate Change for Companies

Climate change (CC) is one of the most contested and complex issues of the 21st century with potentially devastating effects upon the natural habitat and its inhabitants. This refers to alterations in temperature and other atmospheric conditions on Earth as a result of increases in greenhouse gases caused by human activity (Allen et al., 2018). As highlighted above by Wallace-Wells, it has quickly become apparent that many sectors of the economy will suffer the consequences of climate change if industries fail to radically cut their carbon emissions. As a result, a growing number of companies are recognizing the need to integrate climate-related concerns into their strategic decision making. However, many businesses encounter resistance to sustainable reforms within their organizational environment. One of the main obstacles to sustainable development goals is the disbelief in climate change, or climate change scepticism. The goal of this chapter is to describe and synthesize research on the causes of climate change scepticism and recommendations to combat it. We first look at measures that assess CC, then the

DOI: 10.4324/9781003212157-4

forms of scepticism and arguments employed by people who espouse these beliefs. Next, we look at psychological causes for the phenomenon, such as different forms of motivated reasoning and system justification strategies. We also take a look at the characteristics of sceptics in terms of individual differences, political philosophy, and conspiracy theories that may affect people's openness to the idea that climate change is real. Finally, we discuss best practices to counter climate change scepticism.

Attitudes to Climate Change

To get a good idea about the various attitudes and beliefs about CC, it is perhaps best to examine a few of the many measures that attempt to comprehensively assess them. Three things are worth noting. First, most of these measures are about attitudes rather than knowledge. Second, they highlight very different dimensions. Third, most are constructed from those who are more alarmist-concerned, rather than cynical or sceptical.

Attitudes towards Climate Change and Science Instrument (ACSI) from Dijkstra and Goedhart (2012):

1   People should care more about climate change.
2   Climate change should be given top priority.
3   It is annoying to see people do nothing for the climate change problems.
4   People worry too much about climate change.
5   The seriousness of climate change has been exaggerated.
6   Climate change is a threat to the world.

Pro-environmental behaviour

1   I am careful not to waste water.
2   I am careful not to waste food.
3   I separate most of my waste for recycling.
4   I prefer to use public transport or bicycle over car.
5   I always switch off the lights when I leave a room.
6   I always turn off the computer when I do not use it.
7   I try to save energy.
8   I feel it is important to take good care of the environment.

Climate change knowledge test

1   Most of the current climate change is due to greenhouse gases generated by human activity. If my city will have a heat wave this summer, it means climate is changing.
2   Climate change is only defined as the rising of temperature of the earth's surface.
3   Climate change is a result of the ozone layer becoming thinner.

4 Climate change is partly caused by the increase in the emission of heavy metals.
5 Rise in sea level and drought are some of the consequences of climate change.
6 There is a direct link between climate change and skin cancer.
7 The ocean can absorb CO_2 emitted by humans.
8 Because of climate change, an oxygen deficiency can arise.
9 Because of climate change, the water in seas and oceans will expand.
10 The acidification of the forest is a result of climate change.
11 Because of climate change, certain plants and animals may become extinct

Attitudes to Climate Change instrument from Beattie et al. (2011):
Motivation

1 I am more concerned about climate change after seeing these messages.
2 Climate change is a threat to me personally.
3 I will personally be affected by climate change.
4 I am prepared to make lifestyle changes to reduce climate change.
5 I am prepared to change my everyday behavior to reduce climate change.
6 I am prepared to do more to help reduce climate change.

Empowerment

1 The UK can make a difference in the fight against climate change.
2 Climate change is a problem to be solved by my generation.
3 I can personally help reduce climate change.
4 Everyone can do their bit in the fight against climate change.
5 I feel empowered in the fight against climate change.
6 I am already doing something to help reduce climate change.

Shifting responsibility

1 Climate change is mainly a threat to other countries.
2 It is the responsibility of other countries, not the UK, to reduce climate change.
3 Climate change will only affect future generations.
4 Climate change is a problem to be solved by future generations.
5 It is not my responsibility to reduce climate change.
6 I would do more to try and reduce climate change if other people did more as well.

Fatalism

1 I have no control over climate change.
2 There is no point in me trying to do anything to reduce climate change.

3 I feel helpless in the fight against climate change.
4 Climate change is too difficult to overcome.
5 I feel powerless in the fight against climate change.
6 Some people do not care about climate change.

Climate Change Attitude Survey from Christensen and Knezek (2015):

1 I believe our climate is changing.
2 I am concerned about global climate change.
3 I believe there is evidence of global climate change.
4 Global climate change will impact our environment in the next ten years.
5 Global climate change will impact future generations.
6 The actions of individuals can make a positive difference in global climate change.
7 Human activities cause global climate change.
8 Climate change has a negative effect on our lives.
9 We cannot do anything to stop global climate change.
10 I can do my part to make the world a better place for future generations.
11 Knowing about environmental problems and issues is important to me.
12 I think most of the concerns about environmental problems have been exaggerated.
13 Things I do have no effect on the quality of the environment.
14 It is a waste of time to work to solve environmental problems.
15 There is not much I can do that will help solve environmental problems.

Attitudes to Climate Change from Sinatra et al. (2012):

1 Scientific evidence points to a warming trend in global climate.
2 Human activity has been the driving force behind the warming trend over the last 50 years.
3 The release of CO_2 (carbon dioxide) from human activity (such as smoke stacks and car emissions) has played a central role in raising the average surface temperature of the earth.
4 The surface temperature of the earth has risen by more than 1 degree Fahrenheit since 1900.
5 The Greenland ice cap is melting faster than had previously been thought.
6 Human activity is responsible for the continuing rise in average global temperature.
7 The speed with which the melting ice caps may raise sea levels is uncertain.
8 The likelihood that emissions are the main cause of the observed warming trend of the last 50 years is between 90% and 99%.
9 Former Vice President Al Gore's documentary about global climate change, *An Inconvenient Truth*, is just propaganda.
10 Natural phenomena, such as solar variations combined with volcanic activity, are the real cause of the warming effect.

11   Humans have very little effect on climate temperature.
12   An increase in CO_2 (carbon dioxide) is directly related to an increase in global temperature.
13   It is arrogant to assume that humans can influence climate temperature.

What is Climate Scepticism?

The problematic nature of public perceptions towards climate change is typically talked of in terms of climate scepticism. Climate scepticism implies a level of disbelief in the notion, particularly the causes, of climate change (Poortinga et al., 2011). Scepticism is used to describe doubts about scientific aspects of climate change, such as doubts about whether warming is occurring, what caused it, and the harmfulness of climate change's many effects. Scepticism is also used to address concerns about societal, political, and personal responses to climate change. In the majority of cases, scepticism is used to describe a level of uncertainty regarding the notion of CC. However, in research and the media, climate scepticism is used interchangeably with the concepts of contrarianism and denial (Capstick & Pidgeon, 2014).

People can have a sceptical stance towards CC but still be open to considering evidence, or they can be in complete denial, with their minds made up. Some authors suggest that it is more appropriate to conceptualize climate scepticism as a continuum (Dunlap, 2013). On the one end are those who actively reject climate science, and on the other are those who are uncertain about the actuality, causes, and consequences of climate change.

Washington and Cook (2011) note that a healthy dose of scepticism is at the heart of good science and truth-seekers. However, denial is a distinct mental state whereby one refuses to accept the veracity of a claim regardless of evidence. As such, to deny is not to seek the truth, but rather to deny a truth that one finds unpalatable. Thus, there is an asymmetry between climate scepticism and denial.

There is little doubt that some individuals are in full attack on climate science, which appears to be especially true of the core actors of the so-called denial machine (Dunlap, 2013). This includes representatives from conservative think tanks, contrarian scientists, bloggers, and their followers.

Scholars are studying both phenomena, conducting studies of scepticism among the public as well as the denial-machine that perpetuates the denialist stance (Leiserowitz et al., 2012; McCright & Dunlap, 2011; Poortinga et al., 2011; Whitmarsh, 2011).

The following sections elaborate on both ends of the denial-scepticism continuum in the public and try to illuminate differences between outright denial of climate change and doubts about scientific claims.

Prevalence of Scepticism

National polling companies provide the most credible statistics on climate doubt in the community. Essential Research in Australia and Gallup in the

US run frequent climate change polls. These have shown that only 56% of Australians and 55% of Americans believed in human-caused climate change in 2015. A slight change was reported in 2018, where 63% of Australians and 64% of Americans said human activity causes climate change. The UK has seen the same decline in scepticism as Australia and the US. Although these polls report good trends in recent years, the number of "climate believers" has plateaued. It is therefore noteworthy that a third of the people in the two nations with the biggest per capita carbon-output footprint remain agnostic or suspicious about the evidence.

Scepticism Types

According to early work done by (Rahmstorf, 2004), climate change scepticism can be categorized as: *trend sceptics*, who maintain that global warming is not happening; *attribution sceptics*, who do not believe that humans are the culprits in global warming; and *impact sceptics*, who do not believe that global warming will have serious impacts. The typology of trend attribution and impact is widely used. This has also been articulated as "stages" of denialism, in which a sceptic may begin as a trend sceptic but then shift to an attribution or impact sceptic as evidence of human influence on the climate accumulates.

Differing opinions on climate change have also been studied via audience segmentation analyses, which categorize different portions of the population based on two dimensions: *attitudinal valence* and *issue involvement*. Attitudinal valence refers to the propensity to accept or reject climate science. It comprises beliefs regarding the anthropogenic nature of climate change, its harmful impacts, and scientific agreement on climate change, which are main predictors of support for climate policies and activism (Ding et al., 2011; Roser-Renouf et al., 2016). Issue involvement refers to cognitive and affective engagement with the topic of climate change. It is thought of in terms of attitudinal certainty and the amount of thought devoted to the issue.

One of the best-known segmentation programs is the *Yale Climate Change Project* (2009) led by Anthony Leiserowitz. Leiserowitz and colleagues (2021) have identified six audience segments based on their attitudes and beliefs towards climate change information, which they have termed the Six Americas: *Alarmed, Concerned, Cautious, Disengaged, Doubtful*, and *Dismissive*. Those who fall under the *Alarmed* category are staunch advocates for climate policy because they believe global warming is real, caused by humans, and an immediate threat. The *Concerned* share the view that global warming is occurring due to human activity and poses a significant hazard, and they advocate for climate measures. Climate change is not as high of a priority for them because they think its effects will only be felt far in the future. *Cautious* people are still on the fence about whether or not global warming is real, whereas the *Disinterested* tend to be poorly informed on climate change. They often attribute the phenomenon to chance and are typically politically conservative older males (Leiserowitz et al., 2021). Finally, the *Dismissive* hold the view that global warming is not occurring, is not human-caused, and poses no concern.

In terms of issue involvement, both the Alarmed and Dismissive are sure of their ideas, but the Alarmed comprehend the fundamental facts concerning climate change and embrace scientific claims, while the Dismissive reject them. The Concerned, Cautious, Disengaged, and Doubtful are less engaged in climate change issues (Roser-Renouf et al., 2014).

Independently of the type of scepticism employed, a common thread amongst the climate disbelievers are the methods used to deny scientific evidence. These have been summarized by Diethlem and McKee (2009) as the five science-denialism strategies: (1) *conspiracy theories*, (2) trusting *fake experts*, (3) *cherry picking* (or selectivity) of evidence in line with one's attitudes, (4) *impossible expectations* of research outcomes, and (5) *logical fallacies* and *misrepresentation*. In the next section we go into more detail on the drivers of climate change scepticism, focusing on how denialist strategies, such as conspiracy theories and worldviews, perpetuate the denialist rhetoric.

Drivers of Climate Scepticism

Worldviews

The global economy will need to undergo radical adjustment if we are to successfully combat climate change. While there are a variety of tools available for reducing greenhouse gas emissions, the transition from a fossil fuel-based economy to one that relies on renewable energy sources will require new rules and regulations, such as carbon taxes or explicit emission limits. Those who have built their identities and worldviews around free-market economics will find mitigation to be a difficult task. Given this, it should come as no surprise that research has found a number of worldviews/ideologies play a significant role in shaping people's perspectives on climate change (Hornsey, 2021).

The most consistent finding in climate change scepticism research lies in the role of political worldviews in climate change scepticism. Regardless of how worldviews are measured (e.g., political conservatism or free-market libertarianism), a strong and robust correlation (up to 50% of variance) emerges between right-wing political attitudes and climate change scepticism (Lewandowsky, Gignac, & Oberauer, 2013). Indeed, despite the scientific consensus on CC, the ideological polarization around the subject still remains a pervasive phenomenon. This divide is particularly acute in the US, where 84% of Conservatives can be described as sceptics, but it has also been reported globally.

Ideological polarization has been an important barrier to the advancement of climate change mitigation measures and suggests that climate science facts may be related to motivated reasoning, discussed in the next section.

Conspiracy

There is also a considerable relationship between climate denial and conspiratorial ideation (Leiserowitz et al., 2013). When climate sceptics are pushed to reply to climate change, conspiracies theories are nearly always mentioned. Conspiratorial ideation is the belief that seemingly unrelated events have been perpetrated by bad actors with malevolent agendas. In line with this, conspiratorial rhetoric in the climate change domain maintains that the widespread scientific consensus on anthropogenic climate change is manufactured by the UN, communists, or authoritarians in order to control the populace (Uscinski et al., 2017). Indeed, the notion that climate change is a hoax is one of the most endorsed of all theories (Hornsey & Fielding, 2020).

People are motivated to feel that they understand why things happen. This feeling, however, does not require the pursuit of accurate knowledge and facts (Brick et al., 2021).The attractiveness of climate change conspiracy theories is therefore partially explained by the need to have a coherent narrative of events. However, there are many dangers associated with this type of misinformation in the climate sphere. A particularly insidious aspect of conspiracy theories is that they are "self-sealing" and immune to refutation: when confronted with evidence against a conspiracy, deniers tend to regard it as part of the conspiracy (Lewandowsky, 2020). Moreover, people tend to underestimate the impact that conspiracies have on their beliefs. This makes climate change conspiracies particularly problematic for sustainable development goals, as they reduce people's willingness to reduce their carbon footprint as well as their trust in government and mitigation efforts (Jolley & Douglas, 2014; van der Linden et al., 2015).

Psychological Dynamics of Climate Change Scepticism

When faced with an immediate danger that might lead to the end of society as we know it, how can we make sense of denialism and climate change scepticism? First, we must consider that CC represents a unique threat: occurring on a global scale and stretching over centuries. Second, CC represents a cognitive challenge: changes in the climate are impossible to see, and much less verify, through direct personal experience. This renders CC an abstract statistical phenomenon (Weber, 2016). As a result, people's beliefs and motivations play a major role in a how they approach the phenomenon. Thus, to understand the woeful responses to the climate change crisis, we must turn to human psychology.

Motivated Reasoning

Central to the question of climate change denial is the concept of motivated reasoning. Motivated reasoning theory suggests that the more closely people's views are related to their values, attitudes, identity, and lifestyle, the more likely they are to reject evidence that contradicts them and readily accept evidence that supports them. Thus, in a way, motivated reasoning is a case of biased processing: people draw conclusions, form preferences, or make judgments in ways that are in line with their wants, beliefs, and aspirations (Kunda, 1990).

Motivated reasoning is guided by a goal to reach a specific, desirable conclusion. For instance, the desire to hold onto previous beliefs is a significant motivation biasing reasoning. In such cases, encountering contradictory information can even cause people to cling more strongly to their beliefs (Kerr & Wilson, 2018) – also known as the 'backfire effect' (Cook & Lewandowsky, 2016; Druckman & McGrath, 2019).

Motivated reasoning can be driven by many different goals and values: maintaining a sense of identity or status with a group (social identity protection); maintaining group coherence (social consensus seeking); being consistent with scientific norms and evidence (scientific consensus seeking); maintaining a moral or ideological belief system (value affirmation); and maintaining a prior belief (belief consistency seeking) (Bayes & Druckman, 2021). Many of these identities carry with them prescriptions about what is normative. For instance, a 'Republican' is expected to have certain attitudes about national security, government interventions, individual rights, and so forth. This forms part of their social identity and aids self-definition. Espousing different beliefs entails abandoning this identity and group membership. Faced with this, there is great motivation for members of a certain group to assimilate the group beliefs and attitudes as well as reject ideas that deviate from them. As such, many political conservatives reject climate change claims because they see it as a way for the government to curb freedom of enterprise.

Other researchers have claimed that directionally motivated thinking might be driven by a desire to preserve one's ego; that is, if people's sense of self is threatened, they instinctively reject and fight against that knowledge (Klaczynski & Narasimham, 1998). The consequences of CC are threatening in nature, and the associated individual and social sacrifices in CC mitigation efforts are costly. For instance, acknowledging the reality of CC entails acknowledging that, as a society, we are behaving unsustainably, and radical changes ought to ensue. Accordingly, individuals may be highly motivated to discount the risks.

System Justification Theory

There is strong evidence that motivated reasoning also plays a part in the climate change ideological polarization (Kahan, 2015). For instance, conservatives who read climate science news are less likely to support climate change mitigation legislation than liberals (Hart, Nisbet, & Myers, 2015).

According to Feygina et al. (2010), this is a result of system justification tendencies – the motivation to defend and justify existing socioeconomic systems and institutions – which lead to greater CC denial and less will-ingness take action. Climate change is especially threatening to current sys-tems, as it shines light on the inadequacy of current economic structures, industrial practices, and political systems for sustainable development and collective well-being (Wong-Parodi & Feygina, 2020). Thus, the motivation to preserve the status quo may be particularly high for those with vested inter-ests in current systems.

Socio-Structural and Personality Correlates of Climate Change Beliefs

A number of social psychology and sociological studies have examined associa-tions between demographic variables, Big-Five personality traits, and climate change beliefs. Although at times results have been mixed, some patterns have emerged.

The Big Five traits comprise *Openness, Conscientiousness, Extraversion, Agreeableness*, and *Neuroticism*. Greater environmentalism and climate change beliefs have been frequently associated with higher levels of Agreeableness and Openness to experience. Moreover, greater concern for the environment has also been associated with higher levels of Neuroticism (Milfont et al., 2015).

On the socio-structural side, high levels of religious fundamentalism, especially those endorsing Christian religious traditions of human dominance over nature, have been associated with climate change denial (McCright & Dunlap, 2011).

Finally young, educated females with greater socio-economic status and liberal political beliefs tend to be more environmentally engaged and tend to express more climate change worry than their white male peers. These find-ings have led to the notion of a "conservative white man" effect, in which conservative white males are disproportionately more inclined to deny climate change (Whitmarsh, 2011).

Recommendations for Organizations

In light of the above, we offer five methods to deal with climate change denial in organizational environments: communicating the scientific consensus on climate change, correcting or debunking climate myths, inoculation from misinformation, strategic communication, and value-based messaging.

Scientific Consensus

A consistent finding in the scientific literature is that the communication of the scientific consensus on human-caused climate change is one of the most potent interventions in shifting beliefs about the veracity of anthropogenic climate change (van der Linden, 2021; van der Linden et al., 2015). The *Gateway Belief Model* (GBM) posits that trust in scientific agreement is in fact so crucial as to act as a 'gateway belief' to other key beliefs about climate change (Lewandowsky, et al., 2013; van der Linden et al., 2015). In other words, all misconceptions about climate change are likely to be corrected if this one belief is updated. The GBM model describes a two-step cascading process whereby the effect of consensus messaging on belief about climate change is mediated by the perceived level of agreement. Hence, the effect of perceived level of agreement on support for climate policies and action is mediated by beliefs in climate change. Thus, a change in perceived consensus impacts beliefs and, as a result, increases support.

Debunking

Another way to counter the erroneous beliefs people hold on climate change facts is by debunking climate change myths. This is achieved by offering corrections to erroneous information. However, the effects of corrections are nuanced and at times unreliable.

A common finding in the literature is that individuals will accept and believe corrections to climate myths, but they may continue to rely on incorrect information in other ways. This is known as the *continued influence effect*. For instance, in studies where participants were informed on climate-related misinformation tweeted by President Trump, they acknowledged the correction, but their policy preferences were left unaffected (Porter et al., 2019).

One way to deal with this phenomenon is by offering logic-based corrections. Logic-based corrections target reasoning flaws in pieces of information and can be applied systematically to different forms of misinformation. This offers a practical way to counter erroneous CC claims.

Inoculation

False pieces of information replicate more quickly than correct ones. So, how do we immunize people from them? Inoculation theory suggests that individuals will be better prepared to reject misinformation if they are made aware of the techniques employed by the groups that spread these doubts. Consequently, herd immunity can be achieved when the spread of inoculation outpaces the spread of fake information. This theory borrows from the way vaccination immunizes people against disease, whereby weakened forms of a virus are injected in order for an organism to develop antibodies to fight the real disease. Applying the same logic to climate change misinformation, weak forms of denialist arguments are presented to people in order to equip them with the tools to spot climate change misinformation in the media.

Many inoculation tools and guidelines exist (Cook & Lewandowsky, 2012). For instance, inoculation has been employed in interactive choice-based games, such as *Bad News* developed by Roozenbeek and van der Linden (2019) and *Cranky Uncle* developed by (Cook, 2020). In such games people learn the techniques employed in the spread of misinformation and the logical fallacies found in denialist arguments. Studies have shown that participants are more apt to recognize misinformation after gameplay (Roozenbeek & van der Linden, 2019). Moreover, this cognitive immunity is upheld with regular tests and boosts participants' confidence in their ability to spot misinformation – a central feature in resisting persuasion tactics. Organizations may wish to employ this type of training in order to inoculate their workforce against climate change misinformation.

Strategic Communication

An effective strategy to increase engagement with climate change information is to strategically target the various opinion segments. For instance, Roser-Renouf & Myers (2022) designed three messages with different emphasis on the scientific consensus on climate change, impacts of climate change for communities, and solutions to climate change. They found that targeted messages were more effective in increasing engagement that non-targeted messages. For instance, messages underlining the scientific agreement about anthropogenic climate change had more impact on the Doubtful and Dismissive, who are sceptical or deny climate change entirely; and messages emphasizing the catastrophic impact of climate change on nature and society were more effective on the Cautious and Dismissive segments, who tend to discount the harmful effects of climate change. As such, profiling belief segments might be useful for understanding belief compositions within organizations. Hence, messages that assuage the concerns of each segment might be employed in organizational communications to boost engagement.

Value-based Messaging or Jiu-jitsu Persuasion

A first response to climate change science rejection is to repeat the evidence in clear and digestible formats. However, the ideological divide in climate change suggests that this may be ineffective in changing minds, since people have underlying motivations for holding on to their beliefs. A solution to this is value-based messaging – a strategy called Jiu-jitsu Persuasion – inspired by the martial art of using an opponent's force as an asset in combat.

In the climate sphere, this involves uncovering people's motivations, ideologies, and values and framing sustainable initiatives in ways that align with them (Hornsey & Fielding, 2017). For instance, climate change messages targeted at political conservatives were more effective in fostering policy support when they were framed in terms of free-market belief values, security, and patriotism (Wolsko, 2017). The same principle could be applied to a variety of social identities by emphasizing values that people might feel are threatened by the reality of climate change.

Conclusion

In the absence of strong visible signals of climate change or government regulations and policies, organizational beliefs about the veracity of anthropogenic climate change constitute an essential ingredient for any sustainable development initiatives. Therefore, the pervasiveness of climate change denial and scepticism is still a significant impediment to sustainable goals. People's attitudes about climate change are impacted by a variety of motivations, personality factors, and ideologies. As such, no single approach or strategy will be sufficient to dismantle all obstacles to a cohesive view of the reality of climate change. However, attempts to change minds can benefit from an understanding of those who deny climate change and the reasoning behind this denial. A combination of inoculation training, strategic communications, and value-based messages may be key to reducing scepticism and achieving more sustainable practices and processes in business organizations.

References

Allen, M. R., Dube, O. P., Solecki, W., Aragón-Durand, F., Cramer, W., Humphreys, S., ... & Zickfeld, K. (2018). Chapter 1: Framing and context. In V. Masson-Delmotte, P. Zhai, H.-O. Pörtner, D. Roberts, J. Skea, P. R. Shukla, A. Pirani, W. Moufouma-Okia, C. P. Pidcock , & ... T. Waterfield (Eds.), Global warming of 1.5° C: An IPCC special report on the impacts of global warming of 1.5°C above pre-industrial levels and related global greenhouse gas emission pathways, in the context of strengthening the global response to the threat of climate change, sustainable development, and efforts to eradicate poverty (pp. 49–91). IPCC. https://www.ipcc.ch/sr15/chapter/chapter-1.Bayes, R., & Druckman, J. N. (2021). Motivated reasoning and climate change. *Current Opinion in Behavioral Sciences*, 42, 27–35.

Beattie, G., Sale, L., & McGuire, L. (2011). An inconvenient truth? Can a film really affect psychological mood and our explicit attitudes towards climate change? *Semiotica*, 187, 105–125.

Brick, C., Bosshard, A., & Whitmarsh, L. (2021). Motivation and climate change: A review. *Current Opinion in Psychology*, 42, 82–88.

Capstick, S. B., & Pidgeon, N. F. (2014). What is climate change scepticism? Examination of the concept using a mixed methods study of the UK public. *Global Environmental Change*, 24(1), 389–401.

Christensen, R., & Knezek, G. (2015). The climate change attitude survey: Measuring middle school student beliefs and intentions to enact positive environmental change. *International Journal of Environmental and Science Education*, 10(5), 773–788.

Cook, J. (2020). *Cranky Uncle vs climate change: How to understand and respond to climate science deniers*. Citadel Press.

Cook, J., & Lewandowsky, S. (2012). *The Debunking Handbook*. University of Queensland.

Cook, J., & Lewandowsky, S. (2016). Rational irrationality: Modeling climate change belief polarization using Bayesian networks. *Topics in Cognitive Science*, 8(1), 160–179.

Diethlem, P., & McKee, M. (2009). Denialism: What it is and how should scientists respond? *European Journal of Public Health*, 19(1), 2–4.

Dijkstra, E. M., & Goedhart, M. J. (2012). Development and validation of the ACSI: Measuring students' science attitudes, pro-environmental behaviour, climate change attitudes and knowledge. *Environmental Education Research*, 18(6), 733–749.

Ding, D., Maibach, E. W., Zhao, X., Roser-Renouf, C., & Leiserowitz, A. (2011). Support for climate policy and societal action are linked to perceptions about scientific agreement. *Nature Climate Change*, 1, 462–466. https://doi.org/10.1038/nclimate1295.

Druckman, J. N., & McGrath, M. C. (2019). The evidence for motivated reasoning in climate change preference formation. *Nature Climate Change*, 9(2), 111–119.

Dunlap, R. E. (2013). Climate Change Skepticism and Denial: An Introduction. *American Behavioral Scientist*, 57(6), 691–698.

Feygina, I., Jost, J. T., & Goldsmith, R. E. (2010). System justification, the denial of global warming and the possibility of "system-sanctioned change". *Personality and Social Psychology Bulletin*, 36(3), 326–338.

Hart, P. S., Nisbet, E. C., & Myers, T. A. (2015). Public attention to science and political news and support for climate change mitigation. *Nature Climate Change*, 5, 541–545.

Hornsey, M. J. (2021). The role of worldviews in shaping how people appraise climate change. *Current Opinions in Behavioral Sciences*, 42, 36–41.

Hornsey, M. J., & Fielding, K. S. (2017). Attitude roots and jiu jitsu persuasion: Understanding and overcoming the motivated rejection of science. *American Psychologist*, 72(5), 459–473.

Hornsey, M. J., & Fielding, K. S. (2020). Understanding (and Reducing) Inaction on Climate Change. *Social Issues and Policy Review*, 14(1), 3–35.

Jolley, D., & Douglas, K. M. (2014). The social consequences of conspiracism: Exposure to conspiracy theories decreases intentions to engage in politics and to reduce one's carbon footprint. *British Journal of Psychology*, 105(1), 35–56.

Kahan, D. M. (2015). Climate-science communication and the measurement problem. *Political Psychology*, 36(S1), 1–43.

Kerr, J. R., & Wilson, M. S. (2018). Changes in perceived scientific consensus shift beliefs about climate change and GM food safety. *PLOS ONE*, 13(7), e0200295.

Klaczynski, P. A., & Narasimham, G. (1998). Development of scientific reasoning biases: Cognitive versus ego-protective explanations. *Developmental Psychology*, 34(1), 175–187.

Kunda, Z. (1990). The Case for Motivated Reasoning. *Psychological Bulletin*, 108(3), 480–498.

Leiserowitz, A., Maibach, E., Roser-Renouf, C., & Hmielowski, J. (2012). *Global warming's six Americas*. Yale University and George Mason University, Yale Project on Climate Change Communication.

Leiserowitz, A., Maibach, E. W., Roser-Renouf, C., Smith, N., & Dawson, E. (2013). Climategate, public opinion, and the loss of trust. *American Behavioral Scientist*, 57(6), 818–837.

Leiserowitz, A., Roser-Renouf, C., Marlon, J., & Maibach, E. (2021). Global Warming's Six Americas: A review and recommendations for climate change communication. *Current Opinion in Behavioral Sciences*, 42, 97–103.

Lewandowsky, S. (2020). Climate Change Disinformation and How to Combat It. *Annual Review of Public Health*, 42, 1–21.

Lewandowsky, S., Gignac, G. E., & Oberauer, K. (2013). The Role of Conspiracist Ideation and Worldviews in Predicting Rejection of Science. *PLoS ONE*, 8(10), e75637.

Lewandowsky, S., Gignac, G. E., & Vaughan, S. (2013). The pivotal role of perceived scientific consensus in acceptance of science. *Nature Climate Change*, 3(4), 399–404.

McCright, A. M., & Dunlap, R. E. (2011). Cool dudes: The denial of climate change among conservative White males. *Global Environmental Change*, 21, 1163–1172.

Milfont, T. L., Milojev, P., Greaves, L. M., & Sibley, C. G. (2015). Socio-structural and psychological foundations of climate change beliefs. *New Zealand Journal of Psychology*, 44(1), 17–30.

Poortinga, W., Spence, A., Whitmarsh, L., Capstick, S., & Pidgeon, N. F. (2011). Uncertain climate: An investigation into public scepticism about anthropogenic climate change. *Global Environmental Change*, 21(3), 1015–1024.

Porter, E., Wood, T. J., & Bahador, B. (2019). Can presidential misinformation on climate change be corrected? Evidence from internet and phone experiments. *Research & Politics*, 6(3). https://doi.org/10.1177/2053168019864784.

Rahmstorf, S. (2004). The climate sceptics. *Potsdam Institute for Climate Impact Research*, 76–82.

Roozenbeek, J., & van der Linden, S. (2019). The fake news game: Actively inoculating against the risk of misinformation. *Journal of Risk Research*, 22(5), 570–580.

Roser-Renouf, C., Atkinson, L., Maibach, E., & Leiserowitz, A. (2016). The consumer as climate activist. *International Journal of Communication*, 10, 4759–4783.

Roser-Renouf, C., Stenhouse, N., Rolfe-Redding, J., Maibach, E. W., & Leiserowitz, A. (2014). Engaging Diverse Audiences with Climate Change: Message Strategies for Global Warming's Six Americas. *SSRN Electronic Journal*, 1–33.

Sinatra, G. M., Kardash, C. M., Taasoobshirazi, G., & Lombardi, D. (2012). Promoting attitude change and expressed willingness to take action toward climate change in college students. *Instructional Science*, 40(1), 1–17.

Uscinski, J. E., Douglas, K., & Lewandowsky, S. (2017, September 26). Climate Change Conspiracy Theories. In *Oxford Research Encyclopedia of Climate Science*. https://doi.org/10.1093/acrefore/9780190228620.013.328.

van der Linden, S. (2021). The Gateway Belief Model (GBM): A review and research agenda for communicating the scientific consensus on climate change. *Current Opinion in Psychology*, 42, 7–12.

van der Linden, S. L., Leiserowitz, A. A., Feinberg, G. D., & Maibach, E. W. (2015). The scientific consensus on climate change as a gateway belief: Experimental evidence. *PLoS ONE*, 10(2), 2–9.

Wallace-Wells, D. (2018). The Uninhabitable Earth. In S. Holt (Ed.), *The Best American Magazine Writing 2018* (pp. 271–294). Columbia University Press.

Washington, H., & Cook, J. (2011). *Climate change denial: Heads in the sand*. Earthscan.

Weber, E. U. (2016). What shapes perceptions of climate change? New research since 2010. *Wiley Interdisciplinary Reviews: Climate Change*, 7(1), 125–134.

Whitmarsh, L. (2011). Scepticism and uncertainty about climate change: Dimensions, determinants and change over time. *Global Environmental Change*, 21(2), 690–700.

Wolsko, C. (2017). Expanding the range of environmental values: Political orientation, moral foundations, and the common ingroup. *Journal of Environmental Psychology*, 51, 284–294.

Wong-Parodi, G., & Feygina, I. (2020). Understanding and countering the motivated roots of climate change denial. *Current Opinion in Environmental Sustainability*, 42, 60–64.

4 From Precarious Jobs to Sustainable Livelihoods

Stuart C. Carr, Darrin Hodgetts, Veronica Hopner, Pita King, James H. Liu, Molefe Maleka, Ines Meyer, Minh Hieu Nguyen, Johan Potgieter, Mahima Saxena and Charles L. Tchagnéno

> Radical intervention is needed to ensure that future generations not only survive but develop, grow and express themselves meaningfully through decent work.
>
> (Di Fabio & Maree, 2016, p. 1)

In its first 100 years, Work and Organizational Psychology (WOP) has been following Economics. We have placed faith in 'the job' as an engine not only for economic growth, but also human wellbeing (Carr, 2022a; Carr, Hopner, & Hodgetts, 2023). In its second century, major United Nations (UN) institutions like the International Labor Organization (ILO, 2019) and the World Bank (2019) have challenged this pliant act of faith (in jobs). These UN agencies have recently performed spectacular U-turns on 'the job.' Respectively, they have (a) identified poor working conditions as the main challenge for the world of work, and (b) presaged a need, going forward into (and out of) a pandemic, to 'protect people, *not* jobs.' In light of the Di Fabio and Maree quote above, protecting people *from* jobs, which is what this call implies, requires a new, broader, and more inclusive concept than 'the job' for capturing the diverse ways that people make, can make, and will make their livelihoods.

Our chapter argues that *Sustainable Livelihoods* is that concept. Relatable and sensible to most workers, it is an idea that arguably predates 'the job' by millennia (Macrosty, 1898), giving it durable legs to carry humanity into the 21st century – including a new century for WOP. A 'livelihood' entails all forms of work, not just jobs, and it must, broadly speaking, provide decent work conditions, including opportunities for people to expand their skills and capabilities. A livelihood is 'sustainable' only when it protects people from shocks like COVID-19 and when it supports livelihoods for others, by contributing to their wellbeing and skills, now and for future generations. A social and relational span like this recognizes, more than any individualized 'job' from which people now require protecting, that your livelihood is connected to mine, and mine to yours.

Pre-existing concepts in WOP, like portfolio careers, social identity theory, and work-life balance, have scratched the surface of these variegated,

DOI: 10.4324/9781003212157-5

stratified, and communing aspects of work. Sustaining Livelihoods goes considerably deeper. Livelihoods that are sustainable de facto connect us (WOPs), and our work (in Humanitarian Work Psychology), to the UN Sustainable Development Goals (SDGs). In particular, they would boost and extend the goal of SDG-8 – decent work and economic development (United Nations, 2022).

After a brief introduction to sustainable livelihoods via its history, this chapter illustrates how a humanitarian Work and Organizational Psychology (WOP), based around Sustainable Livelihoods, would embrace the following: (1) living wages and fair trade; (2) livelihoods across the vast and frequently 'illegal' informal sector; (3) inclusive social enterprises; (4) interfaces with digital automation and Basic Income; (5) multi-faceted gift economies; and (6) shifts to livelihoods that help to protect ecosystems, including flora and fauna on and in land and sea (Tansley, 1935). Synthesizing (1) through (6), the chapter concludes by calling on the UN to make Sustainable Livelihoods a global development goal in the next round of goals post–2030.

From Precarious Jobs to Sustainable Livelihoods

In the past, throughout its own history, WOP was founded and grounded, both conceptually and practically, on and in 'the job': job analysis, job description, job evaluation, job selection, job performance, job retention, and turnover – the list goes on inexorably towards job wellbeing and job-less ill-being. Throughout the post-World War II period, livelihoods were seen as *depending* on steady, secure, and possibly even lifetime jobs (St-Denis, 2020). Gaining or losing one's job had pretty immediate, and demonstrably so, effects on mental health (Murphy & Athanasou, 1999). Thus, at the turn of this century and up to less than a decade ago, the World Bank (2012), in a landmark *World Development Report*, was touting 'jobs' as a key, core pillar in the fight against poverty.

However, the very next year another caveat was added to the anti-poverty panacea that jobs were supposed to be – to work for people, the job itself had to be of good *quality* (World Bank, 2013). By the mid-2010s, countless numbers of livelihoods from around the world were recognized as simply not sustainable but, instead, 'precarious' (Standing, 2016). By the eve of the 2010s and the dawn of COVID-19, it was becoming clear that 'the job' was a panacea neither for poverty eradication nor for general wellbeing. The numbers do not lie: two out of every three of the 3.3 billion workers across the world were working informally in 'own-account,' 'vulnerable' roles (ILO, 2019); most of the remaining third were 'struggling to make ends meet' (ITUC, 2018). Then came a UN sea-change from jobs as the solution to world poverty to a call to protect *people*, [but] *not* jobs (World Bank, 2019). Jobs had thus become the *culprit* from whom people needed protection (Seubert et al., 2019).

Since Seubert et al. (2019) were writing, COVID-19 has added nails in the coffin of 'the job' as a cure-all. According to the International Monetary

Fund (IMF), the people most likely to bear the brunt of lockdown policies were precisely those people on the lowest wages, whose 'job' was often deemed 'non-essential' and mostly did not allow them a particular choice of working remotely (IMF, 2020). *Because* of their jobs, these workers had to risk their health and wellbeing at work. They had to self-isolate from their family at home. They risked losing their full wage temporarily because of reduced hours and furloughs, or losing it altogether from being laid-off permanently. Problematising 'the job,' the common denominator for exposure to such risks (IMF, 2020) was "to be more *economically* vulnerable: workers that are young, with fewer years of education, engaging in part-time work, and with earnings toward the bottom of the distribution" (IMF, 2020, p. 17). Recalling Hart's (1971) Inverse Care Law, people working in the most precarious jobs, with the greatest need for material and social support, got the least of it.

A further accelerant on the bonfire of jobs, in addition to a pandemic, is automation. This was already threatening 'the job' even before the pandemic began. Globally, an estimated 60% of occupations in 2017 already had almost a third of core work specifications that could, in principle, be automated (McKinsey Global Institute, 2017). During the pandemic, according to the OECD (Organization for Economic Cooperation and Development), COVID lockdown measures forced the adoption of information and communications technology "at a pace never seen before, and … firms may be pushed to replace frontline workers with machines to avoid the risk of infection and disruption" (Scarpetta, 2020, p. 3). Since 2020, the ILO (2021b) has further highlighted the role of digital platforms as new forms of organization that have transformed the world of work, often bringing even further precariousness to 'the job,' which has been uberized to 'the gig', in no less than a 'gig economy' (Kuhn, 2023).

In the wake of jobs, the world of work needs a more robust concept that is far more fit-for-purpose (Morse & McNamara, 2013). Sustainability research and policy has arguably overlooked longer-standing, traditional wisdoms about how to have sustainable livelihoods, even as the term 'sustainability' has become chic and fashionable (Yap & Watene, 2019).

The modern English term *Sustainable Livelihood* originally grew out of a report on environmental sustainability in economically poor rural communities in the "developing" world (World Commission on Environment and Development, 1989). That anchorage point in the Brundtland Report (as the Commission's report remains more popularly known) is ironic since we know from COP26 (2021) that 'developed' countries were (by far) the main carbon polluters. Nevertheless, since the 1980s the term has acquired a frequently cited self-explanatory definition:

> a livelihood comprises the capabilities, assets … and activities required for a means of living, a livelihood is sustainable which can cope with and recover from stress and shocks, maintain or enhance its capabilities and

assets, and provide sustainable livelihood opportunities for the next generation; and which contributes net benefits to other livelihoods at the local and global levels and in the short and long term.

(Chambers & Conway, 1991, p. 6)

When it was first mooted in the Brundtland Report during the 1980s, nobody could have envisaged that this definition of sustainable livelihoods would come to reflect back on all countries, including the richest ones. In the 1990s, the concept was applied from rural towards urban environments, where most of the world's population now dwells – and works (United Nations, 2014a). In the 2000s, it extended again – spanning natural and man-made disasters, where it was seen as a buffer for people in need (Blaikie et al., 2004). In the 2010s, it fanned into a landmark 2012 United Nations Conference in Rio, Brazil, where it was linked to sustainable development more widely (United Nations, 2014b). Today, its footings in sustainability (not precarity) and livelihoods (not jobs) are more salient than ever.

Living Wages, Fair Trades

The foundations of the present-day ILO are embedded in the 1919 Treaty of Versailles, in which a living wage was posited as a fundamental element in securing humanity's future:

> Whereas the League of Nations has for its object the establishment of universal peace, and such a peace can be established only if it is based upon social justice; And whereas conditions of labor exist involving such injustice, hardship and privation to large numbers of people as to produce unrest so great that the peace and harmony of the world are imperiled; and an improvement of the conditions is urgently required: as, for example, by the regulation of the hours of work, including the establishment of a maximum working day and week, the regulation of the labor supply, the prevention of unemployment, the *provision of an adequate living wage.*
>
> (ILO, 1923, p. 332, emphasis added)

Thus, a living wage is historically integral to the concept of sustainable livelihoods.

In the 21st century, most living wage campaigns have gone further than the ill-fated Treaty of Versailles (Carr, 2023). Typically, a living wage provides more than just an 'adequate' wage. For example, it must include enough disposable income to live above bare subsistence and enable dignified participation in society, quality leisure time away from work, savings for the future, and general freedom of choice (Searle & McWha-Hermann, 2021). In this sense, the living wage can be distinguished not only economically and econometrically from a legal minimum wage, but also psychologically. The living wage is an aspiration for the future, whilst meeting costs of living in the present.

Psychological theory of living wages, and their links to sustainable livelihoods, has been developed by Carr and colleagues (2016). Most of the literature preceding this theoretical synthesis had assumed that the link between wage and wellbeing was linear. Yet, both Just Noticeable Difference (JND) and Poverty Trap theories, according to Carr et al. (2016), predict a non-linear linkage: JND theory predicts that any wage is a good wage, with the greatest psychological returns resulting at the lowest end of the wage continuum, in support of low-wage economies; whereas, poverty trap theory predicts that at very low levels increments of wage will make zero difference to working poverty until and unless the wage level passes a critical cusp or threshold, beyond which wellbeing will transform from negative to positive (Carr, 2022a).

Corroborating the concept and practice of setting living wage thresholds, most evidence on wage and wellbeing, ranging from job satisfaction and work engagement through work-life balance and on to anxiety and depression, fits poverty trap theory, not simply JNDs or simple linear dynamics (Carr et al., 2018). Much of this evidence comes from mixed-method studies across a diversity of countries, cultures, and economies within Project Global Living Organizational Wage (Project GLOW, 2021). An illustrative GLOW analysis of living wages across the global coffee industry showed how the concept of a living wage transcends individual jobs and single employers. Paying living wages across whole supply chains – to production, processing, retail, and hospitality workers – boosts the taste for consumers (Carr et al., 2021). Hence, living wages link to Fair Trade and to SDG-12 – Sustainable production and consumption (United Nations, 2022).

Summing up, living wages are an instantiated element of Sustainable Livelihoods. They are reflections of the inter-connectedness of lives and livelihoods. They transcend the formal job by including own-account (e.g., coffee) farming work across the (in)formal sector(s). Regardless of sector, they keep people above a choppy poverty waterline.

Informal work

Recognizing Skills (M. Saxena)

Over 61% of the world's population lives and works in the informal sector (ILO, 2022). Work in the informal sector is irregular, unprotected by organizational or government policies, often poorly paid, prone to occupational safety hazards, and unable to sustain individuals and families. Psychological research has found that working informally tends to be associated with economic tenuousness and income precarity (Saxena, 2021). When viewed purely from an economic standpoint, it appears as though the best way to encourage sustainable growth would be to somehow *minimize informal work* and transition individuals to *formal jobs* (Saxena, 2017).

However, when viewed from a psychological standpoint, nuances start to emerge that reveal core insights that determine the lived experience of those who work informally (Groot & Hodgetts, 2015).

For instance, it is often *assumed* that informal work is low-skilled and that individuals who work in the informal sector do so due to a lack of choice or opportunity to work in the formal sector (Saxena, 2017). However, it has been argued that these are stereotypes that are far removed from the ground reality of worker experiences and tend to white-wash the realities of millions of workers worldwide (Saxena & Tchagnéno, 2023). In India, for instance, it was found that informal workers were *highly skilled* inter-generational artisans who worked in their family occupation, not for lack of opportunities, but rather because it was their expressed, explicit desire to want to continue to do so. Their occupational status and work were part of a continued cultural legacy (referred to as *cultural skills*; Saxena, 2021) and were based on indigenous knowledge that had been passed down for millennia across multiple generations.

This work was a fundamental part of the personal identity and lived experience of the highly skilled informal artisans, illuminated by traditional knowledge that owed a deep sense of gratitude to natural resources, the planet that we live on, and society.

The most remarkable finding was that all of this was nested within the broader realities of serious economic deficits. It was the ecosystem that surrounded the informal work, i.e., lack of infrastructural support, difficulty in procuring raw materials, lack of supply lines, neglect via state and multilateral policy, and bulk availability of inexpensive factory-made but bad for the environment plastic goods, that threatened the livelihoods of the skilled artisans. This was an important investigation, as it revealed that the solution lies not in transitioning to formal 'jobs' but rather in providing infrastructural support for the highly enriching work and occupations that have been around for millennia.

Resisting Formalization (C. Tchagnéno)

Informal work is frequently defined pejoratively, as work evading control and regulation by governmental institutions (Tchagnéno & Doutre, 2021). Yet, its characteristics include underemployment, precariousness, lack of social protection, and exposure to professional and psychosocial risks. Such precariousness or vulnerability is proportional to the exponential growth of the global workforce. Among the world's most 'underdeveloped' regions (West Asia, Latin America and sub-Saharan Africa), sub-Saharan Africa is where the labor force is growing fastest, at 2.9% per year (Filmer & Fox, 2014).

In sub-Saharan Africa, it appears that policies do not always take into account what these actors may really think or want. This is the consequence of negative stereotypes and prejudices that surround the informal work sector, which have often justified its being defined in opposition to the formal one

(Mutukwa & Tanyanyiwa, 2021). The formal sector has often been idealized and presented as the voice of salvation for the informal workers. As a result, informal actors do not recognize themselves in the measures and programs addressed to them. All of which may help to explain the frequent resistance to observing public policies aimed at formalizing informal work (Tchagnéno Téné, 2018; Tchagnéno & Doutre, 2021).

Counteracting Slavery (V. Hopner)

The case for the need to secure sustainable livelihoods in the informal sector is greatest for those at risk of or already enslaved through human trafficking. People with the greatest vulnerability to human trafficking are most likely to live in countries that are politically and economically unstable, have high levels of environmental degradation, and where employment is typically low paid, subject to long hours, and largely informal (UNODC, 2008). In 2021, the ILO estimated that nearly 50 million people live in contemporary slavery. This figure equates to around 27.6 million people in forced labor and 22 million in forced marriages. Of the approximately 27 million people in forced labour, 17.3 million are labourers in the private sector, 3.9 million are under government control, and 6.3 million are in commercial sexual exploitation (ILO, 2021a). The forced labor market, which exploits vulnerable and trafficked people, takes place in the agricultural, construction, textile, mining, domestic servitude, forestry, and fishing industries or sectors (Zimmerman et al., 2011).

This work is at best indecent and at worst obscene. It is typically degrading, dangerous, and dirty. Trafficked people often have histories of trauma, abuse, and poor physical and psychological health, which are exacerbated by the continuing violations that they encounter in forced labor environments (Zimmerman et al., 2011). Once enslaved, people are routinely subject to sexual and physical violence, legal insecurity, deprivation of food and sleep, debt bondage, poor pay, long hours, and hazardous conditions (Baldwin et al., 2015). Such work is clearly not sustainable physically, psychologically, or spiritually. Tackling it will require a concerted focus, through SDG-17 Partnerships, on stopping the unsustainable livelihoods of the traffickers and on providing alternative pathways towards decent work (Hopner, 2022).

Social Enterprises (M. H. Nguyen)

Social enterprises are defined as organizations that pursue both commercial and social goals simultaneously (Dees, 2018). By generating their revenue from commercial activities, social enterprises are able to create good quality employment and buffer communities against the harshest impacts of economic downturns (e.g., COVID-19), especially for vulnerable groups (Estrin et al., 2016).

Social enterprises are making efforts to promote more equitable and sustainable livelihoods for people around the world (Littlewood & Holt, 2018).

The United Nations Development Programme (UNDP, 2015) has recognized them as a key model for poverty reduction, economic growth, and fostering all 17 SDGs. Thus, many social enterprises aim to reduce poverty, protect the planet through the promotion of sustainable food production practices, and generate employment with social inclusion for marginalized persons through a sustainable livelihood (Nguyen et al., 2021b).

In OECD countries, the rising number of social enterprises is partly a response to punitive and failing welfare (Hodgetts & Stolte, 2017). For example, in 2020, social enterprises in the UK were one of the fastest-growing forms of business, creating 2 million jobs, while across European countries they created 13.6 million jobs (Whitfield, 2021). For emerging economies like Morocco, Indonesia, Jamaica, Ethiopia, Sudan, India, and Vietnam, the majority of social enterprises are led by women, with more than 50% of their employees being women (British Council et al., 2021). Social enterprises have provided sustainable incomes for vulnerable people and supported members of these groups to take on leadership roles.

A key feature of social enterprises is their respect for local social and cultural context (McMullen, 2018). The case of Vietnam is an example. The number of social enterprises in the country has increased by five times, to 22,000, since 2015, and they are ranked number one in Southeast Asia for social enterprises making profit (British Council et al., 2021; McMullen, 2018). Social enterprises in Vietnam were built from their traditional values (Nguyen et al., 2021b). The core value of village community has helped the country survive and remain independent through 4,000 years of upheaval and hardship history (more than 1,000 years under colonization and occupation by China, France, and America) (Vu' ộ' ng, 1992; Mus, 1952).

Accordingly, social enterprises in this country are set up as village-styled organizations, which commit to work on the pain points of their community with high attention to the inclusion and livelihoods of as many beneficiaries as possible (Nguyen et al., 2021b). They have a strong emphasis on fair compensation and comfortable working conditions to enhance employee mental and physical health (Nguyen et al., 2021a). The contribution of social enterprises to Vietnam has been underscored most recently in the COVID-19 pandemic: eighty percent of social enterprises in the country reported positive performance at this time, with more than half of their profit contributing back to their staff and their beneficiaries (British Council et al., 2021). Hence, promoting social enterprises has been a key way to promote sustainable livelihoods and achieve the UN SDGs.

Digital Equity (J. Liu, S. Carr)

The pandemic, the automation of work, and the advent of digital platforms have transformed the world of work (ILO, 2021b). The uberization of transportation and hospitality as well as the Zoomification of education and medicine are just a few everyday examples. In their global report on the implications of digital platforms as key 'mediators' of everyday work, the ILO (2021b) highlight its double-edgedness: Yes, digital platforms generate new pathways for earning a livelihood – via gigs, for instance; but, they can also dehumanize work conditions through the "algorithmic management of workers" (ILO, 2021b, p. 4).

Digitalization in wealthier countries is increasingly characterized by experiences of such technology as exploitative (e.g., the hours and wage structures of call centers; the piecemeal and insecure nature of employment for digital-service-oriented companies, i.e., taxis; and data-entry work) or involving surveillance (e.g., computer programs dictating what information is required to determine who gets welfare benefits). Thus, according to Bach et al. (2018), digital technology should be considered as part of a global economy that inscribes inequality.

A bellwether for what digital platforms might deliver, especially in countries still on the wrong side of a digital divide, is China's Belt and Road Initiative (He, 2022). As He (2022) points out, standardization in vehicles, measures, currency, and so forth helped the Qin Empire successfully transform China into a united Middle Kingdom. Fast-forward 2,000 years, and Chinese President Xi Jinping is promoting standard connectivity as one important component of the Belt and Road Initiative. His signature foreign policy proposal is to "serve the ambitious goal of connecting Africa, Asia, Europe and countries throughout the world" (He, 2022, p. 2).

At an everyday level, the original Silk Road arguably created the world of work as we know it today, e.g., via the exchange of crops and ideas (like millet and multi-cropping). These, in turn, enabled the expansion of 'livelihoods' to include occupations, jobs, and inter-connected supply chains. The original Silk Road also weathered pandemics and other global (at the time) crises, including wars and famines. It was able to do so because people were communicating and trading across distances in a way that coordinated benefits across vast distances. Cell phones are a much more efficient way to coordinate such efforts today, especially in places lacking in built infrastructure, like Africa (see Aker & Mbiti, 2010).

To date, however, China's investment in Africa, with the advent of President Xi Jinping's Belt and Road Initiative, has been focused more on heavy construction of buildings and roads (Large, 2021), rather than digital investment and communications. A key *everyday* livelihoods challenge for the Belt and Road Initiative is therefore delivering sustainable livelihoods, not only for workers from China working on the road, but also for country nationals all along the girth of its digital silk belt and road system (Hillman & Tippett, 2021).

As well as accelerating (i) digitalization, the pandemic also reignited a discussion about (ii) social protection via Universal Basic Income (UBI). As (i) advances, the need for (ii) does too. UBI is a tax-funded, recurring monetary payment made to every individual in every household in society with no strings (like having to work for it) attached (Hasdell, 2020). Since the pandemic, public support for such previously 'radical' initiatives has demonstrably grown (Nettle et al., 2021). A recent meta-review (Hasdell, 2020) of UBI trials to date finds that basic income boosted household expenditure (e.g., on durable assets), had "minimal impact on labor market participation" (p. 16), lifted school enrolments (at least in the short-term), and improved health status (apart from social stigma, which a 'universal' basic income would remove). UBIs may stimulate depressed economies by boosting purchasing power (Standing, 2020), including for unpaid domestic (Carr, 2022a) and community work (Atkinson, 1996). UBIs may thereby address both halves of SDG-8 (decent work AND economic development). In *conjunction* with living wages, they have the potential to protect and lift human wellbeing (Huffmeier & Zacher, 2021).

Gift Economies (P. King)

Within the context of Aotearoa/New Zealand, Māori are the indigenous people who, like many other indigenous peoples globally, have experiences of colonization at the hands of the British (Walker, 2004). Amongst these complex histories, social, political, cultural, and economic domination coupled with mass displacement from ancestral homelands have been prominent features. As a result, Māori today are disproportionately affected by issues of poverty, precarity, homelessness, and un(der)employment, all of which negatively impact on people's ability to attain a sustainable livelihood. Within this context, the concept of Sustainable Livelihoods is difficult to understand without the concept of *whenua* or land. For Māori, the *whenua* is not a commodity, it is what gives us life, meaning that we have a duty to care for it as it cares for us (King et al., 2018). To emphasize the significance of this connection further, the word *whenua* itself also refers to the placenta that nurtures and sustains the next generation within the womb (Mead, 2003). These relationships form a metaphor for how Māori see their connections to the *whenua*.

Connection to the *whenua* and the sustainable livelihoods that often emerge from this relationship, however, are not, in a practical sense, a viable option for many Māori today, as urbanization has meant that Māori often find themselves displaced from ancestral homelands and indigenous economies as well as being woven into the fabric of the settler society through capitalism (Walker, 2004). Of use here are Bourdieu's (2000) observations of Algerian society, which was, as a result of French colonialism,

> submitted to a kind of historical acceleration which caused two forms of economic organizations, normally separated by a gap of several centuries and making contradictory demands on their participants, to coexist, or to be telescoped, under the eye of the observer.
>
> (p. 18)

Similar observations can be made within the context of Aotearoa/New Zealand, in that although Māori society experienced massive upheavals, critical pieces of cultural infrastructure have been maintained, such as *marae* (village center/cultural epicenter), the Māori language, and, more importantly, relational networks of gift economies, or what Māori often refer to as *tikanga* (appropriate protocol, cultural way of doing things).

Between these often-contradictory economies, Māori are able to take a dual approach to attaining sustainable livelihoods. The first is to seek structural change of the settler society, in an effort to bring about more equitable outcomes, or to work within the settler system/formal economy. The second is to work outside the formal economy and rely more on local knowledge, emplaced relationships, connections to the environment, and, in some cases, a turn to radical commerce. This is where notions of the gift economy can be particularly useful. The gift economy is less about monetary transactions as an exercise of accounting and more about maintaining social connections, ties, and obligations with others. For example, you may be granted access to ancestral lands to hunt, after which, when you return, it is customary to stop off at the homes of prominent community members/leaders to share some of the hunt to acknowledge the access that has been granted, to show respect for the local peoples, and to further develop these social ties. among other things.

Access to land clearly helps in the establishment, maintenance, and continued reproduction of the gift economy, though it is not always an option for Māori, particularly within urban landscapes. Ways of being and caring for others outside the purview of the formal economy through *tikanga* or culturally patterned social practices have been maintained to an extent, however, the economic deprivation that accompanies colonization has meant that the materiality of how these culturally patterned social practices manifest has had to adapt and make do with what is available at hand (King et al., 2018). In times of increased precarity and economic insecurity (Hodgetts & Stolte, 2017; Standing, 2016), whether it be austerity, automation, climate change/ "natural" disasters, economic catastrophe, or global conflict, the idea of a single job as a means of providing a sustainable livelihood increasingly looks less attainable, and understanding how these networks work and how to support and grow them becomes of greater importance.

Sustainable Livelihoods and the Ecosystem – Clean S.L.A.T.E. (V. Hopner, S. Carr)

Humanity is one species in a global ecosystem upon which all of us depend, not only for our livelihoods, but also our lives (Tansley, 1935). In the age of the "Anthropocene: a term proposed to describe the era in which humans have become central drivers of planetary change, radically altering the earth's biosphere, people have good reason to feel insecure" (UNDP, 2022, p. iii). Contemporary rhetoric about protecting and preserving the ecosystem for future generations, including SDG-13 ("Take urgent action to combat climate change and its impacts"; United Nations, 2022), includes everyday 'jobs.' Protecting jobs in coal 'versus' protecting the environment is a prominent case-in-point, but the same juxtaposition applies equally to farming vs.

rainforest or fishing vs. fish stocks, e.g., with respect to SDGs 14 and 15 ("Life below water" and "Life on land"; United Nations, 2022).

There is no more pressing need to protect the ecosystem and provide sustainable livelihoods as that highlighted by human trafficking and forced labour (above). For instance, the enslaved fishing crews operating in fleets overfishing and plundering the oceans are destroying the marine ecologies that provide these hazardous, abusive, dangerous jobs that violate human rights on a daily basis (UNDP, 2022) A primary challenge with respect to these goals is thus to find win-wins in which livelihoods can be created AND the ecosystem preserved for future generations.

A second challenge concerns the locus of responsibility for replacing unsustainable jobs in these sectors with sustainable livelihoods. Most of the responsibility naturally falls on those with most of the economic power to change policy settings – namely, governments and large corporations. At a more everyday level, though, millions of people will face dilemmas in the light of economic vs. ecological necessities. At this level, the conversation about sustainable livelihoods and the ecosystem is yet to be had. Thus, project Clean S.L.A.T.E. (Sustainable Livelihoods and the Ecosystem) has been set up to research 'how' the transition to cleaner, sustainable livelihoods can be and is being made.

S.L.A.T.E. is developing a rating system to complement the current O*Net classification of occupations, which will rate livelihoods according to their sustainability (Saner & Yiu, 2014). A related focus is exploring the social facilitation of risk over conservatism in making livelihood choices (Stoner, 1961; Estes & Thompson, 2020). Another focus is following community initiatives that localize change at the sub-assemblage level, for example, towns that were built on jobs in a polluting industry but have shifted to sustainable livelihoods under SDGs 6 ("Clean water and sanitation"; United Nations, 2022) and 7 ("Affordable and clean energy"; United Nations, 2022).

Conclusion: Goaling Sustainable Livelihoods

The primary UN goal of eradicating poverty in all its forms everywhere presents enormous challenges and opportunities to those who seek to improve people's lives through access to decent work, which is a stepping-stone towards Sustainable Livelihoods (above; Di Fabio & Maree, 2016). None of the above forms of work are covered adequately by the narrow concept of a job. All of them, though, are relevant to sustainability. Hence, a major international initiative, turning on a psychological revolution in how we think about work and living, life and livelihoods, is right now – today – vital to address these challenges and opportunities. This necessity for a radical change is made ever-more pressing by the pandemic, cost-of-living crisis, and climate (entire ecosystem) destruction.

The international community of Work and Organizational Psychologists (WOP) wishes to work in partnership with others who have similar interests to help develop a post-2030 work agenda focused on Sustainable Livelihoods (Carr, 2022). Far broader in scope than formal jobs, Sustainable Livelihoods recognize working in the informal sector as well as work that is unpaid, irregular, and/or illegal. They/we further recognize that livelihoods are human and relational – they connect us with each other, including with future generations, and the biosphere that supports all life on Earth.

We therefore call on the UN to establish a new development goal in the post-2030 Agenda for Human Development. For most workers today, jobs have become a threat to our wellbeing. Precarious jobs are to sustainable livelihoods as coal is to green hydrogen. While some important work has already been done in areas such as living wages, the potential contribution of WOP to Sustainable Livelihoods is greatly underdeveloped. We in WOP ask the UN to create a new rallying goal post-2030 – *Sustainable Livelihoods.*

References

Aker, J. C., & Mbiti, I. M. (2010). Mobile phones and economic development in Africa. *Journal of Economic Perspectives*, 24(3), 207–232.

Atkinson, A. B. (1996). The case for a Participation Income. *The Political Quarterly*, 67(1), 67–70.

Bach, A. J., Wolfson, T., & Crowell, J. K. (2018). Poverty, Literacy, and Social Transformation: An Interdisciplinary Exploration of the Digital Divide. *Journal of Media Literacy Education*, 10, 22–41.

Baldwin, S. B., Fehrenbacher, A. E., & Eisenman, D. P. (2015). Psychological coercion in human trafficking: An application of Biderman's framework. *Qualitative Health Research*, 25(9), 1171–1181.

Blaikie, P., Cannon, T., Davis, I., & Wisner, B. (2004). *At risk: Natural hazards, people's vulnerability, and disasters.* New York: Routledge.

Bourdieu, P. (2000). Making the Economic Habitus: Algerian Workers Revisited. *Ethnography*, 1(1), 17–41. doi:10.1177/14661380022230624.

British Council, UN-ESCAP, Social Enterprise UK, & HSBC. (2021). *The state of social enterprises in South East Asia.* United Nations.

Carr, S. C. (2022, October 25). *Humanitarian Work Psychology: Goaling Sustainable Livelihoods?* Special Conference on Decent Work, University of Florence.

Carr, S. C. (2023). *Wage and wellbeing: Toward sustainable livelihoods.* New York: Springer.

Carr, S. C., Hopner, V., & Hodgetts, D. (Eds.). (2023). *Tackling precarious work.* New York: Routledge/SIOP New Frontiers Series.

Carr, S. C., Maleka, M., Meyer, I., Barry, M. L., Harr, J., … & Naithani, A. (2018). How can wages sustain a living? By getting ahead of the curve. *Sustainability Science*, 13, 901–917.

Carr, S. C., Meyer, I., Saxena, M., Seubert, C., Hopfgartner, L., Arora, B., Jyoti, D., Rugimbana, R. O., & Kempton, H. (2021). "Our Fair-Trade coffee tastes better": It might, but under what conditions? *Journal of Consumer Affairs*, 56(2), 597–612.

Carr, S. C., Parker, J., Arrowsmith, J., & Watters, P. A. (2016). The Living Wage: Theoretical integration and an applied research agenda. *International Labour Review*, 155, 1–24.

Chambers, R. C., & Conway, G. R. (1991). *Sustainable rural livelihoods: Practical concepts for the 21st century.* IDS (Institute of Development Studies), Discussion Paper 296. Brighton, UK: University of Sussex.

Dees, J. G. (2018). The meaning of social entrepreneurship 1, 2. In J. Hamschmidt & M. Pirson (Eds.), *Case Studies in Social Entrepreneurship and Sustainability* (pp. 22–30). Routledge.

Di Fabio, A., & Maree, S. (2016). Using a transdisciplinary interpretive lens to broaden reflections on alleviating poverty and promoting decent work. *Frontiers in Psychology*, 7, 503.

Estes, K. D., & Thompson, R. T. (2020). Preparing for the aftermath of COVID-19: Shifting risk and downstream health consequences. *Psychological Trauma*, 12, 31–32.

Estrin, S., Mickiewicz, T., & Stephan, U. (2016). Human capital in social and commercial entrepreneurship. *Journal of Business Venturing*, 31(4), 449–467.

Filmer, D., & Fox, L. (2014). *Youth employment in sub-Saharan Africa.* Washington, DC: World Bank Publications.

Groot, S., & Hodgetts, D. (2015). The infamy of begging: A case-based approach to street homelessness and radical commerce. *Qualitative Research in Psychology*, 12, 349–366.

Hart, T. (1971). The Inverse Care Law. *The Lancet*, 1, 405–412.

Hasdell, R. (2020). *What we know about Universal Basic Income: A cross-synthesis of reviews.* Stanford, CT: Basic Income Lab.

He, A. (2022). *The Digital Silk Road and China's Influence on Standard-Setting.* Waterloo, ON: Centre for International Governance Innovation.

Hillman, J., & Tippett, A. (2021). *Who built that? Labor and the Belt and Road Initiative.* Washington, DC: Council on Foreign Relations.

Hodgetts, D., & Stolte, O. (2017). *Urban Poverty and Health Inequalities.* London: Routledge.

Hopner, V. (2022, October 25). *Looking at decent work through a human security lens.* Invited address, Special Conference on Decent Work, University of Florence.

Huffmeier, J., & Zacher, H. (2021). The basic income: Initiating the needed discussion in industrial, work, and organizational psychology. *Industrial and Organizational Psychology*, 14, 531–562.

ILO (International Labour Organization). (1923). *International Labour Office: Official Bulletin Vol. 1 April 1919 – August 1920.* Geneva: ILO.

ILO (International Labour Organization). (2019). *Poor working conditions are main global employment challenge.* Geneva: ILO.

ILO (International Labour Organization). (2021a). *Forced labour, modern slavery and human trafficking.* https://www.ilo.org/global/topics/forced-labour/lang–en/index.htm.

ILO (International Labour Organization). (2021b). *The role of digital labour platforms in transforming the world of work.* Geneva: ILO.

ILO (International Labour Organization). (2022). *World employment and social outlook: trends 2022.* Geneva: ILO.

IMF (International Monetary Fund). (2020). *Who will bear the brunt of lockdown policies? Evidence from tele-workability measures across countries* (IMF Working Paper, WP/20/88). Washington, DC: IMF.

ITUC (International Trade Union Confederation). (2018). *Policy Brief: The Gender Wage Gap.* London: ITUC.

King, P., Hodgetts, D., Rua, M., & Morgan, M. (2018). When the marae moves into the city: Being Māori in urban Palmerston North. *City and Community*, 17(4), 1189–1208.

Kuhn, K. K. (2023). Making a go of it in the gig economy: Understanding risk in platform-based work. In S. C.Carr, V.Hopner, & D. J. Hodgetts (Eds.), *Tackling precarious work: Advancing Sustainable Livelihoods*. New York: Routledge.

Large, D. (2021). *China and Africa: The New Era*. John Wiley & Sons.

Littlewood, D., & Holt, D. (2018). How social enterprises can contribute to the Sustainable Development Goals (SDGs) – A conceptual framework. In N. Apostolopoulos, H. Al-Dajani, D. Holt, P. Jones, & R. Newberry (Eds.), *Entrepreneurship and the Sustainable Development Goals* (pp. 33–46). Emerald Publishing Limited.

Macrosty, H. W. (1898). The recent history of the living wage movement. *Political Science Quarterly*, 13, 413–441.

McKinsey Global Institute. (2017). *Jobs lost, jobs gained: Workforce transitions in a time of automation*. New York: McKinsey Global Institute.

McMullen, J. S. (2018). Organizational hybrids as biological hybrids: Insights for research on the relationship between social enterprise and the entrepreneurial ecosystem. *Journal of Business Venturing*, 33(5), 575–590.

Mead, H. M. (2003). *Tikanga Māori: Living by Māori values*. Wellington, NZ: Huia.

Morse, S., & McNamara, N. (2013). *Sustainable livelihood approach: A critique of theory and practice*. New York: Springer.

Murphy, G. C., & Athanasou, J. A. (1999). The effect of unemployment on mental health. *Journal of Occupational and Organizational Psychology*, 72, 83–99.

Mus, P. (1952). *Vietnam: Sociologie d'une guerre*. Paris: Seuil.

Mutukwa, M. T., & Tanyanyiwa, S. (2021). De-stereotyping Informal Sector Gendered Division of Work: A Case Study of Magaba Home Industry, Harare, Zimbabwe. *African Journal of Public Affairs*, 12, 188–206.

Nettle, D., Johnson, E., Johnson, M., & Saxe, R. (2021). Why has the COVID-19 pandemic increased support for Universal Basic Income? *Humanities and Social Sciences Communications*, 8(1), 79.

Nguyen, M. H. T., Carr, S. C., Hodgetts, D., & Fauchart, E. (2021a). Why do some social enterprises flourish in Vietnam? A comparison of human and ecosystem partnerships. *Sustainability Accounting, Management and Policy Journal*, 12(6), 1312–1347.

Nguyen, M. H. T., Hodgetts, D. J., & Carr, S. C. (2021b). Fitting Social Enterprises for Sustainable Development in Vietnam. *Sustainability*, 13(19), 10630.

Project GLOW (Global Living Organisational Wage). (2021). International perspectives on living wages for sustainable livelihoods: Some lessons from Project GLOW. In W. F. Filho, T. Wall, et al. (Eds.), *Encyclopaedia of the UN Sustainable Development Goals: Decent Work and economic growth* (pp. 1–9). Oxford: Oxford University Press.

Saner, R., & Yiu, L. (2014). Business Diplomacy Competence: A requirement for implementing the OECD's Guidelines for Multinational Enterprises. *The Hague Journal of Diplomacy*, 9, 311–333.

Saxena, M. (2017). Workers in poverty: An insight into informal workers around the world. *Industrial and Organizational Psychology*, 10(3), 376–379. http://dx.doi.org/10.1017/iop.2017.29.

Saxena, M. (2021). Cultural skills as drivers of decency in decent work: An investigation of skilled workers in the informal economy. *European Journal of Work and Organizational Psychology*, 30(6), 824–836. https://doi.org/10.1080/1359432X.2021.1918760.

Saxena, M., & Tchagnéno, C. (2023). Informal work as sustainable work: Pathways to sustainable livelihoods. In S. C.Carr, V.Hopner, & D. Hodgetts (Eds.). *Tackling Precarious Work*. New York: Routledge/SIOP New Frontiers Series.

Scarpetta, S. (2020, June 12). Rebuilding a future that works for all. *Future of Work*. https://www.businessandindustry.co.uk/future-of-work/rebuilding-a-future-that-works-for-all/#. Accessed August 28, 2022.

Searle, R., & McWha-Hermann, I. (2021). "Money's too tight (to mention)": A review and psychological synthesis of living wage research. *European Journal of Work and Organizational Psychology*, 30(3), 428–443. doi:10.1080/1359432X.2020.1838604.

Seubert, C., Hopfgartner, L., & Glaser, J. (2019). Beyond job insecurity: Concept, dimensions, and measurement of precarious employment. *Psychology of Everyday Activity*, 12, 33–45.

Standing, G. (2016). *The precariat: The new dangerous class*. London: Bloomsbury Publishing.

Standing, G. (2020, November). "The case for a basic income": Opening essay for GTI Forum "Universal Basic Income: Has the Time Come?", *Great Transition Initiative*, 1–9. https://www.greattransition.org/gti-forum/basic-income-standing.

St-Denis, X. (2020). The changing importance of lifetime jobs in the United Kingdom. *International Labour Review*, 160(2), 243–269. https://doi.org/10.1111/ilr.12190.

Stoner, J. A. F. (1961). *A comparison of individual and group decisions involving risk*. Cambridge, MA: Massachusetts Institute of Technology.

Tansley, A. G. (1935). The use and abuse of vegetational concepts and terms. *Ecology*, 16, 284–307.

Tchagnéno, C. L. & Doutre, É. (2021). Explaining the intention to engage in informal work restructuring programs using the Theory of Planned Behavior. *Bulletin de psychologie*, 574(4), 297–316. https://doi.org/10.3917/bupsy.574.0297.

Tchagnéno Téné, C. L. (2018). *Analysis of the socio-cognitive determinants of the intention to engage in informal work restructuring programmes in Cameroon*. Doctoral dissertation, Université Grenoble Alpes (ComUE).

UNDP (United Nations Development Programme). (2015). *Social Enterprise: A new model for poverty reduction and employment generation* (ISBN: 978-992-9504-9278-0). UNDP Regional Bureau for Europe and CIS.

UNDP (United Nations Development Programme). (2022). *2022 Special Report: New threats to human security in the Anthropocene: Demanding greater solidarity*. New York: UNDP. https://hdr.undp.org/system/files/documents//srhs2022pdf.pdf.

United Nations. (2014a). *Revision of world urbanization prospects*. New York: United Nations.

United Nations. (2014b). *Future We Want – Outcome Document from Rio +20 United Nations Conference on Sustainable Development*. New York: United Nations.

United Nations. (2022). *The 17 Goals – Sustainable Development Goals*. New York: United Nations.

UNODC (United Nations Office on Drugs and Crime). (2008). *Human trafficking, A crime that shames us all: An introduction to human trafficking: Vulnerability, impact and action*. New York: United Nations. https://www.unodc.org/documents/human-trafficking/An_Introduction_to_Human_Trafficking_-_Background_Paper.pdf.

Vu' ọ' ng, T. Q. (1992). Popular culture and high culture in Vietnamese history. *Crossroads: An Interdisciplinary Journal of Southeast Asian Studies*, 7(2), 5–37.

Walker, R. (2004). *Ka whawhai tonu mātou: Struggle without end*. Auckland, NZ: Penguin.

Whitfield, G. (2021, October 17). Record number of social enterprises formed during the pandemic. *BusinessLive*. https://www.business-live.co.uk/enterprise/record-number-social-enterprises-formed-21876352. Accessed November 24, 2021.

World Bank. (2012). *World Development Report 2013 – Jobs*. Washington, DC: World Bank.

World Bank. (2013). *World Development Report 2014 – Developing with Jobs*. Washington, DC: World Bank.

World Bank. (2019). *World Development Report 2018 – WDR 2019 Presentations*. Washington, DC: World Bank. http://pubdocs.worldbank.org/en/808261547222082195/WDR19-English-Presentation.pdf. Accessed April 9, 2020.

World Commission on Environment and Development. (1989, March). *Our common future*. Oslo: Brundtland Commission.

Yap, M .L. M., & Watene, K. (2019). The Sustainable Development Goals (SDGs) and Indigenous Peoples: Another missed opportunity? *Journal of Human Development and Capabilities*, 20, 451–467.

Zimmerman, C., Hossain, M., & Watts, C. (2011). Human trafficking and health: A conceptual model to inform policy, intervention and research. *Social Science & Medicine*, 73, 327–335.

5 Decent Work and Decent Lives in Organizations for Healthy Lives

Maureen E. Kenny and Annamaria Di Fabio

The Psychology of Working Theory (PWT)

The psychology of working theory (PWT), which was developed by Duffy, Blustein, Diemer, and Autin (2016), has generated substantive research since its inception. Drawing from the previous vocational psychology research of Blustein (2001, 2006, 2013) articulating the psychology of working framework (PWF), Duffy et al. (2016) proposed a PWT theoretical model that could be empirically verified. In contrast with traditional vocational psychology theories, which focused on persons with high volition and work opportunities, Blustein (2001, 2006, 2013) called for an inclusive framework that would consider the needs of persons who had been marginalized based on gender, race, social class, or other identities and that would address the contextual factors that contribute to and sustain their marginalized status (Blustein, 2001, 2006, 2008, 2013). In response to this call, PWT (Duffy et al., 2016) integrates individual factors, reflective of traditional vocational theories of career choice, with social, contextual and sociocultural factors that shape work access and work meaning, particularly among persons experiencing social and economic marginalization. PWT (Duffy et al., 2016) embraces values of social justice and multiculturalism and depicts how access to decent work is shaped through the interaction of psychological, contextual and economic factors. Moreover, PWT (Duffy et al., 2016) seeks to identify psychological factors that may support persons in navigating barriers of marginalization and economic constraints to develop work volition and career adaptability in the pathway to decent work.

Access to decent work is a central variable in the PWT model. The definition of decent, as conceptualized in PWT (Duffy et al., 2016), is inspired by the vision of the International Labour Organization (ILO, 2012) and aligned with the following ILO assumptions:

> Work is central to people's well-being. In addition to providing income, work can pave the way for broader social and economic advancement, strengthening individuals, their families and communities. Such progress, however, hinges on work that is decent. Decent work sums up the aspirations of people in their working lives.

DOI: 10.4324/9781003212157-6

PWT highlights the role of contextual factors on the individual psychological experience of work. In this perspective, decent work includes:

> (a) physical and interpersonally safe working conditions (e.g., absent of physical, mental, or emotional abuse), (b) hours that allow for free time and adequate rest, (c) organizational values that complement family and social values, (d) adequate compensation, and (e) access to adequate health care.
>
> (Duffy et al., 2016, p. 130)

Decent Work

Following from the initial conceptualization of PWF (Blustein, 2001, 2006, 2013) and the above delineation of PWT (Duffy et al., 2016), the conceptualization of decent work in the PWT model highlights the psychological experience of the individual. While PWT was designed to promote research on decent work, progress was hampered by the lack of a measure to assess decent work from a psychological perspective. To remedy this gap, Duffy et al. (2017) developed the Decent Work Scale (DWS; Duffy et al., 2017), with a focus on assessing "how people experienced their working life." The dimensions of the DWS included: Physically and interpersonal safe working conditions; Access to health care; Adequate compensation; Hours that allow for free time and rest; and Organizational values that complement family and social values.

Adequate compensation is one of the five dimensions of decent work in the PWT model that is also connected to the broader value and meaning of work (Duffy et al., 2017). The concept of minimum wage was introduced by the ILO (2020) to consider the minimum pay that is needed to facilitate economic growth by enhancing the labor income distribution, encouraging domestic consumption, and creating local occupation. Consistent with the psychological approach of PWT, Carr, Parker, Arrowsmith, and Watters (2016) consider the value of a living wage not only in terms of economic subsistence, but also in terms of quality of life and adequate participation in organizational and social life. The perceptions of a decent level of remuneration and perceived just processes in determining wages are associated with employee motivation, performance, and productivity in the workplace (Carr et al., 2018). These perceptions are also fundamental aspects of decent work related to well-being for individuals, organizations, and the broader society (Carr ct al., 2016). As noted by Blustein, Kenny, Di Fabio, and Guichard (2019b), decent work that satisfies an array of human needs, including economic survival needs, is critical not only in fostering individual well-being, but also in advancing the welfare of communities.

The PWT model (Duffy et al., 2016) proposes contextual and psychological factors that serve as predictors of decent work. Marginalization and economic constraints are identified at the forefront of the model as contextual factors that reduce access to decent work. Work volition and career adaptability are specified as psychological factors that mediate the relationship between contextual constraints and decent work and proactive personality. Critical consciousness, social support, and economic conditions are proposed as moderators that might reduce the negative effects of contextual constraints on work volition and career adaptability. With regard to the benefits of decent work, decent work is specified as meeting a variety of human needs, including survival needs, needs for social connection and social contribution, and needs for self-determination. It is through the satisfaction of these needs that decent work is hypothesized to contribute to work fulfilment and personal well-being.

A growing body of research lends empirical support for the PWT model. In one of many studies assessing PWT, Duffy et al. (2018) tested the fundamental aspects of the PWT among employed adults from diverse racial and ethnic backgrounds. Consistent with PWT expectations, experiences of marginalization and economic constraints were inversely related to work volition and career adaptability and to decent work. Research on PWT has also been conducted in varied international contexts. Kozan, Işık, and Blustein (2019), for example, examined PWT in the non-Western, collectivist context of Turkey. The findings affirm the contributions of social class to both work volition and career adaptability as well as in access to decent and fulfilling work and well-being in varied cultural contexts where social and economic inequities exist (Kozan, Işık, & Blustein, 2019).

PWT has also inspired research that extends the heuristic value of the model for enhancing understanding of decent work in the US and other international contexts, especially among persons who have experienced some type of marginalized identity. In order to understand how workers understand work-related crises in the United States, Kozan, Blustein, Paciorek, Kilbury, & Işık (2019) interviewed forty-two American adults from different backgrounds. Using modified consensual qualitative research, participant interviews revealed three interrelated themes: government and corporate policies, social justice, and values. These themes reveal workers' sense of the causes, impact, and solutions for work crises related to technology, globalization, and macroeconomic factors. The workers' perspectives were understood additionally by their level of emotional reaction, loci of causality, and political ideology, highlighting how the experience of work is shaped by their psychological, social, and economic contexts. Also following from PWT, Kozan, Gutowski, and Blustein (2020) adopted a PWT lens to study women's work aspirations and beliefs on meritocracy as related to decent work. Participants came from diverse racial, educational, and work backgrounds. Qualitative content analysis revealed that (1) women aspire for work that fulfills essential human needs, (2) women's work aspirations are influenced by multiple factors, and (3) women strive to make sense of their work aspirations in relation to beliefs about the American Dream. The findings highlighted the importance and role of relationships and systemic factors in shaping the work aspirations of US women. This research reveals, consistent with the basic premises of PWT, how one's understandings and experiences of work are inherently shaped by the broader social context and the social location one occupies within that context.

In an effort to better understand dimensions of work that are aligned with and contrast with decent work, Blustein et al. (2020b) delineated the uncertain state of work in the US. Through a person-centered approach, the study defined profiles of decent work and precarious work through administration of the Decent Work Scale (Duffy et al., 2017) and the Precarious Work Scale (Vives et al., 2010). Five profiles were identified among 492 American workers, including: (1) Indecent-Precarious, (2) Highly Decent, (3) Low Health Care-Low Rights, (4) Vulnerability-Dominant, and (5) Health Care-Stability. The results showed that the satisfaction of PWT needs was strongest for the Highly Decent Work profile and lowest for the Indecent-Precarious Work profile. Satisfaction of the PWT need for autonomy was strongest in the Highly Decent Work profile. The Vulnerability-Dominant Work profile was characteristic of independent high-skilled workers who have precarious professions but also exercise more control over their own work. The study findings suggest the need for continued in-depth study to better understand variations in the experience of decent work and precarious work and how they satisfy or fail to meet human needs as specified by PWT.

Precarious Work and Psychology of Working Theory

Many workers across every part of the world navigate an uncertain and precarious work environment (Blustein et al., 2019b). In this regard, Guichard (2009) distinguishes between central and peripheral workers. Central workers are qualified multipurpose employees who guarantee the permanence of the organization over time and allow its rearrangement in the event of a crisis. Peripheral workers, on the other hand, are generally low-skilled, hired with a fixed-term contract when the economic situation is positive, and then fired when it worsens; therefore, they are constantly confronted – much more than central workers – with unstable and precarious work conditions. Peripheral workers can be seen among the unemployed, underemployed, immigrants, the poor, and people with disabling conditions (Blustein et al., 2014).

Given that precarious and peripheral work represent the antithesis of decent work, precarious work has generated interest among PWT researchers. Drawing from existing interdisciplinary research on precarious work in the 21st century, Allan, Autin, and Wilkins-Yel (2021) sought to elaborate the psychological aspects of precarious work. Allan et al. (2017) adopted a definition of precarious work that is consistent with the conditions of peripheral work and reduced employment and includes underemployment, poverty wage employment, and involuntary temporary work (Allan et al., 2017). More specifically, "precarious work includes uncertain working conditions and unpredictable job continuity combined with restricted rights, protections, and freedoms that allow workers to advocate for organizational and social change" (Allan et al., 2021, p. 2). In their research, Allan et al. (2021) identified three broad categories of work precarity: precarity of work, precarity at work, and precarity from work. "Precarity *of* work reflects fears and uncertainty related to the continuity of work, including the continuity of workers' employment, income, and social relationships" (Allan et al., 2021, p. 3). "Precarity *at* work reflects uncertainty and unpredictability in workers' psychosocial or physical safety, including fear of bullying, discrimination, social rejection, harassment, or physically unsafe working conditions" (Allan et al., 2021, p. 3). "Precarity *from* work reflects uncertainty and insecurity in the ability to meet basic survival needs" (Allan et al., 2021, p. 3). The latter two categories include persons who are employed, but they illustrate how the experience of employment itself is not enough to meet standards of decency. Allan et al. (2021) hoped that their research would provide a foundation for further study of precarious work with recognition of how structural and historical changes in organizations, the economy, and the labor market contribute to precarity in its various forms. The authors also called for continued integration of psychological perspectives on precarious work with related literature in other disciplines, such as sociology, history, economics, and public health.

The COVID-19 pandemic provides an example of how public health impacts precarious work. COVID-19 has increased existing inequalities in the world of work and has generated high levels of chronic stress and insecurity that contribute to problems in relationships, mental health, and physical well-being across large segments of the population (Blustein et al., 2020a). While many privileged central workers were able to work remotely in safety and security from their homes throughout the pandemic, many peripheral workers experienced job loss. Other workers, both peripheral and central, were deemed as essential and were required to go into the workplace, even when they felt that this jeopardized their health through potential exposure to the virus. The COVID-19 pandemic thus exacerbated work precarity and various inequities that existed before the current crisis started (Blustein et al., 2020a). Autin, Blustein, Ali, and Garriott (2020) adopted a PWT lens to consider career-development policies and practices that could be applied to resolve problems arising from the pandemic. In efforts to frame the COVID-19 crisis as an opportunity for career-development professionals to strengthen their commitment to promoting decent work and the well-being of workers, recommendations were formulated across four distinct areas, including unemployment, worker mental health, work-family interface, and employment disparities (Autin et al., 2020). Career-development and organizational professionals can take a social justice stance through policy and practice to improve the lives of workers and their families.

Decent Work, Vulnerable Workers, and Preventive Intervention

The well-being of vulnerable workers warrants the attention of career development and organizational psychology. Research has identified a range of vulnerable workers who are most at-risk in the workforce for being excluded from decent work. More positively and proactively, this research has also identified the role of preventive initiatives for enhancing opportunities for vulnerable workers and increasing their access decent work (Di Fabio & Svicher, 2021; Svicher & Di Fabio, 2021). This research is aligned with Blustein et al.'s (2019a, 2019b) call for research and intervention in the field of vocational psychology to enhance decent work as an essential right for all human beings, including those who may be most vulncrable as related to age, gender, race, religion, poverty, and migrant status. The psychology of sustainability and sustainable development framework (Di Fabio, 2017a; 2017b; Di Fabio & Rosen, 2018) complements the PWT model in considering the design of research and preventive intervention at the organizational level to promote decent work as an essential right for all human beings (Blustein et al., 2019b; Duffy et al., 2017). In alignment with the United Nations goals for sustainable development, the psychology of sustainability aims to enhance the quality of life for all human beings through paying specific attention to factors that promote well-being at the organizational level as well as to concerns for the health of the broader economic, social, and ecological environments (Di Fabio, 2017b). We propose an integrated framework to guide the design of preventive interventions at the organizational level to support vulnerable workers. This integrated framework would include the psychology of sustainability and sustainable development (Di Fabio, 2017a), goals for social justice promotion (ILO, 2020; United Nations, 2021), decent work and inclusivity (Blustein, 2019), processes for building strengths (Di Fabio 2017b; Di Fabio & Blustein, 2016; Di Fabio & Kenny, 2015, 2016, 2018, 2019a, 2019b; Di Fabio & Saklofske, 2014, 2021), and the design of positive and healthy organizations that highlight equality and dignity in the workplace (Di Fabio, 2017a; Di Fabio et al., 2020; Di Fabio & Peiró, 2018).

With regard to strengths-based prevention perspectives at the organizational level (Di Fabio & Kenny, 2021; Di Fabio & Saklofske, 2021), job crafting, or attention to tailoring the design features of work and the workplace, represents one possible strategy for promoting decent work among vulnerable workers (Svicher & Di Fabio, 2021). Svicher and Di Fabio (2021) analyzed the literature related to job crafting among vulnerable workers with specific attention to variables included in the PWT model. Job crafting was highlighted in studies of different groups of vulnerable workers, including older workers (Kooij et al., 2020; Nagy et al., 2019; Zacher & Rudolph, 2019), unemployed workers (Hulshof et al., 2020a, 2000b), workers with disabilities (Brucker & Sundar, 2020), and migrant workers (Arasli et al., 2019). Svicher and Di Fabio (2021) identified positive outcomes for job crafting that enhances work features aligned with PWT needs for self-determination (Bakker & Oerlemans, 2019; Hornung, 2019; Shin & Jung, 2019) and for work meaning (Petrou et al., 2017; Tims et al., 2016). Studies also reveal how job crafting has focused on promoting job characteristics that are identified in PWT as moderators and mediators for reaching decent work, including proactive personality (Bakker et al., 2012; Rudolph et al., 2017; Zhang et al., 2018), career adaptability (Federici et al., 2019; Woo, 2020), and work volition (Cheung et al., 2020). This review thus highlights the potential for job crafting to promote changes in the workplace that increase the autonomy of vulnerable workers and bring their jobs in closer alignment with their needs, abilities, and preferences. The potential of job crafting as a strengths-based prevention intervention (Di Fabio & Kenny, 2021; Di Fabio & Saklofske, 2021) that potentiates access to decent work among vulnerable workers (Svicher & Di Fabio, 2021) is a promising area for further research and practice in organizational settings.

Successful organizations that promote decent work for all workers need to foster diversity, equity, and inclusion across race, ethnicity, gender, social class, religion, sexual identity, ableism, and other marginalized social identities (Di Fabio, 2016). Diverse perspectives offered by persons from different backgrounds serve to strengthen and enrich the talent base, creativity, and productivity of organizations. Diversity and inclusion efforts have sought to maximize the capacity for all employees to contribute to organizational goals and to advance to their fullest potential (Cox, 1994). In this regard, the workplace and work environment need to ensure all workers unobstructed opportunities to exercise voice and contribute to the strategic and competitive advantage of their organization (Harris et al., 2007; Leroy et al., 2022; Roberson, 2019; Triana et al., 2021; Van Knippenberg & van Ginkel, 2022). Organizational leaders need to be representative of the diverse workforce they lead, cultivate the contributions of all workers, and create work environments characterized by equity, inclusion, and a sense of belonging for all. Diversity management initiatives have focused on enhancing the performance of a heterogeneous workforce, but with greatest attention to gender, ethnicity, nationality, culture, and educational backgrounds (Yadav & Lenka, 2020). Equal attention has not been afforded to all categories of vulnerable workers as defined by Svicher and Di Fabio (2021), and thus future initiatives in diversity management should enhance the range and inclusivity of strength-based prevention programs for all vulnerable workers.

With regard to promoting inclusion and access to sustainable decent work for vulnerable workers, Di Fabio and Svicher (2022) also emphasize the need to reorganize and revise career counseling services for the 21st century. The authors refer to four key reforms (Di Fabio & Svicher, 2022, p. 1477):

> (1) Enrich career counselling interventions with the processes of self-identity, reflection, and reflexivity on what constitutes actual sustainability for vulnerable workers in terms of professional and personal development; (2) Promote the use of an evidence-based methodology in accordance with the accountability principles for the 21st century; (3) Advocate to enrich available services with positive primary preventive strength-based actions and interventions through timely differentiated career counselling strategies; (4) Encourage applied research and

practices to find new ways to balance resources with evidence-based efficacy; for example, by using the power of the audience in group-based life design counselling (Di Fabio & Maree, 2012).

Researchers and practitioners in vocational psychology and career counseling need to assume an ethical stance, promoting the right to decent work for vulnerable workers and creating and offering specific, differentiated, and tailored interventions on the basis of specific needs.

Decent Lives

The world of work is changing rapidly in ways that often threaten the sense of connection and meaning that people optimally derive from their work life (Blustein et al., 2019b; Di Fabio & Blustein, 2016). In this context, it is important to understand how people construct their work and life meaning. Di Fabio and Blustein (2016) maintain that the current challenges in constructing decent work and decent lives require a shift from motivation to a focus on meaning: "The passage from the paradigm of motivation to the paradigm of meaning, where the sustainability of the decent life project is anchored to a meaningful construction" (Di Fabio & Blustein, 2016, p. 1). The shift towards meaning defines decent lives that are anchored in a personal sense of authenticity and meaning in work and beyond.

Decent lives, however, require more than the realization of individual meaning through engagement in decent work. Guichard (2022) explains this by referring to Arendt's (1958) conceptualization of the "active life," which includes not only work, but also labor and action. According to Arendt (1958), work is productive activity through which individuals recognize themselves; labor includes all of the activities that allow people to sustain their lives (as, for example, personal care work); action concerns the varied collective organizational activities that must be fulfilled because labor and work always produce more than their immediate outcomes. Guichard (2022) maintains that each component of the active life necessitates a different question: "What 'laboring' could I immediately find to ensure my daily (over) living?" (labor); "What job would allow me to become who I expect to be?" (work); "By what forms of action could we together contribute to solving some of the problems (economic, social, political, etc.) that we encounter?" (action). Preventive and career interventions are thus needed to support the design of active lives and to equip people to cope effectively with the complex economic, ecological, social, and political issues of the 21st century. Individuals need to plan beyond their personal goals and consider how they can construct fully active lives where they can work with others to solve the problems of the current global crisis (Guichard, 2022). Creating opportunities for all to engage in decent work and creating workplaces where all individuals can thrive necessitate a movement beyond satisfying individual needs to creating a culture where individuals are prepared and committed to work together to co-construct lives that will be decent for all.

This broad scenario, moving beyond decent work to foster decent and active lives that meet the challenges of sustainability and sustainable development, calls for evolving theories and practices along with revised career and life interventions. Career and life interventions are needed that enable persons to construct and manage personal projects for decent work and for decent life that are grounded in authentic connection and meaning (Di Fabio, 2017a, 2017b; Di Fabio & Blustein, 2016). Life and professional projects are more sustainable, moreover, if they are deeply rooted in meaningful constructions defined by coherence, direction, significance, and belonging (Di Fabio, 2017b; Schnell et al., 2013).

For decent lives to be sustained, people need to collaborate to build healthy communities and healthier societies that go beyond concern for self. Healthy societies are characterized not only by hedonic well-being, but above all by eudaimonic well-being. Hedonic well-being entails the affective components of positive and negative affect (Watson et al., 1988) as well as the cognitive component of life satisfaction (Diener et al., 1985). Life satisfaction represents a positive global evaluation of one's life (Diener et al., 1985). Eudaimonic well-being, on the other hand, entails optimal functioning and self-realization, life meaning and purposefulness (Ryan & Deci, 2001; Waterman et al., 2010), and flourishing across the social (extrapersonal) and psychological (intrapersonal) dimensions of life (Diener et al., 2010). From the perspective of work and organizational psychology, this requires an emphasis on building healthy organizations (Di Fabio, 2017b; Di Fabio et al., 2020) that value the health and safety of all workers as well as the contributions of all workers to organizational effectiveness. This is sound practice for organizations, as workers' well-being and safety are inherently and positively related to organizational productivity and effectiveness (Gracia et al., 2020; Peiró et al., 2019). In this way, building healthy workplaces, which include access to decent work for all, promote healthy lives and nurture a virtuous healthy circle of meaning, authenticity, purpose and productivity. This perspective is also promoted by the well-being movement (Robertson & Cooper, 2010; Johnson et al., 2018), which emphasizes the value of enhancing resources in organizations in order to improve the well-being of workers.

Conclusions

We are now facing unprecedented health, economic, and social challenges that exceed those confronted at the beginning of the 21st century (Blustein et al., 2019b). The current challenges are accelerating and expanding in scope and intensity as we simultaneously experience precarity in work, viral pandemic, war, and the dangerous effects of climate change, including melting glaciers, fires, floods, and severe storms. Meeting these challenges effectively calls for resilience (Borquez et al., 2017; Raymond & Raymond, 2019) as well as hope and optimism (Grund & Brock, 2019).

In addressing these challenges from a positive psychology perspective, the psychology of sustainability and sustainable development (Di Fabio, 2017a,

2017b; Di Fabio & Rosen, 2018) can be integrated with PWT to consider how to build decent work and decent and healthy lives. Harmonization (Di Fabio & Tsuda, 2018) is needed to offer an inclusive and generative perspective that extends from the past, to the present, and towards the future and new generations. Career and life planning should embrace a primary strengths-based prevention perspective (Di Fabio & Kenny, 2021; Di Fabio & Saklofske, 2021; Kenny & Tsai, 2020) to design decent work and decent and healthy lives with a sense of urgency and responsibility concerning the future and future generations. Career and life counseling interventions can attend to constructing sustainable life projects for decent work and decent lives that encompass meaning, social purpose, authentic values, and the realization of eudaimonic well-being for self and others. In the context of the current crises, we need to pivot and focus on the construction of decent and healthy lives and healthier societies, where responsible and sustainable development at the personal, social, organizational, and community levels is taken into account. Organizational psychology can assume a central role in these efforts in collaboration with the fields of primary prevention and vocational and counseling psychology. The need for close and productive collaboration is needed now more than ever in the face of inevitable, new, and complex challenges.

References

Allan, B. A., Autin, K. L., & Wilkins-Yel, K. G. (2021). Precarious work in the 21st century: A psychological perspective. *Journal of Vocational Behavior*, 126, 103491. doi:10.1016/j.jvb.2020.103491.

Allan, B. A., Tay, L., & Sterling, H. M. (2017). Construction and validation of the Subjective Underemployment Scales (SUS). *Journal of Vocational Behaviour*, 99, 93–106. doi:10.1016/j.jvb.2017.01.001.

Arasli, H., Arici, H. E., & Ilgen, H. (2019). Blackbox between job crafting and job embeddedness of immigrant hotel employees: a serial mediation model. *Economic research – Ekonomska Istrazivanja*, 32, 3935–3962. doi:10.1080/1331677X.2019.1678500.

Arendt, H. (1958). *The Human Condition*. University of Chicago Press.

Autin, K. L., Blustein, D. L., Ali, S. R., & Garriott, P. O. (2020). Career development impacts of COVID-19: Practice and policy recommendations. *Journal of Career Development*, 47(5), 487–494. doi:10.1177/0894845320944486.

Bakker, A. B., & Oerlemans, W. G. M. (2019). Daily job crafting and momentary work engagement: A self-determination and self-regulation perspective. *Journal of Vocational Behavior*, 112, 417–430. doi:10.1016/j.jvb.2018.12.005.

Bakker, A. B., Tims, M., & Derks, D. (2012). Proactive personality and job performance: the role of job crafting and work engagement. *Human Relations*, 65, 1359–1378. doi:10.1177/0018726712453471.

Blustein, D. L. (2001). Extending the reach of vocational psychology: Toward an inclusive and integrative psychology of working. *Journal of Vocational Behavior*, 59 (2), 171–182. doi:10.1006/jvbe.2001.1823.

Blustein, D. L. (2006). *The psychology of working: A new perspective for career development, counseling, and public policy*. Mahwah, NJ: Erlbaum.

Blustein, D. L. (2008). The role of work in psychological health and well-being: A conceptual, historical, and public policy perspective. *American Psychologist*, 63(4), 228–240. doi:10.1037/0003-066X.63.4.228.

Blustein, D. L. (2013). *The psychology of working: A new perspective for career development, counseling, and public policy.* Routledge.

Blustein, D. L. (2019). *The Importance of Work in an Age of Uncertainty: The Eroding Work Experience in America.* New York: Oxford University Press.

Blustein, D. L., DeVoy, J., Connors-Kellgren, A., & Olle, C. (2014). Self-construction in an unstable world: Guichard's theory in the era of the great recession. In A. Di Fabio & J.-L. Bernaud (Eds.), *The Construction of the Identity in 21st Century: A Festschrift for Jean Guichard* (pp. 75–86). Nova Science.

Blustein, D. L., Duffy, R., Ferreira, J. A., Cohen-Scali, V., Cinamon, R. G., & Allan, B. A. (2020a). Editorial: Unemployment in the time of COVID-19: A research agenda. *Journal of Vocational Behavior*, 119, 103436. doi:10.1016/j.jvb.2020.103436.

Blustein, D. L., Kenny, M. E., Autin, K., & Duffy, R. (2019a). The psychology of working in practice: A theory of change for a new era. *Career Development Quarterly*, 67, 236–254. doi:10.1002/cdq.12193.

Blustein, D. L., Kenny, M. E., Di Fabio, A., & Guichard, J. (2019b). Expanding the impact of the psychology of working: Engaging psychology in the struggle for decent work and human rights. *Journal of Career Assessment*, 27, 3–28. doi:10.1177/1069072718774002.

Blustein, D. L., Perera, H. N., Diamonti, A. J., Gutowski, E., Meerkins, T., Davila, A., … & Konowitz, L. (2020b). The uncertain state of work in the US: Profiles of decent work and precarious work. *Journal of Vocational Behavior*, 122, 103481. doi:10.1016/j.jvb.2020.103481.

Borquez, R., Aldunce, P., & Adler, C. (2017). Resilience to climate change: From theory to practice through co-production of knowledge in Chile. *Sustainability Science*, 12(1), 163–176. doi:10.1007/s11625-016-0400-6.

Brucker, D. L., & Sundar, V. (2020). Job crafting among American workers with disabilities. *Journal Occupational Rehabilitation*, 30, 575–587. doi:10.1007/s10926–10020–09889–09889.

Carr, S. C., Maleka, M., Meyer, I., Barry, M. L., Haar, J., Parker, J., … & Naithani, A. (2018). How can wages sustain a living? By getting ahead of the curve. *Sustainability Science*, 13(4), 901–917. doi:10.1007/s11625-018-0560-7.

Carr, S. C., Parker, J., Arrowsmith, J., & Watters, P. A. (2016). The Living Wage: Theoretical integration and an applied research agenda. *International Labour Review*, 155(1), 1–24.

Cheung, F., Ngo, H. Y., & Leung, A. (2020). Predicting work volition among undergraduate students in the United States and Hong Kong. *Journal of Career Development*, 47, 565–578. doi:10.1177/0894845318803469.

Cox, T. (1994). *Cultural diversity in organizations: Theory, research and practice.* Berrett-Koehler Publishers.

Diener, E. D., Emmons, R. A., Larsen, R. J., & Griffin, S. (1985). The satisfaction with life scale. *Journal of Personality Assessment*, 49(1), 71–75. https://doi.org/10.1207/s15327752jpa4901_13.

Diener, E., Wirtz, D., Tov, W., Kim-Prieto, C., Choi, D. W., Oishi, S., & Biswas-Diener, R. (2010). New well-being measures: Short scales to assess flourishing and positive and negative feelings. *Social Indicators Research*, 97(2), 143–156. doi:10.1007/s11205-009-9493-y.

Di Fabio, A. (2016). Diversity Management Questionnaire: Primo contributo alla versione italiana [Diversity Management Questionnaire: First contribution to the Italian version]. *Counseling: Giornale Italiano di Ricerca e Applicazioni*, 9(2). doi:10.14605/CS921616.

Di Fabio, A. (2017a). Positive Healthy Organizations: Promoting well-being, meaningfulness, and sustainability in organizations. *Frontiers in Psychology: Organizational Psychology*, 8, 1938. doi:10.3389/fpsyg.2017.01938.

Di Fabio, A. (2017b). The psychology of sustainability and sustainable development for well-being in organizations. *Frontiers in Psychology: Organizational Psychology*, 8, 1534. doi:10.3389/fpsyg.2017.01534.

Di Fabio, A., & Blustein, D. L. (2016). Editorial: "From Meaning of Working to Meaningful Lives: The Challenges of Expanding Decent Work". *Frontiers in Psychology: Organizational Psychology*, 7, 1119. doi:10.3389/fpsyg.2016.01119.

Di Fabio, A., Cheung, F., & Peiró, J.-M. (2020). Editorial Special Issue Personality and individual differences and healthy organizations. *Personality and Individual Differences*, 166. doi:10.1016/j.paid.2020.110196.

Di Fabio, A., & Kenny, M. E. (2015). The contributions of emotional intelligence and social support for adaptive career progress among Italian youth. *Journal of Career Development*, 42, 48–49. doi:10.1177/0894845314533420.

Di Fabio, A., & Kenny, M. E. (2016). From decent work to decent lives: Positive Self and Relational Management (PS&RM) in the twenty-first century. *Frontiers in Psychology*, 7(361). doi:10.3389/fpsyg.2016.00361.

Di Fabio, A., & Kenny, M. E. (2018). Intrapreneurial Self-Capital: A Key Resource for Promoting Well-Being in a Shifting Work Landscape. *Sustainability*, 10(9), 3035. doi:10.3390/su10093035.

Di Fabio, A., & Kenny, M. E. (2019a). Decent work in Italy: Context, conceptualization, and assessment. *Journal of Vocational Behavior*, 110(Part A), 131–143. doi:10.1016/j.jvb.2018.10.014.

Di Fabio, A., & Kenny, M. E. (2019b). Resources for enhancing employee and organizational wellbeing beyond personality traits: The promise of Emotional Intelligence and Positive Relational Management. *Personality and Individual Differences* (Special Issue Personality, Individual Differences and Healthy Organizations), 151, 109278. doi:10.1016/j.paid.2019.02.022.

Di Fabio, A., & Kenny, M. E. (2021). Positive and negative affects and meaning at work: Trait emotional intelligence as a primary prevention resource in organizations for sustainable and positive human capital development. In A. Di Fabio (Ed.), *Cross-cultural Perspectives on Well-Being and Sustainability in Organizations* (pp. 139–152). Switzerland: Springer.

Di Fabio, A., & Maree, J. G. (2012). Group-based Life Design Counseling in an Italian context. *Journal of Vocational Behavior*, 80, 100–107. doi:10.1016/j.jvb.2011.06.001.

Di Fabio, A., & Peiró, J. M. (2018). Human Capital Sustainability Leadership to promote sustainable development and healthy organizations: A new scale. *Sustainability*, 10(7), 2413. doi:10.3390/su10072413.

Di Fabio, A., & Rosen, M. A. (2018). Opening the Black Box of Psychological Processes in the Science of Sustainable Development: A New Frontier . *European Journal of Sustainable Development Research*, 2(4), 47. doi:10.20897/ejosdr/3933.

Di Fabio, A., & Saklofske, D. H. (2014). Promoting individual resources: The challenge of trait emotional intelligence. *Personality and Individual Differences*, 65, 19–23. doi:10.1016/j.paid.2014.01.026.

Di Fabio, A., & Saklofske, D. H. (2021). The relationship of compassion and self-compassion with personality and emotional intelligence. PAID 40th anniversary special issue. *Personality and Individual Differences*, 157. doi:10.1016/j.paid.2020.110109.

Di Fabio, A., & Svicher, A. (2021). The Psychology of Sustainability and Sustainable Development: Advancing Decent Work, Inclusivity, and Positive Strengths-based Primary Preventive Interventions for Vulnerable Workers. *Frontiers in Psychology*, 12, 718354. doi:10.3389/fpsyg.2021.718354.

Di Fabio, A., & Svicher, A. (2022). Precariousness in the Time of COVID-19: A Turning Point for Reforming and Reorganizing Career Counselling for Vulnerable Workers. *Cypriot Journal of Educational Sciences*, 17(5), 1477–1494. doi:10.18844/cjes.v17i5.6676.

Di Fabio, A., & Tsuda, A. (2018). The psychology of harmony and harmonization: Advancing the perspectives for the psychology of sustainability and sustainable development. *Sustainability*, 10(12), 4726. doi:10.3390/su10124726.

Duffy, R. D., Allan, B. A., England, J. W., Blustein, D. L., Autin, K. L., Douglass, R. P., Ferreira, J., & Santos, E. J. R. (2017). The development and initial validation of the Decent Work Scale. *Journal of Counseling Psychology*, 64(2), 206–221. doi:10.1037/cou0000191.

Duffy, R. D., Blustein, D. L., Diemer, M. A., & Autin, K. L. (2016). The psychology of working theory. *Journal of Counseling Psychology*, 63(2), 127–148. doi:10.1037/cou0000140.

Duffy, R. D., Velez, B. L., England, J. W., Autin, K. L., Douglass, R. P., Allan, B. A., & Blustein, D. L. (2018). An examination of the Psychology of Working Theory with racially and ethnically diverse employed adults. *Journal of Counseling Psychology*, 65(3), 280–293. doi:10.1037/cou0000247.

Federici, E., Boon, C., & Den Hartog, D. N. (2019). The moderating role of HR practices on the career adaptability-job crafting relationship: A study among employee-manager dyads. *International Journal of Human Resource Management*, 32, 1339–1367. doi:10.1080/09585192.2018.1522656.

Gracia, F.J., Tomás, I., Martínez-Córcoles, M., & Peiró, J.M. (2020). Empowering leadership, mindful organizing and safety performance in a nuclear power plant: A multilevel structural equation model. *Safety Science*, 123, 104542. doi:10.1016/j.ssci.2019.104542.

Grund, J., & Brock, A. (2019). Why we should empty Pandora's box to create a sustainable future: Hope, sustainability and its implications for education. *Sustainability*, 11(3), 893. doi:10.3390/su11030893.

Guichard, J. (2009). Self-constructing. *Journal of Vocational Behavior*, 75, 251–258. doi:10.1016/j.jvb.2009.03.004.

Guichard, J. (2022). How to support the design of active lives that meet the challenges of the twenty-first century (economy, ecology and politics)? *Australian Journal of Career Development*, 31(1), 5–13. https://doi.org/10.1177/10384162221090815.

Harris, C., Rousseau, G. G., & Venter, D. (2007). Employee perceptions of diversity management at a tertiary institution. *South African Journal of Economic and Management Sciences*, 10(1), 51–71. doi:10.4102/sajems.v10i1.536.

Hornung, S. (2019). Crafting task and cognitive job boundaries to enhance self-determination, impact, meaning and competence at work. *Behavioral Sciences*, 9(12), 136. doi:10.3390/bs9120136.

Hulshof, I. L., Demerouti, E., & Le Blanc, P. M. (2020a). A job search demands-resources intervention among the unemployed: Effects on well-being, job search behavior and reemployment chances. *Journal of Occupational Health Psychology*, 25, 17–31. doi:10.1037/ocp0000167.

Hulshof, I. L., Demerouti, E., & Le Blanc, P. M. (2020b). Reemployment crafting: Proactively shaping one's job search. *Journal of Applied Psychology*, 105, 58–79. doi:10.1037/apl0000419.

ILO (International Labour Organization). (2012). *Decent work indicators: Concepts and definitions*. Retrieved from http://www.ilo.org/wcmsp5/groups/public/—dgrep orts/– integration/documents/publication/wcms_229374.pdf.

ILO (International Labour Organization). (2020). *Global Wage Report 2020–21: Wages and Minimum Wages in the Time of COVID-19*. Geneva: International Labour Office. Retrieved from https://www.ilo.org/wcmsp5/groups/public/—dgrep orts/—dcomm/—publ/documents/publicat ion/wcms_762534.pdf.

Johnson, S., Robertson, I., & Cooper, C. L. (2018). *Wellbeing: Productivity and Happiness at Work* (2nd ed.). London: Palgrave Macmillan.

Kenny, M. E., & Tsai, B.W. (2020). Person and System Focused Prevention in Preparing Youth to Navigate an Uncertain Work Future. *Journal of Prevention and Health Promotion*, 1(2), 155–182. https://doi.org/10.1177/2632077020965568.

Kooij, D. T. A. M., Nijssen, H., Bal, P. M., & van der Kruijssen, D. T. F. (2020). Crafting an interesting job: Stimulating an active role of older workers in enhancing their daily work engagement and job performance. *Work, Aging, and Retirement*, 6 (3), 165–174. doi:10.1093/workar/waaa001.

Kozan, S., Blustein, D. L., Paciorek, R., Kilbury, E., & Işık, E. (2019). A qualitative investigation of beliefs about work-related crises in the United States. *Journal of Counseling Psychology*, 66(5), 600–612. https://doi.org/10.1037/cou0000343.

Kozan, S., Gutowski, E., & Blustein, D. L. (2020). A qualitative exploration of women's work aspirations and beliefs on meritocracy. *Journal of Counseling Psychology*, 67(2), 195–207. doi:10.1037/cou0000409.

Kozan, S., Işık, E., & Blustein, D. L. (2019). Decent work and well-being among low-income Turkish employees: Testing the psychology of working theory. *Journal of Counseling Psychology*, 66(3), 317–327. doi:10.1037/cou0000342.

Leroy, H., Buengeler, C., Veestraeten, M., Shemla, M., & Hoever, I. J. (2022). Fostering team creativity through team-focused inclusion: The role of leader harvesting the benefits of diversity and cultivating value-in-diversity beliefs. *Group & Organization Management*, 47(4), 798–839. doi:10.1177/10596011211009683.

Nagy, N., Johnston, C. S., & Hirschi, A. (2019). Do we act as old as we feel? An examination of subjective age and job crafting behaviour of late career employees. *European Journal of Work and Organizational Psychology*, 28, 373–383. doi:10.1080/1359432X.2019.1584183.

Peiró, J. M., Kozusznik, M., Molina, I. R., & Tordera, N. (2019). The happy-productive worker model and beyond: Patterns of wellbeing and performance at work. *International Journal of Environmental Research and Public Health*, 16(3), 479. doi:10.3390/ijerph16030479.

Petrou, P., Bakker, A. B., & van den Heuvel, M. (2017). Weekly job crafting and leisure crafting: Implications for meaning-making and work engagement. *Journal of Occupational and Organizational Psychology*, 90, 129–152. doi:10.1111/joop.12160.

Raymond, I. J., & Raymond, C. M. (2019). Positive psychology perspectives on social values and their application to intentionally delivered sustainability interventions. *Sustainability Science*, 14(5), 1381–1393. doi:10.1007/s11625-019-00705-9.

Roberson, Q. M. (2019). Diversity in the workplace: A review, synthesis, and future research agenda. *Annual Review of Organizational Psychology and Organizational Behavior*, 6, 69–88. doi:10.1146/annurev-orgpsych-012218-015243.

Robertson, I., & Cooper, C. L. (2010). *Wellbeing: Productivity and Happiness at Work*. London: Palgrave Macmillan.

Rudolph, C. W., Katz, I. M., Lavigne, K. N., & Zacher, H. (2017). Job crafting: a meta-analysis of relationships with individual differences, job characteristics, and work outcomes. *Journal of Vocational Behavior*, 102, 112–138. doi:10.1016/j.jvb.2017.05.008.

Ryan, R. M., & Deci, E. L. (2001). To be happy or to be self-fulfilled: A review of research on hedonic and eudaimonic well-being. *Annual Review of Psychology*, 52, 141–166. doi:10.1146/annurev.psych.52.1.141.

Schnell, T., Höge, T., & Pollet, E. (2013). Predicting meaning in work: Theory, data, implications. *The Journal of Positive Psychology*, 8(6), 543–554. doi:10.1080/17439760.2013.830763.

Shin, I., & Jung, H. (2019). Differential roles of self-determined motivations in describing job crafting behavior and organizational change commitment. *Current Psychology*, 40, 3376–3385. doi:10.1007/s12144-019-00265-2.

Svicher, A., & Di Fabio, A. (2021). Job Crafting: A Challenge to Promote Decent Work for Vulnerable Workers. *Frontiers in Psychology*, 12, 1827. doi:10.3389/fpsyg.2021.681022.

Tims, M., Derks, D., & Bakker, A. B. (2016). Job crafting and its relationships with person-job fit and meaningfulness: A three-wave study. *Journal of Vocational Behavior*, 92, 44–53. doi:10.1016/j.jvb.2015.11.007.

Triana, M. D. C., Gu, P., Chapa, O., Richard, O., & Colella, A. (2021). Sixty years of discrimination and diversity research in human resource management: A review with suggestions for future research directions. *Human Resource Management*, 60(1), 145–204. doi:10.1002/hrm.22052.

United Nations. (2021). *Transforming Our World: the 2030 Agenda for Sustainable Development*. New York: United Nations. Retrieved from https://sdgs.un.org/2030agenda.

Van Knippenberg, D., & van Ginkel, W. P. (2022). A diversity mindset perspective on inclusive leadership. *Group & Organization Management*, 47(4), 779–797. doi:10.1177/1059601121997229.

Vives, A., Amable, M., Ferrer, M., Moncada, S., Llorens, C., Muntaner, C., Benavides, F. G., & Benach, J. (2010). The Employment Precariousness Scale (EPRES): Psychometric properties of a new tool for epidemiological studies among waged and salaried workers. *Occupational and Environmental Medicine*, 67(8), 548–555. doi:10.1136/oem.2009.048967.

Waterman, A. S., Schwartz, S. J., Zamboanga, B. L., Ravert, R. D., Williams, M. K., Bede Agocha, V., ... & Brent Donnellan, M. (2010). The Questionnaire for Eudaimonic Well-Being: Psychometric properties, demographic comparisons, and evidence of validity. *The Journal of Positive Psychology*, 5(1), 41–61. doi:10.1080/17439760903435208.

Watson, D., Clark, L. A., & Tellegen, A. (1988). Development and validation of brief measures of positive and negative affect: The PANAS scales. *Journal of Personality and Social Psychology*, 54(6), 1063–1070. doi:10.1037//0022-3514.54.6.1063.

Woo, H. R. (2020). Perceived overqualification and job crafting: The curvilinear moderation of career adaptability. *Sustainability*, 12(24), 1–17. doi:10.3390/su122410458.

Yadav, S., & Lenka, U. (2020). Diversity management: A systematic review. *Equality, Diversity and Inclusion: An International Journal*, 39(8), 901–929. doi:10.1108/EDI-07-2019-0197.

Zacher, H., & Rudolph, C. W. (2019). Why do we act as old as we feel? The role of occupational future time perspective and core self-evaluations in the relationship between subjective age and job crafting behaviour. *European Journal of Work and Organizational Psychology*, 28, 831–844. doi:10.1080/1359432X.2019.1677609.

Zhang, L., Lu, H., & Li, F. (2018). Proactive personality and mental health: The role of job crafting. *PsyCh Journal*, 7, 154–155. doi:10.1002/pchj.214.

Psychology of Sustainability and Sustainable Development in the Context of Organizational Behaviour

6 Human Capital Sustainability Leadership and Healthy Organizations

Its Contribution to Sustainable Development

Annamaria Di Fabio and José María Peiró

Interest in sustainability and sustainable development has increased in the 21st century due to the features of the current global world of work, which is characterized by complexity, uncertainty, and accelerated changes (Blustein et al., 2019). The psychology of sustainability and sustainable development (Di Fabio, 2017a, 2017b; Di Fabio & Rosen, 2018) introduced a new focus using a psychological lens to study the processes connected with sustainability and sustainable development. A positive sustainability perspective was delineated, where the attention is on resources in terms of respect and regeneration. The focus is on renewable resources as a form of purification/oxygenation to improve health and well-being. In organizations, the psychology of sustainability and sustainable development calls for an assumption of organizational and managerial responsibility to renew, invigorate, and improve the flourishing of human resources promoting health and well-being. Relevant processes are individuated to create and enhance well-being for the sustainable development of resources for positive, healthy organizations (Di Fabio, 2017a; Di Fabio et al., 2020). In strengths-based prevention perspectives (Di Fabio & Saklofske, 2021), it is fundamental to individuate, construct, and reinforce strengths in terms of resources to accompany the flourishing of processes, workers, and organizations. An innovative approach is proposed, with a focus on the well-being of individuals, groups, and organizations in different types of environment(s), ranging from natural to personal, social, organizational, community, digital, and global environments. The psychology of sustainability and sustainable development promotes positive, healthy organizations through preventive perspectives (Di Fabio & Kenny, 2021; Di Fabio & Saklofske, 2021) as well as by centering on development, positive experiences, and narratives to build optimal results starting from strengths. Positive, healthy organizations (Di Fabio, 2017a) engage in anticipating solutions for possible problems, promoting well-being, and valorizing resources at the individual, group, inter-group, organizational, and inter-organizational levels. This framework is crucial for promoting the sustainability of human resources, sustainable development, and the flourishing of organizations' talents (Di Fabio, 2017a, 2021). The framework places an emphasis on integrating new ingredients into leadership styles.

DOI: 10.4324/9781003212157-8

Human Capital Sustainability Leadership (Di Fabio & Peiró, 2018a) is centered on "healthy people as flourishing and resilient workers [as well as] on healthy organizations as thriving and successful environments characterized by the positive circle of long-term well-being and performance" (p. 3). It is a higher-order construct, which includes ethical, sustainable, mindful, and servant leadership, and it is evaluated from the leaders' perspective (leaders' version) or from the followers' perspective (followers' version). Ethical leadership aims to "engender fair and just aims, empower an organisation's members, create consistency of actions with espoused values, use behavior to communicate or enforce ethical standards, fair decisions and rewards, kindness, compassion and concern for others" (Di Fabio & Peiró, 2018a, p. 3). Sustainable leadership produces and maintains

> lifelong learning, safeguards achievement in the short and long terms, supports others' leadership, includes themes linked to social justice, promotes growth without depleting human and material resources, enhances different abilities and resources towards the well-being of environments, and is also enthusiastically involved in environmental issues.
> (Di Fabio & Peiró, 2018a, p. 3)

Mindful leadership is

> a style based on paying attention to the present moment, recognizing personal feelings and emotions and keeping them under control, especially under stress; [and having an] awareness of an individual's own presence at a given time and its impact on other people.
> (Di Fabio & Peiró, 2018a, p. 3)

Servant leadership is centered on "the development of human resources, principally considering their interests and not only the advantages for their organizations or leaders, [and also] accepting their answers/requests and supporting them due to a moral responsibility" (Di Fabio & Peiró, 2018a, p. 3).

To assess this higher-order construct, the Human Capital Sustainability Leadership Scale (HCSLS; Di Fabio & Peiró, 2018a) was developed. The scale is composed of 16 items, with responses ranging from 1 = *none* to 5 = *very much*. Two versions of the scale exist: a version for leaders and a version for followers. An analysis of the psychometric properties of the HCSLS in Italian workers showed a higher-order structure with a second-order factor and four first-order factors (ethical, sustainable, mindful, and servant leadership). The scale showed a good reliability and concurrent validity, presenting positive relationships with the Workplace Relational Civility Scale (WRCS; Di Fabio & Gori, 2016), both part A (me with others) and part B (others with me), as well as the Entrepreneurship/Leadership/Professionalism Questionnaire (ELPQ; Di Fabio et al., 2016). Leaders with higher Human Capital Sustainability Leadership seem more committed to applied relational civility at the workplace, and they seem to perceive more relational civility towards themselves by others. Furthermore, leaders with higher Human Capital Sustainability Leadership seem to perceive themselves as more flourishing in terms of social and psychological prosperity, and this psychological prosperity is a relevant base for promoting the flourishing of followers. Moreover, leaders with higher Human Capital Sustainability Leadership perceive themselves as having the characteristics of entrepreneurship, leadership, and professionalism, which are features that facilitate their function as a role model in their leadership position.

Interest in Human Capital Sustainability Leadership also extended to other countries, particularly in Eastern countries. The psychometric properties of the Malaysian version of Human Capital Sustainability Leadership were reported (Seok et al., 2021). The Malaysian version confirmed the higher-order structure with good reliability, and concurrent validity showed positive associations with flourishing. A Malaysian version of the HCSLS could open promising opportunities for research and intervention in the management of resources for healthy people and healthy organizations (Di Fabio et al., 2020) in a cross-cultural perspective. Interest in this higher-order construct of Human Capital Sustainability Leadership is also testified by works in progress to realize different versions of the scale – for example, a Japanese version, a Korean version, and an Indonesian version. On another front, a Ghanaian version is also in progress. All these versions could open interesting possibilities for cross-cultural comparisons.

Human Capital Sustainability Leadership: Empirical Evidence

Human Capital Sustainability Leadership (Di Fabio & Peiró, 2018a) was empirically studied in two international research and intervention laboratories at the University of Florence, Italy: (1) Cross-Cultural Positive Psychology, Prevention, and Sustainability, and (2) Work and Organizational Psychology for Vocational Guidance, Career Counseling, Career Development, Talents, and Healthy Organizations. Empirical studies considered Human Capital Sustainability Leadership both as a dependent and an independent variable. Human Capital Sustainability Leadership as a dependent variable was connected to independent variables, such as trait emotional intelligence and workplace relational civility. Human Capital Sustainability Leadership as an independent variable was examined in relation to eudaimonic well-being and decent work.

A study by Di Fabio and Svicher (2021) of a sample of Italian workers showed that trait emotional intelligence (Petrides & Furnham, 2000, 2001) was able to explain additional variance in the Human Capital Sustainability Leadership of leaders, controlling for the effects of personality traits. A greater perception of emotional intelligence, in terms of positive emotional resources, control of emotions, recognition of emotions in oneself and others, and expression of emotions, seems to characterize leaders with higher Human Capital Sustainability Leadership.

In another study, workplace relational civility (Di Fabio & Gori, 2016) was able to explain additional variance in the Human Capital Sustainability Leadership of leaders, controlling for the effects of personality traits in Italian workers (Di Fabio and Gori, 2021). Leaders with higher Human Capital Sustainability Leadership were characterized by the perception that the leaders act with greater relational civility (i.e., relational decency, relational culture, relational readiness) in the workplace as well as a perception of greater relational civility from others towards the leaders in the workplace.

Furthermore, Human Capital Sustainability Leadership in Italian workers was able to explain additional variance in eudaimonic well-being in terms of meaning in life (Diener et al., 2010) and flourishing (Morgan & Farsides, 2009), controlling for personality traits (Di Fabio and Peiró, 2018b). Leaders with higher Human Capital Sustainability Leadership perceive themselves as more flourishing in terms of psychological and social well-being, and they perceive themselves as having greater meaning in life.

In the study by Di Fabio (2018) conducted with Italian workers, the Human Capital Sustainability Leadership of followers was able to explain additional variance in decent work (Duffy et al., 2017), controlling for personality traits. Followers who perceive greater Human Capital Sustainability Leadership in their leaders have the perception that their work is more decent in terms of the physical and interpersonal safety of working conditions; the hours, which allow free time and adequate rest; organizational values, which complement family and social values; adequate remuneration; and adequate access to health care.

Human Capital Sustainability Leadership (Di Fabio & Peiró, 2018a) could be a promising resource for workers and organizations from a healthy organization perspective (Di Fabio, 2017a; Di Fabio et al., 2020), from the psychology of sustainability and sustainability development perspective (Di Fabio, 2017b; Di Fabio & Rosen, 2018), and from the psychology of decent work perspective (Duffy et al., 2017).

Human Capital Sustainability Leadership: Healthy Organizations and Cross-cultural Perspectives

Healthy organizations promote the health and safety of workers jointly with organizational effectiveness (Di Fabio, 2017a; Di Fabio et al., 2020; Di Fabio & Peiró, 2018a; Peiró & Rodríguez, 2008; Tetrick & Peiró, 2012). Healthy organizations establish a positive circle for improving the well-being of workers as well as organizational productivity, underlining that the workers' and organization's well-being are strongly associated for their flourishing (Di Fabio. 2017a). Organizational success, effectiveness, and safety are deeply connected to the health and well-being of workers and organizations (Di Fabio, 2017a; Peiró, 2008; Peiró & Tetrick, 2011).

In this framework, it is relevant that the contribution by Tetrick and Peiró (2012) introduces a fundamental shift from an ill-health perspective to a positive-health perspective. The authors suggest enhancing the promotion of health and well-being, including paying specific attention to talents, performance, and effectiveness (Peiró & Tetrick, 2011; Tetrick & Peiró, 2012). They introduce a positive perspective for achievement and excellence that considers various levels ranging from workers to group, organizational, and inter-organizational levels (Henry, 2005; Tetrick & Peiró, 2012).

This perspective takes into account both a preventive framework (Di Fabio, 2017a; Di Fabio & Kenny, 2016) and strengths-based prevention practices (Di Fabio & Saklofske, 2021) with the aim of promoting strength in workers and organizations. Cross-level interactions between workers and organizational perspectives are taken into consideration and centered on promoting positive experiences and narratives in organizations (Di Fabio, 2017a). The focus is on building or enhancing the strengths of workers, working groups, and organizations to promote safer and healthier working environments (Tetrick & Peiró, 2012). This perspective is connected with occupational health psychology (Cox et al., 2000; Raymond et al., 1990; Tetrick & Peiró, 2012), which also emphasizes the value of prevention and points out the relevance of fostering positive work experiences and strengthening resources.

In light of occupational health psychology (Cox et al., 2000; Raymond et al., 1990; Tetrick & Peiró, 2012) and the positive psychology perspective in organizations, positive organizational health psychology (Di Fabio, 2017a; Di Fabio & Peiró, 2018a) was introduced. This perspective is focused on the preventive enhancement of resources in organizations, instead of centering on the negative aspects of weakness and failure, and it is also in line with the well-being movement (Johnson et al., 2018; Robertson & Cooper, 2010). This framework underlines the value of leadership styles aimed at promoting positive organizational environments that are characterized by flourishing and the valorization of human resources (Hart & Cooper, 2001). Human Capital Sustainability Leadership (Di Fabio & Peiró, 2018a) belongs to this category.

Positive organizational health psychology (Di Fabio & Peiró, 2017, 2018a) also suggests the value of successful performance as a fundamental basis for healthy workers, healthy businesses, and healthy organizations (Di Fabio, 2017a). This perspective fits very well with the psychology of sustainability and sustainable development (Di Fabio, 2017b; Di Fabio & Rosen, 2018). Along this line, a recent study emphasized the value of work characteristics that are related to job performance as well as the mediating role of individual values in the relationship between work design and performance (Peiró et al., 2020). This research underlined the value of considering both the environmental attributes of the work and the preferences of the workers to promote flourishing and sustainable performance. These results highlight the need to pay attention to sustainable organizational and management processes as well as resources, especially during selection processes and work (re)design.

Regarding leadership for sustainable development, System Innovation (SI) is a critical approach for motivating individuals and collective actions for sustainable development (Peiró et al., 2021). Within the Climate-KIC Professional

Competence Framework for sustainable development, leadership competences are not only fundamental to managing sustainable development changes but, above all, they are a catalyst for promoting collective actions for sustainable development. Leadership styles that support sustainable development are valuable, and Human Capital Sustainability Leadership could be of particular value for sustainability in organizations.

Positive organizational health psychology (Di Fabio & Peiró, 2017, 2018a) also points out the great value of relationships in organizations (Blustein, 2011). Organizational life is shaped by relationships from the start, and it is important that they are progressively flanked by the construction of meaning at work to increase organizational well-being (Di Fabio, 2017a; Di Fabio et al., 2020). In the positive organizational health psychology for healthy organizations framework (Di Fabio et al., 2020; Tetrick & Peiró, 2012), relationships are fundamental for leadership processes. It is possible to underline the value of promoting leadership styles that are attentive to managing positive relationships in organizations with a focus on promoting the well-being of workers. In this regard, Human Capital Sustainability Leadership (Di Fabio & Peiró, 2018a) has great relevance, as it represents a style characterized by organizational as well as managerial sensibility, which answers current challenging organizational needs and guarantees sustainable organizational development. A leadership style attentive to meaningful details, aware of the relevance of relationships, and committed in the creation of positive narrative is a key element for healthy organizations (Di Fabio, 2017a). Currently in organizations, leaders have the responsibility to create, promote, and maintain positive narratives about work and relationships to nurture a positive and healthy organizational environment (Di Fabio, 2017a; Di Fabio et al., 2020) for sustainable development of human resources (Di Fabio & Peiró, 2018a). Human Capital Sustainability Leadership is a promising approach to the success of healthy businesses and asks for progressive steps in organizational and managerial awareness as a crucial ingredient for promoting positive relational management in organizations (Di Fabio, 2016). Thus, Human Capital Sustainability Leadership (Di Fabio & Peiró, 2018a) could represent a new way for enhancing good organizational relationships by adopting a preventive perspective to lead to healthy organizations (Di Fabio, 2017a; Di Fabio et al., 2020), because this type of leadership also promotes human resources sustainable development in organizations.

Relationships also represent a starting point for reflecting jointly on sustainable development in organizations from a cross-cultural perspective. Respect and caring for oneself, others, and connectedness are fundamental components of positive relational management (Di Fabio, 2016) within and outside of organizations. From a cross-cultural perspective, we can reflect on the relationship between individualism (me) and collectivism (we) to find a new me/us/organization/people/world balance for flourishing relationships (Di Fabio, 2017b). This cross-cultural reflection is expanded by the psychology of harmonization (Di Fabio & Tsuda, 2018, p. 1), which includes both "geographical and temporal perspectives, including meaningful construction processes from the past, to the present, and into the future using reflexivity processes at the individual, group, community, social, and national levels" for sustainability and sustainable development. It underlines the value of strengths-based prevention perspectives (Di Fabio & Saklofske, 2021), including the primary prevention perspective (Di Fabio & Kenny, 2015, 2016; Hage et al., 2007) for building the strengths of people and environments in different cultural contexts. According to this preventive framework, a positive cross-cultural preventive perspective (Di Fabio, 2019) valorises the effort to increase resources in different cultural contexts for positive cross-cultural strengths-based prevention from the occupational perspective of healthy organizations (Di Fabio, 2018, 2021). Human Capital Sustainability Leadership could be a promising opportunity in this framework, as shown by international research (Seok et al., 2021), that could open up future work in this direction by taking into account cross-cultural perspectives. Thus, in the globalized, complex, accelerating, and fluid world of work, to foster healthy organizations we need continuous dialogue based on the psychology of sustainability and sustainable development (Di Fabio, 2017a, 2017b; Di Fabio & Rosen, 2018) as well as cross-cultural, strengths-based, preventative perspectives (Di Fabio, 2021; Di Fabio & Peiró, 2017). Both these two approaches highlight the value of preventive and cross-cultural approaches. The latter proposes reflection upon a universal as well as a global perspective for interventions (Di Fabio, 2019). The universal perspective highlights that prevention is a universal value, whereas the global perspective underlines that, while preventative interventions consider all people, they need to be determined on the basis of different contexts and cultures. Thus, if the universal promotion of preventative actions is fundamental, then it is also globally relevant to decide upon (or decline) actions based on different context and cultures. Therefore, cross-cultural research on Human Capital Sustainability Leadership (Di Fabio & Peiró, 2018a) is of great value for calibrating tailored interventions based on different contexts and cultures in order to build healthy organizations.

Conclusions

Human Capital Sustainability Leadership (Di Fabio & Peiró, 2018a) is a core construct of leadership that integrates aspects of traditional leadership styles to face the challenges of the world of work in the 21st century. Human Capital Sustainable Leadership asks for workers' increased autonomy and self-determination as well as calls for positive relational management in the workplace to promote healthy workers and healthy organizations (Di Fabio, 2017a; Di Fabio et al., 2020). Human Capital Sustainable Leadership could also enable strategic actions to create a more sustainable human environment in organizations, thereby enhancing the sustainable development of workers and organizations as well as promoting healthy organizations and healthy businesses from a cross-cultural perspective. The precise focus on the value of taking care to build positive relationships at work and in the organizational environment does not mean being unable to broaden the scope to encompass sustainable relationships between organizations and the natural environment or the sustainable development of organizations in a way that considers the ecological environment. On these bases, the core construct of leadership is promising for promoting sustainable development – in all of its multifaceted complexity – in organizations.

Future possibilities for research and intervention could be opened via cross-cultural studies on the HCSLS (Di Fabio & Peiró, 2018a). Therefore, Human Capital Sustainability Leadership is a promising resource for healthy organizations around the world as well as for sustainable development.

References

Blustein, D. L. (2011). A relational theory of working. *Journal of Vocational Behavior*, 79(1), 1–17. doi:10.1016/j.jvb.2010.10.004.

Blustein, D. L., Kenny, M. E., Di Fabio, A., & Guichard, J. (2019). Expanding the impact of the psychology of working: Engaging psychology in the struggle for decent work and human rights. *Journal of Career Assessment*, 27, 3–28; doi:10.1177/1069072718774002.

Cox, T., Baldursson, E. B., & Rial-González, E. (2000). Occupational health psychology. *Work and Stress*, 14(2), 101–104.

Diener, E., Wirtz, D., Tov, W., Kim-Prieto, C., Choi, D. W., Oishi, S., & Biswas-Diener, R. (2010). New well-being measures: Short scales to assess flourishing and positive and negative feelings. *Social Indicators Research*, 97(2), 143–156. doi:10.1007/s11205-009-9493-y.

Di Fabio, A. (2016). Positive Relational Management for healthy organizations: Psychometric properties of a new scale for prevention for workers. *Frontiers in Psychology: Organizational Psychology*, 7, 1523. doi:10.3389/fpsyg.2016.01523.

Di Fabio, A. (2017a). Positive Healthy Organizations: Promoting well-being, meaningfulness, and sustainability in organizations. *Frontiers in Psychology: Organizational Psychology*, 8, 1938. doi:10.3389/fpsyg.2017.01938.

Di Fabio, A. (2017b). The psychology of sustainability and sustainable development for well-being in organizations. *Frontiers in Psychology: Organizational Psychology*, 8, 1534. doi:10.3389/fpsyg.2017.01534.

Di Fabio, A. (2018). *Human Capital Sustainability Leadership and Decent Work*. Poster presented at the second international cross-cultural conference "Healthier societies fostering healthy organizations: A cross-cultural perspective" organized by the Department of Education and Psychology, University of Florence, Florence, Italy, August 30–September 1, 2018.

Di Fabio, A. (Ed.). (2019). *Positive psychology for healthy organizations: The challenge of primary prevention in a cross-cultural perspective*. Nova Science Publishers.

Di Fabio, A. (Ed.). (2021). *Cross-cultural Perspectives on Well-Being and Sustainability in Organizations*. Springer.

Di Fabio, A., Bucci, O., & Gori, A. (2016). High Entrepreneurship, Leadership, and Professionalism (HELP): Towards an integrated, empirically based perspective.

Frontiers in Psychology: Organizational Psychology, 7, 1842. doi:10.3389/fpsyg.2016.01842.

Di Fabio, A., Cheung, F., & Peiró, J.-M. (2020). Editorial: Special Issue Personality and individual differences and healthy organizations. *Personality and Individual Differences*, 166. doi:10.1016/j.paid.2020.110196.

Di Fabio, A., & Gori, A. (2016). Assessing Workplace Relational Civility (WRC) with a new multidimensional "mirror" measure. *Frontiers in Psychology: Section Organizational Psychology*, 7, 890. doi:10.3389/fpsyg.2016.00890.

Di Fabio, A., & Gori, A. (2021). Workplace Relational Civility and Human Capital Sustainability Leadership for sustainable development in organizations: Empirical Evidence. *Counseling: Giornale Italiano di Ricerca e Applicazioni,14*(2), 32–40. doi:10.14605/CS1422103.

Di Fabio, A., & Kenny, M. E. (2015). The contributions of emotional intelligence and social support for adaptive career progress among Italian youth. *Journal of Career Development*, 42, 48–59. doi:10.1177/0894845314533420.

Di Fabio, A., & Kenny, M. E. (2016). From decent work to decent lives: Positive Self and Relational Management (PS&RM) in the twenty-first century. *Frontiers in Psychology: Section Organizational Psychology*, 7, 361. doi:10.3389/fpsyg.2016.00361.

Di Fabio, A., & Kenny, M. E. (2021). Positive and negative affects and meaning at work: Trait emotional intelligence as a primary prevention resource in organizations for sustainable and positive human capital development. In A. Di Fabio (Ed.), *Cross-cultural Perspectives on Well-Being and Sustainability in Organizations* (pp. 139–152). Switzerland: Springer.

Di Fabio, A., & Peiró, J. M. (2017). *Conclusion.* First International Cross-cultural Conference "Healthier societies fostering healthy organizations: A cross-cultural perspective" organized by the Department of Education and Psychology (Psychology Section), University of Florence, Florence, Italy, May 26–27, 2017.

Di Fabio, A., & Peiró, J. M. (2018a). Human Capital Sustainability Leadership to promote sustainable development and healthy organizations: A new scale. *Sustainability*, 10(7), 2413. doi:10.3390/su10072413.

Di Fabio, A., & Peiró, J. M. (2018b). *Human Capital Sustainability Leadership and Eudaimonic Well-being.* Poster presented at the Second international cross-cultural conference "Healthier societies fostering healthy organizations: A cross-cultural perspective" organized by the Department of Education and Psychology, University of Florence, Florence, Italy, August 30–September 1, 2018.

Di Fabio, A., & Rosen, M. A. (2018). Opening the Black Box of Psychological Processes in the Science of Sustainable Development: A New Frontier . *European Journal of Sustainable Development Research*, 2(4), 47. https://doi.org/10.20897/ejosdr/3933.

Di Fabio, A., & Saklofske, D. H. (2021). The relationship of compassion and self-compassion with personality and emotional intelligence. *PAID 40ᵗʰ Anniversary Special Issue: Personality and Individual Differences*, 169, 110109. doi:10.1016/j.paid.2020.110109.

Di Fabio, A., & Svicher, A. (2021). Emotional intelligence: A key for Human Capital Sustainability Leadership beyond personality traits. *Counseling: Giornale Italiano di Ricerca e Applicazioni*, 14(3), 73–82. doi:10.14605/CS1432105.

Di Fabio, A., & Tsuda, A. (2018). The psychology of harmony and harmonization: Advancing the perspectives for the psychology of sustainability and sustainable development. *Sustainability*, 10(12), 4726. https://doi.org/10.3390/su10124726.

Duffy, R. D., Allan, B. A., England, J. W., Blustein, D. L., Autin, K. L., Douglass, R. P., & ... Santos, E. J. (2017). The development and initial validation of the Decent Work Scale. *Journal of Counseling Psychology*, 64(2), 206–221. doi:10.1037/cou0000191.

Hage, S. M., Romano, J. L., Conyne, R. K., Kenny, M., Matthews, C., Schwartz, J. P., & Waldo, M. (2007). Best practice guidelines on prevention practice, research, training, and social advocacy for psychologists. *The Counseling Psychologist*, 35(4), 493–566. doi:10.1177/0011000006291411.

Hart, P. M., & Cooper, C. L. (2001). Occupational stress: Towards a more integrated framework. In N. Anderson et al. (Eds.), *Handbook of Work, Industrial and Organizational Psychology* (Vol. 2, pp. 93–114). Sage.

Henry, J (2005). The healthy organization. In A. S. G. Antoniou, & C. L. Cooper (Eds.), *Research companion to organizational health psychology* (pp. 382–391). Edward Elgar.

Johnson, S., Robertson, I., & Cooper, C. L. (2018). *Wellbeing: Productivity and Happiness at Work* (2nd ed.). Palgrave Macmillan.

Morgan, J., & Farsides, T. (2009). Psychometric evaluation of the meaningful life measure. *Journal of Happiness Studies*, 10(3), 351–366. doi:10.1007/s10902-008-9093-6.

Peiró, J. M. (2008). Stress and coping at work: New research trends and their implications for practice. In K. Näswall, J. Hellgren, & M. Sverke (Eds.), *The individual in the changing working life* (pp. 284–310). Cambridge University Press.

Peiró, J. M., Bayonab, J. A., Caballer, A., & Di Fabio, A. (2020). Importance of work characteristics affects job performance: The mediating role of individual dispositions on the work design-performance relationships. *PAID 40th Anniversary Special Issue: Personality and Individual Differences*, 157, 109808. doi:10.1016/j.paid.2019.109808.

Peiró, J. M., Martínez-Tur, V., Nagorny-Koring, N., & Auch, C. (2021). A framework of professional transferable competences for system innovation: Enabling leadership and agency for sustainable development. *Sustainability*, 13(4), 1737. https://doi.org/10.3390/su13041737.

Peiró, J. M., & Rodríguez, I. (2008). Work stress, leadership and organizational health. *Papeles del Psicólogo*, 29(1), 68–82.

Peiró, J. M., & Tetrick, L. (2011). Occupational health psychology. In P. R. Martin, F. M. Cheung, M. C. Knowles, M. Kyrios, L. Littlefield, J. B. Overmier, & J. M. Prieto (Eds.), *Wiley-Blackwell IAAP handbooks of applied psychology: IAAP handbook of applied psychology* (pp. 292–315). Wiley-Blackwell.

Petrides, K. V., & Furnham, A. (2000). On the dimensional structure of emotional intelligence. *Personality and Individual Differences*, 29(2), 313–320. doi:10.1016/S0191-8869(99)00195-6.

Petrides, K. V., & Furnham, A. (2001). Trait emotional intelligence: Psychometric investigation with reference to established trait taxonomies. *European Journal of Personality*, 15(6), 425–448. https://doi.org/10.1002/per.416

Raymond, J. S., Wood, D. W., & Patrick, W. K. (1990). Psychology doctoral training in work and health. *American Psychologist*, 45(10), 1159–1161. doi:10.1037/0003-066X.45.10.1159.

Robertson, I., & Cooper, C. L. (2010). *Wellbeing: Productivity and Happiness at Work*. Palgrave Macmillan.

Seok, C. B., Ching, P. L., & Ismail, R. (2021). Human Capital Sustainability Leadership Scale: Psychometric proprieties of the Malaysian version. In A. Di Fabio (Ed.), *Cross-cultural perspectives on well-being and sustainability in organizations* (pp. 111–120). Springer.

Tetrick, L. E., & Peiró, J. M. (2012). Occupational safety and health. In S. W. J. Kozlowski (Ed.), *The Oxford handbook of organizational psychology* (Vol. 2, pp. 1228–1244). Oxford: Oxford University Press.

7 Driving Sustainable Development Transformations with Emotional Leadership

Thomas A. Norton, Neal M. Ashkanasy and Jo da Silva

Human development in recent centuries transformed how we live. The nature of this transformation left a legacy of social inequality and environmental damage, however, the effects of which we experience today. We now know with hindsight that the manner of this progress was unsustainable and, therefore, requires a new approach to development to address this historic damage and create a society that provides a social foundation for all, without exceeding environmental boundaries (Raworth, 2017).

As Bansal (2019) notes, sustainable development presents a new paradigm that recognises the interconnections between natural and social systems; Bansal argues that we can transition away from unsustainable policies and towards a healthier and equitable society. Whereas sustainability describes a state where meeting present needs does not compromise the ability to meet future needs, sustainable development entails an understanding of how we can create this state (da Silva, 2019) by building safe, inclusive, and resilient communities, infrastructures, and cities. This, in turn, will regenerate ecosystems, conserve resources, increase biodiversity, and help to maintain stable economic growth and social progress.

A paradigm shift is necessary considering the scale of the challenge we face, which requires transformational change in every aspect of society, such as policy and legislation, financing, and, for businesses, the expectations of clients and customers. Organizations face pressure from regulatory bodies, competitors, and the public to move away from practices that we now know to create more harm than good (e.g., see Marshall et al., 2005). Consequently, leading consulting firms such as PwC (2022) maintain that sustainable development has transitioned from a fringe issue to a mainstream concern for business leaders.

Consistent with that idea, organizations today are now joining governments in declaring a climate emergency, committing to change, and delivering new strategies to align with sustainable development (e.g., see da Silva, 2019). The responsibility to deliver these strategies falls to leaders throughout companies and involves changes to technical and behavioural aspects of organizational life. The Intergovernmental Panel on Climate Change (IPSS, 2022) argues that the technology we require exists today, but we lack the determination to

DOI: 10.4324/9781003212157-9

make the behavioural changes. Leaders need to consider their role in enabling a psychological and behavioural transition among their teams. In this chapter, we focus on emotions as an important micro-foundation to manage change resistance and drive the change. We begin with discussion of the specific role leaders play in transitioning organizations and challenges they face.

Identify Leaders' Roles in Transitioning Organizations and the Challenges They Face

For many, if not most, organizations, the sustainable development imperative implies transformational change, as some of the fundamental rules of the game change in step with tighter regulations, increased public scrutiny, institutional competition, and emerging opportunities. Naturally, leaders have a responsibility to guide and to drive the necessary adaptations to policy and processes through their people. In this area, leaders face three challenges, some of which we capture below, and each of which has an emotional component.

First, leaders need to address any knowledge gap around sustainable development and develop a reference point to understand (1) where they are, and (2) where they need to go. This includes the emotional climate towards sustainable development. From here, leaders can diagnose the precise impact for the company, specific teams within it, employees, and them personally. This can be particularly challenging for leaders with relatively low levels of literacy in this area and those who find it difficult to detach from the business of the day.

Second, leaders need to define the new normal and to motivate people towards this. In many cases, this will require people to create or to adopt new ways of working when existing methods are still seen as fit-for-purpose, though incompatible with sustainable development. This requires leaders to demonstrate the courage to challenge the things that need to change and the determination to overcome roadblocks (Polman & Winston, 2021). This also points to systemic (rather than piecemeal) interventions to overcome the organizational inertia that emerges from years and decades of operating without the degree of scrutiny or accountability for social, environmental, and economic costs (when sustainability was regarded as a fringe issue, not the mainstream priority it is today). In effect, the status quo that emerged leaves a legacy of self-reinforcing interdependencies among different parts of the system and an organizational inertia leaders must overcome to effect change.

Third, leaders need to reconcile goals that relate to sustainable development with the rusted-on priorities that are deeply engrained in how they think and make decisions. Without effective framing, the inclusion of new requirements previously seen as nice-to-have can lead to frustration, where people interpret sustainability either as requiring extra effort or as coming at the expense of already accepted requirements. Leaders can mitigate this by framing sustainability development as a catalyst for resolving existing issues that frustrate people in their work and create an inspiring vision of the future with which to motivate people (Polman & Winston, 2021). A clear and engaging justification for change can promote people throughout the company to take ownership, which means leaders can focus on strategic coordination rather than technical minutiae (Willink & Babin, 2017).

In view of this, transitioning a business towards sustainable development requires a change in how people in the business think, feel, and behave. Decades of scientific research points to the anthropogenic origins of climate change (e.g., see. Hansen & Stone, 2016); it is a problem rooted in human behaviour. Effectively addressing this to create a world where human activity exists within a social foundation and an ecological ceiling necessitates behaviour change on a large scale, both in terms of the breadth and the longevity of these changes. Leaders who attempt this without due consideration of the emotional dimensions of behaviour and change greatly increase the degree of difficulty they face (Katzenbach et al., 2018).

Emotions as a Mechanism for Sustainable Development Transitions

Katzenbach and his colleagues (2018) write that, in their experience, successful organizational transformations require leaders to leverage the emotional energy that exists within a company's culture. More specifically, "connecting strategic choices and operational shifts to the company's people in ways that motivate and energize them" (Katzenbach et al., 2018, pp. 8–9). In this regard, and consistent with Russell and Barrett (1999), we define emotions as a set of physiological factors that underlie behavioural decisions. In the context of sustainability, these in turn articulate the relationship between decisions and sustainable development behaviour at work, which we define as actions that integrate sustainable development principles into the technical, social, and commercial aspects of an organization and contribute to sustainable development goals (Grijalvo Martín et al., 2020). Moreover, our (human) emotional sensitivity can trigger pro-social behaviour that seeks to provide benefit to others with little or no direct benefit to ourselves (cf. Nummenmaa et al., 2012). In this regard, and consistent with Trope & Liberman's (2003) concept of temporal construal theory, we note that people tend to experience the present emotionally and the future hypothetically. Using overly rational arguments reinforces the view that the future is in the distant. Integrating with emotional content might help bring the future closer (Wittmann & Sircova, 2018), and emotions are a strong motivator for behaviour (either to generate desired emotions or to avoid undesirable emotions).

The question arises at this point as to the types of emotions that might arise in connection with sustainable development and the different effects they might have. In the following, we identify and discuss six possibilities in this regard.

Negative versus positive emotions. As Nummenmaa et al. (2012) point out, negative emotions tend to narrow our focus, whereas positive emotions are associated with trying new behaviours and creativity (cf. broaden-and-build theory; Frederickson, 2001). Interpersonal emotional synchronization means the narrowing effect of negative emotions promotes homogeneity (i.e., high inter-subject correlations), whereas positive emotions promote heterogeneity (i.e., low inter-subject correlations).

Emotional overload. Francoeur and Paillé (2022) note that employees tend to withdraw from pro-social behaviours when their work environment is overly taxing on their emotional resources.

Anxiety and disgust. Smith and Leiserowitz (2014) found that being anxious about global warming relates strongly with people's policy support for global warming issues, while a feeling of disgust tends paradoxically to go in the opposite direction, such that people develop strong negative reactions to such initiatives. O'Neill and Nicholson-Cole (2009) found similarly that fearful messages about climate change have perverse (negative) effects on people's engagement with global warming. These findings seem to support the notion that "fear appeals" fail to garner positive support, especially when there is a lack of perceived self-efficacy for the proposed policy (Witte & Allen 2000).

Sadness. Prior research on pro-social behaviour has shown that sadness tends to trigger pro-social behaviour, including proenvironmental decision-making and policies. Sadness seems to elicit actions to help others, perhaps to repair or regulate emotions (Small & Verrochi, 2009) and can even result in negative responses to appeals for action (cf. Small et al., 2007).

Guilt. Bissing-Olson et al. (2013) found that guilt can arise in employees who do not take advantage of opportunities to engage in proenvironmental behaviour, and this emotion can motivate future behaviour.

Arousal. Russell & Ashkanasy (2021) investigated emotions with differing valence (positive, negative) and arousal (high, low), and they found that communications featuring anger, fear, contentment, and hope produce positive effects on workplace sustainable behaviour, but sadness suppresses such behaviour. Their research illustrates the complexity of emotions, even as other research shows sadness can motivate this type of behaviour (Schwartz & Lowenstein, 2017).

In this chapter, we argue further that the nature of sustainable development might account for a relative lack of research on the role of emotions. Schwartz and Lowenstein (2017) suggest issues that are easily discernible in our immediate environment and show rapid change elicit strong emotional responses. Nonetheless, the factors that underpin the need for sustainable development do not necessarily share these characteristics, as satirised in the film *Don't Look Up* (McKay, 2021), although more recent political and economic instability and increasingly frequent extreme weather events are likely to change this.

Despite this, emotions account for approximately half the variance in environmental policy support (Smith & Leiserowitz, 2014), which indicates this is an important consideration for organizations trying to align themselves with sustainable development. Emotional experiences offer opportunities for behaviour change (Hökkä et al., 2020). We therefore propose that leaders who create the right emotional conditions will be more effective in transitioning their teams and organizations to be in line with sustainable development. To understand the emotional processes that underpin sustainable behaviour, we argue that emotions must be considered at multiple levels of analysis. To address this, we refer to the Ashkanasy (2003a, 2003b) Five-Level Model of Emotions at Work (FLMEW; see also Ashkanasy & Dorris, 2017).

The Five-Level Model of Emotions at Work

Ashkanasy (2003a, 2003b) argues that emotion in organizational contexts is inherently multi-level in nature, and, moreover, the effects at each level interact to produce a complex picture of the effects at each level. At the lowest level in the model (Level 1), emotions are ephemeral, varying moment-by-moment depending on the occurrence of "affective events" in the environment (Weiss & Cropanzano, 1996) that result in emotional reactions leading to the formation of affect-driven behaviours and attitudes. Level 2 in the model refers to individual differences in the means by which affect and emotions are perceived and managed, including personality, positive versus negative affectivity (Watson & Tellegen, 1985), and emotional intelligence (Mayer & Salovey, 1997). At Level 3 of the model, the focus is on inter-personal aspects of emotions, including communication and regulation of emotion in self and others, and it includes the concept of emotional regulation and emotional labour (Grandey, 2000; Gross, 1998; Hochschild, 1983; Troth et al., 2018). Groups and teams are the focus of Level 4 in the model, which also addresses leadership, which is defined as a process of managing emotional contagion among team members (Sy et al., 2005). At the top level of the model (Level 5), attention turns to considering the organization as a whole (cf. Ashkanasy & Härtel, 2014).

Level 1: Within-Person Temporal Variations in Emotions

This level of the model is rooted in the notion that, across a typical day, our emotions fluctuate in response to our internal experience of the external world. Weiss and Cropanzano (1996) note in their model of Affective Events Theory that these moment-to-moment variations can result in "affect-driven" behavioural responses (i.e., impulsive behaviour) or accumulate to form more stable attitudes and behaviours that later result in "judgement-driven" (i.e., considered) behaviour. A full picture of the emotional dimension of an organizational transition towards sustainable development must therefore be grounded in this level of analysis. Importantly, Snippe et al. (2018) found that, at this level of analysis, a reciprocal relationship exists between positive mood and pro-social behaviour, whereby positive moods induce helping behaviour, which in turn maintains a positive mood that, in turn, leads to more proenvironmental behaviour (cf. Russell & Ashkanasy, 2021).

This idea is supported in findings by Bissing-Olson and her colleagues (2013) demonstrating that daily positive affect accounts for approximately

30% of the variance in daily proenvironmental behaviour. Using a daily diary methodology, these researchers found a positive relationship between positive affect and proenvironmental behaviour, particularly for people with less positive attitudes towards the natural environment. It appears that the degree of affective arousal influences the type of behaviour people engage in. Specifically, high arousal positive affect (e.g., feeling energetic) correlates with extra-role behaviour, whereas low arousal positive affect (e.g., feeling calm) correlates with performing required work tasks in an environmentally friendly way.

Because of the dynamic nature of emotions, the impact an emotion can have on behaviour appears to reduce with time as people experience other emotions. Schwartz and Lowenstein (2017) found in this regard that emotive videos prompt people to spend more time researching their personal environmental impact and donate more to environmental organizations than non-emotive videos, but this effect weakens where there was a delay between the stimulus and the opportunity for behaviour. In this way, the impact of emotions themselves appears fleeting, which points to the need for another mechanism to encourage a pattern of behaviour to emerge.

One such mechanism is motivation, where broaden-and-build theory (Frederickson, 2001) holds that positive emotional feedback from a behaviour can build intrinsic motivation to repeat the behaviour in the future. There is empirical evidence of such a relationship with behaviours associated with sustainable development. For example, Løvoll and her colleagues (2017) reported finding a bidirectional positive relationship between positive emotions and intrinsic motivation in the context of enjoying nature. Compared with other types of motivation, intrinsic motivation ends up being more resilient over time (Gagne & Deci, 2005), likely because it does not require external regulation (e.g., rewards, evaluation from others). Where positive emotional feedback creates intrinsic motivation, behaviour can transition from being a feature of a particular moment in time to being a characteristic of an individual that exists in a huge number of moments across their lifetime.

The Leadership Challenge at Level 1

Our emotional state influences our sustainability development behaviours from one moment to the next. Creating a stable, positive emotional environment at work increases people's propensity to engage in sustainable development behaviour (AlSuwaidi et al., 2021). Employees also need the right capabilities and opportunities to leverage the emotional motivation for sustainable development behaviour, however. Leaders who can identify or create emotive events, whilst providing the necessary opportunities and capabilities to capitalise on these, are likely to be more effective than others in facilitating behavioural change. Effective use of emotions to catalyse sustainable development behaviour at this level can establish the groundwork for more stable patterns of behaviours over time.

Level 2: Between-Person Individual Differences

While our experience of affective events and subsequent emotional responses fluctuates from moment to moment, stable patterns start to emerge over time, and these traits can distinguish individuals from others. The transformational change implicit in the concept of sustainable development requires the emergence of stable patterns of cognition and behaviour to improve social, environmental, and economic outcomes. Organizations where between-person variability in sustainable development-related behaviour is minimal will observe group-level behaviour change faster than those where such variability is pronounced.

We argue that the critical personal characteristic at this level of analysis is emotional intelligence (EI). While this variable remains controversial, especially in the context of leadership research (see Antonakis et al., 2009; Dasborough et al., 2022), multiple meta-analyses have now established that EI accounts for significant variance in key organizational behaviour variables, including job attitudes and performance (e.g., see O'Boyle et al., 2011). Much of the controversy surrounding EI, however, derives from measurement issues. In this regard, Ashkanasy and Daus (2005) identified three "streams" of EI thought and research. Stream 1 models of EI are based on the four-branch "ability" model of EI as defined by Mayer and Salovey (1997), which holds that EI is the ability (1) to perceive emotions in the self and others accurately, (2) to use this information in decision-making, (3) to understand emotions, and (4) to regulate (manage) emotions in the self and others. Stream 1 measures use an IQ-like "ability measure, the MSCEIT" (Mayer et al., 2002). Stream 2 models are also based in the four-branch definition, but measurement is based on self- or peer-report measures (e.g., "I am able to read emotions accurately."). Examples of self-report measures include the Workgroup Emotional Intelligence Profile (WEIP; Jordan et al., 2002) and the Wong and Law Emotional Intelligence Scale (WLEIS; Wong & Law, 2002); Jordan and Ashkanasy (2005) also developed a peer-report measure of the WEIP. Stream 3 models, e.g., use self-report scales to assess a range of EI-like attributes; examples include the Emotional Competence Inventory (ECI; Sala, 2002), which is based on the Goleman (1995) concept of EI, and the Emotional Quotient Inventory (EQ-i; Bar-On, 1997). As Ashkanasy (2021) argues, however, Stream 2 and 3 models of EI tend to be confounded with personality characteristics (see also Dasborough et al., 2022), leaving the ability models of EI as the most credible measure of the construct (cf. Daus & Ashkanasy, 2005).

These individual differences are relevant for the present context to the extent that they influence attitudes and behaviour related to sustainable development. Where individual differences do exist, this can in turn influence the support or resistance a leader faces in transitioning a business to be in line with sustainable development.

EI influences our perceptions of events and how we respond to these (Ciarrochi et al., 2001; Daus & Ashkanasy, 2005). Ashkanasy (2021) argues further that EI is a driver of proactive attitudes, including environmental awareness. On the one hand, people with different levels of EI exposed to the same event can interpret these in different ways; on the other hand, two people with similar levels of EI who perceive events in the same way may experience similar emotions yet choose to respond differently depending on how they manage these emotions (Aguilar-Luzón et al., 2014). Aguilar-Luzón and her co-authors reported finding that people with strong abilities in managing their own emotions are more open to sustainable behaviour, develop stronger intentions, and follow through to a greater degree than those with weaker EI abilities.

Another relevant individual difference is trait affect (Watson & Tellegen, 1985). Recall, we described earlier the influence of individuals' affective states from one moment to the next, but people's general affective (positive or negative) disposition is another relevant factor for leading a sustainable development transformation. In this regard, Snippe et al. (2018) found that positive affective disposition is related to people's proclivity to engage in pro-social behaviour. This effect may be explained in terms of Kuiper et al.'s (2000) finding that people with high positive trait affect tend to have more favourable expectations and approach uncertainty with enthusiasm relative to others with high negative affect. This finding is consistent with findings by Lyubomirsky et al. (2005) that people prioritise protecting their personal resources and avoiding harm. In the organizational context, Forgas and George (2001) argue further that trait affect is a key driver of altruistic and pro-social behaviour at work, which could facilitate a transition in line with sustainable development (see also Ashkanasy, 2021).

The Leadership Challenge at Level 2

Despite detractors, the overwhelming weight of evidence tells us that EI is important for leadership (cf. Dasborough et al., 2022). We also know that positive trait affect links to positive proactivity and pro-social behaviour. Moreover, managing the variety of emotional orientations to sustainable development in general as well as people's attachment to the things implicated in a transition to a more sustainable way of working will require deliberate effort. To start with, leaders need to look inward and to align their emotions to this strategic imperative so that they can communicate and role-model authentically and consistently. Looking outward, effective leaders need to recognise and to manage the emotions of others to encourage the individual-level cognition and behaviour that underpin an organization-level transformation (cf. Troth et al., 2018). Finally, leaders who create a positive emotional environment at work can foster positive job attitudes that support employee engagement and organizational commitment more generally, making it more likely that individual employees demonstrate support for strategic priorities such as sustainable development.

Level 3: Emotional Communication

Humans use emotions to communicate with each other, and mimicry is an evolved process to facilitate affiliation and liking (Lakin et al., 2003).

Moreover, emotions are contagious (Hatfield et al., 1994; Wild et al., 2001), and the neural activation of highly arousing emotions (e.g., pain, disgust, pleasure) is similar whether we experience these ourselves or view them in others. Evidence indicates that people in social settings (e.g., in conversation, watching the same scene) can experience emotional synchronization (Kauppi et al., 2010), which could reduce between-person emotional variance from moment to moment (Nummenmaa et al., 2012) and facilitate an emotional climate within a group.

People also prefer to display socially acceptable emotions. This is the basis of "emotional labour" (Hochschild, 1983), especially when such displays are intended to satisfy organizational rules regarding emotional expression (Diefendorff et al., 2011). Using emotions to communicate effectively with others about sustainable development requires an understanding of the individual's own emotions towards it and, ideally, the emotions of the other person(s). In this way, employees can act as role models to others. Russell and Ashkanasy (2021) investigated the effectiveness of communicating different emotions on workplace sustainability-related behaviour. These authors found that messages containing positive (e.g., contentment, hope) and negative (e.g., anger, fear) emotions can encourage these behaviours better than messages with no emotional content, which in turn perform better than messages featuring negative emotions with low arousal (e.g., sadness).

Interpersonal intelligence (the ability to understand and react to interpersonal cues; Gardner, 1985) also appears to support behaviour associated with sustainable development, including pro-social and proenvironmental behaviour (Han et al., 2022). Individuals with high interpersonal intelligence are more likely to demonstrate positive behaviours, and their ability to communicate and cooperate with others can help such behaviour spread throughout a team. Helping others is fundamental to group inclusion and, for social species like humans, fundamental to long-term survival (Caporeal & Brewer, 1991).

Finally, we note that passion for sustainable development tends to manifest in interpersonal exchanges and can trigger contagion effects, whereby this passion spreads throughout a social network (Cardon, 2008). Fostering, encouraging, or otherwise enabling people to demonstrate passion towards social and environmental issues creates an opportunity for passionate individuals to engage in positive emotional displays that others can witness and emulate. Cultivating passionate members is an important precursor to sustainable development in organizations (Saifulina & Caballo-Penela, 2017).

The Leadership Challenge at Level 3

The prominence of leaders provides substantial opportunity for interpersonal influence, and role-modelling is an effective way to promote ethical and pro-social behaviour (Brown et al., 2005). Robertson and Barling (2013) found that the proenvironmental behaviour of leaders demonstrating transformational leadership traits, including charisma, has a positive influence on followers' environmental passion, a positive emotion providing autonomous motivation for proenvironmental behaviour (Vallerand et al., 2007). The emotional content in how a leader communicates verbally and behaviourally can also have negative consequences for sustainable development transformations. A leader who lacks emotional engagement with the change is unlikely to project emotions that followers can interpret as an endorsement; we note further that the research indicates positive and negative emotions (e.g., fear, embarrassment) can be effective (Fineman, 1996; Lord, 1994).

Leadership is fundamentally about managing interpersonal relationships (Sy et al., 2005). Effective leadership involves bringing emotional expression and control front-and-centre (Martin et al., 1998). For example, a leader may need to have difficult conversations with people for whom transitioning to a more sustainable organization will have significant consequences. Whether stakeholder engagement results in opposition or enthusiasm towards the change may rest on a leader's ability to manage the emotional dimension of the engagement. Effective leaders who can read the emotions of followers (i.e., demonstrate EI) create the opportunity to adapt to and to manage others' emotions to facilitate interpersonal exchanges and enhance relationships.

Leaders also need to consider how the work environment in general might influence employees' capacity for interpersonal emotional exchange and the types of emotions that might be communicated. For example, Karatepe et al. (2021) found that emotional exhaustion can inhibit sustainable behaviours and facilitate counterproductive behaviour. Support from leaders is an effective way to alleviate emotional exhaustion (Chen et al., 2021), and leaders can use their authority to address the underlying causes of emotional exhaustion to create a workplace conducive to positive interpersonal emotional communication.

Level 4: Groups and Teams

At Level 4 of the FLMEW (Ashkanasy, 2003a), the focus is on groups and teams, and explicitly includes leadership. Key processes at the level of analysis include emotional contagion (Hatfield et al., 1994) and group affective tone (Collins et al., 2013). As Sy et al. (2005) argue, team leaders must "infect" team members with the appropriate emotions that are, in turn, reflected in the group's affective tone. Moreover, as Tee et al. (2013) showed, leaders can "catch" team members' emotional states in a reciprocal process (cf. Dasborough et al., 2009).

At the individual level, the direct impact from behaviour scales longitudinally across time. At the group or team level, the direct impact also scales across the membership. Thus, rapid and meaningful contributions to sustainable development require collective contributions. Creating a team climate for sustainable development requires collective commitment to the organization's moral sensitivity, motivation, judgment, and responsibility towards ethical, social, and environmental issues (Arnaud & Sekerka, 2010). Positive emotions can facilitate this by encouraging social cohesion and shared ownership among team members as well as by internalising group values related to sustainable development. An important consequence of positive emotions at the group level in the context of change is an increase in pro-social behaviour (Aknin et al., 2018), including helping behaviour (Deckop et al., 2003). Such behaviour tends to replicate, building a group's capacity to support transformational goals (Sekerka & Fredrickson, 2008).

The question that arises at this point is whether positive emotions at the group level can make a tangible contribution to an organization's sustainable development transformation, however. Research by Paillé and his colleagues (2020) indicates that it can, either through employee-led eco-initiatives (see also Paillé & Raineri, 2015; Raineri & Paillé, 2016) or via discrete actions where employees take charge to improve the environmental performance of an organization through functional change (Ramus & Killmer, 2007; Ramus & Steger, 2000). These behaviours are an important indicator of employee engagement and of organic transformation (Katzenbach et al., 2018).

The Leadership Challenge at Level 4

A primary concern for leaders is translating an organization-level sustainable development strategy into team-level objectives. We advocate that this needs to be done in such a way that it enables team members to form an emotional connection to the overall goal and, in doing so, generate more internalised forms of motivation to catalyse initial changes and persevere when obstacles inevitably arise (Graves & Sarkis, 2018).

Generally, a key function of leaders is to create and to maintain functional relationships among team members with varying degrees of emotional attachment to one another (Kahn, 1998; Ozcelik et al., 2008). Building and maintaining familiarity among team members can facilitate an emotional contagion (Ashkanasy et al., 2020; Petitta et al., 2017). Importantly, leaders need to ensure the content of an emotional contagion supports the strategic objective (i.e., sustainable development transformation), and they should seek to generate and encourage team members to share constructive group emotions (Krzeminska et al., 2018; Ozcelik et al., 2008). We note, however, that constructive emotions are not necessarily positive emotions and acknowledge the role that negative emotions, like fear and anger, can play in producing positive behavioural outcomes.

Leaders also need to provide the right type of support to their teams through the transformation, support that is emotional in nature and manifests in encouragement and respect for employees' views on sustainable development. This can complement more instrumental forms of support (such as allocating resources). As such, leaders need to be aware that members are sensitive to whether emotional support is genuine or superficial, in which case it can undermine support for the change (Paillé et al. 2020). Supervisory relationships that feature abusive traits can undermine positive emotions, which otherwise facilitate extra-role sustainable development-related behaviour (Chen et al., 2021).

Level 5: Organization-Wide

Scaling to the organizational level is a requirement for any meaningful sustainable development transformation. If transformation attempts are unable to encapsulate the organization as a whole, it is likely that the efforts of leaders and employees will be ineffective at changing the underlying system that governs organizational behaviour. In the FLMEW (Ashkanasy, 2003a), Level 5 encapsulates the idea of a "palpably sensed" emotional atmosphere (de Rivera, 1992). Ashkanasy and Härtel (2014) subsequently differentiated affective climate from culture; while affective culture is rooted in employees' deeply felt feelings and values, emotional climate tends to be variable and fluctuates depending on environmental exigencies, which Ashton-James and Ashkanasy (2008) liken to an organizational level "affective event". For example, an organization may experience a positive affective climate following an ostensibly successful organizational outcome, but then they many experience a negative affective climate if the apparent success comes to be seen as unsustainable. In this regard, Carr et al. (2003) found that affective climate has stronger relationships with employee job satisfaction and organizational commitment (compared to cognitive and instrumental climate), resulting in higher job performance and wellbeing as well as lower withdrawal.

Based on this evidence, it seems that the organizational affective climate and culture acts as an important enabler of new patterns of behaviour, including those related to sustainable development. In this regard, Norton and his colleagues (2015) used established models of culture (Schein, 1990; Hatch, 1993) to propose that the artifacts that manifest from cultural assumptions, beliefs, and values serve as cues for employees regarding what is expected and endorsed within the work context. These artifacts include the decisions, language, and behaviour of others, which all have an emotional component. In this case, the conduct of organizational leaders, who are seen by employees to represent the organization, (see Schein, 2010) carries disproportionate influence on employees and, therefore, the organization as a whole.

Empirical research from many domains, including safety (Neal & Griffin, 2006), ethics (Dey et al., 2022), and environmental sustainability (Mouro & Duarte, 2021), confirms this view and demonstrates a reliable effect of organizational climates on collective behaviour. A key ingredient for an organizational climate is leader behaviour, and research indicates that the emotional environment within a business determines whether that behaviour will manifest in similar employee behaviour (Dasborough et al., 2009).

In another study, Menges and his colleagues (2011) found that the consistent demonstration of transformational leadership within an organization interacts with the affective climate to support workforce performance, including citizenship behaviour. Importantly, affective climate acts as an organizational-level mediator; this implies that leadership behaviour without the right emotional environment may well be ineffective. Interestingly, a climate for environmental sustainability, a subcomponent of sustainable development, also appears necessary for a positive relationship between a corporate policy for sustainability and related employee behaviours (Mouro & Duarte, 2021; Norton et al., 2014).

Empirical data also support the influence of leader behaviour on climate in the context of sustainable development (Robertson & Barling, 2013). We propose that, within this context, transformational leadership could lead to a climate featuring both positive affect and support for sustainable development and, subsequently, employee behaviour aligning to this agenda.

The Leadership Challenge at Level 5

The clear message from the foregoing discussion is that leaders must create an organizational climate conducive to sustainable development to enable a sustainable transformation. This hinges on creating a shared perception among members that sustainable development is something the organization endorses, values, and actively demonstrates. Leaders who can demonstrate a coherent pattern of behaviour facilitate sense-making, which leads to stronger climates (Zohar & Luria, 2005). Integrating emotional content into attributes such as language, behaviour, and other symbols (including policies, procedures, and practices for sustainable development) should help organizational members form an emotional connection to this aspect of the organization's strategic direction and activities.

At the same time, leaders need to attend to the emotional or affective climate in their organization. Practices, such as accommodating members' emotional needs, providing positive feedback where possible, encouraging teamwork, and role-modelling positive emotional-display norms, can encourage a positive emotional climate characterised by psychological safety (Ozcelik et al., 2008). In such a climate, members are more likely to view change as an opportunity, rather than as a threat, and proactively take ownership over creating new ways of working that support the organization's sustainable development transformation. Research shows that strategic growth is stronger in companies with positive emotional climates.

With the right climate conditions, organizations can enable individual- and group-level engagement to scale and effect meaningful change. Leaders need to channel this latent energy deliberately to deliver a systemic transformation within the organization, leveraging emotions to support the perseverance of people and teams trying to achieve systemic change—so they can overcome the organizational inertia preserving the status quo. Such a transformation would align the core function of the business to sustainable development and avoid reinventing corporate social responsibility, which is criticised for promoting superficial action that in some cases directly contradicts a company's business practices (Mullerat, 2009).

How Leaders Can Integrate Emotions into the Processes They Use to Lead a Transition

To conclude, we identify four key means for leaders to augment their style to acknowledge the critical emotional dimension of leading a sustainable development transformation across the five levels in the FLEMW (Ashkanasy, 2003a).

First, leaders can embed emotional content into their verbal and non-verbal communications at every level of the FLEMW. Managing and leveraging own emotions when communicating about sustainable development helps followers appreciate the importance of the transformation, thereby building commitment and change readiness (Martin et al., 1998). Boiral and colleagues (2013) demonstrate that employees can emulate managers' behaviour, creating a multiplier effect that facilitates organizational change. One specific action is to describe the future state (i.e., when the organization has transitioned into a business that aligns to the principles of sustainable development) in a way that triggers positive emotions. Alternatively, leaders can articulate the negative emotions that might arise if the company fails to adapt (e.g., lose ground to competitors, become less attractive to customers/clients, be unable to do the things that make us proud, fear of redundancies).

Naturally, not everyone will respond positively to the prospect of a transformational change, and leaders should acknowledge the negative emotions often associated with change (e.g., fear, grief). Leaders who can detect the emotions in others' communications can use this insight to help address change resistance and demonstrate empathy (Hunt et al., 2017). In this case, leaders clearly need to take the time to talk with people and identify the various emotional drivers in their team and use this understanding to supplement more rational arguments in support of the change (Katzenbach et al., 2018).

Second, leaders need to demonstrate their commitment to the transformation through their actions at all five levels of the FLMEW. On the one hand, this refers to role-modelling the behaviour required of others to drive the transformation. Inconsistencies between what a leader says and what they do can produce cynicism and undermine change engagement (Polman & Winston, 2021). On the other hand, leaders can demonstrate their (and by association, the organization's) commitment by setting a new standard and holding members to it, for example, by refusing to release funding to support a new project until it satisfies new requirements for social and environmental benefits, by managing others' emotions by acknowledging their frustrations, by emphasising why the change is necessary, or by explaining what they need to do to avoid this frustration in the future (i.e., by meeting the new standard).

Third, leaders can create "affective events" that generate emotions conducive to the transformation, both at the individual level and at the organizational level. This can involve symbolic acts to create or to leverage affective events when opportunities arise (Katzenbach et al., 2018). On the one hand, these events can highlight positives, for example, by connecting sustainable development to an event that makes people proud (e.g., winning a new contract, gaining industry recognition) or by celebrating change milestones (e.g., moving away from clients or sectors that do not align with sustainable development). On the other hand, the leaders may sometimes need to highlight negative emotions, such as the shared frustration felt towards an incident that does not align with sustainable development or represents an obstacle to the transformation.

Fourth and finally, leaders can take deliberate steps to ensure that the way they support followers acknowledges and attends to the followers' emotional needs. This may be a challenge for many leaders whose positions reflect a technical proficiency while they are yet to develop people-oriented capabilities. Effective leaders provide the instrumental support that enables followers to meet their objectives through allocating resources; and the emotional support that provides the motivation to persist when obstacles arise (Paillé et al., 2020).

References

Aguilar-Luzón, M. C., Calvo-Salguero, A., & Salinas, J. M. (2014). Beliefs and environmental behavior: The moderating effect of emotional intelligence. *Scandinavian Journal of Psychology*, 55, 619–629. https://doi.org/10.1111/sjop.12160.

Aknin, L. B., Van de Vondervoort, J. W., & Kiley Hamlin, J. (2018). Positive feelings reward and promote prosocial behavior. *Current Opinions in Psychology*, 20, 55–59. https://doi.org/10.1016/j.copsyc.2017.08.017.

AlSuwaidi, M., Eid, R., & Agag, G. (2021). Understanding the link between CSR and employee green behaviour. *Journal of Hospitality and Tourism Management*, 46, 50–61. https://doi.org/10.1016/j.jhtm.2020.11.008.

Antonakis, J., Ashkanasy, N. M., & Dasborough, M. T. (2009). Does leadership need emotional intelligence? *The Leadership Quarterly*, 20, 247–261. https://doi.org/10.1016/j.leaqua.2009.01.006.

Arnaud, A., & Sekerka, L. E. (2010). Positively ethical: The establishment of innovation in support of sustainability. *International Journal of Sustainable Strategic Management*, 2, 121–137. https://doi.org/10.1504/IJSSM.2010.032556.

Ashkanasy, N. M. (2003a). Emotions in organizations: A multilevel perspective. In F. Dansereau & F. J. Yammarino (Eds.), *Research in multi-level issues, volume 2: Multilevel issues in organizational behavior and strategy* (pp. 9–54). Bingley, UK: Emerald. https://doi.org/10.1016/s1475-9144(03)02002-2.

Ashkanasy, N. M. (2003b). Emotions at multiple levels: An integration. In F. Dansereau & F. J. Yammarino (Eds.), *Research in multi-level issues, volume 2: Multilevel issues in organizational behavior and strategy* (pp. 71–81). Bingley, UK: Emerald. https://doi.org/10.1016/s1475-9144(03)02005-8.

Ashkanasy, N. M. (2021). A multilevel model of emotions and proactive behaviour. In K. Z. Peng & C.-H. Wu (Eds.) *Emotion and proactivity at work: Prospects and dialogues* (pp. 79–99). Bristol, UK: Bristol University Press. https://doi.org/10.2307/j.ctv1ks0hcg.10.

Ashkanasy, N. M., & Daus, C. S. (2005). Rumors of the death of emotional intelligence in organizational behavior are vastly exaggerated. *Journal of Organizational Behavior*, 26(4), 441–452. https://doi.org/10.1002/job.320.

Ashkanasy, N. M., & Dorris, A. D. (2017). Emotion in the workplace. *Annual Review of Organizational Psychology and Organizational Behavior*, 4, 67–90. https://doi.org/10.1146/annurev-orgpsych-032516-113231.

Ashkanasy, N. M., & Härtel, C. E. J. (2014). Positive and negative affective climate and culture: The good, the bad, and the ugly. In B. Schneider & K. Barbera (Eds.), *The Oxford handbook of organizational culture and climate* (pp. 136–152). New York: Oxford University Press. https://doi.org/10.1093/oxfordhb/9780199860715.013.0008.

Ashkanasy, N. M., Härtel, C. E. J., & Bialkowski, A. (2020). Affective climate and organization-level emotion management. In L.-Q. Yang, R. S. Cropanzano, V. Martinez-Tur, & C. A. Daus (Eds.), *The Cambridge Handbook of Workplace Affect* (pp 375–385). New York: Cambridge University Press. https://doi.org/10.1017/9781108573887.029.

Ashton-James, C. E., & Ashkanasy, N. M. (2008). Affective events theory: A strategic perspective. In W. J. Zerbe, C. E. J. Härtel, & N. M. Ashkanasy (Eds.), *Research on emotion in organizations* (vol. 4, pp. 1–34). Bingley, UK: Emerald Group Publishing. https://doi.org/10.1016/s1746-9791(08)04001-7.

Bansal, P. (2019). Sustainable development in an age of disruption. *Academy of Management Discoveries*, 5, 8–12. https://doi.org/10.5465/amd.2019.0001.

Bar-On, R. (1997). *Bar-On Emotional Quotient Inventory (EQ-i): Technical manual.* Toronto, Canada: Multi-Health Systems Inc.

Bissing-Olson, M. J., Iyer, A., Fielding, K. S., & Zacher, H. (2013). Relationships between daily affect and pro-environmental behavior at work: The moderating role of pro-environmental attitude. *Journal of Organizational Behavior*, 34, 156–175. https://doi.org/10.1002/job.1788.

Boiral, O., Talbot, D., & Paille, P. (2013). Leading by example: A model of organizational citizenship behavior for the environment. *Business Strategy and the Environment*, 24, 532–550. https://doi.org/10.1002/bse.1835.

Brown, M. E., Treviño, L. K., Harrison, D. A. (2005). Ethical leadership: A social learning perspective for construct development and testing. *Organizational Behavior and Human Decision Processes*, 97, 117–134. https://doi.org/10.1016/j.obhdp.2005.03.002.

Caporeal, L. R., & Brewer, M. B. (1991). Reviving evolutionary psychology: Biology meets society. *Journal of Social Issues*, 47, 187–195. https://doi.org/10.1111/j.1540-4560.1991.tb01830.x.

Cardon, M. S. (2008). Is passion contagious? The transference of entrepreneurial passion to subordinates. *Human Resource Management Review*, 18, 77–86. https://doi.org/10.1016/j.hrmr.2008.04.001.

Carr, J. Z., Schmidt, A. M., Ford, J. K., & DeShon, R. P. (2003). Climate perceptions matter: A meta-analytic path analysis relating molar climate, cognitive and affective states, and individual level work outcomes. *Journal of Applied Psychology*, 88, 605–619. https://doi.org/10.1037/0021-9010.88.4.605.

Chen, H., Green, Y., & Williams, K. (2021). Does perceived manager support reduce hotel supervisors' emotional exhaustion? The mediating role of control over time and negative emotions. *International Hospitality Review.* https://doi.org/10.1108/IHR-03-2021-0024.

Ciarrochi, J., Forgas, J., & Mayer, J. (2001). *Emotional intelligence in everyday life: A scientific inquiry.* Philadelphia, PA: Psychology Press.

Collins, A. L., Lawrence, S. A., Troth, A. C., & Jordan, P. J. (2013). Group affective tone: A review and future research directions. *Journal of Organizational Behavior,* 34(S1), S43–S62. https://doi.org/10.1002/job.1887.

da Silva, J. (2019). Toward increasingly sustainable development. *Domus Ecoworld,* 1038, 14–15.

Dasborough, M. T., Ashkanasy, N. M., Humphrey, H. H., Harms, P. D., Credé, M., & Wood, D. (2022). Does leadership still not need emotional intelligence? Continuing "The great EI debate." *The Leadership Quarterly,* 33(6), 101539. https://doi.org/10.1016/j.leaqua.2021.101539.

Dasborough, M. T., Ashkanasy, N. M., Tee, E. E. J., & Tse, H. H. M. (2009). What goes around comes around: How meso-level negative emotional contagion can ultimately determine organizational attitudes toward leaders. *The Leadership Quarterly,* 20, 571–585. https://doi.org/10.1016/j.leaqua.2009.04.009.

Daus, C. S., & Ashkanasy, N. M. (2005). The case for the ability-based model of emotional intelligence in organizational behavior. *Journal of Organizational Behavior,* 26, 453–466. https://doi.org/10.1002/job.321.

de Rivera, J. (1992). Emotional climate: Social structure and emotional dynamics. *International Review of Studies of Emotion,* 2, 197–218.

Deckop, J. R., Cirka, C., & Andersson, L. M. (2003). Doing unto others: The reciprocity of helping behavior in organizations. *Journal of Business Ethics,* 47, 101–113. https://doi.org/10.1023/A:1026060419167.

Dey, M., Bhattacharjee, S., Mahmood, M., Uddin, M. A., & Biswas, S. R. (2022). Ethical leadership for better sustainable performance: Role of employee values, behavior and ethical climate. *Journal of Cleaner Production,* 337, 130527. https://doi.org/10.1016/j.jclepro.2022.130527.

Diefendorff, J. M., Erickson, R. J., Grandey, A. A., & Dahling, J. J. (2011). Emotional display rules as work unit norms: A multilevel analysis of emotional labor among nurses. *Journal of Occupational Health Psychology,* 16, 170–186. https://doi.org/10.1037/a0021725.

Fineman, S. (1996). Emotional subtexts in corporate greening. *Organization Studies,* 17, 479–500. https://doi.org/10.1177/017084069601700306.

Forgas, J. P., & George, J. M. (2001). Affective Influences on Judgments and Behavior in Organizations: An Information Processing Perspective. *Organizational Behavior and Human Decision Processes,* 86, 3–34. https://doi.org/10.1006/obhd.2001.2971.

Francoeur, V., & Paillé, P. (2022). *Green behaviors in the workplace: Nature, complexity, and trends.* Cham, Switzerland: Palgrave Macmillan.

Frederickson, B. L. (2001). The role of positive emotions in positive psychology: The broaden-and-build theory of positive emotions. *American Psychologist,* 56, 218–226. https://doi.org/10.1037.0003–0066X.56.3.218.

Gagne, M., & Deci, E. L. (2005). Self-determination theory and work motivation. *Journal of Organizational Behaviour.* 26, 331–362. https://doi.org/10.1002/job.322.

Gardner, H. (1985). *Frames of mind: The theory of multiple intelligences.* New York: Harper & Row.

Goleman, D. (1995). *Emotional intelligence: Why it can matter more than IQ.* New York: Bantam Books.

Grandey, A. A. (2000). Emotion regulation in the workplace: A new way to conceptualize emotional labor. *Journal of Occupational Health Psychology*, 5, 95–110. https://doi.org/10.1037/1076-8998.5.1.95.

Graves, L. M., & Sarkis, J. (2018). The role of employees' leadership perceptions, values, and motivation in employees' proenvironmental behaviors. *Journal of Cleaner Production*, 196, 576–587. https://doi.org/10.1016/j.jlepro.2018.06.013.

Grijalvo Martín, M., Pacios Álvarez, A., Ordieres-Meré, J., Villalba-Díez, J., & Morales-Alonso, G. (2020). New business models from prescriptive maintenance strategies aligned with sustainable development goals. *Sustainability*, 13(1), 216. https://doi.org/10.3390/su13010216.

Gross, J. J. (1998). The emerging field of emotion regulation: An integrative review. *Review of General Psychology*, 2, 271–299. https://doi.org/10.1037/1089-2680.2.3.271.

Han, L., Zhou, H., & Wang, C. (2022). Employees' belief in a just world and sustainable organizational citizenship behaviors: The moderating effect of interpersonal intelligence. *Sustainability*, 14, 2943. https://doi.org/10.3390/su14052943.

Hansen, G., & Stone, D. (2016). Assessing the observed impact of anthropogenic climate change. *Nature Climate Change*, 6, 532–537. https://doi.org/10.1038/nclimate2896.

Hatch, M. J. (1993). The dynamics of organizational culture. *Academy of Management Review*, 18, 657–693. https://doi.org/10.2307/258594.

Hatfield, E., Cacioppo, J. T., & Rapson, R. L. (1994). *Emotional Contagion*. Cambridge, UK: Cambridge University Press. https://doi.org/10.1017/CBO9781139174138.

Hochschild, A. R. (1983). *The Managed Heart: Commercialization of Human Feeling*. Berkeley, CA: University of California Press.

Hökkä, P., Vähäsantanen, K., & Paloniemi, S. (2020). Emotions in learning at work: A literature review. *Vocations and Learning*, 13, 1–25. https://doi.org/10.1007/s12186-019-09226-z.

Hunt, P. A., Denieffe, S., & Gooney, M. (2017). Burnout and its relationship to empathy in nursing: A review of the literature. *Journal of Research in Nursing*, 22, 7–22. https://doi.org/10.1177/1744987116678902.

Intergovernmental Panel on Climate Change. (2022). *Climate change 2022: Impacts, adaptation, and vulnerability*. Cambridge, UK: Cambridge University Press. https://doi.org/10.1017/9781009325844.

Jordan, P. J., & Ashkanasy, N. M. (2005). Emotional intelligence, emotional self-awareness, and team effectiveness. In V. U. Druskat, F. Sala, & G. J. Mount (Eds.), *The impact of emotional intelligence on individual and group performance* (pp. 145–163). Mahwah, NJ: Lawrence Erlbaum Associates.

Jordan, P. J., Ashkanasy, N. M., Härtel, C. E. J., & Hooper, G. S. (2002). Workgroup emotional intelligence: Scale development and relationship to team process effectiveness and goal focus. *Human Resource Management Review*, 12, 195–214. https://doi.org/10.1016/s1053-4822(02)00046-3.

Kahn, W. A. (1998). Relational systems at work. In B. M. Straw & L. L. Cummings (Eds.), *Research in Organizational Behavior* (vol. 20, pp. 39–76). Greenwich, CT: JAI Press.

Karatepe, O. M., Rezapouraghdam, H., & Assannia, R. (2021). Sense of calling, emotional exhaustion and their effects on hotel employees' green and non-green work outcomes. *International Journal of Contemporary Hospitality Management*, 33, 3705–3728. https://doi.org/10.1108/IJCHM-01-2021-0104.

Katzenbach, J., Thomas, J., & Anderson, G. (2018). *The critical few: Energize your company's culture by choosing what really matters.* Oakland, CA: Berrett-Koehler.

Kauppi, J.-P., Jääskeläinen, I. P., Sams, M., & Tohka, J. (2010). Inter-subject correlation of brain hemodynamic responses during watching a movie: Localization in space and frequency. *Frontiers in Neuroinformatics*, 4, 5. https://doi.org/10.3389/fninf.2010.00005.

Krzeminska, A., Lim, J., & Härtel, C. E. (2018). Psychological capital and occupational stress in emergency services teams: Empowering effects of servant leadership and workgroup emotional climate. In L. Petitta, C. E. J. Härtel, N. M. Ashkanasy, & W. J. Zerbe (Eds.) *Research on emotion in organizations* (vol. 14, pp. 189–198). Bingley, UK: Emerald Group Publishing.

Kuiper, N. A., McKee, M., Kazarian, S. S., & Olinger, J. L. (2000). Social perceptions in psychiatric inpatients: Relation to positive and negative affect levels. *Personality and Individual Differences*, 29, 479–493. http://doi.org/10.1016/S0191-8869(99)00209-3.

Lakin, J. L., Jefferis, V. E., Cheng, C. M., & Chartand, T. L. (2003). The chameleon effect as social glue: Evidence for the evolutionary significance of nonconscious mimicry. *Journal of Nonverbal Behavior*, 27, 145–162. https://doi.org/10.1023/A:1025389814290.

Lord, K. R. (1994). Motivating recycling behavior: A quasiexperimental investigation of message and source strategies. *Psychology & Marketing*, 11, 341–358. https://doi.org/10.1002/mar.4220110404.

Løvoll, H. S., Røysamb, E., & Vittersø, J. (2017). Experiences matter: Positive emotions facilitate intrinsic motivation. *Cogent Psychology*, 4(1), 1340083. https://doi.org/10.1080/23311908.2017.1340083.

Lyubomirsky, S., King, L., & Diener, E. (2005). The benefits of frequent positive affect: Does happiness lead to success? *Psychological Bulletin*, 131(6), 803–855. https://doi.org/10.1037/0033-2909.131.6.803.

Marshall, R. S., Cordano, M., & Silverman, M. (2005). Exploring individual and institutional drivers of proactive environmentalism in the US wine industry. *Business Strategy and the Environment*, 14, 92–109. https://doi.org/10.1002/bse.433.

Martin, J., Knopoff, K., & Beckman, C. (1998). An alternative to bureaucratic impersonality and emotional labor: Bounded emotionality at The Body Shop. *Administrative Science Quarterly*, 43(2), 429–469. https://doi.org/10.2307/2393858.

Mayer, J. D., & Salovey, P. (1997). What is emotional intelligence? In P. Salovey & D. J. Sluyter (Eds.), *Emotional Development and Emotional Intelligence: Educational Implications* (pp. 3–31). New York: Basic Books.

Mayer, J. D., Salovey, P., & Caruso, D. R. (2002). *Mayer-Salovey-Caruso Emotional Intelligence Test (MSCEIT) user manual.* Toronto, Canada: Multi-Health Systems.

McKay, A. (Director). (2021). *Don't look up* [movie]. Los Angeles, CA: Hyperobject Industries and Bluegrass Films.

Menges, J. I., Walter, F., Vogel, B., & Brush, H. (2011). Transformational leadership climate: Performance linkages, mechanisms, and boundary conditions at the organizational level. *The Leadership Quarterly*, 22, 893–909. https://doi.org/10.1016/j.leaqua.2011.07.010.

Mouro, C., & Duarte, A. P. (2021). Organisational climate and pro-environmental behaviours at work: The mediating role of personal norms. *Frontiers in Psychology*, 12, 635739. https://doi.org/10.3389/fpsyg.2021.635739.

Mullerat, R. (2009). *International Corporate Social Responsibility.* The Netherlands: Kluwer Law International.

Neal, A., & Griffin, M. A. (2006). A study of the lagged relationships among safety climate, safety motivation, safety behavior, and accidents at the individual and group levels. *Journal of Applied Psychology*, 91, 946–953. https://doi.org/10.1037/0021-9010.91.4.946.

Norton, T. A., Zacher, H., & Ashkanasy, N. M. (2014). Organisational sustainability policies and employee green behaviour: The mediating role of work climate perceptions. *Journal of Environmental Psychology*, 38, 49–54. https://doi.org/10.1016/j.jenvp.2013.12.008.

Norton, T. A., Zacher, H., & Ashkanasy, N. M. (2015). Pro-environmental organizational culture and climate. In J. L. Robertson & J. Barling (Eds.), *The Psychology of Green Organizations* (pp. 322–348). Oxford: Oxford University Press. https://doi.org/10.1093/acprof:oso/9780199997480.003.0014.

Nummenmaa, L., Glerean, E., Viinikainen, M., Jääskeläinen, I. P., Hari, R., & Sams, M. (2012). Emotions promote social interaction by synchronizing brain activity across individuals. *Proceedings of the National Academy of Sciences*, 109, 9599–9604. https://doi.org/10.1073/pnas.1206095109.

O'Boyle Jr, E. H., Humphrey, R. H., Pollack, J. M., Hawver, T. H., & Story, P. A. (2011). The relation between emotional intelligence and job performance: A meta-analysis. *Journal of Organizational Behavior*, 32, 788–818. https://doi.org/10.1002/job.714.

O'Neill, S., & Nicholson-Cole, S. (2009). Fear won't do it: Promoting positive engagement with climate change through visual and iconic representations. *Science Communication*, 30, 355–379. https://doi.org/10.1177/1075547008329020.

Ozcelik, H., Langton, N., & Aldrich, H. (2008). Doing well and doing good: The relationship between leadership practices that facilitate a positive emotional climate and organizational performance. *Journal of Managerial Psychology*, 23, 186–203. https://doi.org/10.1108/02683940810850817.

Paillé, P., Mejía-Morelos, J. H., Amara, N., & Halilem, N. (2020). Greening the workplace through supervisory behaviors: Assessing what really matters to employees. *The International Journal of Human Resource Management*, 33, 1–28. https://doi.org/10.1080/09585192.2020.1819857.

Paillé, P., & Raineri, N. (2015). Linking perceived corporate environmental policies and employees' eco-initiatives: The influence of perceived organisational support and psychological contract breach. *Journal of Business Research*, 68, 2404–2411. https://doi.org/10.1016/j.jbusres.2015.02.021.

Petitta, L., Jiang, L., & Härtel, C. E. J. (2017). Emotional contagion and burnout among nurses and doctors: Do joy and anger from different sources of stakeholders matter? (SMI-2016–0125). *Stress and Health*, 33, 358–369. https://doi.org/10.1002/smi.2724.

Polman, P., & Winston, A. S. (2021). *Net positive: How courageous companies thrive by giving more than they take.* Boston, MA: Harvard Business Review Press.

PwC (PricewaterhouseCoopers). (2022). *25th annual global CEO survey.* Downloaded 4 October 2022 from https://www.pwc.com/gx/en/ceo-agenda/ceosurvey/2022.html.

Raineri, N., & Paillé, P. (2016). Linking corporate policy and supervisory support with environmental citizenship behaviors: The role of employee environmental beliefs and commitment. *Journal of Business Ethics*, 37, 129–148. https://doi.org/10.1007/s10551–10015–2548-x.

Ramus, C. A., & Killmer, A. B. C. (2007). Corporate greening through prosocial extrarole behaviours: A conceptual framework for employee motivation. *Business Strategy and the Environment*, 16, 554–570. https://doi.org/10.1002/bse.504.

Ramus, C. A., & Steger, U. (2000). The roles of supervisory support behaviors and environmental policy in employee "ecoinitiatives" at leading-edge European companies. *Academy of Management Journal*, 43, 605–626. https://doi.org/10.2307/1556367.

Raworth, K. (2017). *Doughnut economics: How to think like a 21st century economist.* White River Junction, VT: Chelsea Green Publishing.

Robertson, J. L., & Barling, J. (2013). Greening organizations through leaders' influence on employees' pro-environmental behaviors. *Journal of Organizational Behavior*, 34, 176–194. https://doi.org/10.1002/job.1820.

Russell, J. A., & Barrett, L. F. (1999). Core affect, prototypical emotional episodes, and other things called emotion: Dissecting the elephant. *Journal of personality and social psychology*, 76, 805–819. https://doi.org/10.1037/0022-3514.76.5.805.

Russell, S. V., & Ashkanasy, N. M. (2021). Pulling on the heartstrings: Three studies of the effectiveness of emotionally framed communication to encourage workplace pro-environmental behavior. *Sustainability*, 13, 10161. https://doi.org/10.3390/su131810161.

Saifulina, N., & Carballo-Penela, A. (2017). Promoting sustainable development at an organization level: An analysis of the drivers of workplace environmentally friendly behaviour of employees. *Sustainable Development*, 25, 299–310. https://doi.org/10.1002/sd.1654.

Sala, F. (2002). *Emotional competence inventory: Technical manual.* Philadelphia, PA: McClelland Center for Research, HayGroup.

Schein, E. H. (1990). Organizational culture. *American Psychologist*, 45, 109–119. https://doi.org/10.1037/0003-066X.45.2.109.

Schein, E. H. (2010). *Organizational culture and leadership* (4th ed.). San Francisco: Jossey-Bass.

Schwartz, D., & Loewenstein, G. (2017). The chill of the moment: Emotions and proenvironmental behavior. *Journal of Public Policy Marketing*, 36, 255–268. https://doi.org/10.1509/jppm.16.132.

Sekerka, L. E., & Fredrickson, B. L. (2008). Establishing positive emotional climates to advance organizational transformation. In N. M. Ashkanasy & C. L. Cooper (Eds.), *Research Companion to Emotion in Organization* (pp. 531–545). Cheltenham, UK: Edward Elgar. https://doi.org/10.4337/9781848443778.00046.

Small, D. A., Loewenstein, G., & Slovic, P. (2007). Sympathy and callousness: The impact of deliberative thought on donations to identifiable and statistical victims. *Organizational Behavior and Human Decision Processes*, 102, 143–153. https://doi.org/10.1016/j.obhdp.2006.01.005.

Small, D. A., & Verrochi, N. M. (2009). The face of need: Facial emotion expression on charity advertisements. *Journal of Marketing Research*, 46, 777–787. https://doi.org/10.1509/jmkr.46.6.777_JMR6F.

Smith, N., & Leiserowitz, A. (2014). The role of emotion in global warming policy support and opposition. *Risk Analysis*, 34, 937–948. https://doi.org/doi.org/10.1111/risa.12140.

Snippe, E., Jeronimus, B. F., Aan Het Rot, M., Bos, E. H., de Jonge P., & Wichers, M. (2018). The reciprocity of prosocial behavior and positive affect in daily life. *Journal of Personality*, 86, 139–146. https://doi.org/10.1111/jopy.12299.

Sy, T., Côté, S., & Saavedra, R. (2005). The Contagious Leader: Impact of the Leader's Mood on the Mood of Group Members, Group Affective Tone, and Group

Processes. *Journal of Applied Psychology*, 90, 295–305. https://doi.org/10.1037/0021-9010.90.2.295.

Tee, E. Y. J., Ashkanasy, N. M., & Paulsen, N. (2013). The influence of follower mood on leader mood and task performance: Evidence for an affective, follower-centric perspective of leadership. *The Leadership Quarterly*, 24, 496–515. https://doi.org/10.1016/j.leaqua.2013.03.005.

Trope, Y., & Liberman, N. (2003). Temporal construal. *Psychological Review*, 110(3), 403–421. https://doi.org/10.1037/0033-295X.110.3.403.

Troth, A. C., Lawrence, S. A., Jordan, P. J., & Ashkanasy, N. M. (2018). Interpersonal emotion regulation in the workplace: A conceptual and operational review and future research agenda. *International Journal of Management Reviews*, 20, 523–543. https://doi.org/10.1111/ijmr.12144.

Vallerand, R. J., Salvy, S. J., Mageau, G. A., Elliot, A. J., Denis, P. L., Grouzet, F. M. E., & Blanchard, C. (2007). On the role of passion in performance. *Journal of Personality* 75, 505–533. https://doi.org/10.1111/j.1467-6494.2007.00447.x.

Watson, D., & Tellegen, A. (1985). Toward a consensual structure of mood. *Psychological Bulletin*, 98, 219–235. https://doi.org/10.1037/0033-2909.98.2.219.

Weiss, H. M., & Cropanzano, R. (1996). Affective events theory: A theoretical discussion of the structure, causes, and consequences of affective experiences at work. In B. M. Staw & L. L. Cummings (Eds.), *Research in Organizational Behavior* (vol. 18, pp. 1–74). Greenwich, CT: JAI Press.

Wild, B., Erb, M., & Bartels, M. (2001). Are emotions contagious? Evoked emotions while viewing emotionally expressive faces: Quality, quantity, time course and gender differences. *Psychiatry Research*, 102, 109–124. https://doi.org/10.1016/s0165-1781(01)00225-6.

Willink, J., & Babin, L. (2017). *Extreme ownership: How U.S. Navy SEALs lead and win.* New York: St Martin's Press.

Witte, K., & Allen, M. (2000). A meta-analysis of fear appeals: Implications for effective public health campaigns. *Health Education & Behavior*, 27, 591–615. https://doi.org/10.1177/109019810002700506.

Wittmann, M., & Sircova, A. (2018). Dispositional orientation to the present and future and its role in pro-environmental behavior and sustainability. *Heliyon*, 4, e00882. https://doi.org/10.1016/j.heliyon.2018.e00882.

Wong, C. S., & Law, K. S. (2002). The effect of leader and follower emotional intelligence on performance and attitude: An exploratory study. *Leadership Quarterly*, 13, 243–274. https://doi.org/10.1016/s1048-9843(02)00099-1.

Zohar, D., & Luria, G. (2005). A multilevel model of safety climate: Cross-level relationships between organization and group-level climates. *Journal of Applied Psychology*, 90, 616–628. https://doi.org/10.1037/0021-9010.90.4.616.

8 Organizational Change towards Sustainability

From Ambition to Impact through Mindsets and Communities of Practice

Olga Tregaskis, James Graham, Marijana Baric, Viki Harvey, Duncan Maguire, George Michaelides, Rachel Nayani and David Watson

The trans-disciplinary field of sustainability science aims to bridge the boundaries between human and environmental systems to create a holistic understanding of this complex dynamic and its consequences for planetary and human wellbeing (Di Fabio & Rosen, 2018; Howard-Grenville & Lahneman, 2021). The Brundtland Report's (United Nations, 1987) definition of sustainable development, as that which 'meets the needs of the present without compromising the ability of the future generations to meet their needs too' has enjoyed preeminent status for nearly 30 years, but failure to address the multiple challenges outlined by the Brundtland Report questions the value and application of this concept. Now, as then, what sustainability is, and how it can be achieved, might be the single most important question for society and organizations confronted with the existential crisis of climate and ecological emergency.

In this chapter, we aim to contribute to the growing body of work concerned with how human action on sustainability might address the environmental shifts we are experiencing. By taking a psychological lens to our examination of organizational-level sustainability literature we discuss how mindsets form and evolve through situated learning drawing on theory of communities of practice. We suggest a sustainability mindset can operate as a bridge to transform organizational sustainability ambitions into positive sustainability actions and impacts. We begin by considering the definitional limitations that have impacted the organizational sustainability literature. We review key concepts underpinning organizational models of sustainability and the lack of attention paid to individual-level research on sustainability competences necessary to move organizations more rapidly from ambition to implementation. Within the theoretical framework of communities of practice, we propose a circular and recursive model of learning that promotes a sustainability mindset that enables a dynamic interplay between the organizational member and their wider sustainability context, leading to positive sustainability actions and employee performance.

DOI: 10.4324/9781003212157-10

The organizational literature on sustainability is expansive. Whilst it has its roots in systems thinking, the academic critique points to boundaries often set around the organization that have limited theorisation (Williams et al., 2017) and practice (Hahn & Tampe, 2021). Howard-Grenville & Lahneman (2021) argue that organizational theories of change based on conceptualisations of organizational structures and strategy generated in more stable environmental conditions are now no longer fit for purpose. To address these criticisms, much of the contemporary organizational literature on sustainability has focused on adaptation and resilience to bring greater attention to the dynamics within ecosystems and a recognition of the near and far time frames. Adaptation refers to how organizations are changing to meet shifting external demands, and thus the focus is on this process(es) and how it is/they are integrated across an organization (Schein, 1983). Resilience, by contrast, is understood as capabilities to adapt and outcomes of adaptation (Howard-Grenville & Lahneman, 2021; Walker et al., 2006). Resilience bridges the conceptual divide between approaches toward mitigation, i.e., reducing emissions and levels of greenhouse gases, and adaptation, i.e., adapting to the external changes already happening. However, the role of the individual is often marginalised because of the focus on technological systems and organizational structures. Disciplinary silos mean that psychological perspectives of sustainable change are not captured within organizational models. However, the organization is also a social structure which provides a critical site for learning and experimentation, and, as such, a holistic understanding of sustainable transitions requires greater multilevel theoretical integration. We aim to enrich the conceptualisation of organizational sustainability by highlighting the role of the individual as a learner and the process of learning in converting organizational sustainability ambition into impact.

What is Organizational Sustainability?

The expansive scope of organizational sustainability has made consensus around a single definition elusive. A useful anchoring point for much of the research since the 1990s has been *Our Common Future*, or the Brundtland Report (United Nations, 1987), in which sustainability is identified in terms of an ability to meet four challenges arising from human degradation of the world's ecosystem through the growing world population and consumption behaviours:

1   Depletion of natural resources, e.g., energy, waste, land, and material;
2   Equitable access to constrained resources;
3   Inter- and intra-generational equity to resources and associated opportunities and risks; and
4   Progressive transformation of the economy and society in support of the health and wellbeing of the natural and social world.

However, since this seminal work there has been a plethora of interpretations of the concept of sustainability. In a bid to generate greater clarity and coherence around the definition of the concept, Meuer, Koelbel, and Hoffman (2020) reviewed the way in which sustainability has been defined in the academic literature over the past three decades. Based on a systematic review of the organizational sustainability literature between 1987 and 2018, they identified a set of criteria for refining the concept of sustainability. They identified 33 definitions and, based on content analysis, identified two types of definitions and three key attributes that distinguished between the definitions. The two types were those that (a) identify the organizational design (i.e., practices, processes, strategies) and those that (b) identify how an organization does business (i.e., the approach or paradigm). The three attributes of organizational sustainability are:

1   The level of ambition to enhance or create a change, for example, where efforts to innovate may be focused on improving or adapting processes and products so they become more sustainable, whilst at the more ambitious extreme organizations are concerned with value creation through sustainable action, i.e., redefining the business model.

2   The level of integration between the internal functions and processes within organizations whereby environmental concerns become part of the core business activity. Here a distinction is often drawn between organizations that separate social or environmental interventions from other work processes compared with those that integrate sustainability into the vision and mission for the organization.

3   Degree of specificity of sustainable development in terms of whether the organization captures all four of Brundtland's challenges (low specificity) or only one or two (high specificity and thus a restrictive definition). Differing levels of specificity are often reflected in the expansion of sub-themes in the sustainability field, for example, with research focusing on social aspects through Corporate Social Responsibility (CSR) and a focus on climate through Environmental Management.

Meuer et al. (2020) suggest that the lack of conceptual clarity has hampered theoretical advances and, consequently, limited evidence-based recommendations to support organizational interventions. The implication of this definitional framework is that, in using these criteria, it is possible to map an organization in terms of its relative position, and doing so can aid a firm's understanding of its progress or lack of. It can help an organization identify its level of ambition, for example, the extent to which it is concerned with adaptation of its products and processes to external factors through innovation and/or building resilience and the capacity to adapt through changing the value proposition. Further, the criteria correspond to areas of empirical evidence, thereby providing a framework for the greater integration of the empirical evidence with the conceptualisation of sustainability. For example, ambitious goals are argued to be required to achieve greater impact (GRI et al., 2015); using Meuer et al.'s (2020) definitional framework would guide scholars to examine how ambition is impacted by organizational design, internal integration, and specificity of action. Greater understanding of the criteria defining sustainability aids our consideration of how progress might be measured and underlines the need for new and more nuanced measures (Dyllick & Muff, 2016).

Over the years conceptualisations of sustainability have become more complex in attempting to capture the idea of creating value beyond that of financial stakeholders. This conceptualisation requires going beyond the minimization of harm, developing greater systems thinking, proactively engaging stakeholders beyond organizational boundaries (e.g., consumers, customers, social groups, activists, NGOs), and embedding sustainability-led decision-making into the core of why an organization exists and how it operates. This is a challenge that organizations have, on the whole, failed to live up to (Banerjee, 2008, 2011).

Organizational research on sustainability is embedded within systems thinking that recognises the connectedness between the organization and the environment in which it operates as well as the inter-dependency between the health of the organization and the natural and social resources in which the organization is embedded (Gladwin et al., 1995; Whiteman et al., 2013; Starik & Rands, 1995). From a systems perspective sustainability can be understood as 'a normative concept referring to an ideal state of being in which humans are able to flourish within ecological thresholds of the planet alongside other living entities for perpetuity' (Williams et al., 2017, p. 12; Ehrenfeld, 2012). As such, sustainability is dynamic, in a state of flux and co-evolution with the actors within the environment in which it operates. This environment may be spatially local or, as in the case of multinational enterprises (MNEs), it may operate and have impact globally. Williams et al. (2017, p. 13) argue that sustainability reflects the 'ability of systems to persist, adapt, transform and transition in the face of constantly changing conditions'. Despite this dynamic and embedded conceptualisation, sustainability in organizations has often failed to reach, both in practice and in theory, such a fully integrated or multi-level understanding. This failure may be due to the necessity of broadening the systems boundary beyond that typically considered by traditional management theories. For example, Gray (2010, p. 48) offers a systems-based definition of sustainability as follows: 'sustainability is a systems-based concept and, environmentally at least, only begins to make any sense at the level of ecosystems and is probably difficult to really conceptualise at anything below planetary or species levels'. However, traditional management theories have remained linear in their logic (Williams et al., 2017) and overly reliant on assumptions of external market stability. The environment is understood as a pool of resources that the organization exploits and converts into outputs to the environment. Resource-based theories of the firm focus on identification and exploitation of resources, theories of competitive advantage focus on winning market position through the control of resources, whilst institutional theory focuses on isomorphism or convergence in organizational practice as the legitimizing force necessary for organizational survival. While social and environmental concerns have been added to financial outcomes as indicators to distinguish sustainable organizations, debate continues over the primacy of financial outcomes often depicted in the Greenwashing debates (Delmas & Burbano, 2011). A further critique of the lack of systemic consideration is the focus on short-term returns for organizations at the expense of considering longer-term socio-environmental impacts and how they, in fact, underpin the conditions for organizational resilience and performance.

The more recent interpretation of the theory of competitive advantage has shifted organization framing of environmental responses from being a cost to being a source of strategic advantage because of the economic efficiencies and reputational enhancement created (Porter & Kramer, 2002). Whilst this framing still drives organizational action towards sustainability on the basis of financial considerations, it represents a step forward from more problematic exploitative approaches. Over the past 20 years, organizational sustainability has matured, becoming progressively proactive, with the development of new Business Models for Sustainability that come closer to encapsulating the systems thinking inherent in the Brundtland report. Notwithstanding the limitations, the extant research on organizational sustainability provides valuable contributions and a platform for further work.

Organizational Models of Sustainability: Transforming from Reducing Harm to Creating Value through Sustainable Organizations

The innovation literature has been a primary source of insight on how organizations have approached sustainability challenges. This field of study grew out of engineering-based innovation and, whilst initially highly technology based, it is more accurate to view it in terms of innovation of socio-technical systems in recognition of the people aspects of technology delivery. Eco-innovation is focused on minimizing an organization's impact on the environment through technological advances or changing products and production processes. As such, the focus was traditionally on minimizing harm through incremental improvements in the production processes and technology already in use, enhancing employee skills in the use of new technologies and processes (for a review see Adams et al., 2016). Many organizations are still working within this more constrained conceptualisation of sustainability, but Adams et al. (2016) argue that while 'these approaches make an important contribution at the firm-level, their impact is limited ... and insufficient to address the sustainability challenge', for whilst they may increase the efficiency of an organization and its negative impact, these benefits may be off-set by higher levels of growth, what Carrillo-Hermonsilla et al. (2010) refer to as the rebound effect. Additionally, the focus on the isolated innovation efficiency of processes or products/services ignores the systematic nature of sustainability.

Given these limitations, organizationally driven sustainability requires transformational change that is consistent with holistic and systemic conceptualisations of sustainability. Research on Sustainable Business Models reflects both a paradigm shift with regards to why an organization exists, i.e., its purpose, and identifies relational-based features of organizational practice as being fundamental to the theoretical extensions required to support the challenges of sustainable organization. In the sections that follow, we consider the key features proposed in the literature and the implications these have for a research agenda that incorporates a greater understanding of a relational context for transformation.

Sustainable Organizations

A burgeoning literature on Sustainable Business Models captures a paradigm shift from business as usual to a reframing of why an organization exists and how it operates. The thrust of these models is to reframe sustainability from a business model based on responding to external market pressures that legitimize sustainability practices for competitive advantage to one that gives equal saliency to triple bottom line (TBL) priorities of people, planet, and profit (Elkington, 1994). These models increase the ambition of organizational sustainability in terms of one that adopts a broad and all-encompassing approach and actively seeks to create shared value for business, society, and nature from sustainability (Dyllick & Muff, 2016).

These models are focused on enhancing the resilience of the whole (socio-ecological) system (Adams et al., 2016, p. 35); and they are focused more on resilience than adaptation, where resilience refers to the capacity of an organization to absorb shocks and adjust to ongoing changes within the ecosystem in which it operates (Westley et al., 2011), whether on a geographically local or global scale (Folke et al., 2010; Steffen et al., 2015). This greater systemic conceptualisation of sustainability encourages and is more amenable to the growing trans-disciplinary nature of Sustainability Science (Di Fabio, 2017). There is strong alignment with theories in ecology that identify change in planetary systems as a constant (Howard-Grenville & Lahneman, 2021), with the biophysical world relying on a dynamic set of properties to foster adaptation, renewal, transformability, and thus resilience in ecosystems over time (Holling, 2001; Walker et al., 2004).

Whilst the TBL paradigm shifts (Elkington, 1994) from a focus on financial outcomes as the dominant purpose, mission, and measure of performance to one that gives people and planet equal saliency, it is not without challenges (Bertens & Statema, 2011; George et al., 2012; Esslinger, 2011, Stubbs & Cocklin, 2008; Nosratabadi et al., 2019). The empirical evidence remains contentious regarding the attainment of equality between these three domains (Birkin et al., 2009; Adams et al., 2016; Christina et al., 2017), although Adams et al. (2016) identify a common set of organizational-level characteristics that are associated with the TBL aspiration. These include the integration of planetary and social concerns with the purpose of the organization; use of planetary and social outcomes as organizational performance indicators; proactive engagement with the interests of planetary and social stakeholders alongside shareholders; proactive stakeholder engagement; organizational cultural and structural mechanisms that leverage sustainability leaders and change agents; and systems thinking not only inside the organization, but in terms of how the organization is embedded within its wider environment. TBL models could be conceived as an evolution of traditional business models in that they are largely concerned with extending the range of performance indicators to social and environmental concerns, allowing a combined focus on efficiency and innovation. This means that traditional structural and cultural tools for enhanced organizational performance remain relevant. For example, the power of aligning organizational priorities with stakeholder interests to improve performance, and internal alignment between production processes and organizational and employee learning and capacity building are necessary to change performance outcomes (Christina et al., 2017). However, TBL models also bring into focus a more novel mechanism of transformation, which is the meaningfulness of organizational goals to individual stakeholders, whether these be internal stakeholders, such as the employee, line manager, senior manager, or external stakeholders, such as the customer, consumer, or citizen.

TBL thinking is also apparent in how organizations approach process innovation. One of the more pronounced shifts evidenced is how resources are managed through the move to closed-loop manufacturing and the extension of circular-economy principles to organization practice. The closed-loop borrows from biological thinking based on the reduction of waste and reuse of high-quality by-products of the production process. Advanced manufacturing spearheaded closed-loop innovation. Correspondingly, the circular-economy concept signals a move from conventional linear economic thinking. Sometimes referred to as 'take-make-use-destroy', where the social and environmental consequences and resource used are not factored in, yet it is how business is done and how organizations and supply chains operate (Govindan & Hassanagic, 2018, p. 278; Jawahir & Bradley, 2016). Circular economy thinking explicitly manages a product function in a closed loop, whereby there is less reliance on the need for new raw materials and the outputs from the product, the production process can be reused (Kok et al., 2013), and where both environmental protection and social wellbeing are part of the economic system (Jawahir & Bradley, 2016). The circular economy principles are reflected in organizational practices based on the '3Rs' of reduce-reuse-recycle (Yuan et al., 2008), with evidence demonstrating the cost and energy use for recycling is significantly less compared to the traditional linear product life cycle, and even greater for reuse. The need to innovate and build human competencies around reusing materials and recycling waste are further argued as key drivers of quality work and jobs and, thus, part of the policy agenda for advocating economic growth through green jobs and a green economy (Govindan & Hasanagic, 2018; MacArthur, 2021).

More recently, there have been conceptualisations of regenerative models. Taking a trans-interdisciplinary approach to sustainability, researchers are beginning to introduce ideas from urban planning and the built environment, where organizations have, at their core, value propositions concerned with the generation of value to society – socially and environmentally. Regenerative thinking offers an outside-in systems thinking lens on how organizations relate to the environment (du Plessis, 2012; Folke et al., 2010; Zhang & Wu, 2015; Slawinski et al., 2019; Hahn & Tampe, 2021). Whilst many of these models are normative and aspirational, they nevertheless provide conceptual tools on the relational context that can help the research community theorise, assess, and evaluate sustainability practices.

Despite the developments on Sustainable Business Models, a core critique remains the perpetual linear and static nature of much of the conceptualisation and resulting practice. Organizational research and theorisation on sustainability has its origins in systems thinking, as illustrated above, which recognises the role of firms in the consumption and extraction from the natural world and the local or global environment in which the firm operates. However, translating conceptualisations of sustainability into strategies for action have tended to lead to silos between bodies of research and practice and an overwhelming and fragmented literature base (for reviews see Luo et al., 2020; Gond et al., 2017). Successive reviews have consistently identified siloed sub-themes and definitions. There is now growing recognition that moving beyond actions that limit harm to the natural world to more rapid responses to the climate emergency requires a step change evolution in organizational action. Building on the calls for a stronger role for psychology within sustainability science (Di Fabio & Rosen, 2018; Di Fabio, 2017) we offer, in the next section, a framework based on individual skills and relational competencies that are developed through communities of practice as a tool for bridging an organization's sustainability ambition with impact.

Bridging Sustainability Ambition and Impact through Mindsets and Communities of Practice

Research attempting to define the nature of sustainability offers clarity for individuals in organizations in that it identifies the need to consider sustainability actions in a systems framework that looks both outward from the organization as well as inward on internal processes. This requires recognition of the interplay and inter-dependencies between macro-level (global-local scale), meso-level (intra- and inter-organizational structures and processes), and micro-level (individual-level psycho-social processes) constructs. The research on new models of sustainable organization has identified organizational structure and process change as fundamental, but it also highlights challenges in affecting this change both upwards (macro level) and downwards (micro level). Core to new sustainable organizational models is the ambition to shift to a value-creating purpose of why organizations exist that is derived from a sustainability ethos in which economic, social, and ecological concerns are equitable, synergistic, and resource positive.

As organizations are social entities, the individual is a critical decision-maker and behaviour change agent. However, the lack of competence or know-how is often identified as a key barrier to moving organization-centric sustainability objectives forward (Hengst et al., 2020; Demers & Gond, 2020). We suggest that it is important to consider both what and how individual competencies are created in tandem to better understand sustainable practice. We draw on communities of practice thinking, which conceptualises how individuals learn as a social process (Lave & Wenger, 1991). Through communities of practice, we suggest individuals create and develop a sustainability mindset that offers an important bridge between organizational ambition and action (Figure 8.1).

Communities of practice arise through *collaborative effort* over time to bring together individuals across a domain of practice. Communities attract diverse knowledge bases and skill sets but are tied to each other through a common endeavour or domain of practice, such as sustainability. But,

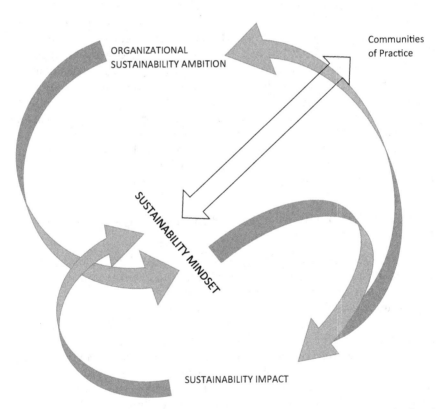

Figure 8.1 A Sustainability Mindset that bridges the gap between organizational ambition and action

importantly, the community of practice is not a task-focused group or narrowly defined by a task. As such, a community is not the ownership of an organization or outside entity but, instead, is negotiated and constituted of social relationships that coalesce around a domain. The communities of practice enable members to learn through experience and relationships with others. Through communities of practice, members co-create meaning, new understandings, and identity. The community of practice goes beyond thinking of learning as the identification and acquisition of information. Knowledge embedded and embodied within experiences and practices is the foci for learning. New members on the periphery of a community learn from the core members, bringing in new ideas, thinking, and values. The dynamic and social context of learning provides an ideal vehicle for individuals in organizations to create the values, identity, and know-how to support organizational sustainability goals and translate these into practice with impact.

To further elaborate on how communities of practice enable individuals in organizations to move sustainability practice forward, we suggest communities of practice are critical in creating mindset shifts. A mindset can be defined as a

> combination of perceptions, attitudes, beliefs, thoughts, dispositions, which can explain personal actions and/or choices. Thus, a mindset is reflective of the identity of individuals – how they perceive themselves – which in turn influences how they interact with others, and they perceive their environment and responsibilities.
>
> (Nadelson et al., 2020, p. 1)

Situating the mindset concept within the sustainability domain, we suggest that the sustainability mindset reflects an understanding of the mutual interdependencies between the components of the TBL and the strategies and actions pursued by the individual, which reflect the process through which a sustainability mindset forms and evolves – what and how. Sustainability proponents argue that changing from a focus on eco-innovations for business and financial returns to creating value through addressing sustainability concerns (Dyllick & Muff, 2016) and regenerative resource thinking (Hahn & Tampe, 2021) requires mindset changes at the individual and organizational levels. Systems thinking and collaborative behaviours are core to how those mindsets shift in the sustainability domain.

A sustainability mindset grows through systems thinking, which requires individuals to understand how the organization fits within its wider environment in relation to the impact of decisions around what and how products or services are created, produced, and used across their entire life cycle. It is this understanding that enables the individual to seek information and solutions amongst the relevant stakeholders (Broland et al., 2016; Ryan et al., 2012). However, as sustainability solutions and knowledge are still developing and growing, then communities of practice offer a learning route that connects individuals across disciplines and enables the joint construction of the meaning and value of that knowledge to joint concerns. Strategies that enable and support openness to enquiry and to transdisciplinary learning (Dibrell et al., 2015) can thus enhance systems thinking, and communities of practice can provide a vehicle for learning in this regard.

A sustainability mindset demands an understanding of the scale complexity of the environment in which the firm embeds, as this is core to conceptualisations of sustainability. This suggests that individuals need to use strategies and practices that enable them to access a wide set of stakeholder interests – from employees to customers, suppliers, and policy actors. Bridging these different, often contested, interests requires cognitive frames that are sufficiently malleable to the integration of divergent interests (Tregaskis & Almond, 2018). For international organizations, or organizations embedded within global production networks and policy networks, transnational scale issues bring to the fore the need to understand different cultural, social, and institutional norms (Tregaskis & Almond, 2018). Cultural awareness and exposure provide an opportunity for actors to integrate embedded and embodied cultural knowledge into their cognitive frames for sense-making and problem-solving (Tregaskis, 2003; Tregaskis et al., 2010). Communities of practice can scale these knowledge landscapes, coalescing around a sustainability domain of practice.

Relationality is a core part of a sustainable mindset in terms of making connections between others, valuing outcomes, and getting others to see viewpoints. Understanding the value of different types of expertise is more likely to encourage actors to create relationships and networks that support collaboration (Waddock, 2007). Empowering individuals to be able to take responsibility, innovate, and experiment supports collaboration and mindset growth (Dweck, 2016). Collaborative problem-solving involving organizationally located expertise combined with external stakeholder interests and expertise is empirically documented in the eco-innovation literature as being associated with positive environmental impacts and organizational sustainability performance (Verhulst & Van Doorsselaer, 2015; Dangelico et al., 2017). However, there is less evidence of this collaborative capability for sustainability objectives across non-technical, beyond one-off interventions, or across different types of organizational actors. Having a holistic perspective on the organization's processes and functions for positive sustainability outcomes (Gluch et al., 2009) arguably requires collaborative skills amongst the whole of the workforce, not just within pockets of the organization via specific groups of employees or a defined innovation project or industry (Dweck, 2016). Looking beyond traditional conceptions of stakeholders to consider others – for example, consumers of services or citizens – widens our understanding of the sustainability impacts. Looking beyond the boundaries of the organization and reframing how value is co-created with external stakeholders becomes imperative. Collaborative engagement with stakeholders is therefore not only confined to the acquisition of knowledge and know-how or the sharing of information with stakeholders for instructional or educational purposes, but it can be about fundamental co-creation of new knowledge in line with regenerative resource cognitive reframing. Learning through communities of practice provides a route for mindset growth in this regard.

A future orientation and ability to envision future scenarios is a central critique of much economic-driven organizational-based action. By implication, sustainability mindsets will bring temporal dimensions to the fore in problem-solving and planning (De Haan, 2006; Wiek et al., 2011). As such, future orientation is argued as a key capacity needed by individuals, i.e., the 'capacity to deal with uncertainty and future prognoses, expectations and plans ... being able to think beyond the present' (De Haan, 2006, p. 22). In addition, it is necessary to consider future orientations within a much longer time frame than is often the case in much organizational strategy and planning. Because communities of practice do not belong to an individual organization, they have the potential to address sustainability practice that is more future orientated and, as such, they can operate as a learning resource for both individuals and organizations to address near and far sustainability practice concerns.

The understanding of this new sustainability mindset means a complex interplay between the sustainability framing at an organizational/institutional level and how individuals within and between organizations are responding to it. This difficulty is exemplified by individuals reverting back to market- and profit-based motives at work when facing tensions with managing sustainability objectives (Lo et al., 2012; Wright & Nyberg, 2017; Kok et al., 2019). There is a plurality of mindsets at play in modern organizations, and this is exacerbated by sustainability agendas (Besharov & Smith, 2014). This results in 'tough moral reasoning' to make sense of the consequences of going beyond the regulatory compliance to be truly environmentally sustainable but at the cost of losing competitive advantages (Hengst et al., 2020, p. 258). This is important, as mindsets are sources of legitimacy for individuals that 'provide a sense of order and ontological security' (Thornton & Ocasio, 2008, p. 108), allowing individuals to make sense of these tensions through their pre-existing assumptions (Maitlis & Christianson, 2014). As organizations have to balance multiple objectives, such as 'people, profit and planet', the associated mindsets create tension between the different ways of thinking about sustainability, as there is a perpetual tension between market-based (financial) thinking and other 'sustainability' worldviews at work (civic/ social/ecological) (Wright & Nyberg, 2017; Kok et al., 2019; Demers & Gond, 2020; Franco-Torres et al., 2020; Hengst et al., 2020; Luo et al., 2020). The tension between a market-based and the heterogenous types of sustainability-based thinking seem to constantly come into conflict. Groups within and between organizations enacted different logics that have been derived from different 'cultural toolkits', and these 'underlying worlds' are justified through the moral stance of their logic (Demers & Gond, 2020). When confronted with environmental sustainability phenomena, individuals fall back into their familiar logics, reinforced by their organizational (sub)culture, to legitimise their choices and render their experiences meaningful (Thornton & Ocasio, 2008; Smith & Tracey,

2016; Kok et al., 2019). The result of this can be seen in relation to sustainability tensions as individuals engage in legitimising strategies in different contexts that exploit their own existing competencies (Hengst et al., 2020).

Developing capabilities, competencies, and capacity to manage these tensions and provide a space that allows individuals in organizations the scope to make and implement sustainability-based decisions that are not stymied by financial objectives remains a challenge; these objectives have historically overwhelmed the progress of sustainability thinking within organizations.

Conclusions

We suggest that sustainability communities of practice are an important vehicle for learning processes through which individuals can develop and grow their sustainability mindset. In turn, a sustainability mindset helps bridge organizational ambition with impactful action. The organizational sustainability literature calls for a mindset paradigm shift at the organizational level but says little about the learning processes that may underpin or enable such a mindset shift. Through unpacking the organizational sustainability debate and empirical evidence, it is apparent that innovation in the sustainability domain is dependent on the construction of new knowledge that involves meaning making in a multi-level, multi-disciplinary situated context. Given this, a fruitful avenue for further research is understanding the constitution, construction, and growth of a sustainability mindset at individual, group, and organizational levels. Communities of practice coalesce around sustainability interests and permeate organizational and inter-disciplinary boundaries to offer a space for sustainability mindset growth. However, there are tensions in the process of mindset formation that are not clearly understood. Are there triggers that tip the balance in how individuals evaluate sustainable value and the logics they draw upon to legitimise their actions? How do sustainability communities of practice form, how do individuals access them, and to what extent are these driven by personal values and relationships or/and professional values and relationships? Allied to mindset growth, how does the process of identity formation challenge or resolve conflict in personal and professional values? Organizations have focused on technological solutions to sustainable transitions, with little attention paid to the capacity and agency of the individual. However, taking a mindset perspective brings to the fore a systemic understanding of the role of the individual and the attitudinal, social, motivational, and behavioural capacities and strategies required to underpin a paradigm shift in the sustainability domain.

References

Adams, R., Jeanrenaud, S., Bessant, J., Overy, P., & Denyer, D., (2016). *Innovating for sustainability: A systematic review of the body of knowledge.* Network for Business Sustainability.

Banerjee, S. B. (2008). Corporate social responsibility: The good, the bad and the ugly. *Critical Sociology*, 34(1), 51–79.

Banerjee, S. B. (2011). Embedding sustainability across the organization: A critical perspective. *Academy of Management Learning & Education*, 10(4), 719–731.

Bertens, C. , & Statema, H. (2011). *Business Models of eco-innovations: An exploratory study into the value network of the business models of eco-innovation and some Dutch case studies.* Zoetermeer, NL: Dutch Ministry of Infrastructure and Environment.

Besharov, M. L., & Smith, W. K. (2014). Multiple institutional logics in organisations: Explaining their varied nature and implications. *Academy of Management Review*, 39(3), 364–381.

Birkin, F., Polesie, T., & Lewis, L. (2009). A new business model for sustainable development: An exploratory study using the theory of constraints in Nordic organizations. *Business Strategy and the Environment*, 18, 277–290.

Broland, H., Ambrosini, V., Lindgreen, A., & Vanhamme, J. (2016). Building theory at the intersection of ecological sustainability and strategic management. *Journal of Business Ethics*, 135(2), 293–307.

Carrillo-Hermosilla, J., Del Rio, P., & Könnölä, T. (2010). Diversity of econ-innovation: Reflections from selected case studies. *Journal of Cleaner Production*, 18(10/11), 1073–1083.

Christina, S., Dainty, A., Daniels, K., Tregaskis, O., & Waterson P. (2017). Shut the fridge door!: HRM alignment, job redesign and energy performance. *Human Resource Management Journal*, 27(3), 382–402.

Dangelico, R. M., Pujari, D.& Pontrandolfo, P. (2017). Green product innovation in manufacturing firms: A sustainability-oriented dynamic capability perspective. *Business Strategy and the Environment*, 26(4), 490–506.

De Haan, G. (2006). The BLK '21' programme in Germany: a 'Gestaltungskometenz'-based model of education for sustainable development. *Environmental Education Research*, 12(1), 19–32.

Delmas, M. A., & Burbano, V. C. (2011). The Drivers of Greenwashing. *California Management Review*, 54(1), 64–87.

Demers, C., & Gond, J-P. (2020). The moral microfoundations of institutional complexity: sustainability implementation as compromise-making at an oil sands company. *Organization Studies*, 41(4), 561–586.

Dibrell, C., Craig, B., Kim, J., & Johnson, A. (2015). Establishing how natural environmental competency, organisational social consciousness and innovativeness relate. *Journal of Business Ethics*, 127(3), 591–605.

Di Fabio, A. (2017). The psychology of sustainability and sustainable development for well-being in organizations. *Frontiers in Psychology: Organizational Psychology*, 8, 1534. https://doi.org/10.3389/fpsyg.2017.01534.

Di Fabio, A., & Rosen, M. A. (2018). Opening the Black Box of Psychological Processes in the Science of Sustainable Development: A New Frontier. *European Journal of Sustainable Development*, 2(4), 47.

du Plessis, C. (2012). Towards a regenerative paradigm for the built environment. *Building Research & Information*, 40(1), 7–22.

Dweck, C. (2016, Jan 13). What having a 'growth mindset' actually means. *Harvard Business Review*.

Dyllick, T., & Muff, K. (2016). Clarifying the meaning of sustainable business: Introducing a typology from business-as-usual to true business sustainability. *Organization & Environment*, 29(2), 156–174.

Ehrenfeld, J. R. (2012). Beyond the brave new world: Business for sustainability. In P. Bansal & A. J. Hoffman (Eds.), *The Oxford Handbook of Business & the Natural Environment* (pp. 611–619). Oxford Academic.

Elkington, J. (1994). Towards the sustainable corporation: Win-win-win business strategies for sustainable development. *California Management Review*, 36(2), 90–100.

Esslinger, H. (2011). Sustainable Design: Beyond the innovation-driven business model. *Journal of Production Innovation Management*, 28(3), 401–404.

Folke, C., Carpenter S. R., Walker, B., et al. (2010). Resilience thinking: Integrating resilience, adaptability and transformability. *Ecology and Society*, 15(4), 20.

Franco-Torres, M., Rogers, B. C., & Ugarella, R. M. (2020). A framework to explain the role of boundary objects in sustainability transitions. *Environmental Innovation and Societal Transitions*, 36, 34–48.

George, G., McGahan, A. M., & Prabhu, J. (2012). Innovation for inclusive growth: Towards a theoretical framework and a research agenda. *Journal of Management Studies*, 49(4), 661–683.

Gladwin, T. N., Kennelly, J. J., & Krause, T. S. (1995). Shifting paradigms for sustainability development: Implications for management theory and research. *Academy of Management Review*, 20(4), 874–907.

Gluch, P., Gustafsson, M, & Thuvander, L, (2009). An absorptive capacity model for green innovation and performance in the construction industry. *Construction Management and Economics*, 27(2), 451–464.

Gond, J.-P., Akremi, A. E., Swaen, V., & Babu, N. (2017). The psychological microfoundations of corporate social responsibility: A person-centric systematic review. *Journal of Organizational Behaviour*, 38, 225–246.

Govindan, K., & Hasanagic, M. (2018). A systemic review on drivers, barriers, and practices towards circular economy: A supply chain perspective. *International Journal of Production Research*, 56(1–2), 278–311.

Gray, R. (2010). Is accounting for sustainability actually accounting for sustainability … and how would we know? An exploration of narratives of organisations and the planet. *Accounting, Organizations, and Society*, 35(1), 47–62.

GRI, UN Global Compact, & WBCSD. (2015). *SDG Compass: The guide for business action on the SDGs.* www.sdgcompass.org.

Hahn, T., & Tampe, M. (2021). Strategies for regenerative business. *Strategic Organization*, 19(3), 456–477.

Hengst, I.-A., Jarzabkowski, P., Hoegl, M., & Muethel, M. (2020). Strategies Legitimate in Action. *Academy of Management Journal*, 63(1), 246–271.

Holling, C. S. (2001). Understanding the complexity of economic, ecological, and social systems. *Ecosystems*, 4, 390–405.

Howard-Grenville, J., & Lahneman, B. (2021). Bringing the biophysical to the fore: Re-envisioning organizational adaptation in the era of planetary shifts. *Strategic Organization*, 19(3), 478–493.

Jawahir, I. S., & Bradley, R. (2016). Technological elements of circular economy and the principles of 6R-based closed-loop material flow in sustainable manufacturing. *Procedia CIRP*, 40, 103–108.

Kok, A. M., de Bakker, F. G. A., & Groenewegen, P. (2019). Sustainability struggles: Conflicting cultures and incomparable logics. *Business & Society*, 58 (8), 1496–1532.

Kok, L., Wurpel, G., & Ten Wolde, A. (2013). *Unleashing the Power of the Circular Economy.* IMSA Amsterdam.

Lave, J., & Wenger, E. (1991). *Situated learning: Legitimate peripheral participation.* Cambridge University Press.

Lo, S. H., Peters, G.-J. Y., & Kok, G. (2012). Energy-related behaviours in office buildings: A qualitative study on individual and organisational determinants. *Applied Psychology*, 61(2), 227–249.

Luo, B. N., Tang, Y., Chen, E. W., Li, S., & Luo, D. (2020). Corporate sustainability paradox management: a systematic review and future agenda . *Frontiers in Psychology*, 11, 1–15.

MacArthur, E. (2021). *Towards the Circular Economy, Vol 1: Economic and Business Rationale for a Circular Economy.* Ellen MacArthur Foundation.

Maitlis, S., & Christianson, M. (2014). Sensemaking in organizations: Taking stock and moving forward. *The Academy of Management Annals*, 8(1), 57–125.

Meuer, J., Koelbel, J., & Hoffman, V. H. (2020). On the nature of corporate sustainability. *Organization & Environment*, 33(3), 319–341.

Nadelson, L. S., Albritton, S., Couture, V. G., Green, C., Loyless, S. D., & Shaw, E. O. (2020). Principals' perceptions of education equity: A mindset for practice. *Journal of Education and Learning*, 9(1), 1–19.

Nosratabadi, S., Mosavi, A., Shamshirband, S., Zavadskas, E. K., Rakotonirainy, A., & Chau, K. W. (2019). Sustainable Business Models: A review. *Sustainability*, 11, 1663–1693.

Porter, M. E., & Kramer, M. R. (2002). The competitive advantage of corporate philanthropy. *Harvard Business Review*, 80(12), 56–68.

Ryan, A., Millar, C., Kajzer Mitchell, I., & Daskou, S. (2012). An interaction and networks approach to developing sustainable organisations. *Journal of Organizational Change Management*, 25(4), 578–594.

Schein, E. H. (1983). *Organizational Culture: A Dynamic Model.* Cambridge, MA: Alfred P Sloan School of Management.

Slawinski, N., Winsor, B., Mazutis, D., Schouten, J. W., & Smith, W. K. (2019). Managing the paradoxes of place to foster regeneration. *Organization & Environment*, 34(4), 595–618.

Smith, W. K., & Tracey, P. (2016). Institutional complexity and paradox theory: Complementarities of competing demands. *Strategic Organization*, 14(4), 455–466.

Starik, M., & Rands, G. P. (1995). Weaving an integrated web: Multilevel and multisystem perspectives of ecologically sustainable organisations. *Academy of Management Review*, 20(4), 908–935.

Steffen, W., Richardson, K., Rockström, J., Cornell, S. E., et al. (2015). Planetary boundaries: Guiding human development on a changing planet. *Science*, 347(6223), 1259855.

Stubbs, W., & Cocklin, C. (2008). Conceptualizing a 'sustainability business model'. *Organization and Environment*, 21(2), 103–127.

Thornton, P. H., & Ocasio, W. C. (2008). Institutional logics. In R. Greenwood, C. Oliver, K. Sahlin, & R. Suddaby (Eds.), *Handbook of Organizational Institutionalism* (pp. 99–129). Sage.

Tregaskis, O. (2003). Learning networks, power and legitimacy in multinational subsidiaries. *International Journal of Human Resource Management*, 14(3), 1–17.

Tregaskis, O., & Almond, P. (2018). Multinationals and skills policy networks: HRM as a player in economic and social concerns. *British Journal of Management*, 30(3), 593–609. doi:10.1111/1467-8551.12276.

Tregaskis O., Edwards T., Edwards P., Ferner A., & Marginson, P. (2010). Transnational learning structures in multinational firms: Organisational context and national embeddedness. *Human Relations*, 63(4), 471–499.

United Nations. (1987). *Our Common Future: Report of the World Commission Environment and Development* [Brundtland Report]. http://www.un-documents.net/our-common-future.pdf.

Verhulst, E, & Van Doorsselaer, K. (2015). Development of a hands-on toolkit to support integration of ecodesign in engineering programmes. *Journal of Cleaner Production*, 108, 772–783.

Waddock, S. (2007). Leadership integrity in a fractured knowledge world. *Academy of Management Learning and Education*, 6(4), 543–557.

Walker, B., Gunderson, L. H., Kinzig, A. P., Folke, C., Carpenter, S. R., & Schultz, L. (2006). A handful of heuristics and some propositions for understanding resilience in social-ecological systems. *Ecology and Society*, 11(1), 13.

Walker, B., Holling, C. S., Carpenter, S. R., & Kinzig, A. (2004). Resilience, adaptability and transformability in social-ecological systems. *Ecology & Society*, 9(2), 5.

Westley, F., Olsson, P., Folke, C., Homer-Dixon, T., Vredenburg, H., Loorbach, D., Thompson, J., Nilsson, M., Lambin, E., Sendzimir, J., Banergee, B., Galaz, V., & Van Der Leeuw, S. (2011). Tipping toward sustainability: emerging pathways of transformation. *AMBIO: A Journal of the Human Environment*, 40(7), 762–780.

Whiteman, G., Walker, B., & Perego, P. (2013). Planetary boundaries: Ecological foundations for corporate sustainability. *Journal of Management Studies*, 50(2), 307–336.

Wiek, A., Withycombe, L., & Redman, C., (2011). Key competencies in sustainability: A reference framework for academic programme development. *Sustainability Science*, 6(2), 203–218.

Wiliams, A., Kennedy, S., Philipp, F. et al. (2017). Systems thinking: a review of sustainability management research. *Journal of Cleaner Production*, 148, 866–881.

Wright, C., & Nyberg, D. (2017). An inconvenient truth: How organizations translate climate change into business as usual. *Academy of Management Journal*, 60(5), 1633–1661.

Yuan, Z., Bi, J., & Moriguichi, Y. (2008). The circular economy: A new development strategy in China. *Journal of Industrial Ecology*, 10(1–2), 4–8.

Zhang, X., & Wu, Z. (2015). Are there future ways for regenerative sustainability? *Journal of Cleaner Production*, 109, 39–41.

9 The Psychology of Employee Owners

Why Launching New Employee Ownership Schemes Can Signal Organizational Resilience During Crises

Aneesh Banerjee, Joseph Lampel and Ajay Bhalla

Introduction

The study of organizational resilience and the long-term sustainability of businesses has emerged as a major topic of research – especially in times of economic turbulence (Di Fabio, 2017; Rai et al., 2021; Shepherd & Williams, 2022). Organizational resilience – the ability of an organization to successfully cope with a crisis – is a systemic property of the organization. It is a combination of factors, such as strong culture, operational efficiency, robust supply chains, and close relationships with external stakeholders, that allow organizations to generate additional resources when they face threats to their viability (Christianson et al., 2009; Salanova et al., 2012). In this context, organizational sustainability refers to how an organization balances short- and long-term needs as it builds "the present in such a way as not to put the future at risk" (Di Fabio, 2017, p. 2).

During a crisis, external stakeholders, such as customers, suppliers, or external shareholders, pay close attention to how an organization responds to the challenges. As they do not have complete information, they rely on information signals generated by managerial actions that are salient to the organization's ability to recover from the crisis – therefore, indicating resilience (Sanders & Boivie, 2004; Musteen et al., 2010). Such decisions generate what we shall call 'resilience signals' because they provide information about the strength of the organization when facing threats to its viability and long-term sustainability.

In this chapter, we examine one such resilience signal – the launch of a new Employee Stock Ownership Program (ESOP). We propose that the decision to launch a new ESOP not only conveys to external stakeholders, especially capital markets, what top managers think about the prospects of the firm but also provides information about what the employees, who often have first-hand knowledge of the state of the firm, think about the future prospects of the firm and their willingness to invest their own capital in building a sustainable future for the business (Pierce & Rodgers, 2004; Wagner et al., 2003). Using concepts in signaling theory, we further argue that external shareholders would perceive the launching of ESOPs during a crisis as a proxy of

DOI: 10.4324/9781003212157-11

organizational resilience since it meets key conditions set out by the theory: (a) the launch and magnitude of employee uptake of the ESOPs are publicly reported and, hence, are easy to observe externally; (b) the launch of an ESOP carries potential penalty costs for a firm in terms of damage to the perception of resilience if the offer is not taken up by employees, and likewise, there are potential costs for participating employees if the firm does not recover its valuation; and (c) launching ESOPs meets the condition for effective signals by creating a separating equilibrium between resilient and non-resilient organizations (Bergh et al., 2014).

This chapter contributes to our understanding of how managerial actions that enable employees to increase their ownership stake in the organization can be a resilience signal (Van Der Vegt et al., 2015; Williams & Shepherd, 2016; Williams et al., 2017). To build our argument, we draw upon organizational research in signaling theory (Bergh et al., 2014; Connelly et al., 2011), stakeholder theory with an emphasis on changes in ownership (Donaldson & Preston, 1995), and research on the psychology of ownership and employees' actions based on their outlook on the firm (Pierce & Rodgers, 2004; Babenko & Sen, 2015; Luthans et al., 2007).

Theoretical Background

Organizational Resilience

Developed by ecological system theorists, resilience is a measure of "the persistence of systems and of the ability to absorb change and disturbance and still maintain the same relationships between state variables" (Holling, 1973, p. 14). More recently, organizational theorists extended the concept to organizations, focusing attention on resilience as the ability of some organizations to absorb the impact of a crisis (Van Der Vegt et al., 2015).

Researchers have identified a variety of mechanisms that allow firms to develop resilience (Sabatino, 2016). These include developing managerial competencies that enable decision-makers to respond quickly to crises situations (Lampel et al., 2019; Lengnick-Hall et al., 2011), positive affect and transformational leadership (Sommer et al., 2016), developing 'healthy' organizational resources and practices (Salanova et al., 2012), learning from rare events that improve the organization's ability to deal with future crises (Christianson et al., 2009; Lampel et al., 2009; Williams et al., 2017), evolving organizational capabilities that allow organizations to reconstruct activities during environmental change (Hamel & Valikangas, 2003), capabilities for rapid change (McDonald, 2006), designing enterprise systems that absorb shocks such as redundancies in supply chains (Christopher & Peck, 2004), and engaging in business continuity planning that prepares organizations for disruptions in critical systems (Riolli & Savicki, 2003). These mechanisms are internal to the organization. Their relative strength can be assessed by managers as well as employees, who can observe operations on a day-by-day basis, but they are relatively invisible to outside observers. Furthermore, assessing whether these mechanisms confer resilience on the organization is, normally speaking, not a top priority for these observers unless the viability, if not very the survival of the organization, is at stake.

Signaling Theory and ESOP as a Resilience Signal

Signaling is essentially concerned with reducing information uncertainty in interactions between two parties – where one party (receiver) relies on the actions of another party (sender) to credibly infer certain information about it (sender). For instance, in a job market recruiters need to make assessments about the abilities of applicants. In this situation, recruiters can consider an applicant's educational attainment as a signal of their abilities. The credibility of the signal lies in the recruiter's belief that educational achievement is cor-related with ability, allowing them to distinguish between applicants with high and low abilities (Spence, 1973, 2002). Management scholars have used this theoretical lens to explain decision-making under information asymmetry in several contexts across strategic management, entrepreneurship, and organizational behavior (Connelly et al., 2011). For instance, Turban and Cable (2003) use signaling theory to show that students in business schools use a firm's reputation for socially responsible practices as a signal of that organization's working conditions. They show that this is reflected in the higher quality and quantity of job applications to firms with higher reputations.

It is worth noting that in these examples, as in the case of resilience signals, the signal is not created for the receiver who interprets the signal. The educational attainment of applicants may reflect an interest in the subject rather than a signaling decision to a future employer. Organizations may engage in responsible social practices because managers subscribe to a set of values, rather than a conscious design to attract a certain type of employee. What is crucial for the receiver is whether the signal is credible, not whether it was intentionally created or whether it distinguishes between parties that have or do not have the desired characteristics.

During crises, external stakeholders pay more attention to organizational resilience, making them particularly sensitive to resilience signals that convey information about the organization's ability to deal with the crisis (Abrahamson & Park, 1994). Such signals are not necessarily created by managers with the primary purpose of conveying resilience, but they are often the by-product of actions that address other issues facing the organization. Nevertheless, actions that are undertaken purely for organizational purposes may contain information that external stakeholders may find useful when it comes to assessing the resilience of the organization as a whole. The usefulness, however, will depend on the relationship of the external stakeholders to the organization: suppliers may be sensitive to a potential fall in demand that may affect the ability of the organization to meet its payment obligations; buyers of products that require long-term servicing may be focused on the survivability of the organization; and shareholders are likely to pay close attention to any changes in the firm's financial structure during a crisis, as this will negatively impact their own investments.

A key premise of this theory is that external shareholders are keenly aware of the information asymmetries that exist between their knowledge about the firm and the knowledge that is available to organizational insiders (Petit, 2007). It is important to bear in mind that signaling theory makes a distinction between the observability of signals and their credibility. Signals must be observable to be interpreted accurately, but they will not be taken as credible unless they are costly to produce (Spence, 1973). An illustration of a costly signal that observers are more likely to take seriously is quality certification programs, such as ISO 14001. As Montiel et al. (2012) demonstrate, to become ISO 14001 certified firms must comply with strict, costly quality and environmentally responsible practices. In essence, the upfront costs of implementing ISO 14001 make it a credible information signal to stakeholders in general but, in particular, for customers that seek information on which firms produce quality products and are environmentally responsible and which firms do not. The precise reasons that motivate firms to implement ISO 14001 are less important to external stakeholders than the fact that the organization is willing to bear the upfront costs associated with the program, since motivations may vary. Firms may wish to outdo their competitors in a reputation for quality or merely avoid falling behind the rest of the industry. Regardless of the motivation, these upfront costs lend legitimacy to the information signals and credibly confirm the program's substantial impact on the organization.

In addition to discussing information signals that are credible because they involve upfront costs, signaling theory also argues that information signals can be credible when they do not involve significant upfront costs but, instead, communicate future scenarios that can impose substantial penalties on the decision-maker. For example, when a CEO buys shares in her own company, external shareholders see the move as a credible signal of a higher probability of positive future performance. They take this view because they assume that the CEO, a rational self-interested actor with insider knowledge of the firm, will not take this risk if there was a significant probability of the firm doing poorly in the future (Jain & Tabak, 2008). In other words, they attribute credibility to the information signal generated by the action of the CEO because such an action creates potential costs for the CEO if the actual state of the firm turns out to be much worse than what management discloses to the market in its current business announcements and formal financial reporting. This assumption gains even greater credibility during a crisis, when the CEO's or top management's purchase of shares occurs during a downturn. A downturn confronts the CEO and top management with a stark choice: they can preserve their personal wealth by acting in a manner that is consistent with their knowledge of the state of the firm, or they can behave inconsistently and suffer substantial financial losses. From the point of view of external shareholders, therefore, personal purchases of shares by top-management insiders during a downturn generates credible resilience signals because these actions represent an undertaking of personal risk at a time when the organization confronts conditions that will test its ability to deal with the crisis.

ESOP Adoption as a Signal of Employees' Insider Knowledge

Insider knowledge of how well a firm can cope with a severe economic crisis is not just confined to the CEO or even top management. Employees who deal with daily operations and interact with customers are often the first to see problems and strengths that influence an organization's future performance. For instance, Babenko and Sen (2015, p. 1878) argue that lower-level employees often have information about the prospects of the firm, such as future sales growth and innovation. They show that "aggregate purchases of company stock by lower-level employees predict future stock returns" and, crucially for our argument, their analysis also suggests that the relationship between employees' stock purchases and future stock returns is stronger in firms where employees are likely to have a greater informational advantage over external shareholders when there is less publicly available information – notably, in the case of smaller firms, in firms that are followed by fewer analysts, or in times of crisis when information asymmetries are likely to rise.

Studies of the influence of employees' equity ownership, such as those carried out by Chang (1990), Faria et al. (1993), and Beatty (1995), demonstrate a positive influence of the level of employee ownership on shareholder value. In contrast, other studies, notably Gordon and Pound (1990) and Poulain-Rehm and Lepers (2013), failed to detect an influence of employee ownership on shareholder value. A comprehensive analysis of studies on this issue by Blasi et al. (2003, pp. 155–157) analyzed seventy empirical studies, effectively all studies published on the topic at that time. They found that the evidence of a positive influence of employees' equity ownership is exceptionally strong. Indeed, the evidence is so strong that they concluded with the observation that the "results surprised even us, not because they were so positive, but because they were so extensive and so uniform. Investors came out ahead if their company adopted key elements of partnership capitalism."

Extant evidence that shares of firms with employee ownership perform better in equity markets is based on normal trading conditions. By and large, this evidence supports the hypothesis that external shareholders view a certain level of employee ownership as correlating with better long-term share performance (Lampel et al., 2017). During crises, however, investors are much more concerned with the firm's near-term ability to avoid debilitating losses rather than long-term returns. Here, too, research suggests that employee ownership can make a positive contribution to a firm's longevity. Blair et al. (2000) track publicly traded companies from 1983 to 1995, finding that companies with substantial employee stakes are 20% more likely to survive in their respective industries. Park et al. (2004) track data from all U.S. public companies from 1988 to 2001, finding that employee-owned firms disappear at a slower rate and, hence, are less vulnerable than non-employee-owned firms, which disappear at a faster rate. In a more recent study of firm performance from 1999 to 2011, which covers the last two recessions, Kurtulus and Kruse (2017) also argue that employee-owned businesses provided more stable employment and were more likely to survive the crises.

To sum up, evidence shows that the level of employee ownership is a predictor of future financial performance and, hence, also a predictor of long-term share performance. During a crisis, the level of employee ownership is also a good predictor of the firm's ability to address the issues that arise as a result of the crisis. Building on this body of evidence, we propose that, keeping everything else equal, an increase in employee ownership during a crisis by launching a new ESOP can generate a signal of organizational resilience. We use the response of external shareholders to test this proposition. What is important to bear in mind is that we are not arguing that firms strategically use ESOPs to influence the behavior of external shareholders. Rather, in line with signaling theory, we argue that ESOPs are launched primarily for organizational reasons and, thus, constitute an unintentional rather than an intentional signal (Vasudeva et al., 2018).

In the following section, we derive three propositions that are based on this argument that launching new ESOPs is a resilience signal. First, we argue firms that launch new ESOPs during a crisis would have more resilience. Second, if the signal has greater salience in times of a crisis, a key part of our argument is that organizational resilience is more relevant in times of crisis compared to relatively normal times. Third, we argue that the credibility of the signal to external shareholders is proportionately greater if it comes from firms that have lower levels of employee ownership rather than firms that are already largely employee owned.

Propositions

Our central argument in this chapter is that the action of launching an ESOP is a resilience signal that provides information on organizational resilience to external shareholders. The signal is particularly meaningful during a crisis, when the solvency of the organization, and hence resilience, is of salience to external shareholders. Therefore, if launching an ESOP communicates resilience during a crisis, external shareholders are more likely to view firms that launch ESOPs more positively than firms that do not.

Separating Equilibrium Due to ESOP Launch

As discussed before, external shareholders are attentive to any changes in the equity ownership by internal employees. If employees buy shares in the firm during the crisis, it is likely to indicate employees' confidence in the resilience of the firm; conversely, if employees sell their equity stake or are given an opportunity prefer not to increase their equity stake, it is likely to indicate their lack of confidence in the firm's ability to recover. External stakeholders can form their own assessment of the resilience of the firm by obtaining readily available information on insiders' share purchases. Information on ESOPs is routinely made available to external shareholders via investor reports. A firm's decision to launch ESOPs and employees' subsequent decisions to purchase or decline to purchase shares through an ESOP are therefore visible to external shareholders because such schemes are launched formally and openly, and the uptake by employees is noted publicly.

Launching a new ESOP, therefore, meets the first and second conditions for credible signaling stipulated by Bergh et al. (2014). The first is clear signal observability, and the second is costly signaling due to potential penalty costs on both the firm and employees should uptake of the ESOP offer fail to meet expectations. The two conditions must work together. In other words, the launch of an ESOP on its own will not communicate a strong organizational resilience signal unless it is clear to external shareholders that the firm will incur potential penalty costs in the form of lower share prices should employees decline to participate in the ESOP.

A board's decision to incur the costs of launching an ESOP and employees' uptake of the share offer are together, therefore, a credible resilience signal precisely because, during a crisis, both the board and employees risk exceptionally high penalty costs – the board by virtue of its fiduciary responsibility to shareholders, and the employees because the firm's failure will wipe out their own investments. Put differently, neither the board nor the employees would participate in a new employee ownership scheme unless they were confident of the firm's ability to deal with the crisis.

Bergh et al. (2014), however, point out that although potential penalty costs may be necessary, they are not sufficient to ensure the credibility of a signal. For the signal to be useful to shareholders, it must create a 'separating equilibrium' – a relative difference in the market valuation of firms that launch ESOPs and those that do not. In the context of a crisis, if the launching of a new ESOP is a resilience signal, then everything else remains equal, and external shareholders are likely to view the prospects of firms that launch new ESOPs more positively than firms that do not. Therefore, our first proposition is the relationship between the launching of a new ESOP and organizational resilience:

Proposition 1: During an economic crisis, only firms with greater resilience would launch new ESOPs. Therefore, the launching of an ESOP can be a resilience signal.

The Salience of Launching an ESOP During a Crisis and Normal Conditions

Extant research argues that a signal's salience depends on the context in which it is interpreted by a receiver (Connelly et al., 2011; Kotha et al., 2018). For instance, Davila, Foster, and Gupta (2003) argue that Venture Capital

(VC) funding for an early-stage start-up is a signal of its financial need as well as quality. However, in the job market potential employees may still be reluctant to commit to a start-up that has not yet secured financing over multiple rounds. For potential employees, VC funding in a later stage is likely to have more salience, as they are more likely to be interested in joining the growth phase of the firm, rather than the start-up phase when risks may be greater. In essence, the same signal (VC funding) has more salience for a job applicant in a growth stage start-up than in an early-stage start-up.

Our first proposition argues that external shareholders are likely to view the decision to launch a new ESOP as a signal of employees' insider information about organizational resilience in the face of the crisis. In practice, this means that during a crisis ESOPs impact market valuation of the firm because external shareholders are attentive to solvency issues when making investment decisions. However, as we mentioned earlier, Blasi et al. (2003) suggest that firms that launch ESOPs during normal economic conditions have a higher market valuation relative to firms that do not act similarly. The difference between launching ESOPs during normal times and during crises is the importance of firm solvency. During normal economic conditions, solvency of a business in not a major concern and, therefore, external stakeholders' interpretations of the launch of ESOPs and its influence on share prices is less likely to be focused on solvency. In large part this is because employees with insider knowledge are less likely to consider immediate solvency as an issue when deciding on whether to buy into an ESOP. Instead, as researchers have suggested, in normal times employees' decisions to participate in ESOPs are motivated by various reasons, such as trust in corporate governance, tenure with the firm, exit intention, long-term retirement savings, or even knowledge of future product launches (Babenko & Sen, 2015; Caramelli & Carberry, 2014). Therefore, during normal conditions, while external shareholders, who are motivated to maximize returns, are likely to consider the launch of ESOPs as a positive indication, they are also likely to consider a variety of other measures to assess how the firm meets their own investment objectives. In essence, we argue that when firms face adverse business conditions, the launching of an ESOP becomes more credible as a resilience signal, as external stakeholders are far more focused on the risk of organizational failure and, therefore, are more sensitive to actions, such as the launching of ESOPs, which help them bridge the information asymmetry, and they need to assess this risk more accurately.

Putting the two together, we can compare the impact of launching ESOPs during normal times and during an economic crisis to determine its salience as a resilience signal. If ESOPs signal organizational resilience, and thus lead to greater market valuation, we would expect the gap in market valuation that exists between firms that are more and less resilient to increase when ESOPs are launched during an economic crisis. Put differently, during an economic crisis we would expect external shareholders to place an even greater significance on the launch of ESOPs than they would during normal economic conditions, thereby leading to relatively higher market valuation if they judge the information positively. This gives us our second proposition regarding the salience of the signal in times of crisis compared to non-crisis:

Proposition 2: The relative difference in resilience between firms that launch new ESOPs and those that do not launch new ESOPs will be greater during a crisis compared to non-crisis periods.

Credibility of New ESOPs in Relation to Existing Levels of Employee Ownership

Extant research on signaling theory argues that costly signals are more credible (Cohen & Dean, 2005; Connelly et al., 2011). Thus far, we have contrasted the response of shareholders to firms that launched ESOPs versus firms that do not launch ESOPs. However, the binary distinction does not take into account the level of employee ownership at the time of the launch of ESOPs. In our theoretical discussion, we point out that the potential penalty costs that employees may incur when purchasing shares play an important role in employees' willingness to take up the ESOP offer. Thus, the rate of ESOP uptake constitutes a resilience signal that is strong when a high percentage of the share offer is purchased by employees and weak when employees decline to take advantage of the offer.

Because the rate of ESOP uptake determines the strength of the resilience signal, it is a factor that top management must consider when deciding on whether to launch an ESOP. Moving ahead with an ESOP launch will therefore reflect risk assessment of the rate at which the ESOP offer will be taken up by the employees to whom it is offered. The existing level of employee ownership will influence this risk assessment: Employees that do not have previous experience with taking up ESOP offers are less likely to respond positively than employees that have purchased shares before and, therefore, are more familiar with the process. Thus, launching an ESOP in a firm where existing employee ownership is low poses a greater risk of low uptake than launching an ESOP in a firm where employee ownership level is high.

The willingness of top management to take this greater risk in terms of a higher penalty cost translates into shareholders perceiving the resilience signal as more credible relative to firms with high levels of employee ownership. This means that external shareholders evaluating ESOPs as a signal are likely to see an ESOP from firms with low levels of existing employee ownership as conveying more credible information about the resilience of the organization than firms with high levels of existing employee ownership. The judgement as to the credibility of the signal, it is worth emphasizing, is relative: shareholders may not necessarily conclude that the future performance of firms with low employee ownership that launch ESOPs is higher than firms with high employee ownership that launch ESOPs. But during a crisis, when uncertainty is high, they are likely to see the information conveyed by ESOPs launched by firms with low employee ownership levels as less ambiguous than the information conveyed by firms with high employee ownership. This means that during a crisis, investors are likely to view more favorably the launch of new ESOPs by firms with a lower proportion of employee ownership, indicating that the relative difference in market valuation between firms that launch new ESOPS and those that do not should be greater for firms that have lower proportion of employee ownership. This gives us our third proposition regarding the credibility of the signal:

Proposition 3: During a crisis, the relative difference in resilience between firms that launch new ESOPs and those that do not launch new ESOPs will be greater for firms with a lower percentage of employee ownership.

Conclusion

In line with current literature, we characterize the acquisition of equity by insiders as a proxy for insider knowledge that external stakeholders and shareholders can employ to make decisions. However, the nature of this knowledge and how it is interpreted is underspecified in the theory. We propose that, since resilience signals involve interpretations regarding a firm's ability to successfully deal with the crisis, it is qualitatively different from interpretations of insiders acquiring equity during normal business cycles. We propose that employees choosing to increase their equity ownership via ESOPs during a crisis is indicative of the underlying psychology of employee ownership – they believe in the long-term sustainability of the business. Under normal business conditions, external shareholders' schema focuses attention on potential profits that can shift share prices when processing information about ESOPs. On the other hand, when firms face adverse business conditions, external stakeholders are far more focused on the risk of organizational failure. They are therefore likely to regard the launching of ESOPs as a resilience signal because employees, who have firsthand knowledge of the organization's ability to sustainably recover, would not be willing to invest their own capital in the businesses.

References

Abrahamson, E., & Park, C. (1984). Concealment of negative organizational outcomes: An agency theory perspective. *Academy of Management Journal*, 37(5), 1302–1334.

Babenko, I., & Sen, R. (2015). Do nonexecutive employees have valuable information? Evidence from employee stock purchase plans. *Management Science*, 62, 1878–1898.

Beatty, A. (1995). The cash flow and informational effects of employee stock ownership plans. *Journal of Financial Economics*, 38, 211–240.

Bergh, D. D., Connelly, B. L., Ketchen, D. J., & Shannon, L. M. (2014). Signalling theory and equilibrium in strategic management research: An assessment and a research agenda. *Journal of Management Studies*, 51, 1334–1360.

Blair, M. M., Kruse, D. L., & Blasi, J. (2000). Employee ownership: An unstable form or a stabilizing force? In M. M. Blair & T. Kochan (Eds.), *The new relationship:*

Human capital in the American corporation (pp. 241–298). Brookings Institution Press.

Blasi, J. R., Kruse, D., & Bernstein, A. (2003). *In the company of owners: The truth about stock options (and why every employee should have them)*. Basic Books.

Caramelli, M., & Carberry, E. J. (2014). Understanding employee preferences for investing in employer stock: Evidence from France. *Human Resource Management Journal*, 24, 548–566.

Chang, S. (1990). Employee stock ownership plans and shareholder wealth: An empirical investigation. *Financial Management*, 19, 48–58.

Christianson, M. K., Farkas, M. T., Sutcliffe, K. M., & Weick, K. E. (2009). Learning through rare events: Significant interruptions at the Baltimore & Ohio Railroad Museum. *Organization Science*, 20, 846–860.

Christopher, M., & Peck, H. (2004). Building the resilient supply chain. *The International Journal of Logistics Management*, 15, 1–14.

Cohen, B. D., & Dean, T. J. (2005). Information asymmetry and investor valuation of IPOs: Top management team legitimacy as a capital market signal. *Strategic Management Journal*, 26, 683–690.

Connelly, B. L., Certo, S. T., Ireland, R. D., & Reutzel, C. R. (2011). Signaling theory: A review and assessment. *Journal of Management*, 37, 39–67.

Davila, A., Foster, G., & Gupta, M. (2003). Venture capital financing and the growth of startup firms. *Journal of Business Venturing*, 18(6), 689–708. doi:10.1016/S0883-9026(03)00127-1.

Di Fabio, A. (2017). The psychology of sustainability and sustainable development for well-being in organizations. *Frontiers in Psychology*, 8, 1534.

Donaldson, T., & Preston, L. E. (1995). The stakeholder theory of the corporation: Concepts, evidence, and implications. *Academy of Management Review*, 20(1), 65–91.

Faria, H. J., Trahan, E., & Rogers, R. C. (1993). ESOPs in public companies: Firm characteristics, shareholder wealth, and impact on performance. *Journal of Employee Ownership Law and Finance*, 5, 75–92.

Gordon, L. A., & Pound, J. (1990). ESOPs and corporate control. *Journal of Financial Economics*, 27, 525–555.

Hamel, G., & Valikangas, L. (2003). The quest for resilience. *Harvard Business Review*, 81, 52–65.

Holling, C. S. (1973). Resilience and stability of ecological systems. *Annual Review of Ecology and Systematics*, 4, 1–23.

Jain, B. A., & Tabak, F. (2008). Factors influencing the choice between founder versus non-founder CEOs for IPO firms. *Journal of Business Venturing*, 23, 21–45.

Kotha, R, Crama, P., & Kim, P. H. (2018). Experience and signaling value in technology licensing contract payment structures. *Academy of Management Journal*, 40(1), 59–78.

Kurtulus, F. A., & Kruse, D. (2017). *How Did Employee Ownership Firms Weather the Last Two Recessions? Employee Ownership, Employment Stability, and Firm Survival: 1999–2011*. W.E. Upjohn Institute for Employment Research.

Lampel, J., Banerjee, A., & Bhalla, A. (2017). The ownership effect inquiry: What does the evidence tell us? Retrieved on 30 May 2023 from http://theownershipeffect.co.uk/the-evidence/.

Lampel, J., Banerjee, A., & Bhalia, A. (2019). The Resilient Decision Maker: Navigating Challenges in Business and Life. Lioncrest Publishing.

Lampel, J., Shamsie, J., & Shapira, Z. (2009). Experiencing the improbable: Rare events and organizational learning. *Organization Science*, 20, 835–845.

Lengnick-Hall, C. A., Beck, T. E., & Lengnick-Hall, M. L. (2011). Developing a capacity for organizational resilience through strategic human resource management. *Human Resource Management Review*, 21, 243–255.

Luthans, F., Avolio, B. J., Avey, J. B., & Norman, S. M. (2007). Positive psychological capital: Measurement and relationship with performance and satisfaction. *Personnel Psychology*, 60(3), 541–572.

McDonald, N. (2006). Organisational resilience and industrial risk. In E. Hollnagel & D. D. Woods (Eds.), *Resilience engineering: Concepts and precepts.* (pp. 155–179). Aldershot: Ashgate.

Montiel, I., Husted, B. W., & Christmann, P. (2012). Using private management standard certification to reduce information asymmetries in corrupt environments. *Strategic Management Journal*, 33, 1103–1113.

Musteen, M., Datta, D. K., & Kemmerer, B. (2010). Corporate reputation: Do board characteristics matter? *British Journal of Management*, 21, 498–510.

Park, R., Kruse, D., & Sesil, J. (2004). Does employee ownership enhance firm survival? *Advances in the Economic Analysis of Participatory and Labor-Managed Firms*, 8, 3–33.

Pierce, J. L., & Rodgers, L. (2004). The psychology of ownership and worker-owner productivity. *Group & Organization Management*, 29(5), 588–613.

Poulain-Rehm, T., & Lepers, X. (2013). Does employee ownership benefit value creation? The case of France (2001–2005). *Journal of Business Ethics*, 112, 325–340.

Rai, S. S., Rai, S., & Singh, N. K. (2021). Organizational resilience and social-economic sustainability: COVID-19 perspective. *Environment, Development and Sustainability*, 23(8), 12006–12023.

Riolli, L., & Savicki, V. (2003). Information system organizational resilience. *Omega*, 31, 227–233.

Sabatino, M. (2016). Economic crisis and resilience: Resilient capacity and competitiveness of the enterprises. *Journal of Business Research*, 69, 1924–1927.

Salanova, M., Llorens, S., Cifre, E., & Martínez, I. M. (2012). We need a hero! Toward a validation of the healthy and resilient organization (HERO) model. *Group & Organization Management*, 37, 785–822.

Sanders, W., & Boivie, S. (2004). Sorting things out: Valuation of new firms in uncertain markets. *Strategic Management Journal*, 25, 167–186.

Shepherd, D. A., & Williams, T. A. (2022). Different response paths to organizational resilience. *Small Business Economics*, 1–36. doi:10.1007/s11187-022-00689-4.

Sommer, S. A., Howell, J. M., & Hadley, C. N. (2016). Keeping positive and building strength: The role of affect and team leadership in developing resilience during an organizational crisis. *Group & Organization Management*, 41, 172–202.

Spence, M. (1973). Job market signaling. *The Quarterly Journal of Economics*, 87, 355–374.

Spence, M. (2002). Signaling in retrospect and the informational structure of markets. *American Economic Review*, 92, 434–459.

Turban, D. B., & Cable, D. M. (2003). Firm reputation and applicant pool characteristics. *Journal of Organizational Behavior: The International Journal of Industrial, Occupational and Organizational Psychology and Behavior*, 24, 733–751.

Van Der Vegt, G. S., Essens, P., Wahlström, M., & George, G. (2015). Managing risk and resilience. *Academy of Management Journal*, 58, 971–980.

Vasudeva, G., Nachum, L., & Say, G. (2018). A signaling theory of institutional activism: How Norway's sovereign wealth fund investments affect firms' foreign acquisitions. *Academy of Management Journal*, 61, 1583–1611.

Wagner, S. H., Parker, C. P., & Christiansen, N. D. (2003). Employees that think and act like owners: Effects of ownership beliefs and behaviors on organizational effectiveness. *Personnel Psychology*, 56(4), 847–871.

Williams, T. A., Gruber, D. A., Sutcliffe, K. M., Shepherd, D. A., & Zhao, E. Y. (2017). Organizational response to adversity: Fusing crisis management and resilience research streams. *Academy of Management Annals*, 11(2), 733–769.

Williams, T. A., & Shepherd, D. A. (2016). Building resilience or providing sustenance: Different paths of emergent ventures in the aftermath of the Haiti earthquake. *Academy of Management Journal*, 59(6), 2069–2102.

Section 3

Prevention in the Context of the Psychology of Sustainable Development in Organizations

10 Towards a Sustainable and Supportive Email Culture

Jean-François Stich

In organizations, email has come to be seen as both a "source and symbol of stress" (Barley et al., 2011), and many dream of replacing it with alternative communication applications (Bertin et al., 2020). Office workers are partly to blame for this negative reputation, having *misused* email in several ways that will be reviewed in the present chapter (e.g., sending too many poor-quality messages to too many recipients). However, decades after its inception, email remains the most "business critical" application (Sumecki et al., 2011), with an estimated 320 billion messages exchanged every day worldwide (Radicati, 2021). As the following review shows, many of these messages could have been improved or even avoided altogether (Understanding Email Misuse) in order to improve individuals' wellbeing, organizations' performance, and our planet (Outcomes of Email Misuse). As an example, individuals tend to deal with incoming emails within six seconds of reception (Jackson et al., 2006); doing so outside of office hours can result in work-life conflict (Derks et al., 2015) and interrupt personal and family activities (Delanoeije et al., 2019). In order to avoid such *email misuse*, this chapter ends by suggesting an agenda towards a sustainable, supportive email culture for both research and practice (Discussion).

Understanding Email Misuse

Email Volume

Email misuse occurs when large, spiraling volumes of email are sent, received, and read. Individuals are often faced with "perceptions that their own email use has gotten out of control" (Dabbish & Kraut, 2006, p. 431) – a phenomenon named *email overload*. Email is easy to use and, for example, transmitting a message to thousands of recipients is effortless thanks to digital 'carbon copies' (Thomas & King, 2006). Despite the existence of alternative communication applications, email is often the default way to communicate in organizations (Tarafdar et al., 2023), resulting in the exchange of large volumes of messages. Email volume then often tends to spiral, as new recipients and tasks are added to email threads, and because individuals have difficulty

DOI: 10.4324/9781003212157-13

switching to other applications once a communication has been initiated using email (Thomas & King, 2006).

Email misuse is further assessed in terms of the frequency and times at which emails are exchanged. Given that emails are often checked as they arrive (Barley et al., 2011), rather than periodically, receiving email often leads to productivity losses (Jackson et al., 2006) and calls for frequent email replies, thereby worsening the problem across the organization. Emails exchanged after working hours can damage the work-life balance for both senders and receivers (Wright et al., 2014) and create an overall sense of "telepressure" (Barber & Santuzzi, 2015) and expectations for constant availability (Barley et al., 2011).

However, individuals have different tolerance levels and preferences regarding the number of emails they can process (Kalman & Ravid, 2015; Stich et al., 2019) and the point at which they start considering email to be a threat to their work-life balance (Wright et al., 2014). Email volume thus mainly turns into email misuse when individuals perceive such volumes to be threatening or overloading (Dabbish & Kraut, 2006).

Paradoxically, email misuse can also originate from a lack of email, rather than an excess. When in situations of "email underload" (Stich et al., 2019), individuals may suffer from the idea of being left out of important communications or a perceived lack of response to their emails. They may lack the timely information that they need to conduct their work and lose performance and productivity as a result (Addas & Pinsonneault, 2015). As will be seen in the next sub-section, the actual content of email also matters in the perception of email misuse. For instance, receiving emails that are critical to undertake the task at hand may be perceived as an opportunity rather than a threat (Mano & Mesch, 2010; Sobotta & Hummel, 2015; Sumecki et al., 2011).

Email Quality

Email misuse can also take the form of an exchange of poor-quality emails. Part of the problem resides in the reduced visual cues, co-presence, or synchronicity of email (Friedman & Currall, 2003; Taylor et al., 2008). In the absence of such cues in real time, individuals have difficulty clarifying the message they wish to convey, which may ultimately lead to the message being erroneously interpreted by the receiver (Byron, 2008). However, individuals tend to overestimate their ability to convey emotional messages and may thus not be aware of this difficulty (Kruger et al., 2005). Emails can be considered ambiguous and difficult to interpret as a result (Byron, 2008).

Conflict escalation can occur when a message is perceived – correctly or otherwise – as hostile, unfriendly, or aggressive and is responded to in kind (Friedman & Currall, 2003). When the response to the message employs a similar tone, it can in turn be perceived as hostile by the receiver, which results in a spiral of email flaming (Turnage, 2007). Email tone and style is often at the root of such perceptions of hostility, for instance, when emails contain swear words, all capitals, or excessive exclamation points or question marks (Turnage, 2007). Intimidations and insults are considered to be the most common form of hostility in email and can even result in or be a sign of cyberbullying (Baruch, 2005). Given the asynchrony of email, it is hard for victims of cyberbullying to psychologically remove themselves from the negative messages they can continue receiving anytime, anywhere (Coyne et al., 2017).

Furthermore, individuals may not always see the value and usefulness of some of the emails they receive (Mano & Mesch, 2010). Email senders are often unaware of what receivers are currently working on. Sending email is mostly about "dropping" tasks onto other people (Renaud et al., 2006). Thus, emails often do not have immediate usefulness for an individual's tasks at hand (Addas & Pinsonneault, 2015) and are thus not always considered "business critical" enough to be valuable and capable of reducing work stress (Sumecki et al., 2011). The relevance of emails may also be further lost as email threads discursively increase in size, receivers, tasks, updates, and requests (Thomas & King, 2006).

Email Behaviors

Individuals can also 'misuse' email because of poor email management techniques. Most employees have their mailboxes open all day, a practice that has the potential to create stressful disruptions throughout the workday (Renaud et al., 2006). Indeed, incoming emails are often associated with pop-ups alerting the recipients, even when they are using other software. When the receivers see these alerts, they can either immediately handle the incoming emails or ignore them and stay focused on their work at hand. Barley et al. (2011) found that most of the participants in their study handled emails as they arrived in order to feel responsive and on top of their work. This practice can even be considered addictive because of the positive reinforcement mechanism it activates (Mazmanian et al., 2005). Among all the negative and disruptive incoming emails, some are positive and useful. Constant email monitoring can thus act as a lottery in which receivers continue to check email in the hope of finally receiving positive and useful emails (Mazmanian et al., 2005). These expectations for constant availability also create a strong pressure to respond that tends to spread among email receivers, who in turn have heightened expectations of others (Mazmanian et al., 2005), although they tend to overestimate these expectations (Giurge & Bohns, 2021). Expectations for constant availability and prompt responses thus tend to operate at an organizational level (Barley et al., 2011) and constitute the "email culture" of each organization.

Email inboxes are also indicative of misuse, such as when messages pile up in inboxes, thereby reminding their owners of their email overload (Barley et al., 2011). Inefficient use of email filters, flags, reminders, and folders contribute both to email user stress and to the stress of everyone in the organization (Burgess et al., 2005; Soucek & Moser, 2010). Not everyone has the same strategy to deal with inboxes, however, ranging from simple accumulation to constant cleaning (Kalman & Ravid, 2015). Overall, having the ability to manage the emails received can ease the consequences of others' email misuse (Soucek & Moser, 2010).

The preceding sub-sections have discussed that email misuse mostly originates from individuals sending emails that are too numerous and of low quality. Thus, individuals must also question and improve the emails they themselves send. Besides the aforementioned characteristics of email misuse (e.g., sending emails after working hours, sending complex and ambiguous messages) comes the fundamental question of whether email is in fact the appropriate application for the given task or communication (Tarafdar et al., 2023), or for the given interlocutor (Stich et al., 2017). Given all the functions of email, ranging from communication to task management and document archiving (Ducheneaut & Bellotti, 2001), and its ease of use, individuals can be tempted to use "email by default" (Tarafdar et al., 2023) instead of employing more suitable alternative applications (Jung & Lyytinen, 2014). A communication initiated using email is likely to continue by email (Thomas & King, 2006), thus emphasizing the importance of choosing the right application to begin with.

Below we review the outcomes of email misuse at the individual, organizational, and societal levels.

Outcomes of Email Misuse

Individual Impacts

Email misuse is associated with a variety of negative individual outcomes. First, email misuse increases workloads. Individuals commonly feel that their information load is getting out of control (Dabbish & Kraut, 2006), which increases the risk of dissatisfaction, distress (Mano & Mesch, 2010), and emotional exhaustion (Brown et al., 2004), sometimes to the point of burnout (Barber & Santuzzi, 2015; Wright et al., 2014). Information overload further increases work overload (Barley et al., 2011; Stich et al., 2017) because of the time required to handle and process email (e.g., 29 minutes spent reading email every day; Jackson et al., 2006) and the time lost recovering from email interruptions (Jackson et al., 2006).

Second, negative experiences associated with insults and intimidation via email can lead to high blood pressure (Taylor et al., 2005), stress, and stress-related illness (Baruch, 2005). When this 'cyber incivility' (Lim & Teo, 2009) turns into cyberbullying, new consequences may arise, such as increased anxiety (Baruch, 2005) and emotional exhaustion (Farley et al., 2016). When email interactions start replacing physical interactions (e.g., colleagues emailing one another within the same building), psychological and physiological stress may arise (Mark et al., 2012).

Third, the 'constant connectivity' that can result from checking email anytime, anywhere (Mazmanian et al., 2005) is generally detrimental to the work-life balance (Derks et al., 2015), as personal activities are often interrupted to respond to work demands (Delanoeije et al., 2019). Again, such email misuse can cause distress (Mazmanian et al., 2005) and emotional exhaustion (Xie et al., 2018), along with poorer sleep quality (Hu et al., 2019) or other physiological consequences (Akbar et al., 2019) and, ultimately, burnout (Wright et al., 2014).

All of these negative individual outcomes thus point towards an overall experience of work stress due to email misuse in the form of work overload, damaged work relationships, and work-life conflicts. In contrast, the opportunities for email to potentially create stimulating and fulfilling wellbeing outcomes have seldom been mentioned in the literature (Ducheneaut & Bellotti, 2001; Sobotta & Hummel, 2015), besides the empowerment of having accomplished something by "dropping tasks onto others" (Friedman & Currall, 2003) or of having protected one's back with the production of written proof (Romm & Pliskin, 1999).

Organizational Impacts

Email misuse also has consequences for organizations, mainly through reduced employee performance. Individuals can take up to 15 minutes to recover from an email interruption and re-engage in their task at hand (Jackson et al., 2006). A task takes one-third longer with email interruptions than without (Marulanda-Carter & Jackson, 2012). The financial impact of email interruptions alone has been estimated at over $10 million a year for a large organization (Jackson et al., 2006). In addition to interrupting work, email misuse can also reduce employee productivity and performance through the mental strain associated with overload (Dabbish & Kraut, 2006; Karr-Wisniewski & Lu, 2010). In contrast, productivity and performance can be increased by emails that transmit information necessary for task completion (Addas & Pinsonneault, 2015; Mano & Mesch, 2010) and by the acquisition of email management abilities (Soucek & Moser, 2010).

The work-life conflicts caused by email misuse also represent a financial and legal risk for organizations. Although constant connectivity can sometimes increase employee performance, this comes at a personal cost that negates productivity gains (Dén-Nagy, 2014), such as health-related absenteeism and poorer sleep quality (Barber & Santuzzi, 2015). Email cultures involving constant connectivity have even led certain employees to sue their employers (e.g., an organization ordered to pay £53,000; Samuel, 2018). Employee performance may be further reduced by the misunderstandings and conflicts engendered by email misuse. Uncivil email exchanges have been found to diminish task performance and energy (Giumetti et al., 2013), alongside the aforementioned health effects.

Environmental Impacts

Emails and email misuse can also have a certain societal impact. Information communications technology (ICT) in general contributed an estimated 1.8%–

2.8% of global greenhouse gases emissions in 2020 (Freitag et al., 2021). These estimates include user devices (e.g., computers, smartphones – both their energy consumption and manufacturing), data centers, and networks, which each contribute around one-third of the emissions (Freitag et al., 2021). Reports have estimated that around 320 billion emails are sent and received every day worldwide – a number that is forecast to grow to over 376 billion by 2025 (Radicati, 2021). There is currently no consensus on the exact calculation of email's carbon footprint, but it is considered to be quite trivial (McDonnell, 2020), given that computers, networks and datacenters would probably remain on with or without emails. Rough estimates have mentioned an average footprint of around 4g of CO_2 per email (50g with large attachments), but have been challenged since (Berners-Lee, 2020). Writing and reading emails require devices (e.g., computers, smartphones) that consume energy to operate and rare minerals to manufacture. It has been estimated that around two hours are spent every day writing and reading emails (Dietzen, 2017). To reach its destination, an email transits between several datacenters across the globe and dozens of servers, routers, and pieces of equipment, which consume energy to operate and rare minerals to manufacture. Emails then need to be stored in datacenters. Although the energy efficiency of datacenters has doubled in the last decade (Masanet et al., 2020), keeping thousands of emails still involves storing gigabytes of data. In that regard, using email as file storage (Ducheneaut & Bellotti, 2001) is particularly inefficient compared to using document-sharing platforms (e.g., WeTransfer, Google Drive), given that an attachment sent to 100 receivers would need to be stored 100 times instead of just once. Pictures included in email signatures also count as attachments, and some add several megabytes to emails sent. All in all, and despite the minor global carbon footprint of emails, email misuse also comes at an environmental cost (e.g., when carbon copies are over-used, when another application may have been more appropriate to communicate, and when email inboxes are not kept tidy). As implied in the preceding sections, the best emails are probably short, of good quality, and useful to the receivers; they make an appropriate use of attachments; and they are sent to the fewest people possible.

Discussion

Towards a Sustainable and Supportive Email Culture

The review up to this point has painted a relatively negative picture of email use. The many ways in which individuals misuse email have certainly contributed to its reputation as a symbol of all that is wrong in business communication (Barley et al., 2011). Although email has certain characteristics that make misuse more common (e.g., lack of visual cues, ease of use, asynchrony) (Byron, 2008; Friedman & Currall, 2003; Mano & Mesch, 2010), individuals and organizations have a role to play in creating a more sustainable and supportive email culture (see Table 10.1).

Table 10.1 Towards a sustainable and supportive email culture

---

Organizations could train employees to use email efficiently (Burgess et al., 2005; Soucek & Moser, 2010):

- Handling emails: filtering, archiving, sorting;
- Replying to problematic emails;
- Writing emails that are clearer, more concise, and only addressed to the appropriate recipients; and
- Deciding when email is not the most appropriate communication application.

Organizations could implement email policies and circulate guidelines (Barber & Santuzzi, 2015; Leonardi et al., 2010):

- Encouraging limited numbers of emails sent;
- Creating support groups to share experiences of email misuse and constant connectivity;
- Limiting the sending of bulk corporate emails; and
- Conducting campaigns targeting attitudes towards email (e.g., "no email week").

Individuals could set an example when sending emails (Byron, 2008; Renaud et al., 2006; Tarafdar et al., 2023):

- Deciding whether email is the most appropriate application;
- Respecting the preferences and needs of targeted recipients;
- Refraining from sending emails outside of office hours;
- Limiting the size of attachments or using document-sharing platforms; and
- Undertaking or asking for training to improve email management and writing techniques.

First, many forms of email misuse could be avoided by properly training individuals to use email efficiently. For example, Burgess et al. (2005) designed and taught a course that involved writing effective subject lines, getting messages across, and targeting emails to relevant recipients. They found that their training significantly improved the quality of the emails sent by trainees. Soucek and Moser (2010) similarly developed a comprehensive training intervention that included demonstrations of email management techniques (e.g., filtering, archiving), role-playing exercises about managing and replying to fictional problematic emails, and collective writing of email policies. The 16 training sessions they conducted significantly improved trainees' stress levels and productivity. Training aimed at improving email quality seems more relevant than ever nowadays, given that an increasing number of email software programs now incorporate AI-driven suggestions for email replies (e.g., Google Mail, Microsoft Outlook) that are not always appropriate and may thus create further misunderstandings (Robertson et al., 2021). Improving email quality can help reduce misunderstandings and conflicts (Soucek & Moser, 2010) and, thus, go a long way in creating more positive and supportive email cultures.

Second, organizations could implement policies and circulate guidelines to encourage sustainable and supportive email use. Guidelines can encourage individuals to limit the number of emails they send (Soucek & Moser, 2010). Support groups can be created for employees to share their experiences of email misuse and constant connectivity as well as collectively discuss and design best practices (Barber & Santuzzi, 2015; Leonardi et al., 2010). Organizations may also rethink their policies regarding corporate emails sent in bulk to employees. Although such bulk corporate emails are deemed important by executives and communicators, they are often considered unimportant by recipients and quickly discarded (Kong et al., 2021). Organizations may be further tempted to use these policies to lock down email servers after office hours to curtail certain email practices deemed unvirtuous. However, such inflexible policies do not tackle the root of the problem (i.e., the antecedents of email misuse) and may push employees into more questionable practices, such as sharing their personal email addresses with colleagues or printing confidential documents. Instead, campaigns targeting attitudes towards email (e.g., "no email week"; Pillet & Carillo, 2016) could be used to spark long-term behavioral changes.

Third, organizations could encourage a sustainable and supportive email culture by setting an example and by recognizing the imbalance of power between users. As there are very few or no restrictions on incoming emails, most emails sent ultimately reach their destinations. This implies that email senders wield more authority over email receivers (Renaud et al., 2006), for example, by having the power to 'drop' tasks on them (Renaud et al., 2006), by being responsible for the quality of the emails initially sent (Byron, 2008), and by originating response expectations (Barber & Santuzzi, 2015). This is why the studies on email training reviewed in the previous section mostly consisted of training for email senders (Burgess et al., 2005; Soucek & Moser, 2010). Thus, email senders have significant responsibility in setting an example in terms of email volume and quality as well as in choosing one email application rather than another to initiate communication (Tarafdar et al., 2023). For example, they could refrain from sending an email to a colleague they know would prefer a phone call (Stich et al., 2017). Communication preferences can be shared, for instance, in email signatures (Wijngaards et al., 2022). Delaying email delivery may also prove beneficial when written outside office hours. Setting an example is even more important when the email senders are managers, given that their messages could be perceived as more negative (Byron, 2008) and threatening (Taylor et al., 2005) by their subordinates or could create much stronger response expectations within and outside of office hours (Waller & Ragsdell, 2012).

Fourth, technical solutions could be implemented to improve email culture. Given that certain forms of email misuse are due to a lack of adequate alternative communication applications (Tarafdar et al., 2023), organizations should make sure that their employees have access to all the applications they need and prefer. For example, Enterprise Social Networks may prove useful to replace email for certain interactions (Bertin et al., 2020). Generally, care should be taken to identify complementary applications (Ducheneaut & Bellotti, 2001; Jung & Lyytinen, 2014) and ensure that they are easy to use and thus a viable alternative to email (Tarafdar et al., 2023). In order to limit the excessive, unsustainable use of email attachments, document-sharing platforms should be encouraged and made easy to use. For example, attachments to emails sent through Office 365 or Gmail could be stored on OneDrive and Google Drive, respectively. Desktop and mobile email inboxes (e.g., Microsoft Outlook) could be pre-configured to check incoming messages at regular times rather than continuously (every 45 minutes ideally; Gupta et al., 2011), although some employees in certain jobs would still need to check emails continuously to deal with urgent requests (Wijngaards et al., 2022).

Points for Future Research and Applications in Work and Organizational Psychology

This review has identified several characteristics of email misuse (volume, quality, management techniques) and their individual, organizational, and environmental outcomes. However, interesting directions remain for future research on email use and a sustainable, supportive email culture. First, there is currently little research on actual email content (rather than content quality), which is surprising given that content is the reason emails are sent and read in the first place. For example, Thomas and King (2006) recorded emails and conducted textual analyses on their content to explore the discursive evolution of email threads. Second, the stressful potential of *email underload* (Stich et al., 2019) could be further explored quantitatively (as email overload scales do not capture underload) and qualitatively (e.g., emails that receive no timely reply or none at all). Third, the dyadic relationships between email senders and email receivers seem interesting to study, given the nature of email use (e.g., Sender-Message-Receiver; Byron, 2008) and the potential power imbalance between senders and receivers (Renaud et al., 2006). Fourth, research on email misuse may greatly benefit from Big Data and objective measures of email use as recorded by email software (e.g., Kalman & Ravid, 2015). These objective measures could then be compared to self-report measures of email use and subjective measures of email misuse to unveil interesting dynamics. Fifth, the mixed findings on the efficiency of certain email management techniques (e.g., batching) may warrant further research on the appropriate conditions and the individuals for whom each technique works (Wijngaards et al., 2022). Finally, there is room for future study on the positive outcomes and experiences of email use, such as eustress (Tarafdar et al., 2019). Indeed, the longevity of business email (over 40 years) seems peculiar given all the negative experiences and outcomes reported in research. There is undoubtedly more to email than meets the academic eye. Email is here to stay (Radicati, 2021), so continuing to explore its use, misuse, and impacts will remain timely and relevant.

References

Addas, S., & Pinsonneault, A. (2015), "The many faces of information technology interruptions: a taxonomy and preliminary investigation of their performance effects", *Information Systems Journal*, Vol. 25 No. 3, pp. 231–273.

Akbar, F., Bayraktaroglu, A.E., & Buddharaju, P. (2019), *"Email Makes You Sweat: Examining Email Interruptions and Stress with Thermal Imaging"*, presented at the CHI 2019, Glasgow, Scotland, UK.

Barber, L.K., & Santuzzi, A.M. (2015), "Please Respond ASAP: Workplace Telepressure and Employee Recovery", *Journal of Occupational Health Psychology*, Vol. 20 No. 2, pp. 172–189.

Barley, S.R., Meyerson, D.E., & Grodal, S. (2011), "E-mail as a Source and Symbol of Stress", *Organization Science*, Vol. 22 No. 4, pp. 887–906.

Baruch, Y. (2005), "Bullying on the net: adverse behavior on e-mail and its impact", *Information & Management*, Vol. 42 No. 2, pp. 361–371.

Berners-Lee, M. (2020), *How Bad Are Bananas?: The Carbon Footprint of Everything*, Profile Books.

Bertin, E., Colléaux, A., & Leclercq-Vandelannoitte, A. (2020), "Collaboration in the digital age: From email to enterprise social networks", *Systèmes d'information & management*, Vol. 25 No. 1, p. 7.

Brown, S.A., Fuller, R.M., & Vician, C. (2004), "Who's Afraid of the Virtual World?: Anxiety and Computer-Mediated Communication", *Journal of the Association for Information Systems*, Vol. 5 No. 2, pp. 79–107.

Burgess, A., Jackson, T.W., & Edwards, J. (2005), "Email training significantly reduces email defects", *International Journal of Information Management*, Vol. 25 No. 1, pp. 71–83.

Byron, K. (2008), "Carrying Too Heavy a Load?: The Communication and Miscommunication of Emotion by Email", *Academy of Management Review*, Vol. 33 No. 2, pp. 309–327.

Coyne, I., Farley, S., Axtell, C., Sprigg, C., Best, L., & Kwok, O. (2017), "Understanding the relationship between experiencing workplace cyberbullying, employee mental strain and job satisfaction: A dysempowerment approach", *The International Journal of Human Resource Management*, Vol. 28 No. 7, pp. 945–972.

Dabbish, L.A., & Kraut, R.E. (2006), "Email overload at work: an analysis of factors associated with email strain", *Proceedings of the 2006 20th Anniversary Conference on Computer Supported Cooperative Work*, ACM, Banff, Alberta, Canada, pp. 431–440.

Delanoeije, J., Verbruggen, M., & Germeys, L. (2019), "Boundary role transitions: A day-to-day approach to explain the effects of home-based telework on work-to-home conflict and home-to-work conflict", *Human Relations*, Vol. 72 No. 12, pp. 1843–1868.

Dén-Nagy, I. (2014), "A double-edged sword?: A critical evaluation of the mobile phone in creating work–life balance", *New Technology, Work and Employment*, Vol. 29 No. 2, pp. 193–211.

Derks, D., van Duin, D., Tims, M., & Bakker, A.B. (2015), "Smartphone use and work-home interference: The moderating role of social norms and employee work engagement", *Journal of Occupational and Organizational Psychology*, Vol. 88 No. 1, pp. 155–177.

Dietzen, R. (2017), *Email Use 2017 – EMEA Report*, Adobe Systems Incorporated, available at: https://blogs.adobe.com/digitaleurope/files/2017/08/20170815_Email2017_EMEA_Report.pdf.

Ducheneaut, N., & Bellotti, V. (2001), "E-mail As Habitat: An Exploration of Embedded Personal Information Management", *Interactions*, Vol. 8 No. 5, pp. 30–38.

Farley, S., Coyne, I., Axtell, C., & Sprigg, C. (2016), "Design, development and validation of a workplace cyberbullying measure, the WCM", *Work & Stress*, Vol. 30 No. 4, pp. 293–317.

Freitag, C., Berners-Lee, M., Widdicks, K., Knowles, B., Blair, G.S., & Friday, A. (2021), "The real climate and transformative impact of ICT: A critique of estimates, trends, and regulations", *Patterns*, Vol. 2 No. 9, available at: https://doi.org/10.1016/j.patter.2021.100340.

Friedman, R.A., & Currall, S.C. (2003), "Conflict escalation: Dispute exacerbating elements of e-mail communication", *Human Relations*, Vol. 56 No. 11, pp. 1325–1347.

Giumetti, G.W., Hatfield, A.L., Scisco, J.L., Schroeder, A.N., Muth, E.R., & Kowalski, R.M. (2013), "What a rude e-mail! Examining the differential effects of incivility versus support on mood, energy, engagement, and performance in an online context", *Journal of Occupational Health Psychology*, Vol. 18 No. 3, pp. 297–309.

Giurge, L.M., & Bohns, V.K. (2021), "You don't need to answer right away!: Receivers overestimate how quickly senders expect responses to non-urgent work emails", *Organizational Behavior and Human Decision Processes*, Vol. 167, pp. 114–128.

Gupta, A., Sharda, R., & Greve, R.A. (2011), "You've got email!: Does it really matter to process emails now or later?", *Information Systems Frontiers*, Vol. 13 No. 5, pp. 637–653.

Hu, X., Santuzzi, A.M., & Barber, L.K. (2019), "Disconnecting to Detach: The Role of Impaired Recovery in Negative Consequences of Workplace Telepressure", *Revista de Psicología Del Trabajo y de Las Organizaciones*, Vol. 35 No. 1, pp. 9–15.

Jackson, T.W., Burgess, A., & Edwards, J. (2006), "A simple approach to improving email communication", *Communications of the ACM*, Vol. 49 No. 6, pp. 107–109.

Jung, Y., & Lyytinen, K. (2014), "Towards an ecological account of media choice: a case study on pluralistic reasoning while choosing email", *Information Systems Journal*, Vol. 24 No. 3, pp. 271–293.

Kalman, Y.M., & Ravid, G. (2015), "Filing, piling, and everything in between: The dynamics of E-mail inbox management", *Journal of the Association for Information Science and Technology*, Vol. 66 No. 12, pp. 2540–2552.

Karr-Wisniewski, P., & Lu, Y. (2010), "When more is too much: Operationalizing technology overload and exploring its impact on knowledge worker productivity", *Computers in Human Behavior*, Vol. 26 No. 5, pp. 1061–1072.

Kong, R., Zhu, H., & Konstan, J.A. (2021), "Learning to Ignore: A Case Study of Organization-Wide Bulk Email Effectiveness", *Proceedings of the ACM on Human-Computer Interaction*, Vol. 5 No. CSCW1, pp. 80:1–80:23.

Kruger, J., Epley, N., Parker, J., & Ng, Z.-W. (2005), "Egocentrism over e-mail: Can we communicate as well as we think?", *Journal of Personality and Social Psychology*, Vol. 89 No. 6, pp. 925–936.

Leonardi, P.M., Treem, J.W., & Jackson, M.H. (2010), "The connectivity paradox: Using technology to both decrease and increase perceptions of distance in distributed work arrangements", *Journal of Applied Communication Research*, Vol. 38 No. 1, pp. 85–105.

Lim, V.K.G., & Teo, T.S.H. (2009), "Mind your E-manners: Impact of cyber incivility on employees' work attitude and behavior", *Information & Management*, Vol. 46 No. 8, pp. 419–425.

Mano, R.S., & Mesch, G.S. (2010), "E-mail characteristics, work performance and distress", *Computers in Human Behavior*, Vol. 26 No. 1, pp. 61–69.

Mark, G., Voida, S., & Cardello, A. (2012), "A pace not dictated by electrons: an empirical study of work without email", *Proceedings of the SIGCHI Conference on Human Factors in Computing Systems*, ACM, pp. 555–564.

Marulanda-Carter, L., & Jackson, T.W. (2012), "Effects of e-mail addiction and interruptions on employees", *Journal of Systems and Information Technology*, Vol. 14 No. 1, pp. 82–94.

Masanet, E., Shehabi, A., Lei, N., Smith, S., & Koomey, J. (2020), "Recalibrating global data center energy-use estimates", *Science*, Vol. 367 No. 6481, pp. 984–986.

Mazmanian, M., Orlikowski, W.J., & Yates, J. (2005), "Crackberries: The social implications of ubiquitous wireless e-mail devices", in Sørensen, C., Yoo, Y., Lyytinen, K. & DeGross, J. (Eds.), *Designing Ubiquitous Information Environments: Socio-Technical Issues and Challenges*, Springer, New York, pp. 337–343.

McDonnell, T. (2020), "Don't worry about the carbon footprint of your emails", *Quartz*, 25 November, available at: https://qz.com/1937309/dont-worry-about-the-carbon-footprint-of-your-emails (accessed 30 July 2022).

Pillet, J.-C., & Carillo, K.D.A. (2016), "Email-free collaboration: An exploratory study on the formation of new work habits among knowledge workers", *International Journal of Information Management*, Vol. 36 No. 1, pp. 113–125.

Radicati. (2021), *Email Statistics Report, 2021–2025*, The Radicati Group, Inc., available at: https://www.radicati.com/?p=17209.

Renaud, K., Ramsay, J., & Hair, M. (2006), "'You've Got E-Mail!' … Shall I Deal With It Now?: Electronic Mail from the Recipient's Perspective", *International Journal of Human-Computer Interaction*, Vol. 21 No. 3, pp. 313–332.

Robertson, R.E., Olteanu, A., Diaz, F., Shokouhi, M., & Bailey, P. (2021), "'I Can't Reply with That': Characterizing Problematic Email Reply Suggestions", *Proceedings of the 2021 CHI Conference on Human Factors in Computing Systems*, Association for Computing Machinery, New York, pp. 1–18.

Romm, C.T., & Pliskin, N. (1999), "The office tyrant: Social control through e-mail", *Information Technology & People*, Vol. 12 No. 1, pp. 27–43.

Samuel, H. (2018), "British firm ordered to pay €60,000 by French court for breaching employee's 'right to disconnect' from work", *The Telegraph*, 1 August, available at: https://www.telegraph.co.uk/news/2018/08/01/british-firm-ordered-pay-60000-french-court-breaching-employees (accessed 29 January 2019).

Sobotta, N., & Hummel, M. (2015), "A Capacity Perspective on E-Mail Overload: How E-Mail Use Contributes to Information Overload", *System Sciences (HICSS), 2015 48th Hawaii International Conference On*, IEEE, pp. 692–701.

Soucek, R., & Moser, K. (2010), "Coping with information overload in email communication: Evaluation of a training intervention", *Computers in Human Behavior*, Vol. 26 No. 6, pp. 1458–1466.

Stich, J.-F., Tarafdar, M., Cooper, C.L., & Stacey, P. (2017), "Workplace stress from actual and desired computer-mediated communication use: A multi-method study", *New Technology, Work and Employment*, Vol. 32 No. 1, pp. 84–100.

Stich, J.-F., Tarafdar, M., Stacey, P.K., & Cooper, C.L. (2019), "Appraisal of Email Use as a Source of Workplace Stress: A Person-Environment Fit Approach", *Journal of the Association for Information Systems*, Vol. 20 No. 2, pp. 132–160.

Sumecki, D., Chipulu, M., & Ojiako, U. (2011), "Email overload: Exploring the moderating role of the perception of email as a 'business critical' tool", *International Journal of Information Management*, Vol. 31 No. 5, pp. 407–414.

Tarafdar, M., Cooper, C.L., & Stich, J.-F. (2019), "The technostress trifecta – techno eustress, techno distress and design: An agenda for research", *Information Systems Journal*, Vol. 29 No. 1, pp. 6–42.

Tarafdar, M., Wenninger, H., & Stich, J.-F. (2023), "Email Overload: Investigating Technology-fit Antecedents and Job-related Outcomes", *The Data Base for Advances in Information Systems*, Vol. 54 No. 2.

Taylor, H., Fieldman, G., & Altman, Y. (2008), "E-mail at work: A cause for concern?: The implications of the new communication technologies for health, well-being and productivity at work", *Journal of Organisational Transformation & Social Change*, Vol. 5 No. 2, pp. 159–173.

Taylor, H., Fieldman, G., & Lahlou, S. (2005), "The impact of a threatening e-mail reprimand on the recipient's blood pressure", *Journal of Managerial Psychology*, Vol. 20 No. 1, pp. 43–50.

Thomas, G.F., & King, C.L. (2006), "Reconceptualizing E-Mail Overload", *Journal of Business and Technical Communication*, Vol. 20 No. 3, pp. 252–287.

Turnage, A.K. (2007), "Email Flaming Behaviors and Organizational Conflict", *Journal of Computer-Mediated Communication*, Vol. 13 No. 1, pp. 43–59.

Waller, A.D., & Ragsdell, G. (2012), "The impact of e-mail on work-life balance", *Aslib Proceedings*, Vol. 64 No. 2, pp. 154–177.

Wijngaards, I., Pronk, F.R., & Burger, M.J. (2022), "For whom and under what circumstances does email message batching work?", *Internet Interventions*, Vol. 27, 100494.

Wright, K.B., Abendschein, B., Wombacher, K., O'Connor, M., Hoffman, M., Dempsey, M., Krull, C., et al. (2014), "Work-Related Communication Technology Use Outside of Regular Work Hours and Work Life Conflict: The Influence of Communication Technologies on Perceived Work Life Conflict, Burnout, Job Satisfaction, and Turnover Intentions", *Management Communication Quarterly*, Vol. 28 No. 4, pp. 507–530.

Xie, J., Ma, H., Zhou, Z.E., & Tang, H. (2018), "Work-related use of information and communication technologies after hours (W_ICTs) and emotional exhaustion: A mediated moderation model", *Computers in Human Behavior*, Vol. 79, pp. 94–104.

11 Humor Awareness as a Primary Prevention Resource in Organizations for Sustainable Development

*Georgia Marunic, Chloe Lau, Willibald Ruch,
Annamaria Di Fabio and Donald H. Saklofske*

Introduction

Humor in the workplace is considered by employees to be a significant aspect of organizational life, the part that "gets you through the day" (Robert, 2017). After surveying 100 working adults, Robert comments that "given the strength and depth of people's feelings about humor in the workplace, it seems ironic that humor in the organizational environment has received very little attention in the research literature" (par. 8) and notes the paucity of psychological research on organizational humor. However, sustainability within organizations is an important component of today's society that is constantly mutating, and the latest environmental and geopolitical crises have brought critical issues to light in all aspects of our community (Di Fabio, 2017). Modern organizations face many challenges to remain competitive in the market that have a direct impact on the professional lives of employees, who find themselves working in an increasingly stressful and demanding environment (Di Fabio, 2017). The importance of a positive environment and positive individual resources in promoting organizational and individual well-being is emphasized (Di Fabio & Peiró, 2018; Peiró et al., 2020) and considered in the current research area of the psychology of sustainability and sustainable development (Di Fabio & Rosen, 2018, 2020). As strength-based prevention, humor can be considered a preventive resource (Di Fabio & Duradoni, 2020; Di Fabio et al., 2019).

In current psychological research, humor is considered a multifaceted construct that involves both cognitive and emotional elements (Ruch, 2008). Although most humor presupposes an interaction between individuals, it can be purely intrapsychic (e.g., comical perception of life events) and both a state (experiencing amusement) and/or a trait (having a sense of humor). Humor does not equate only to the appreciation or comprehension of jokes. Ruch (1998) points out that humor has been studied for over 100 years from various perspectives and in different cultures and, therefore, the understanding of what humor is can differ considerably. In the current international humor literature, humor is used as an umbrella term, albeit in different countries other umbrella terms exist. It is therefore important to think about humor as a

DOI: 10.4324/9781003212157-14

neutral term incorporating all kinds of comical phenomena, materials, and personalities.

Using a trait-based psychological framework, humor is described as the cognition, behaviors, and affect that constitute amusement, mirth, and exhilaration experienced by the individual and expressed to the surrounding environment (Ruch et al., 1996; Ruch, 1997; Ruch & Hofmann, 2012). More specifically, the sense of humor can be expressed as a style, representing an individual's typical behavior (e.g., cheerfulness, predominant mood, aesthetic perception). Humor can also be expressed as maximal behavior (i.e., humor creativity, humor production), which characterizes the skill or competence to produce humorous remarks that can be measured as quantity (e.g., number of jokes) or quality (i.e., strong agreement content is funny, creative, and witty; Brodzinsky & Rubien, 1976; Ruch & Heintz, 2019a; Ruch & Hofmann, 2012). The quantitative component is seen as a continuum from low to high frequency, while the qualitative component recognizes that "humor might have a different tone (comic tonality), flavor (just as people have different tastes), form, type, distinctive quality, or style" (Ruch, Heintz, et al., 2018, p. 2). Considering the intersection between these two components, humor qualities can be very specific and represent a narrow field of behavior (e.g., teasing), or they can be very general and cover a wide range of behavior (e.g., socially warm humor). When the level of abstraction is low, the humor attribute approximates a specific behavior manifested in a situation. Conversely, when the level of abstraction is high, the humor attribute refers more to a general behavioral disposition (Ruch, 2008; Ruch et al., 2018a).

So far, several approaches have addressed the classification of humor styles: Craik et al. (1996) distinguish ten humor styles; Martin et al., (2003) four; and Ruch, Heintz, et al. (2018) eight comic styles. When Ruch and Heintz (2019b) conducted a hierarchical factor analysis on five bipolar dimensions, they found six common factors of entertaining, canned, reflective/benign, inept, laughter, and mean-spirited/earthy. While Mesmer-Magnus and colleagues (2012) offered that researchers tend to agree that a sense of humor, regardless of style, is a stable personality trait, its dimensions are not necessarily mutually exclusive, and they can operate simultaneously.

To further investigate the conceptualization of humor as a trait, Samson and Ruch (2008) investigated 23 humor-related constructs and qualities (e.g., merry/funny, ingenious/witty, imaginative, absurd) and found that two dimensions of affect ("cute" vs. "macabre") and cognition (e.g., "funny" vs. "sophisticated") accounted for all 23 qualities (as cited in Ruch, 2008). Possessing humorous qualities has been found to be beneficial in producing positive outcomes in many aspects of the human experience, including acquiring mating success, intelligence, positive self-image, decreased distress in illness, and greater self-efficacy in the workplace (Abel, 1998; Carver et al., 1993; Geisler & Weber, 2010; Greengross & Miller, 2011). Although it appears intuitive that not all uses of humor are beneficial (e.g., workplace bullying), little research has investigated the effects of mockery and mean-spirited humor in the workplace (Mesmer-Magnus et al., 2012). Ruch and Stahlmann (2020) noted that gelotophobia, the fear of being laughed at, is associated with decreased job satisfaction, increased work stress, and workplace bullying. Gelotophobia was associated with less access to resources and more stressors (Hofmann et al., 2017). Indeed, gelotophobia amongst workers may be associated with greater social withdrawal and avoidance to deter any potential of being ridiculed (Ruch & Stahlmann, 2020). Although the research is scarce, gelotophobia research may be an area of need for organizational researchers.

Humor at the Workplace

Organizational psychology often focused on studying the use of humor at work perceived as successful. Successful humor in the workplace may be conceptualized as humorous, amusing, and cooperative interpersonal communication (Cooper, 2005; Holmes & Marra, 2002; Lynch, 2002; Robert & Yan, 2007). Cooper (2005) adds to this the act of intentionality, whose function is not amusement itself, but the intention to amuse the target of the interaction. Later, Romero and Cruthirds (2006) expand on this positive conceptualization by better specifying the target and point out that "organizational humor consists of amusing communications that produce positive emotions and cognitions in the individual, group, or organization" (p. 59). Eventually, humor may be operationalized as an intentional act expressed or communicated by the emitter to the receiver (at the individual, group, or organizational level), whose interaction includes both affective and cognitive aspects (Dikkers et al., 2012). These interactions can take place at different social levels, for example, at the individual and group or organizational levels. The former is represented by employees and managers characterized by their sense of humor. The latter by the work group's use of humor and the humor culture that characterizes the organization. This chapter will follow this division to illustrate the role of humor on an individual and group/organizational level. Clearly, there is no neat boundary between levels and the interactions that have repercussions at the organizational level.

Before discussing the effects that the use of humor at work can have at different organizational levels, a preliminary note should be made. Some research has been built on the approach proposed by Martin et al. (2003), who subdivided four humor styles into two benign (i.e., affiliative, self-enhancing) and two deleterious/harmful (i.e., aggressive, self-defeating) styles. The first two are considered lighter, and the latter two are darker humor styles. However, these four styles do not grant for a finer differentiation between them, and it is precisely this that would allow discussing how different styles can be "used" and, thus, modified and trained (Ruch, Hoffman, et al., 2018). In addition, most of this research was conducted using the Humor Styles Questionnaire (HSQ; Martin et al., 2003), but there are serious limitations with the measure (for full review see Heintz, 2017; Heintz & Ruch, 2015,

2016, 2018; Ruch & Heintz, 2013). Ruch & Heintz (2013) concluded that there was low incremental validity of humor styles in predicting psychological well-being beyond broad personality traits. The content of the HSQ also included non-humorous components that largely overlap their humor-specific content (Ruch & Heintz, 2013). In further exploring the item content, Ruch and Heintz (2017) found mixed findings for the construct validity of the self-enhancing and aggressive humor scales and no support for the self-defeating humor scale. The scale also failed to cover all aspects of humorous personality traits. Heintz (2017) revealed seven dimensions of humor, including cheerful, witty, deriding, amused, sarcastic, self-directed, and canned. Of these dimensions, cheerful, amused, and self-directed humor behaviors are positively associated with subjective well-being even when humor styles were controlled for (Heintz, 2017). Hence, recent research has shifted to evaluating light forms of humor (e.g., fun, benevolent humor, nonsense) and mockery styles of humor, like irony, sarcasm, and cynicism (Hofmann et al., 2020). Therefore, readers should interpret findings using the HSQ with caution given recent research on its limitations. In addition, most cross-sectional survey research precludes any conclusive evidence for causal relationships between variables.

Individual Level

Individual employees' humor styles differ and interact with one another (Feng et al., 2014; Marinkovic et al., 2011; Shibata et al., 2017). Many studies have focused on the effects that humor at work can have on individuals by assessing personal and work-related outcomes, such as perceived well-being, general health, self-efficacy, sense of belonging, stress levels, coping abilities, burnout, performance rates, job satisfaction, and many other psychological phenomena (for a detailed review, see Mesmer-Magnus et al., 2012). With a few exceptions, these empirical studies provided evidence that benign/lighter humor styles were associated with positive outcomes, while darker humor and mockery correlated with negative outcomes (Dikkers et al., 2012). Hence, individual differences in humor may influence employee wellness. Specific humor traits may facilitate or impede the stress-moderating effects in the workplace (Wisse & Rietzschel, 2014). Kuiper and Harris (2009) found that humor styles were associated with different coping strategies, while other important psychological variables related to well-being, such as negative affect, were unrelated to coping strategies. In particular, self-enhancing humor was associated with effective coping strategies (e.g., changing perspective, planning), while aggressive humor was correlated with greater denial and less flexibility in a perspective shift when coping with stressors. Specific humor styles also mediated the link between vulnerability factors related to negative biases in depressive cognitive patterns. Self-enhancing humor is associated with greater cognitive reappraisal, which is associated with mitigating psychological distress (Fritz et al., 2017). Benign humor styles were also associated with decreased harmful schema domains, low mood, and cognitive distortions (Dozois et al., 2009; Rnic et al., 2016). Cognitive distortions, rumination, and harmful schemas were associated with reduced use of self-enhancing humor and greater use of self-defeating humor, which correlated with greater levels of depression (Dozois et al., 2009; Olson et al., 2005; Rnic et al., 2016).

Benign humor styles were related to improved social relationships in the workplace. Dyck and Holtzman (2013) found social support fully mediated the association between affiliative humor and depression, which may explain the benefits of affiliative humor with coping. Cheung and Yue (2012) found that affiliative humor, but not self-enhancing humor, interacted with acculturative stress (i.e., language hassles, relational hassles, and cultural hassles), which was associated with depressed mood, but not life satisfaction. Affiliative humor may be associated with better stress-moderating effects, as interpersonal relationships become increasingly important for students moving to a new place (Cheung & Yue, 2012). Di Fabio and Duradoni (2020) found that self-enhancing humor mediated the relationship between emotionality and resistance to change (inverse relationship), whereas affiliative humor mediated the relationship between extraversion and resistance to change (inverse relationship). These findings may extend to the workplace, where benign humor styles facilitate better coping through differential mechanisms.

Humor influences how we perceive others, and workplace situations are no exception. Revealing a sense of humor may be beneficial in the workplace. Finkelstein and colleagues (2017) studied how humor may influence one's perception of others' traits and qualities within the work environment. Their studies focused on impression-formation theories. In particular, humor may create a Halo effect, the style and use of humor could "color" the perception of others when the first impression is formed. People revert to heuristics to position the new information within a more structured framework. Thus, Finkelstein and colleagues postulated, based on Implicit Personality Theories (IPT; Schneider, 1973, as cited in Finkelstein et al., 2017), that

> people develop their own idiosyncratic theories of what qualities go together in people, but because these theories develop over time and experiences within shared contexts (e.g., co-workers have similar experiences with leaders), this gives rise to the typical commonalities that exist across perceivers' theories.
>
> (par. 12)

Furthermore, when a person is of particular importance/interest to another (e.g., when evaluating a candidate for a new position), they tend to pay special attention to even the smallest details (Scholer & Higgins, 2008). Thus, the Halo effect of humor, passing from IPT, may affect the image one creates in a positive or negative manner. To form an overall opinion of a person, people look for indicators of qualities that are of particular interest to them (Finkelstein et al., 2017). In this respect, benign humor styles may have psychosocial benefits beyond individual cognitive and affective shift (Kuiper et al., 2014). When affiliative and self-enhancing humorous comments from a casual acquaintance were presented to unacquainted judges, judges revealed more positive ratings and less social rejection of the acquaintance (Kuiper et al., 2014). Conversely, an aggressive humor style is correlated with a negative evaluation of people, who are seen as pessimistic, introverted, and prone to complaining (Cann & Matson, 2014; Dikkers et al., 2012; Zeigler-Hill et al., 2013). Individuals revealing higher levels of self-defeating and aggressive humor may be perceived less favorably compared to individuals engaging in benign humor styles (Kuiper, Kirsh et al., 2010; Zeigler-Hill et al., 2013). In the workplace, self-defeating humor may provide denial and escape for underlying negative feelings, while aggressive humor allows one to gain power or demonstrate superiority within a social interaction (Martin et al., 2003). Indeed, disinhibition was positively associated with aggressive humor, and self-defeating humor style and antagonism were positively associated with the aggressive humor style (Zeigler-Hill et al., 2016). Sufficiently confident people might use humor at crucial moments during selection or integration into a new workplace to convey a positive or negative self-image. Otherwise, if one is not confident in one's humor abilities, it might be wise to rely on other qualities to make a good first impression (Finkelstein et al., 2017).

A leader's sense of humor uses the same mechanisms and influences the same aspects of humor as that of the employees (Mesmer-Magnus et al., 2012). However, the role and position of managers within an organization bring humor to operate in some other ways too. Although there is a rich body of work that has examined the topic of humor and leadership, most of the work uses humor styles (Cooper & Sosik, 2012; Kong et al., 2019; Mesmer-Magnus et al., 2012; Robert & Wilbanks, 2012; Romero & Cruthirds, 2006; Rosenberg et al., 2021). Mild aggressive humor styles (e.g., mocking or joking about others' weaknesses) have been studied predominantly in the military and sports contexts and correlated with the achievement of behavioral compliance (Dwyer, 1991). Self-enhancing humor in leaders has been shown to be useful if one wants to make a good impression or attract superiors' attention (Romero & Cruthirds, 2006). However, in an organizational context, a leader's decisions and actions may directly influence the performance determinants and other situational variables that will affect his/her co-workers' and organizational effectiveness. Given the influence that a leader could assume within the organization, several researchers have considered recourse to the aforementioned styles as inappropriate (Larsson & Vinberg, 2010; Liden & Antonakis, 2009). Indeed, most of the research in this area has focused on the use of benign humor as aspects, in the organizational sphere, that could prove the promoters of progress are of greater interest.

The results of those studies link a leader's positive use of humor to increased employee satisfaction and commitment (Burford, 1987; Decker, 1987; Mao et al., 2017), reduced social distance between supervisors and subordinates, enhanced employee creativity (Zhang et al., 2022), and increased work group cohesion (Holmes & Marra, 2006; Romero &

Cruthirds, 2006). Benign humor may facilitate learning and organizational change (Vetter & Gockel, 2016) by promoting greater creativity (Lang & Lee, 2010; Thorson & Powell, 1993; Yang, 2021; Zhang et al., 2022) and increasing performance at the individual and group level (Avolio et al., 1999; de Souza et al., 2019; Romero & Cruthirds, 2006). Furthermore, leaders who can effectively harness humor may more easily inspire a sense of trust, boost organizational acceptance, and enhance the endorsement of shared values (Hampes, 1999; Hughes & Avey, 2009; Neves & Karagonlar, 2020). As leaders' actions must ensure the company's effectiveness and achievement of strategic goals by shaping the attitudes and behaviors of their employees, the use of humor could be one of the successful tactics to achieve compliance and increase job performance claims (Rosenberg et al., 2021).

To promote leadership effectiveness, it is also necessary to consider that humor can be trained. In this regard, research results have brought to light evidence that employees react better to a leader's humor expression (using humor appropriately concerning circumstances) than to a leader's humor trait (Kong et al., 2019). Both humorous and non-humorous people benefit from humor interventions (Wellenzohn et al., 2018). Being able to make avail of specific training programs could be a relatively simple and inexpensive means to promote the use of humor in organizational environments and lead to a series of short- and long-term benefits on all levels (individual, group, and organizational).

Group/Organizational Level

"Humor is not an isolated event, but a shared social experience that unfolds during interactions between individuals, often in groups and teams" (Crowe et al., 2016, par. 31). How humor is perceived in an organization largely depends on individual differences. For instance, employees with a fear of being laughed at are generally less satisfied with work and experience more work stress (Hofmann et al., 2017). Moreover, the joy of laughing at oneself is associated with positive evaluations of one's life and work, while the joy of laughing at others is negatively related to work satisfaction (Hofmann et al., 2017). Thus, the outcomes of making jokes may largely depend on how receptive the receivers are to those jokes.

All activities within an organization comprise continuous interactions between its employees and within teams they form. Team members should be aligned by a shared vision and act together to reach desired goals (Senge, 1990, as cited in Yeager & Nafukho, 2012). Some factors have particular weight for these to be achieved (e.g., task management and reduction of work-related stress, perceived social support, and appreciation of different cultural backgrounds).

Humor may help an organization and its members to share the same vision and act together. One mechanism may be through burnout and emotional exhaustion from work commonly contributing to stress. Miczo (2004) found that a sense of humor was associated with a greater willingness to communicate, which led to lower perceived stress. Oktug (2017) also reported that self-enhancing and self-defeating humor moderated the positive and negative association, respectively, between job stress and emotional exhaustion. Ho (2016) found in a sample of primary and secondary school teachers in Hong Kong that affiliative and self-enhancing humor correlated with decreased emotional exhaustion and depersonalization, and this association was mediated through increased perceived social support. These findings suggest the possible beneficial effects of using humor in the workplace in alleviating stress. However, these outcomes may depend on the organizational culture. Humor may compensate for the lack of certain organizational cultural aspects, such as inclusiveness and mutual support among colleagues. In a large sample of Belgium employees, Van den Broeck and colleagues (2012) found that affiliative and self-enhancing humor styles were both negatively associated with burnout. However, these humor styles did not enhance positive qualities in the workplace, but they compensated for lower social support at work. Specifically, benign humor styles did not interact with individual dispositions (i.e., role conflict, social support) in the prediction of burnout. In sum, Van den Broeck et al. (2012) argued that while self-enhancing and affiliative humor may compensate for a lack of social support in the workplace, these traits may not uplift an individual for more positive outcomes under high stress. These findings aligned with Freeman and Ventis's (2010) study, which proposed self-enhancing humor was only adaptive under low stress. Similarly, under high stress, higher self-defeating and aggressive humor scores were associated with optimal health outcomes (Freeman & Ventis, 2010). Thus, the benefits of specific humor styles may depend on the characteristics of the employees, stress levels, and the tasks they are dealing with.

The positive effects humor may produce at the individual level extend among co-workers and may lead to a cascade of beneficial outcomes (e.g., a calmer working climate is fostered, a sense of well-being, cohesion, and cooperation among team members increases) which ultimately may lead to better team job performance (Gully et al., 1995, as cited in Crowe et al., 2016). Empirical research shows team effectiveness can rise because humor improves a group's productivity, learning, and viability (Romero & Pescosolido, 2008). Humor in work groups leads to a faster inclusion of newly arrived employees, strengthened interpersonal relationships, and stronger team bonds (Cooper, 2008; Heidari et al, 2016; Heiss & Carmack, 2012). In addition, employees may communicate more effectively (Romero & Cruthirds, 2006), raise openness to constructive feedback (Karakowsky et al., 2020; Mesmer-Magnus, 2012), increase trust within team members (Hampes, 1999; Romero & Pescosolido, 2008), and facilitate the shaping of group identity (Weick & Westley, 1996). Some researchers consider humor as a "social lubricant" that helps in sharing social experiences (Romero, 2005).

Numerous empirical findings have shown how humor in the workplace is linked to better team performance (Avolio et al., 1999; Lehmann-Willenbrock

& Allen, 2014; Mesmer-Magnus et al., 2012; Romero & Pescosolido, 2008) and how it contributes to developing a positive organizational culture (Clouse & Spurgeon, 1995; Gunning, 2001; Heidari et al., 2016). Humor may not always act as a social lubricant because an amusing message may not necessarily be perceived as such. Personal and cultural differences among team members may create barriers to team cohesion and performance (Yeager & Nafukho, 2012). For a team to be effective, a certain degree of mutual understanding among members is essential. The role of the shared organizational culture is to help this process. Crowe et al. (2016) propose that work meetings represent the ideal situation for spreading organizational culture. During meetings, there can always be a moment dedicated to humor, one can share an "inside" joke or lighten a difficult situation with one. As a result of their research, the authors emphasize the presence of behavioral patterns in such situations, pointing out that following a light moment, team members tend to return to their work agenda, summarize the work done, and proceed with constructive suggestions.

Promotion of Humor within Organizations

How does one recognize whether a joke is appropriate in the workplace? While the trait humor literature provides a comprehensive overview of the nature of a humorous personality in the workplace, other theories point to how to discern the appropriateness of a message. The benign violation theory posits that humor assists with coping through allowing psychological distance to the threat while transforming a tragedy (violation) related or unrelated to an individual into comedy (benign violation; McGraw & Warren, 2010; McGraw et al., 2012; McGraw et al., 2014). McGraw and colleagues (2010, 2012, 2014) found evidence across multiple studies that psychological distance from a threat transformed a violation (e.g., an unpleasant incident) into a benign violation (i.e., a joke). Hence, the threat is not so close that it produces psychological harm, but also not too distant, which makes the threat within the joke uninteresting. These studies suggest that a tragic event is difficult to joke about at first, but the passage of time creates a "sweet spot," until the event becomes less threatening (McGraw et al., 2010, 2012, 2014). Moreover, these findings explain individual differences in commitment to a norm and psychological distance to particular tragedies (i.e., severe violations) and mishaps (mild violations) facilitate laughter and amusement in the workplace for some individuals, whereas others view a humorous approach to certain topics as undesirable and inappropriate (McGraw et al., 2010, 2012, 2014). Evidence from the benign violation theory demonstrates how individuals perceive and process humor at work.

Promoting humor in the workplace may also be effective regardless of individual difference variables. Geisler and Weber (2010) found that individuals randomized in a humor condition (i.e., involving violation and normal appraisal) increased positive affect and produced more external attribution of failure compared to the control condition. Likewise, Samson and Gross (2012) investigated actual uses of benign and harmful humor when put into the experimental context through instruction to use benign humor (e.g., sympathetic, tolerant, benevolent) or harmful humor (e.g., mocking). Individuals using benign humor achieved regulation of positive emotion compared to those instructed to use harmful humor after experiencing a stressor (Samson & Gross, 2012). Moreover, participants in the benign humor condition were also more successful at down-regulating negative emotions and up-regulating positive emotions, which supports findings from the trait differences literature on the benefits of promoting benign humor (Samson & Gross, 2012). Samson and colleagues (2014) later extended the study to find long-term benefits, as participants who used humorous coping (i.e., defined as a humorous appraisal of negative stimuli) were able to continue to down-regulate negative emotions in the long-term compared to those instructed to use serious appraisal. These results suggest benefits to humor beyond simple distraction and requiring greater cognitive demand (Samson et al., 2014). Organizations that encourage a humorous approach may experience these aforementioned benefits in employee well-being.

Future Directions

Although most workplace humor investigations assessed humor using the humor styles questionnaire, the criterion validity of the humor styles has been largely questioned (Heintz, 2017; Heintz & Ruch, 2015, 2016, 2018). Specifically, the limitations of the humor styles questionnaire include small effects for well-being when broader personality traits were controlled for, non-humorous components impacting the perception of the items, and lack of convergence between the conceptualization of humor styles. Heintz and Ruch (2015, p. 611) suggested "that either the constructs and model of the humor styles need to be adjusted or newly developed, or the HSQ does." Findings across these studies should be replicated using other newly developed measures of humor with stronger psychometric properties (Hofmann et al., 2017). Most assessment tools and theories on humor were developed in the Western world and then simply adapted into other languages. Instead, it would be desirable to develop the tools from the bottom up or at least rely on the use of those that pay more attention to different possible facets of humor to ensure a more accurate study of the construct. Current findings should be interpreted with caution given the limitations of the HSQ used in most organizational humor studies, and future studies should replicate findings with other newly developed, reliable, and valid humor measurement scales. For future researchers interested in conducting humor research in organizations, a growing number of theoretical models and validated measures demonstrating strong psychometric properties have been documented for theoretically and empirically distinguishable humor attributes. Ruch and Proyer (2009) proposed three dispositions toward ridicule and laughter, including gelotophobia (i.e., the fear of being laughed at), gelotophilia (i.e., the joy of being laughed at), and katagelasticism (i.e., the joy of laughing at others). These dispositions are commonly measured using the self-report instrument named PhoPhiKat-45, which is short for the phobia (i.e., fear of being laughed at), philia (i.e., love of being laughed at), and katagelasticism (for long version see Ruch & Proyer, 2009; for short version see Hofmann et al., 2017). Ruch, Heintz, and colleagues (2018) have also conceptualized eight individual difference factors of comic styles, including fun, humor, nonsense, wit, irony, satire, sarcasm, and cynicism. These markers can be characterized by laughing with another (e.g., lighter styles of fun, benevolent, nonsense), laughing at others (e.g., sarcasm, cynicism), and mixed styles (e.g., wit, irony, satire), which are associated with differential personality, intelligence, and character strengths. The self-report measure Comic Styles Markers questionnaire has been developed to measure these eight comic styles (Ruch, Heintz, et al., 2018). Humor attributes may also be conceptualized more globally as benevolent or corrective. Benevolent humor defines using humor to treat human weaknesses and wrongdoings compassionately, while corrective humor aims at bettering human weaknesses using humor as temperament and virtue (Heintz et al., 2018, 2019; Ruch & Heintz, 2016). The BENCOR measure assesses benevolent and corrective humor that have demonstrated strong reliability and validity across 25 samples in 22 countries (Heintz et al., 2018, 2019). To encourage humor training, McGhee (2010) has proposed six humor skill factors – enjoyment of humor, laughter, verbal humor, finding humor in everyday life, laughing at yourself, and humor under stress – that can be trained. The Sense of Humor Parallel Version has been developed to promote the assessment of the efficacy of humor-skills training (Heintz et al., 2022). These novel theoretical conceptualizations of individual differences in humor may be extended to future studies on organizational humor.

In addition to encouraging positive humor interactions, organizations may explore how, where, and when to encourage them when looking at cultural factors. Understanding similarities and differences in humor appreciation, comprehension, and production between collectivist and individualist cultures is essential to foster healthy relationships in modern multinational organizations. Future research should investigate cross-cultural differences in humor within organizations to examine whether certain characteristics are culture dependent.

For instance, some studies that addressed these differences evidence how exposure to humorous comments can affect mood states differently between North American and Middle Eastern Lebanese participants (Kuiper et al., 2010). Chinese employees report lower levels of humor than Australian employees (Wang et al., 2018). Similarly, Wu and Chan (2013) also found that Chinese participants reported less use of humor in coping with stress than their Canadian counterparts. Indeed, humor in Chinese culture may have specific functions that differ from individualistic cultures (Lo & Yue, 2017).

Future research should also focus on studying interventions to promote a more open and psychologically safer culture to foster an environment in which playful and positive forms of humor can be used successfully.

Conclusions

This chapter aimed to present how humor, employed in the workplace, can influence a person's career path, the dynamics it triggers in relationships with colleagues, and the effects it can produce at the organizational level. Going back to the remarks of Robert (2017), perhaps the body of research on the topic is still limited, but the evidence is clear and speaks of numerous positive outcomes on all organizational levels. Findings have shown that humor can operate as a moderator and mediator variable in the relationship between stress, mood, and well-being (León-Pérez et al., 2021; Martin & Lefcourt, 1983). Furthermore, there is evidence in support of humor as a behavioral component that can be trained (Kong et al., 2019). Over the years, several humor-based interventions have been proposed, achieving efficacy and effectiveness in different settings (Baisley & Grunberg, 2019; Bartzik et al., 2021; Ruch & McGhee, 2014; Ruch, Hoffman, et al., 2018; Wellenzohn et al., 2016, 2018). However, few studies have addressed humor-based interventions in organizational settings (León-Pérez et al., 2021). Future research should approach the topic from a multidimensional perspective, thinking about agile, easy-to-propose plans within the organizational context that benefit the individual and organization for sustainable development.

References

Abel, M. H. (1998). Interaction of humor and gender in moderating relationships between stress and outcomes. *The Journal of Psychology: Interdisciplinary and Applied*, 132(3), 267–276.

Avolio, B. J., Howell, J. M., & Sosik, J. J. (1999). A funny thing happened on the way to the bottom line: Humor as a moderator of leadership style effects. *Academy of Management Journal*, 42, 219–227.

Baisley, M. C., & Grunberg, N. E. (2019). Bringing humour theory into practice: An interdisciplinary approach to online humor training. *New Ideas in Psychology*, 55, 24–34. https://doi.org/10.1016/j.newideapsych.2019.04.006.

Bartzik, M., Bentrup, A., Hill, S., Bley, M., von Hirschhausen, E., Krause, G., Ahaus, P., Dahl-Dichmann, A., & Peifer, C. (2021). Care for joy: Evaluation of a humor intervention and its effects on stress, flow experience, work enjoyment, and meaningfulness of work. *Frontiers in Public Health*, 9, 667821. https://doi.org/10.3389/fpubh.2021.667821.

Brodzinsky, D. M., & Rubien, J. (1976). Humor production as a function of sex of subject, creativity, and cartoon content. *Journal of Consulting and Clinical Psychology*, 44(4), 597–600.

Burford, C. (1987). Humor of principals and its impact on teachers and the school. *Journal of Educational Administration*, 25(1), 29–54.

Cann, A., & Matson, C. (2014). Sense of humor and social desirability: Understanding how humor styles are perceived. *Personality and Individual Differences*, 66, 176–180. https://doi.org/10.1016/j.paid.2014.03.029.

Carver, C. S., Pozo, C., Harris, S. D., Noriega, V., Scheier, M. F., Robinson, D. S., Ketcham, A. S., Moffat, F. L., Jr., & Clark, K. C. (1993). How coping mediates the effect of optimism on distress: A study of women with early stage breast cancer. *Journal of Personality and Social Psychology*, 65(2), 375–390.

Cheung, C. K., & Yue, X. D. (2012). Sojourn students' humor styles as buffers to achieve resilience. *International Journal of Intercultural Relations*, 36(3), 353–364.

Clouse, R. W., & Spurgeon, K. L. (1995). Corporate analysis of humor. *Psychology: A Journal of Human Behavior*, 32, 1–24.

Cooper, C. (2005). Just joking around? Employee humor expression as an ingratiatory behavior. *Academy of Management Review*, 30(4), 765–776.

Cooper, C. (2008). Elucidating the bonds of workplace humor: A relational process model. *Human Relations*, 61(8), 1087–1115. https://doi.org/10.1177/0018726708094861.

Cooper, C. D., & Sosik, J. J. (2012). The laughter advantage: Cultivating high quality connections and workplace outcomes through humor. In G. M. Spreitzer & K. Cameron (Eds.), *The handbook of positive organizational scholarship* (pp. 474–489). Oxford University Press.

Craik, K. H., Lampert, M. D., & Nelson, A. J. (1996). Sense of humor and styles of everyday humorous conduct. *Humor*, 9(3–4), 273–302. https://doi.org/10.1515/humr.1996.9.3-4.273.

Crowe, J., Allen, J. A., & Lehmann-Willenbrock, N. (2016). Humor in workgroups and teams. In C. Robert (Ed.), *The Psychology of Humor at Work*, (pp. 108–120). Routledge.

Decker, W. H. (1987). Managerial humor and subordinate satisfaction. *Social Behavior and Personality: An International Journal*, 15(2), 225–232.

de Souza, A. M., Felix, B., de Andrade, A. M., & dos Santos Cerqueira, A. (2019). Humor at work: A study about the relationship between humor styles, satisfaction with management and individual job performance. *Revista de Administração da Universidade Federal de Santa Maria*, 12(4), 803–820.

Di Fabio, A. (2017). The psychology of sustainability and sustainable development for well-being in organizations. *Frontiers in Psychology*, 8, 1534. doi:10.3389/fpsyg.2017.01534.

Di Fabio, A., & Duradoni, M. (2020). Humor styles as new resources in a primary preventive perspective: Reducing resistance to change for negotiation. *International Journal of Environmental Research and Public Health*, 17(7), 2485. http://dx.doi.org/10.3390/ijerph17072485.

Di Fabio, A., & Peiró, J. M. (2018). Human Capital Sustainability Leadership to promote sustainable development and healthy organizations: A new scale. *Sustainability*, 10(7), 2413. https://doi.org/10.3390/su10072413.

Di Fabio, A., & Rosen, M. A. (2018). Opening the black box of psychological processes in the science of sustainable development: A new frontier. *European Journal of Sustainable Development Research*, 2(4), 47. https://doi.org/10.20897/ejosdr/3933.

Di Fabio, A., & Rosen, M. A. (2020). An exploratory study of a new psychological instrument for evaluating sustainability: The Sustainable Development Goals Psychological Inventory. *Sustainability*, 12, 7617. https://doi.org/10.3390/su12187617.

Di Fabio, A., Smith, M. M., & Saklofske, D. H. (2019). Perfectionism and a healthy attitude toward oneself: Could humor be a resource? *International Journal of Environmental Research and Public Health*, 17(1), 201. https://doi.org/10.3390/ijerph17010201.

Dikkers, J., Doosje, S., & De Lange, A. (2012). Humor as a human resource tool in organizations. *Contemporary Occupational Health Psychology: Global Perspectives on Research and Practice*, 2, 74–91.

Dozois, D. J. A., Martin, R. A., & Bieling, P. J. (2009). Early maladaptive schemas and adaptive/maladaptive styles of humor. *Cognitive Therapy and Research*, 33(6), 585–596.

Dwyer, T. (1991). Humor, power, and change in organizations. *Human Relations*, 44 (1), 1–19.

Dyck, K. T. H., & Holtzman, S. (2013). Understanding humor styles and well-being: The importance of social relationships and gender. *Personality and Individual Differences*, 55(1), 53–58. doi:10.1016/j.paid.2013.01.023.

Feng, Y. J., Chan, Y. C., & Chen, H. C. (2014). Specialization of neural mechanisms underlying the three-stage model in humor processing: An ERP study. *Journal of Neurolinguistics*, 32, 59–70.

Finkelstein, L. M., Cerrentano, C. A., & Voyles, E. C. (2017). Humor and person perception. In C. Robert (Ed.), *The Psychology of Humor at Work*, (pp. 28–45). Routledge.

Freeman, G. P., & Ventis, W. L. (2010). Does humor benefit health in retirement? Exploring humor as a moderator. *Europe's Journal of Psychology*, 6(3), 122–148.

Fritz, H. L., Russek, L. N., & Dillon, M. M. (2017). Humor use moderates the relation of stressful life events with psychological distress. *Personality and Social Psychology Bulletin*, 43(6), 845–859.

Geisler, F. C., & Weber, H. (2010). Harm that does not hurt: Humour in coping with self-threat. *Motivation and Emotion*, 34(4), 446–456.

Greengross, G., & Miller, G. (2011). Humor ability reveals intelligence, predicts mating success, and is higher in males. *Intelligence*, 39(4), 188–192.

Gunning, B. L. (2001). *The role that humor plays in shaping organizational culture.* [Doctoral dissertation, The University of Toledo]. https://etd.ohiolink.edu/apexprod/rws_etd/send_file/send?accession=toledo1101326392&disposition=attachment.

Hampes, W. P. (1999). The relationship between humor and trust. *Humor*, 12(3), 253–260. https://doi.org/10.1515/humr.1999.12.3.253.

Heidari, H., Khashei, V., & Maroufani Asl, M. (2016). Effect of humor on organizational culture and group cohesion. *Organizational Culture Management*, 14(1), 73–96.

Heintz, S. (2017). Putting a spotlight on daily humor behaviors: Dimensionality and relationships with personality, subjective well-being, and humor styles. *Personality and Individual Differences*, 104, 407–412.

Heintz, S., & Ruch, W. (2015). An examination of the convergence between the conceptualization and the measurement of humor styles: A study of the construct validity of the Humor Styles Questionnaire. *Humor*, 28(4), 611–633.

Heintz, S., & Ruch, W. (2016). Reply to Martin (2015): Why our conclusion hold. *Humor*, 29(1), 125–129.

Heintz, S., & Ruch, W. (2018). Can self-defeating humor make you happy? Cognitive interviews reveal the adaptive side of the self-defeating humor style. *Humor*, 31(3), 451–472.

Heintz, S., Ruch, W., Aykan, S., Brdar, I., Brzozowska, D., Carretero-Dios, H., Chen, H.-C., Chłopicki, W., Choi, I., Dionigi, A., Đurka, R., Ford, T. E., Güsewell, A., Isler, R. B., Ivanova, A., Laineste, L., Lajčiaková, P., Lau, C., Lee, … & Wong, P. S. O. (2019). Benevolent and corrective humor, life satisfaction, and broad humor dimensions: Extending the nomological network of the BenCor across 25 countries. *Journal of Happiness Studies*, 21, 2473–2492. https://doi.org/10.1007/s10902-019-00185-9.

Heintz, S., Ruch, W., Lau, C., Saklofske, D. H., & McGhee, P. (2022). Development and validation of the short version of the Sense of Humor Scale (SHS-S): Paving the way for assessment of humor skills training. *European Journal of Psychological Assessment*, 38(4), 320–331. https://doi.org/10.1027/1015-5759/a000670.

Heintz, S., Ruch, W., Platt, T., Pang, D., Carretero-Dios, H., Dionigi, A., Argüello Gutiér-rez, C., Brdar, I., Brzozowska, D., Chen, H-C., Chłopicki, W., Collins, M., Durka, R., Yahfoufi, N.Y.E., Quiroga-Garza, A., Isler, R.B., Mendiburo-Seguel, A., Ramis, T., Saglam, B., ... & Torres-Marín, J. (2018). Psychometric comparisons of benevolent and corrective humor across 22 countries: The virtue gap in humor goes international. *Frontiers in Psychology*, 9, 92. https://doi.org/10.3389/fpsyg.2018.00092.

Heiss, S. N., & Carmack, H. J. (2012). Knock, knock; Who's there?: Making sense of organizational entrance through humor. *Management Communication Quarterly*, 26 (1), 106–132.

Ho, S. K. (2016). Relationships among Humour, Self-Esteem, and Social Support to Burnout in School Teachers. *Social Psychology of Education: An International Journal*, 19(1), 41–59.

Hofmann, J., Heintz, S., Pang, D., & Ruch, W. (2020). Differential relationships of light and darker forms of humor with mindfulness. *Applied Research in Quality of Life*, 15(2), 369–393.

Hofmann, J., Ruch, W., Proyer, R. T., Platt, T., & Gander, F. (2017). Assessing dis-positions toward ridicule and laughter in the workplace: Adapting and validating the PhoPhiKat-9 questionnaire. *Frontiers in Psychology*, 8, 714. doi:10.3389/fpsyg.2017.00714.

Holmes, J., & Marra, M. (2002). Having a laugh at work: How humour contributes to workplace culture, *Journal of Pragmatics*, 34(2), 1683–1710.

Holmes, J., & Marra, M. (2006). Humor and leadership style. *Humor*, 19(2), 119–138. https://doi.org/10.1515/HUMOR.2006.006.

Hughes, L. W., & Avey, J. B. (2009). Transforming with levity: Humor, leadership, and follower attitudes. *Leadership & Organization Development Journal*, 30, 540–562. doi:10.1108/01437730910981926.

Karakowsky, L., Podolsky, M., & Elangovan, A. R. (2020). Signaling trustworthiness: The effect of leader humor on feedback-seeking behavior. *The Journal of Social Psychology*, 160(2), 170–189.

Kong, D. T., Cooper, C. D., & Sosik, J. J. (2019). The state of research on leader humor. *Organizational Psychology Review*, 9(1), 3–40. https://doi.org/10.1177/2041386619846948.

Kuiper, N. A., Aiken, A., & Pound, M. S. (2014). Humor use, reactions to social comments, and social anxiety. *Humor*, 27(3), 423–439.

Kuiper, N. A., & Harris, A. L. (2009). Humor styles and negative affect as predictors of different components of physical health. *Europe's Journal of Psychology*, 5(1). https://doi.org/10.5964/ejop.v5i1.280.

Kuiper, N. A., Kazarian, S. S., Sine, J., & Bassil, M. (2010). The impact of humor in North American versus Middle East cultures. *Europe's Journal of Psychology*, 6(3), 149–173. https://doi.org/10.5964/ejop.v6i3.212.

Kuiper, N. A., Kirsh, G. A., & Leite, C. (2010). Reactions to Humorous Comments and Implicit Theories of Humor Styles. *Europe's Journal of Psychology*, 6(3), 236–266. https://doi.org/10.5964/ejop.v6i3.215.

Lang, J. C., & Lee, C. H. (2010). Workplace humor and organizational creativity. *The International Journal of Human Resource Management*, 21(1), 46–60.

Larsson, J., & Vinberg, S. (2010). Leadership behaviour in successful organisations: Universal or situation-dependent? *Total Quality Management*, 21(3), 317–334.

Lehmann-Willenbrock, N., & Allen, J. A. (2014). How fun are your meetings? Investigating the relationship between humor patterns in team interactions and team performance. *Journal of Applied Psychology*, 99(6), 1278–1287. https://doi.org/10.1037/a0038083.

León-Pérez, J. M., Cantero-Sánchez, F. J., Fernández-Canseco, Á., & León-Rubio, J. M. (2021). Effectiveness of a humor-based training for reducing employees' distress. *International Journal of Environmental Research and Public Health*, 18(21), 11177. https://doi.org/10.3390/ijerph182111177.

Liden, R. C., & Antonakis, J. (2009). Considering context in psychological leadership research. *Human Relations*, 62(11), 1587–1605.

Lo, T.W., & Yue, X. (2017). *Humor and Chinese Culture: A Psychological Perspective.* Routledge. https://doi.org/10.4324/9781315412450.

Lynch, O. (2002), Humorous communication: finding a place for humor in communication research, *Communication Theory*, 12(4), 423–446.

Mao, J. Y., Chiang, J. T. J., Zhang, Y., & Gao, M. (2017). Humor as a relationship lubricant: The implications of leader humor on transformational leadership perceptions and team performance. *Journal of Leadership & Organizational Studies*, 24(4), 494–506.

Marinkovic, K., Baldwin, S., Courtney, M. G., Witzel, T., Dale, A. M., & Halgren, E. (2011). Right hemisphere has the last laugh: neural dynamics of joke appreciation. *Cognitive, Affective & Behavioral Neuroscience*, 11(1), 113–130.

Martin, R. A., & Lefcourt, H. M. (1983). Sense of humour as a moderator of the relation between stressors and moods. *Journal of Personality and Social Psychology*, 45(6), 1313–1324. https://doi.org/10.1037/0022-3514.45.6.1313.

Martin, R.A., Puhlik-Doris, P., Larsen, G., Gray, J., & Weir, K. (2003). Individual differences in uses of humor and their relation to psychological well-being: Development of the Humor Styles Questionnaire. *Journal of Research in Personality*, 37(1), 48–75.

McGhee, P. (2010). *Humor as survival training for a stressed-out world: The 7 humor habits program.* Author House.

McGraw, A. P., & Warren, C. (2010). Benign violations: Making immoral behavior funny. *Psychological Science*, 21(8), 1141–1149.

McGraw, A. P., Warren, C., Williams, L. E., & Leonard, B. (2012). Too close for comfort, or too far to care? Finding humor in distant tragedies and close mishaps. *Psychological Science*, 23(10), 1215–1223. https://doi.org/10.1177/0956797612443831.

McGraw, A. P., Williams, L. E., & Warren, C. (2014). The rise and fall of humor: Psychological distance modulates humorous responses to tragedy. *Social Psychological and Personality Science*, 5(5), 566–572.

Mesmer-Magnus, J., Glew, D.J., & Viswesvaran, C. (2012). A meta-analysis of positive humor in the workplace. *Journal of Managerial Psychology*, 27(2), 155–190. https://doi.org/10.1108/02683941211199554.

Miczo, N. (2004). Humor ability, unwillingness to communicate, loneliness, and perceived stress: Testing a security theory. *Communication Studies*, 55(2), 209–226.

Neves, P., & Karagonlar, G. (2020). Does leader humor style matter and to whom? *Journal of Managerial Psychology.* 35(2), 115–128. https://doi.org/10.1108/JMP-12-2018-0552.

Oktug, Z. (2017). The moderating role of employees' humor styles on the relationship between job stress and emotional exhaustion. *International Business Research*, 10(4), 131–138.

Olson, M. L., Hugelshofer, D. S., Kwon, P., & Reff, R. C. (2005). Rumination and dysphoria: The buffering role of adaptive forms of humor. *Personality and Individual Differences*, 39(8), 1419–1428.

Peiró, J. M., Bayona, J. A., Caballer, A., & Di Fabio, A. (2020). Importance of work characteristics affects job performance: The mediating role of individual dispositions on the work design-performance relationships. *Personality and Individual Differences*, 157, 109808. https://doi.org/10.1016/j.paid.2019.109808.

Rnic, K., Dozois, D. J. A., & Martin, R. A. (2016). Cognitive Distortions, Humor Styles, and Depression. *Europe's Journal of Psychology*, 12(3), 348–362.

Robert, C. (Ed.). (2017). *The psychology of humor at work*. Routledge.

Robert, C., & Wilbanks, J. E. (2012). The wheel model of humor: Humor events and affect in organizations. *Human Relations*, 65(9), 1071–1099.

Robert, C., & Yan, W. (2007). The case for developing new research on humor and culture in organizations: toward a higher grade of manure. In J. J. Martocchio (Ed.), *Research in Personnel and Human Resources Management* (vol. 26, pp. 205–267). Emerald Group Publishing Limited. https://doi.org/10.1016/S0742-7301(07)26005-0.

Romero, E., & Pescosolido, A. (2008). Humor and group effectiveness. *Human Relations*, 61(3), 395–418.

Romero, E. J. (2005). The effect of humor on work effort and mental state. *International Journal of Work Organization and Emotion*, 1, 137–149.

Romero, E. J., & Cruthirds, K. W. (2006). The use of humor in the workplace. *Academy of Management Perspectives*, 20, 58–69.

Rosenberg, C., Walker, A., Leiter, M., & Graffam, J. (2021). Humor in Workplace Leadership: A Systematic Search Scoping Review. *Frontiers in Psychology*, 12, 610795. https://doi.org/10.3389/fpsyg.2021.610795.

Ruch, W. (1997). State and trait cheerfulness and the induction of exhilaration: A FACS study. *European Psychologist*, 2(4), 328–341. https://doi.org/10.1027/1016-9040.2.4.328.

Ruch, W. (1998). Sense of humor: A new look at an old concept. In W. Ruch (Ed.), *The sense of humor: Explorations of a personality characteristic* (pp. 3–14). Mouton de Gruyter.

Ruch, W. (2008). Psychology of Humor. In V. Raskin (Ed.), *The Primer of Humor Research* (pp. 17–101). Walter de Gruyter & Co. https://doi.org/10.1515/9783110198492.

Ruch, W.& Heintz, S. (2016). The virtue gap in humor: Exploring benevolent and corrective humor. *Translational Issues in Psychological Science*, 2(1), 35–45. https://doi.org/10.1037/tps0000063.

Ruch, W., & Heintz, S. (2017). Experimentally manipulating items informs on the (limited) construct and criterion validity of the humor styles questionnaire. *Frontiers in Psychology*, 8, 616. https://doi.org/10.3389/fpsyg.2017.00616.

Ruch, W., & Heintz, S. (2019a). Humor production and creativity: Overview and recommendations. In S.R. Luria, J. Baer, & J.C. Kaufman (Eds.), *Creativity and humor: Explorations in creativity research* (pp. 1–42). Academic Press. https://doi.org/10.1016/B978-0-12-813802-1.00001-6.

Ruch, W., & Heintz, S. (2019b). On the dimensionality of humorous conduct and associations with humor traits and behaviors. *Humor*, 32(4), 643–666.

Ruch, W., Heintz, S., Platt, T., Wagner, L., & Proyer, R. T. (2018). Broadening humor: comic styles differentially tap into temperament, character, and ability. *Frontiers in Psychology*, 9, 6. https://doi.org/10.3389/fpsyg.2018.00006.

Ruch, W., & Hofmann, J. (2012). A temperament approach to humor. In P. Gremigni (Ed.). *Humor and health promotion* (pp. 79–113). Nova Science.

Ruch, W., Köhler, G., & Van Thriel, C. (1996). Assessing the "humorous temperament": Construction of the facet and standard trait forms of the State-Trait-Cheerfulness-Inventory—STCI. *Humor*, 9(3–4), 303–340. https://doi.org/10.1515/humr.1996.9.3-4.303.

Ruch, W.& McGhee, P. E. (2014). Humor intervention programs. InA. C. Parks& S. M. Schueller (Eds.), *The Wiley Blackwell handbook of positive psychological interventions* (pp. 179–193). Wiley. https://doi.org/10.1002/9781118315927.ch10.

Ruch, W., & Proyer, R. (2009). Extending the study of gelotophobia: On gelotophiles and katagelasticists. *Humor*, 22(1–2), 183–212. https://doi.org/10.1515/HUMR.2009.009.

Ruch, W., & Stahlmann, A. G. (2020). Toward a dynamic model of Gelotophobia: Social support, workplace bullying and stress are connected with diverging trajectories of life and job satisfaction among Gelotophobes. *Current Psychology*, 1–13. https://doi.org/10.1007/s12144-020-01046-y.

Ruch, W. F., & Heintz, S. (2013). Humour styles, personality and psychological well-being: What's humour got to do with it? *The European Journal of Humour Research*, 1(4), 1–24.

Ruch, W. F., Hofmann, J., Rusch, S., & Stolz, H. (2018). Training the sense of humor with the 7 Humor Habits Program and satisfaction with life. *Humor*, 31 (2), 287–309.

Samson, A. C., Glassco, A. L., Lee, I. A., & Gross, J. J. (2014). Humorous coping and serious reappraisal: Short-term and longer-term effects. *Europe's Journal of Psychology*, 10(3), 571–581.

Samson, A. C., & Gross, J. J. (2012). Humour as emotion regulation: The differential consequences of negative versus positive humour. *Cognition and Emotion*, 26(2), 375–384.

Scholer, A. A., & Higgins, E. T. (2008). People as resources: Exploring the functionality of warm and cold. *European Journal of Social Psychology*, 38, 1111–1120.

Shibata, M., Terasawa, Y., Osumi, T., Masui, K., Ito, Y., Sato, A., & Umeda, S. (2017). Time course and localization of brain activity in humor comprehension: An ERP/sLORETA study. *Brain Research*, 1657, 215–222. https://doi.org/10.1016/j.brainres.2016.12.010.

Thorson, J. A., & Powell, F. C. (1993). Sense of humor and dimensions of personality. *Journal of Clinical Psychology*, 49(6), 799–809.

Van den Broeck, A., Vander Elst, T., Dikkers, J., De Lange, A., & De Witte, H. (2012). This is funny: On the beneficial role of self-enhancing and affiliative humour in job design. *Psicothema-Revista de Psicologia*, 24(1), 87–93.

Vetter, L., & Gockel, C. (2016). Can't buy me laughter: Humour in organisational change. *Gruppe. Interaktion. Organisation. Zeitschrift für Angewandte Organisationspsychologie*, 47, 313–320. https://doi.org/10.1007/s11612-016-0341-7.

Wang, R., Chan, D. K. S., Goh, Y. W., Penfold, M., Harper, T., & Weltewitz, T. (2018). Humor and workplace stress: A longitudinal comparison between Australian and Chinese employees. *Asia Pacific Journal of Human Resources*, 56(2), 175–195.

Weick, K. & Westley, F. (1996). Organizational Learning: Reaffirming an oxymoron. In S. Clegg, C. Hardy, & W. Nord (Eds.), *Handbook of Organization Studies* (pp. 440–458). Sage.

Wellenzohn, S., Proyer, R. T., & Ruch, W. (2016). How do positive psychology inter-ventions work? A short-term placebo-controlled humor-based study on the role of the time focus. *Personality and Individual Differences*, 96, 1–6.

Wellenzohn, S., Proyer, R. T., & Ruch, W. (2018). Who benefits from humor-based positive psychology interventions? The moderating effects of personality traits and sense of humor. *Frontiers in Psychology*, 9, 821.

Wisse, B., & Rietzschel, E. (2014). Humor in leader-follower relationships: Humor styles, similarity and relationship quality. *Humor*, 27(2), 249–269.

Wu, J., & Chan, R. M. (2013). Chinese teachers' use of humour in coping with stress. *International Journal of Psychology*, 48(6), 1050–1056.

Yang, G. (2021). Leader positive humor and employee creativity: The mediating role of work engagement. *Social Behavior and Personality: An International Journal*, 49(7), 1–8.

Yeager, K. L., & Nafukho, F. M. (2012). Developing diverse teams to improve per-formance in the organizational setting. *European Journal of Training and Develop-ment*, 36(4), 388–408.

Zeigler-Hill, V., Besser, A., & Jett, S. E. (2013). Laughing at the looking glass: Does humor style serve as an interpersonal signal? *Evolutionary Psychology*, 11(1). https://doi.org/10.1177/147470491301100118.

Zeigler-Hill, V., McCabe, G. A., & Vrabel, J. K. (2016). The dark side of humor: DSM-5 pathological personality traits and humor styles. *Europe's Journal of Psychology*, 12(3), 363–376.

Zhang, Y., Yin, C., Akhtar, M. N., & Wang, Y. (2022). Humor at work that works: A multi-level examination of when and why leader humor promotes employee creativity. *Frontiers in Psychology*, 13, 903281. https://doi.org/10.3389/fpsyg.2022.903281.

12 Perfectionism as a Critical Disadvantage for Sustainable Development in Organizational Contexts

Donald H. Saklofske, Annamaria Di Fabio, Andrea Svicher and Martin M. Smith

Introduction

The psychology of sustainability and sustainable development (Di Fabio, 2017a, 2017b; Di Fabio & Rosen, 2018) stems from the broad, transdisciplinary field of Sustainability Science and includes a focus on effective and sustainable paths for the well-being of individuals and their working environments. Furthermore, positive psychological variables are conceived as vital elements for sustainable developmental processes, having the crucial features to regenerate psychological resources (Di Fabio & Tsuda, 2018), and therefore fueling the sustainability of developmental processes. Among the critical disadvantages that can take away from the flourishing of organizational environments, perfectionism has gained the attention of applied psychologists in the last two decades (see Harari et al., 2018 for review). Research has shown that workplace perfectionism can have an adverse impact on employee well-being and work-related outcomes as well as on the larger organization (Harari et al., 2018; Mohr et al., 2022; Ocampo et al., 2020), albeit with some evidence of cross-cultural variability (Spagnoli et al., 2022). To follow on from previous reviews, we present a focused review of the relationship between perfectionism, which could impede the sustainable development of a healthy organization, and what could be useful to address perfectionism in a more nuanced way, considering its destructive potential in contrast to a healthy organization's framework (Di Fabio, 2017a, Di Fabio et al., 2020). The present chapter reviews the negative impact of perfectionism from two sides: first, elucidating the role of perfectionism in negatively affecting the well-being and job-related 'capacities' of workers; and second, highlighting the role of perfectionism in dysfunctional organizational outcomes. Lastly, viable strategies to prevent and ameliorate the negative effects of perfectionism in organizations are discussed.

Conceptualizing Perfectionism

Early scholars (e.g., Adler, 1956; Bruch, 1988; Horney, 1950) described perfectionism as part of a personality style characterized by a rigid and extreme

DOI: 10.4324/9781003212157-15

drive to achieve perfection, which is accompanied by high expectations, self-evaluations, and concerns. These investigations tended to view several critical, overlapping dimensions of perfectionism as one undifferentiated construct (Smith et al., 2022). Frost et al. (1990) and Hewitt and Flett (1991) concurrently initiated the modern era of perfectionism research and independently created two multidimensional models of perfectionism, drawing upon early definitions of the concept. Frost et al.'s (1990) view extended the unitary concept of perfectionism by proposing six interrelated attitudinal features: personal standards, concern over mistakes, doubts about actions, parental expectations, parental criticism, and organization. They pointed out that personal standards are perfectionistic when linked with excessive concerns over mistakes (Frost et al., 1990) and associated with parental approval or disappointment. These authors also included a sixth dimension labelled "organization", that entails other features of perfectionism dealing with an excessive need for accuracy and order (Frost et al., 1990). Subsequent research supports the validity of this extensively applied model (e.g., Gavino et al., 2019; Parker & Adkins, 1995), while clarifying that parental expectations, parental criticism, and organization are not central or core features of perfectionism (Damian et al., 2013; Smith et al., 2022). Parental expectations and parental criticism were found to be developmental precursors of perfectionism, whereas organization was highlighted as a correlate of perfectionism (Damian et al., 2013).

In comparison to the model and measure proposed by Frost et al. (1990), Hewitt and Flett (1991) also consider insights from attachment theory (e.g., Bowlby, 1988) as well as interpersonal and intrapersonal aspects of psychodynamic theories (e.g., Horney, 1950; Sullivan, 1953). Hewitt and Flett (1991) developed their model distinguishing between the source and target of perfectionistic expectations and highlighting the individual's need for perfection (Flett & Hewitt, 2002). They proposed that trait perfectionism encompasses three dimensions: self-oriented perfectionism (i.e., requiring perfection of the self), other-oriented perfectionism (i.e., requiring perfection of other people), and socially prescribed perfectionism (i.e., belief that others require perfection of the self) (Hewitt et al., 2017). The Hewitt and Flett model has been documented through an extensive body of literature that confirmed its validity, reliability, and utility for both practice and research (Flett & Hewitt, 2014; Hewitt et al., 2017). Subsequently, Hewitt et al. (2017) proposed the Comprehensive Model of Perfectionistic Behavior (CMPB). The CMPB notes that perfectionism is a multidimensional and multilevel personality characteristic that interacts with most behavior (Hewitt et al., 2017) and consists of the aforementioned trait-perfectionism dimensions as well as perfectionistic self-presentation (i.e., the need to appear perfect) and perfectionistic cognitions (i.e., automatic perfectionism-related thoughts) (Hewitt et al., 2017).

In understanding perfectionism, personality researchers (e.g., Smith et al., 2022) suggest that it is critical to determine what perfectionism is not. Perfectionism is not conscientiousness. Unlike self-discipline, organization, goal-seeking, and achievement-striving (Flett & Hewitt, 2016), perfectionism involves a rigid and punitive need for perfection at all costs (Hewitt et al., 2003). Furthermore, perfectionism is not a distinct but rather a multifaceted dimensional concept that varies in severity (Broman-Fulks et al., 2008). Thus, perfectionism is a complex, multidimensional construct that involves intrapersonal and interpersonal attributes (Stoeber & Damian, 2014; Stoeber et al., 2021).

To consolidate the different dimensions and conceptualizations of perfectionism, scholars identified a two-factor model composed of *positive strivings* and *maladaptive evaluation concerns* (Frost et al., 1993), which combined dimensions of the models of Frost et al. (1990) and Hewitt and Flett (1991). *Positive strivings* combine personal standards, organization, self-oriented perfectionism, and other-oriented perfectionism, whereas *maladaptive evaluation* combines concern over mistakes, doubts about actions, parental expectations, and socially prescribed perfectionism (Stoeber & Otto, 2006). Research generally supports the two-factor model (e.g., Bieling et al., 2004; Chang, 2002; Hill et al., 2004; Stairs et al., 2012) that Stoeber and Otto (2006) subsequently relabelled as *perfectionistic strivings* and *perfectionistic concerns*. However, scholars questioned the two-factor model's inclusion of parental expectations, criticism, and organization (Damian et al., 2013; Smith et al., 2018). As well, Harari et al. (2018) further classified the two-factor model for workers as *excellence-seeking perfectionism* and *failure-avoidance perfectionism*, reflecting *perfectionistic strivings* and *perfectionistic concerns*. Nevertheless, Stoeber (2018) questioned these two labels since the degree to which these two dimensions are linked to adaptive and maladaptive work-related outcomes requires further empirical examination beyond labelling them simply as "positive" or "negative" for the workplace.

Starting from research findings that have emerged during the last three decades, Smith et al. (2016) proposed a more recent and alternative multidimensional model, namely the Big Three Perfectionism Scale (BTPS). It includes ten different types of perfectionism facets, which may be split into three main dimensions: rigid, self-critical, and narcissistic perfectionism (Smith et al., 2016). Rigid perfectionism reflects seeking perfection from oneself. It includes *self-oriented perfectionism* (i.e., the pursuit of perfection) and *self-worth contingencies*, which encompass the relationship between self-worth and reaching personal criteria of perfection (Smith et al., 2016). Self-critical perfectionism describes worrying about adverse reactions to inadequate performances and perceiving that others expect one to be perfect. It is composed of *concern over mistakes* (overly adverse responses to errors), *doubts about actions* (uncertainty and performance dissatisfaction), *self-criticism* (self-criticism about perceived imperfections), and *socially prescribed perfectionism* (a tendency to perceive that others expect perfection) (Smith et al., 2016). Lastly, the BTPS is the first model that considers narcissistic perfectionism as a grandiose, hypercritical, and entitled demand for others' perfection (Hewitt & Flett, 2004).

In the next paragraphs, perfectionism will be addressed in the context of the workplace, which will include the relation to personality traits, ill-being correlates in workers, and work-related outcomes. To examine the key research on perfectionism at the workplace, we focus on the extensively studied and well-supported trait-perfectionism dimensions conceptualized by Hewitt and Flett (1991), the attitudinal-perfectionism dimensions posited by Frost et al. (1990), as well as their subsequent reformulation of *perfectionistic strivings* and *perfectionistic concerns*. In addition, we include an overview of the most recent results applying the Smith et al.'s (2016) three-factor model.

Relationship between Perfectionism and Other Personality Traits

In studying the connections between perfectionism and other personality traits, researchers mostly draw from the five-factor model (FFM), encompassing neuroticism, extraversion, openness to experience, agreeableness, and conscientiousness (McCrae & Costa, 1997). Smith et al. (2019) reported meta-analytic results that considered the FFM as a whole. FFM traits explained from 21% to 46% of self-oriented perfectionism and concern over mistakes' variance, with doubts about actions accounting for 72%. This suggests that multidimensional perfectionism should be regarded as different from FFM, with the probable exception of doubts about actions (Smith et al., 2019). Considering each of the FFM traits, conscientiousness and emotional stability have gathered the greater attention since data showed the strongest links between these traits and perfectionism (Barrick et al., 2001). Employees who score high on perfectionistic strivings are focused on organization, order, accomplishment, discipline, and obedience, which are all traits that are connected with conscientiousness (Dunkley et al., 2012; McCrae & Costa, 1997). On the other hand, individuals who score low on conscientiousness are characterized as lazy, irresponsible, and careless (Barrick et al., 2001). These characteristics are opposite to the high standards and concern over mistakes, which are characteristics of perfectionism (Frost et al., 1990). One of the most relevant characteristics that differentiates conscientiousness from perfectionism is rigidity and intense attention to pursuing faultless results (Flett & Hewitt, 2002). Individuals who are high in perfectionism are also likely to be low in emotional stability (high in neuroticism). This is especially true for individuals with high perfectionistic concerns because these individuals experience high levels of concern over mistakes, critical thoughts, and self-doubt, all of which indicate low emotional stability (Frost & DiBartolo, 2002). Differently, high impulsivity and anger are indicative of poor emotional stability and are associated with perfectionism (Dunkley et al., 2012).

Meta-analytic findings for samples of workers (Harari et al., 2018) revealed that the relationship between perfectionistic strivings and conscientiousness was positive but negative for perfectionistic concerns. Differently, the relationship between perfectionism and the neuroticism factor tapping emotional stability received mixed support. Perfectionistic concerns had a negative and strong association with emotional stability, whereas the association between perfectionistic strivings and emotional stability was low. Agreeableness and perfectionistic concerns had a negative and appreciable association, whereas the relationship between perfectionistic strivings and agreeableness was not of significance. Extraversion was positively associated with perfectionistic strivings but not with perfectionistic concerns. Lastly, the association between perfectionism and openness showed that only perfectionistic concerns had a negative and appreciable association with this latter FFM dimension (Harari et al., 2018). Smith et al. (2019) provide further meta-analytic data that supports gender differences in the perfectionism-personality relationship. Specifically, the association between self-oriented perfectionism and neuroticism was found to be stronger in females than in males. A more recent network analysis provided by Di Fabio et al. (2022) investigated the relationships between the Big Three Perfectionism dimensions and the FFM facets, showing that rigid perfectionism and FFM dominance (one of the two extraversion facets) are relevant in linking perfectionism and personality traits in workers.

Relationship between Perfectionism and Ill-being Correlates in Workers

Perfectionism has been shown to have harmful impacts on physical health (Sirois, 2016) to the extreme of predicting early death even after controlling for FFM personality traits (Fry & Debats, 2009). This is not unexpected since individuals with high perfectionism disregard rest and relaxation, which ultimately could harm their physical health (Flaxman et al., 2012; Flett et al., 2015). Of relevance is that perfectionism has the potential to impede daily functioning at work (Ocampo et al., 2020). High perfectionism has been linked with higher cortisol reactivity following stress exposure (Enns et al., 2005), and several studies have highlighted the relationship between perfectionism and somatic stress symptoms (Flett et al., 2015; Molnar et al., 2006; Martin et al., 1996). Perfectionism has been associated with migraine (Bottos & Dewey, 2004), hypertension, and cardiovascular and gastrointestinal illnesses (Albert et al., 2016; Flett et al., 2007; Shanmugasegaram et al., 2014). In a related vein, Molnar and colleagues (2006) reported that socially prescribed perfectionism is linked to various adverse health effects (i.e., fatigue, pains, sleep problems, shortness of breath, upset stomach); as well, individuals high in perfectionism have a greater propensity for a quicker decrease in immunological function (Fry & Debats, 2009, 2011).

Research has additionally found that perfectionism also negatively impacts workers' psychological health and well-being (Bakker & Demerouti, 2007; Harari et al., 2018; Hill & Curran, 2016). Features associated with the need for flawlessness, a characteristic of employees with high perfectionism, may entail significant demands that, in turn, highly impair an array of psychological well-being correlates in workers (Schwenke et al., 2014). Consistently, research has shown that perfectionism and stress are positively associated (Dunkley et al., 2014; Dunn et al., 2006; Mandel et al., 2018). Employees with high perfectionism are more likely to experience stress because, while they are concerned about the quality of their work, they may have a reduced ability to deal with and address perceived difficulties in the workplace (Dunkley et al., 2003; Stoeber & Otto, 2006). Moreover, researchers found that perfectionism is associated with higher depression and anxiety (Harari et al., 2018). Workers with higher perfectionism are likely to constantly strive to achieve their goals while also being concerned about their job performance; the sustained activation of such increased strain over time could lead them to experience high stress and anxiety (Kawamura et al., 2001). Furthermore, providing challenging demands on oneself and feeling unable to reach the high self-imposed standards may result in experiences of unfulfilled expectations, which, if unresolved, may lead workers high in perfectionism to develop depression (Flett et al., 2003). Recent meta-analysis appears to confirm these findings that perfectionism in the workplace has consistent and significant associations with stress, anxiety, and depression (Harari et al., 2018). Furthermore, perfectionism and burnout are thought to be linked (Childs & Stoeber, 2012). Job burnout is a chronic psychological condition that may occur in workers, and it is characterized by emotional exhaustion, cynicism, and a reduction in effectiveness (Maslach, 2003). Employees who score higher on perfectionism traits are more likely to experience greater emotional exhaustion and lower efficacy (Schaufeli & Bakker, 2004). This could be because they tend to set extremely high standards for themselves and frequently doubt their capacity to fulfill the requirements of their jobs (Childs & Stoeber, 2012; Hill & Curran, 2016). In addition, individuals with a high level of perfectionism are also more likely to experience high levels of cynicism toward the job, especially if they feel that other coworkers judge their work as a failure (Bieling et al., 2004; Maslach, 2003). Two meta-analyses have confirmed these trends, highlighting a positive association between perfectionism and burnout (Harari et al., 2018) as well as showing a positive and relevant association with burnout and perfectionistic concerns (Harari et al., 2018; Hill & Curran, 2016).

Studies have also observed that perfectionism is detrimental to workplace well-being and can negatively impact relational aspects of work (Dunkley et al., 2014). This is particularly true for the interpersonal components of perfectionism (e.g., socially prescribed perfectionism), which reflects perfectionists' desire to attain self-worth via the respect of others, often leading to individuals' alienation from other people (Hewitt et al., 2017). Relatedly, reported findings have identified that perfectionism is related to increased experience of conflict in work relationships (Fairlie & Flett, 2003). Furthermore, subordinates with high degrees of socially prescribed perfectionism are concerned with expectations of high standards imposed by others. As a result, they were more inclined to have unpleasant relationships with their coworkers and supervisors (Monck, 2009). Differently, perfectionistic concerns may cause people to view social interactions as a failure, resulting in interpersonal stress, withdrawal from or avoidance of social connections, and a diminished sense of social support (Dunkley et al., 2014). Moreover, leaders and more senior personnel who score high on other-oriented perfectionism were found to be associated with monitoring behaviors and were highlighted as a barrier to building trusting relationships (Otto et al., 2021).

Perfectionism also crosses family role boundaries (Mitchelson, 2009). For example, research shows that perfectionistic concerns are positively associated with more significant work-family conflict, as reflected by higher marital conflict, parental distress, and emotional exhaustion at home (Deuling & Burns, 2017; Mitchelson & Burns, 1998). Men appear to be more prone to exhibit maladaptive levels of perfectionism in conjunction with work-family conflict than women (Ekmekci et al., 2021).

Lastly, workaholism (people's urge to work incessantly and think about work even when they are not at the workplace) has been shown to be positively linked with self-oriented perfectionism (Stoeber et al., 2013) as well as perfectionistic strivings (Spagnoli et al., 2021; Stoeber & Damian, 2016) and concerns (Spagnoli et al., 2021; Stoeber & Damian, 2016). Other studies have investigated the effects of the interaction between managers' perfectionism and employees' perfectionism on workaholism. It was found that employees' socially-prescribed perfectionism and work addiction was strongest when a manager was perceived to be addicted to work (Morkevičiūtė & Endriulaitienė, 2022).

Relationship between Perfectionism and Work-related Outcomes

Existing research has focused on three theoretical approaches to investigate the function of perfectionism in the working environment: the Goal Setting Theory (GST; Locke & Latham, 2002), the Conservation of Resources Theory (COR; Hobfoll, 2001), and the Transactional Model of Stress and Coping (Lazarus, 1966; Lazarus & Folkman, 1987). The core tenet of the goal-setting theory is that the achievement of goals motivates effort, control, and persistence (Locke & Latham, 2002). In line with GST (Locke & Latham, 2002), perfectionism is particularly harmful to the achievement of goals since workers high in perfectionism are unwilling to modify their unrealistic goals, are overly concerned with making mistakes, and have a negative view of their performance (Frost et al., 1990; Hrabluik et al., 2012). Therefore, especially when sustained job performance is required, perfectionism could affect the capability to maintain sustained effort, contributing to emotional exhaustion and substantially impairing performance (Hrabluik et al., 2012).

The COR theory proposes that individuals strive to build, protect, and conserve physical and psychological resources (Hobfoll, 2001). Resources are deemed valuable when they enable people to satisfy demands, accomplish objectives, or prevent possible resource loss (Hobfoll, 2001). Individuals judge something as a resource, either for their intrinsic worth (such as well-being and health) or for their utility in attaining or conserving other resources (such as social support and motivation) resources (Hobfoll, 2001). COR theory includes two core tenets: the primacy of resource loss, according to which a loss of resources was most psychologically relevant than an equivalent gain, and resource investment, illustrating that resource investment is required to acquire further resources as well as to prevent or recover from a loss (Hobfoll et al., 2018). Research on perfectionism in the workplace has used the primacy of resource loss to explain stress and strain raised from perfectionistic demands (e.g., Deuling & Burns, 2017; Flaxman et al., 2012). A systematic review of perfectionism at work (Ocampo et al., 2020) showed that COR theory is mostly used to explain how workers with high levels of perfectionistic concerns manage and use to excess resources to satisfy their high expectations at work. However, the effects of perfectionistic traits (attention to detail and high standards) on resource investment and their effects on workplace opportunities (e.g., sabbatical leave, training programs) and performance have yet to be addressed in the literature (Ocampo et al., 2020).

The transactional paradigm (Lazarus, 1966; Lazarus & Folkman, 1987) posits that interaction between the individual and the environment causes stress. According to Lazarus (1966), stress emerges when a person views the environment as dangerous, hurtful, or troublesome. Two appraisals connect the individual with the environment: a primary appraisal dealing with the evaluation of the stressor in terms of personal efforts and a secondary appraisal encompassing the evaluation of the coping ability to overwhelm the stressor (Lazarus, 1966). Thus, a person's reaction to stress depends on their perception of the stressor and their coping ability (Lazarus & Folkman, 1987). Appraisal theory has been used to show how workers high in perfectionism perceive stress and coping (Ocampo et al., 2020). Workers with high perfectionistic concerns show increased stress anticipation combined with a lower capacity to estimate their coping abilities (Dunkley et al., 2014). Consistently, workers with high perfectionistic concerns tend to experience higher stress and use maladaptive coping techniques, resulting in negative affect and burnout (e.g., Chang, 2002; Crane et al., 2015). Conversely, literature has shown that perfectionistic strivings help workers to enhance their coping skills and capacity to regulate stress (Schwenke et al., 2014).

Meta-analytic results (Harari et al., 2018) focus mainly on work engagement that is frequently linked with perfectionism. The term "work engagement" refers to a psychological state in which workers are fully absorbed in their work, committed to completing their assigned tasks, and filled with renewed energy and enthusiasm (Schaufeli & Bakker, 2004). In this view, it is possible to conceive of work engagement as the opposite of and antidote to burnout (Schaufeli et al., 2006). The perfectionism-engagement connection has received mixed support from meta-analytic results (Harari et al., 2018). The overall relationship was nonexistent (Harari et al., 2018). However, perfectionistic strivings and perfectionistic concerns showed a medium-sized association with engagement but in opposite directions. Excellence-seeking showed a positive association, whereas failure-avoiding perfectionism displayed a negative association (Harari et al., 2018). These findings point to the importance of assessing the different characteristics of perfectionism (perfectionistic strivings versus perfectionistic concerns) in understanding the link between perfectionism and work engagement (Harari et al., 2018).

Results concerning the association between perfectionism and job performance have been extensively reported in the literature (e.g., Beauregard, 2012; Hrabluik et al., 2012; Kobori et al., 2011; Locander et al., 2015; Mor et al., 1995; Sherry et al. 2010; Spence & Robbins, 1992; Zwaan et al., 2009). It has been suggested that perfectionistic strivings could be involved in improving performance (Stoeber, 2012; Stoeber et al., 2018). Accordingly, perfectionistic strivings include most perfectionistic characteristics focused on achieving goals. Thus, results have shown that strivings to achieve perfection are positively associated with approaching orientations (Elliot & Church, 1997) that, in turn, improve work-related performance (see Stoeber et al., 2018, for a review). In addition, research has shown that strivings for perfection are positively associated with more desired pre-performance emotional states (such as enthusiasm), cognitive evaluations (such as challenge), and incentives for participating (e.g., self-regulation in autonomous motivation) (e.g., Hill et al., 2020). Starting for these premises, Stoeber et al. (2012, 2018) indicated that perfectionistic strivings were generally positively linked with better performance at work, whereas perfectionistic concerns were generally uncorrelated to performance. Thus, Stoeber and colleagues (2012, 2018) stated that perfectionistic striving is not always synonymous of poor performance, and it could be an integral element of a healthy pursuit of excellence. However, this positive effect could be considered only when a high perfectionistic strivings standard is not accompanied by equally high levels of perfectionistic concerns (Stoeber et al., 2018).

Studies other than those of Stoeber (2012) examined in depth the relationships between performance and perfectionism in the workplace. Two studies by Hrabluik et al. (2012) partially confirmed the positive link between workplace performance and perfectionistic strivings. They investigated the relationship between perfectionism and maximum workplace performance in police officers, based on how candidates performed on a promotion test. In the first study, the researchers found that perfectionistic strivings had a significant positive and medium association with maximum performance. In the second research, perfectionistic strivings revealed a positive link with regular performance, although the correlation was not significant and was very slight (Hrabluik et al., 2012).

Sherry et al. (2010) investigated the relationship between perfectionism and academic productivity, including first-authored publications, number of citations, and magnitude of impact factor in a sample of psychology university professors. In contrast with Stoeber et al. (2012), perfectionistic strivings were found to have the highest negative correlation with research productivity, whereas perfectionistic concerns indicated a negative but smaller correlation with research output. The pattern of correlations was the same for all of the other proxies of productivity, except for the link between perfectionistic concerns and impact factor rating, which was insignificant (Sherry et al., 2010).

Controlling for conscientiousness and neuroticism, perfectionistic strivings remained significantly negatively and modestly correlated with research output, whereas perfectionistic concerns indicated a nonsignificant association. That said, a recent review (Stoeber et al., 2018) highlighted that perfectionistic concerns are more likely to have a negative impact, either directly or indirectly, on performance. This is because perfectionistic concerns instill a psychological commitment to perfection excluding personally goal-directed components, thus resulting in a pervasive sensation of being powerless in the face of external challenges. In particular, research has shown that perfectionistic concerns are positively associated with avoidance orientations (such as performance-avoidance objectives) (Stoeber et al., 2018). Furthermore, perfectionistic concerns have been found to be positively related to less desirable pre-performance affective states, such as anxiety; cognitive appraisals, such as threats; and minor reasons for participation, including controlled motivation regulations (Hill et al., 2020). These factors are likely to result in worse performance, in contrast to the performance-related factors associated with perfectionistic strivings (e.g., Richardson et al., 2012). Moreover, meta-analytic findings illustrate that workers with high perfectionistic strivings traits are more prone to have higher rates of worked hours and to be more motivated. However, the relationship between motivation and perfectionistic concerns was found to be nil (Harari et al., 2018), again suggesting the prominent role of perfectionistic strivings.

Conclusions and Suggested Strategies to Assess, Prevent, and Ameliorate Perfectionism in Organizations

From an organizational perspective, sustainability experts have advanced the concept of positive healthy organizations (Di Fabio, 2017b; Di Fabio et al., 2020) to bring the central tenets of the psychology of sustainability and sustainable development into the workplace (Di Fabio, 2017a). This is aligned with the positive psychology/well-being movement (Robertson & Cooper, 2011), together with studies of workplace psychological health. Accordingly, in positive, healthy organizations, well-being is promoted rather than viewed as healing from damages (Tetrick & Peiró, 2012). Furthermore, building the strength and capacity of workers also requires having valid and reliable psychological assessment methods that allow both researchers and practitioners to assess psychological resources as well as critical disadvantages in the workplace that could impact the well-being of workers and employees (Di Fabio, 2017b). Thus, according to a positive healthy perspective (Di Fabio, 2017b; Di Fabio et al., 2020) and accountability principle (Whiston, 2001, 2008), such an in-depth assessment of workplace resources and limitations could clarify which levels and kinds of preventive strategies need to be activated.

The research literature has shown that perfectionism has some deleterious effects and should certainly be differentiated from the personality trait of conscientiousness, which, in contrast, is recognized as a positive quality in workers (Barrick et al., 2001). Most important in distinguishing conscientiousness from perfectionism is the rigidity and focused attention in the pursuit of flawless outcomes that is observed in persons scoring high on perfectionism (Flett & Hewitt, 2002). Furthermore, extraversion, another favorable trait in workers, at least in contexts where social and interpersonal relationships are an important aspect (Barrick et al., 2001), is found to be linked with perfectionistic strivings, suggesting that this dimension could be an integral element in the healthy pursuit of excellence (Stoeber, 2012). However, the literature suggests evaluating the balance between perfectionistic strivings and perfectionistic concerns in order to have an overall view of the health of workers and the workplace (Stoeber, 2012). A more recent network analysis (Di Fabio et al., 2022) suggested paying particular attention to the link between the extraversion facet of dominance and rigid perfectionism.

The links between perfectionism and compromised well-being correlates show a consistent body of literature that highlights the association between a high level of perfectionism in workers and several dangers to physical and mental health (e.g., Harari et al., 2018: Ocampo et al., 2020). Thus, an in-depth assessment of the multidimensional components of perfectionism could be appropriate to individuate a relevant proxy for psychological and physical ill-being in the workplace context.

The data concerning the association between work-related outcomes and perfectionism suggest assessing separately perfectionistic concerns and perfectionistic strivings since they have different associations with relevant work-related variables (Stoeber et al., 2018). In particular, perfectionistic strivings could be a marker of behavior related to higher performance and engagement, and again a careful assessment of the balance of this dimension with perfectionist concerns is suggested, since this latter variable is frequently associated with poorer performance and lower engagement (e.g., Harari et al., 2018; Ocampo et al., 2020).

With regards to both intervention and prevention, Di Fabio et al. (2022) suggested focusing and expanding on positive strength-based perspectives (Di Fabio & Saklofske, 2021) to increase the positive psychological resources of workers (Di Fabio & Svicher, 2021, 2022), with implications for reducing and preventing perfectionism from becoming a negative influence in the workforce and workplace. This position could have two advantages: it could enhance psychological resources to achieve optimal performance and satisfaction, and it could also activate strengths to cope with the challenges of this century (Blustein et al., 2019; Cartwright & Cooper, 2014). To this end, positive strength-based perspectives (Di Fabio & Saklofske, 2021) are specifically aimed at building psychological strengths, such as enhancing emotional intelligence, stress management, and resilience, together with promoting psychological health and well-being (Di Fabio & Saklofske, 2014, 2018, 2019a, 2019b). Positive strength-based interventions can be directed at all four levels of the work environment: individual, group, organization, and inter-organization.

This can also be focused on different preventive strategies, including primary preventive (i.e., preventing the insurgence of issues before they start and promoting psychological well-being) (Di Fabio & Kenny, 2016a, 2016b, 2018) as well as secondary and tertiary preventive perspectives (Di Fabio, 2017a). Thus, positive healthy organizations (Di Fabio, 2017b; Di Fabio et al., 2020) should reflect the optimal workplace environment that identifies and addresses the negative impact of perfectionism, thereby promoting the sustainable development of workers and the organizations.

References

Adler, A. (1956). Understanding life. In H. L. Ansbacher & R. R. Ansbacher (Eds.), *The individual psychology of Alfred Adler: A systematic presentation in selections from his writings.* Harper Torch Books.

Albert, P., Rice, K. G., & Caffee, L. (2016). Perfectionism Affects Blood Pressure in Response to Repeated Exposure to Stress. *Stress and health: Journal of the International Society for the Investigation of Stress,* 32(2), 157–166. https://doi.org/10.1002/smi.2591.

Bakker, A. B., & Demerouti, E. (2007). *The job demands-resources model: State of the art. Journal of Managerial Psychology,* 22, 309–328. https://doi.org/10.1108/02683940710733115.

Barrick, M. R., Mount, M. K., & Judge, T. A. (2001). Personality and performance at the beginning of the new millennium: What do we know and where do we go next? *International Journal of Selection and Assessment,* 9, 9–30. http://dx.doi.org/10.1111/1468-2389.00160.

Beauregard, T. A. (2012). Perfectionism, self-efficacy and OCB: The moderating role of gender. *Personnel Review,* 41(5), 590–608. https://doi.org/10.1108/00483481211249120.

Bieling, P. J., Summerfeldt, L. J., Israeli, A. L., & Antony, M. M. (2004). Perfectionism as an explanatory construct in comorbidity of axis I disorders. *Journal of Psychopathology and Behavioral Assessment,* 26(3), 193–201. https://doi.org/10.1023/B:JOBA.0000022112.27186.98.

Blustein, D. L., Kenny, M. E., Di Fabio, A., & Guichard, J. (2019). Expanding the impact of the psychology of working: Engaging psychology in the struggle for decent work and human rights. *Journal of Career Assessment,* 27(1), 3–28. https://doi.org/10.1177/1069072718774002.

Bottos, S., & Dewey, D. (2004). Perfectionists' Appraisal of Daily Hassles and Chronic Headache. *Headache: The Journal of Head and Face Pain,* 44(8), 772–779. https://doi.org/10.1111/j.1526-4610.2004.04144.x.

Bowlby, J. (1988). *A secure base: Parent-child attachment and healthy human development.* Basic Books.

Broman-Fulks, J. J., Hill, R. W., & Green, B. A. (2008). Is perfectionism categorical or dimensional? A taxometric analysis. *Journal of Personality Assessment,* 90(5), 481–490. https://doi.org/10.1080/00223890802248802.

Bruch, H. (1988). Conversations with anorexics. Basic Books.

Cartwright, S., & Cooper, C. L. (2014). Towards Organizational Health: Stress, Positive Organizational Behavior, and Employee Well-Being Bridging Occupational. In G. F. Bauer & O. Hämming (Eds.), *Organizational and Public Health: A Transdisciplinary Approach* (pp. 29–42). Springer Netherlands.

Chang, E. C. (2002). Examining the link between perfectionism and psychological maladjustment: Social problem solving as a buffer. *Cognitive Therapy and Research,* 26(5), 581–595. https://doi.org/10.1023/A:1020329625158.

Childs, J. H., & Stoeber, J. (2012). Do you want me to be perfect? Two longitudinal studies on socially prescribed perfectionism, stress and burnout in the workplace. *Work & Stress,* 26, 347–364. http://dx.doi.org/ 10.1080/02678373.2012.737547.

Crane, M. E., Phillips, J. K., & Karin, E. (2015). Trait perfectionism strengthens the negative effects of moral stressors occurring in veterinary practice. *Australian Veterinary Journal,* 93(10), 354–360. doi:10.1111/avj.12366.

Damian, L. E., Stoeber, J., Negru, O., & Băban, A. (2013). On the development of perfectionism in adolescence: Perceived parental expectations predict longitudinal increases in socially prescribed perfectionism. *Personality and Individual Differences,* 55, 688–693. doi:10.1016/j.paid.2013.05.021.

Deuling, J. K., & Burns, L. (2017). Perfectionism and work-family conflict: Self-esteem and self-efficacy as mediator. *Personality and Individual Differences,* 116, 326–330. https://doi.org/10.1016/j.paid.2017.05.013.

Di Fabio, A. (2017a). The Psychology of Sustainability and Sustainable Development for Well-Being in Organizations. *Frontiers in Psychology,* 8, 1534. https://doi.org/10. 3389/fpsyg.2017.01534.

Di Fabio, A. (2017b). Positive Healthy Organizations: Promoting Well-Being, Meaningfulness, and Sustainability in Organizations. *Frontiers in Psychology,* 8, 1938. https://doi.org/10.3389/fpsyg.2017.01938.

Di Fabio, A., Cheung, F. M., & Peiró, J. M. (2020). Editorial to special issue "Personality and individual differences and healthy organizations". *Personality and Individual Differences,* 166, 110196. https://doi.org/10.1016/j.paid.2020.110196.

Di Fabio, A., & Kenny, M. E. (2016a). Promoting Well-Being: The Contribution of Emotional Intelligence. *Frontiers in Psychology,* 7, 1182. https://doi.org/10.3389/fp syg.2016.01182.

Di Fabio, A., & Kenny, M. E. (2016b). From Decent Work to Decent Lives: Positive Self and Relational Management (PS&RM) in the Twenty-First Century. *Frontiers in Psychology,* 7(361). https://doi.org/10.3389/fpsyg.2016.00361.

Di Fabio, A., & Kenny, M. E. (2018). Intrapreneurial self-capital: A key resource for promoting well-being in a shifting work landscape. *Sustainability (Switzerland),* 10 (9), 3035. https://doi.org/10.3390/su10093035.

Di Fabio, A. & Rosen, M. A. (2018). Opening the Black Box of Psychological Processes in the Science of Sustainable Development: A New Frontier. *European Journal of Sustainable Development Research,* 2(4), 47. https://doi.org/10.20897/ ejosdr/3933.

Di Fabio, A., & Saklofske, D. H. (2014). Promoting individual resources: The challenge of trait emotional intelligence. *Personality and Individual Differences,* 65, 19–23. https://doi.org/10.1016/j.paid.2014.01.026.

Di Fabio, A., & Saklofske, D. H. (2018). The contributions of personality and emotional intelligence to resiliency. *Personality and Individual Differences,* 123, 140–144. https://doi.org/10.1016/j.paid.2017.11.012.

Di Fabio, A., & Saklofske, D. H. (2019a). Positive Relational Management for Sustainable Development: Beyond Personality Traits—The Contribution of Emotional Intelligence. *Sustainability,* 11(2), 330. https://doi.org/10.3390/su11020330.

Di Fabio, A., & Saklofske, D. H. (2019b). The Contributions of Personality Traits and Emotional Intelligence to Intrapreneurial Self-Capital: Key Resources for Sustainability and Sustainable Development. *Sustainability*, 11(5), 1240. https://doi.org/10.3390/su11051240.

Di Fabio, A., & Saklofske, D. H. (2021). The relationship of compassion and self-compassion with personality and emotional intelligence. *Personality and individual differences*, 169, 110109. https://doi.org/10.1016/j.paid.2020.110109.

Di Fabio, A., Saklofske, D. H., Gori, A., & Svicher, A. (2022). Perfectionism: A network analysis of relationships between the Big Three Perfectionism dimensions and the Big Five Personality traits. *Personality and Individual Differences*, 199, 111839. https://doi.org/10.1016/j.paid.2022.111839.

Di Fabio, A., & Svicher, A. (2021). The Psychology of Sustainability and Sustainable Development: Advancing Decent Work, Inclusivity, and Positive Strength-Based Primary Preventive Interventions for Vulnerable Workers. *Frontiers in Psychology*, 12, 718354. https://doi.org/10.3389/fpsyg.2021.718354.

Di Fabio, A., & Svicher, A. (2022). Precariousness in the time of COVID-19: A turning point for reforming and reorganizing career counselling for vulnerable workers. *Cypriot Journal of Educational Science*. 17(5), 1477–1494. https://doi.org/10.18844/cjes.v17iSI.1.6676.

Di Fabio, A., & Tsuda, A. (2018). The Psychology of Harmony and Harmonization: Advancing the Perspectives for the Psychology of Sustainability and Sustainable Development. *Sustainability*, 10(12), 4726. https://doi.org/10.3390/su10124726.

Dunkley, D. M., Blankstein, K. R., & Berg, J. L. (2012). Perfectionism dimensions and the five- factor model of personality. *European Journal of Personality*, 26, 233–244. http://dx.doi.org/10.1002/per.829.

Dunkley, D. M., Mandel, T., & Ma, D. (2014). Perfectionism, neuroticism, and daily stress reactivity and coping effectiveness 6 months and 3 years later. *Journal of Counseling Psychology*, 61(4), 616–633. https://doi.org/10.1037/cou0000036.

Dunkley, D. M., Zuroff, D. C., & Blankstein, K. R. (2003). Self-critical perfectionism and daily affect: Dispositional and situational influences on stress and coping. *Journal of Personality and Social Psychology*, 84, 234–252. http://dx.doi.org/10.1037/0022-3514.84.1.234.

Dunn, J. G. H., Dunn, J. C., Gotwals, J. K., Vallance, J. K. H., Craft, J. M., & Syrotuik, D. G. (2006). Establishing construct validity evidence for the Sport Multidimensional Perfectionism Scale. *Psychology of Sport and Exercise*, 7(1), 57–79. https://doi.org/10.1016/j.psychsport.2005.04.003.

Ekmekci, O. T., Camgoz, S. M., & Karapinar, P. B. (2021). Path to well-being: Moderated mediation model of perfectionism, family-work conflict, and gender. *Journal of Family Issues*, 42(8), 1852–1879. doi:10.1177/0192513X20957041.

Elliot, A. J., & Church, M. A. (1997). A hierarchical model of approach and avoidance achievement motivation. *Journal of Personality and Social Psychology*, 72, 218–232. http://dx.doi.org/10.1037/0022-3514 .72.1.218.

Enns, M. W., Cox, B. J., & Clara, I. P. (2005). Perfectionism and Neuroticism: A Longitudinal Study of Specific Vulnerability and Diathesis-Stress Models. *Cognitive Therapy and Research*, 29(4), 463–478. https://doi.org/10.1007/s10608-005-2843-04.

Fairlie, P., & Flett, G. L. (2003, August). *Perfectionism at work: impacts on burnout, job satisfaction, and depression*. Poster presented at the 111th Annual Convention of the American Psychological Association at Toronto, Ontario, Canada.

Flaxman, P. E., Ménard, J., Bond, F. W., & Kinman, G. (2012). Academics' experiences of a respite from work: Effects of self-critical perfectionism and perseverative cognition on postrespite well-being. *Journal of Applied Psychology*, 97(4), 854–865. https://doi.org/10.1037/a0028055.

Flett, G. L., Besser, A., Davis, R. A., & Hewitt, P. L. (2003). Dimensions of perfectionism, unconditional self-acceptance, and depression. *Journal of Rational-Emotive & Cognitive-Behavior Therapy*, 21, 119–138. http://dx.doi.org/10.1023/A:1025051431957.

Flett, G. L., & Hewitt, P. L. (Eds.). (2002). *Perfectionism: Theory, research and treatment*. American Psychological Association. https://doi.org/10.1037/10458-000.

Flett, G. L., & Hewitt, P. L. (2014). A proposed framework for preventing perfectionism and promoting resilience and mental health among vulnerable children and adolescents. *Psychology in the Schools*, 51(9), 899–912. https://doi.org/10.1002/pits.21792.

Flett, G. L., & Hewitt, P. L. (2016). Still measuring perfectionism after all these years: Reflections and an introduction to the special issue on advances in the assessment of perfectionism. *Journal of Psychoeducational Assessment*, 34(7), 615–619. https://doi.org/10.1177/0734282916651540.

Flett, G. L., Hewitt, P. L., & Molnar, D. S. (2015). Perfectionism in health and illness from a person-focused, historical perspective. In F. M. Sirois & D. S. Molnar (Eds.), *Perfectionism, health, and well-being* (pp. 25–44). Springer.

Flett, G. L., Hewitt P. L., Whelan, T., & Martin, T. R. (2007). The perfectionism cognitions inventory: Psychometric properties and associations with distress and deficits in cognitive self-management . *Journal of Rational-Emotive and Cognitive-Behavior Therapy*, 25(4), 255–277. https://doi.org/10.1007/s10942-007-0055-4.

Frost, R. O., & DiBartolo, P. M. (2002). Perfectionism, anxiety, and obsessive-compulsive disorder. InG. L.Flett& P. L.Hewitt (Eds.),*Perfectionism: Theory, research, and treatment* (pp.341–371). American Psychological Association. https://doi.org/10.1037/10458-014.

Frost, R. O., Heimberg, R. G., Holt, C. S., Mattia, J. I., & Neubauer, A. L. (1993).A comparison of two measures of perfectionism. *Personality and Individual Differences*, 14(1), 119–126. https://doi.org/10.1016/0191-8869(93)90181-2.

Frost, R. O., Marten, P., Lahart, C., & Rosenblate, R. (1990). The dimensions of perfectionism. *Cognitive Therapy and Research*, 14(5), 449–468. doi:10.1007/BF011272967.

Fry, P. S., & Debats, D. L. (2009). Perfectionism and the five-factor personality traits as predictors of mortality in older adults. *Journal of Health Psychology*, 14(4), 513–524. https://doi.org/10.1177/1359105309103571.

Fry, P. S., & Debats, D. L. (2011). Perfectionism and other related trait measures as predictors of mortality in diabetic older adults: a six-and-a-half-year longitudinal study. *Journal of Health Psychology*, 16(7), 1058–1070. https://doi.org/10.1177/1359105311398684.

Gavino, A., Nogueira, R., Pérez-Costillas, L., & Godoy, A. (2019). Psychometric properties of the frost multidimensional perfectionism scale in Spanish children and adolescents. *Assessment*, 26(3), 445–464. https://doi.org/10.1177/1073191117740204.

Harari, D., Swider, B. W., Steed, L. B., & Breidenthal, A. P. (2018). Is perfect good? A meta-analysis of perfectionism in the workplace. *Journal of Applied Psychology*, 103 (10), 1121–1144. https://doi.org/10.1037/apl0000324.

Hewitt, P. L., & Flett, G. L. (1991). Perfectionism in the self and social contexts: Conceptual assessment, and association with psychopathology. *Journal of Personality and Social Psychology*, 60(3), 456–470. https://doi.org/10.1037/0022-3514.60.3.456.

Hewitt, P. L., & Flett, G. L. (2004). *The multidimensional perfectionism scale: Technical manual.* Multi-Health Systems.

Hewitt, P. L., Flett, G. L., Besser, A., Sherry, S. B., & McGee, B. (2003). Perfectionism is multidimensional: A reply to Shafran, Cooper and Fairburn (2002). *Behaviour Research and Therapy*, 41(10), 1221–1236. https://doi.org/10.1016/S0005-7967(03)00021-4.

Hewitt, P. L., Flett, G. L., & Mikail, S. F. (2017). *Perfectionism: A relational approach to conceptualization, assessment, and treatment.* The Guilford Press.

Hill, A. P., & Curran, T. (2016). Multidimensional perfectionism and burnout: A meta-analysis. *Personality and Social Psychology Review*, 20, 269–288. http://dx.doi.org/10.1177/1088868315596286.

Hill, R. W., Huelsman, T. J., Furr, R. M., Kibler, J., Vicente, B. B., & Kennedy, C. (2004). *Perfectionism Inventory (PI)* [Database record]. APA PsycTests. https://doi.org/10.1037/t30103-000.

Hill, A. P., Madigan, D. J., Smith, M. M., Mallison-Howard, S. H., & Donachie, T. C. (2020). Perfectionism. InD.Hackfort& R. J.Schicke(Eds.), *The Routledge International Encyclopaedia of Sport and Exercise Physiology, Vol. 1: Theoretical and Methodological Concepts* (pp.405–413). Routledge.

Hobfoll, S. E. (2001). The influence of culture, community, and the nested-self in the stress process: Advancing Conservation of Resources theory. *Applied Psychology: An International Review*, 50(3), 337–370. https://doi.org/10.1111/1464-0597.00062.

Hobfoll, S. E., Halbesleben, J., Neveu, J.-P., & Westman, M. (2018). Conservation of resources in the organizational context: The reality of resources and their consequences. *Annual Review of Organizational Psychology and Organizational Behaviour*, 5(1), 103–128. https://doi.org/10.1146/annurev-orgpsych-032117-104640.

Horney, K. (1950). *Neurosis and human growth: The struggle toward self-realization.* W.W. Norton.

Hrabluik, C., Latham, G. P., & McCarthy, J. M. (2012). Does goal setting have a dark side? The relationship between perfectionism and maximum versus typical employee performance. *International Public Management Journal*, 15, 5–38. http://dx.doi.org/10.1080/10967494.2012.684010.

Kawamura, K. Y., Hunt, S. L., Frost, R. O., & DiBartolo, P. M. (2001). Perfectionism, anxiety, and depression: Are the relationships independent? *Cognitive Therapy and Research*, 25, 291–301. http://dx.doi.org/10.1023/A:1010736529013.

Kobori, O., Yoshie, M., Kudo, K., & Ohtsuki, T. (2011). Traits and cognitions of perfectionism and their relation with coping style, effort, achievement, and performance Anxiety in Japanese musicians. *Journal of Anxiety Disorders*, 25, 674–679. http://dx.doi.org/10.1016/j.janxdis.2011.03.001.

Lazarus, R. S. (1966). *Psychological stress and the coping process.* McGraw-Hill.

Lazarus, R. S., & Folkman, S. (1987). Transactional theory and research on emotions and coping. *European Journal of Personality*, 1, 141–169. https://doi.org/10.1002/per.2410010304.

Locander, D. A., Weinberg, F. J., Mulki, J. P., & Locander, W. B. (2015). Salesperson lone wolf tendencies: The roles of social comparison and mentoring in a mediated model of performance. *Journal of Marketing Theory and Practice*, 23, 351–369. http://dx.doi.org/10.1080/10696679.2015.1049680.

Locke, E. A., & Latham, G. P. (2002). Building a practically useful theory of goal setting and task motivation: A 35-year odyssey. *American Psychologist*, 57(9), 705–717. https://doi.org/10.1037/0003-066X.57.9.705.

Mandel, T., Dunkley, D. M., & Starrs, C. J. (2018). Self-critical perfectionism, daily interpersonal sensitivity, and stress generation: A four-year longitudinal study. *Journal of Psychopathology and Behavioral Assessment*, 40(4), 701–713. https://doi.org/10.1007/s10862-018-9673-7.

Martin, T. R., Flett, G. L., Hewitt, P. L., Krames, L., & Szanto, G. (1996). Personality correlates of depression and health symptoms: A test of a self-regulation model. *Journal of Research in Personality*, 30(2), 264–277. https://doi.org/10.1006/jrpe.1996.0017.

Maslach, C. (2003). Job burnout: New directions in research and intervention. *Current Directions in Psychological Science*, 12, 189–192. http://dx.doi.org/10.1111/1467-8721.01258.

McCrae, R. R., & Costa, P. T., Jr. (1997). Personality trait structure as a human universal. *American Psychologist*, 52(5), 509–516. https://doi.org/10.1037/0003-066X.52.5.509.

Mitchelson, J. K. (2009). Seeking the perfect balance: Perfectionism and work-family conflict. *Journal of Occupational and Organizational Psychology*, 82, 349–367. doi:10.1348/096317908X314874.

Mitchelson, J. K., & Burns, L. R. (1998). Career mothers and perfectionism: Stress at work and at home. *Personality and Individual Differences*, 25(3), 477–485. https://doi.org/10.1016/S0191-8869(98)00069-5.

Mohr, M., Venz, L., & Sonnentag, S. (2022). A dynamic view on work-related perfectionism: Antecedents at work and implications for employee well-being. *Journal of Occupational and Organizational Psychology*, 95(4), 846–866.

Molnar, D. S., Reker, D. L., Culp, N. A., Sadava, S. W., & DeCourville, N. H. (2006). A mediated model of perfectionism, affect, and physical health. *Journal of Research in Personality*, 40(5), 482–500. https://doi.org/10.1016/j.jrp.2005.04.002.

Monck, L. (2009). *The Impact of Perfectionism on Work Attitudes and Behaviour*. City University of New York.

Mor, S., Day, H. I., Flett, G. L., & Hewitt, P. L. (1995). Perfectionism, control, and components of performance anxiety in professional artists. *Cognitive Therapy and Research*, 19, 207–225. http://dx.doi.org/10.1007/BF02229695.

Morkevičiūtᘢ, M., & Endriulaitienᘢ, A. (2022). Moderating role of perceived work addiction of managers in the relationship between employees' perfectionism and work addiction: A trait activation theory perspective. *Baltic Journal of Management*, 17(5), 586–602. https://doi.org/10.1108/bjm-03-2022-0112.

Ocampo, A. C. G., Wang, L., Kiazad, K., Restubog, S. L. D., & Ashkanasy, N. M. (2020). The relentless pursuit of perfectionism: A review of perfectionism in the workplace and an agenda for future research. *Journal of Organizational Behavior*, 41(2), 144–168. https://doi.org/https://doi.org/10.1002/job.2400.

Otto, K., Geibel, H. V., & Kleszewski, E. (2021). "Perfect Leader, Perfect Leadership?" Linking Leaders' Perfectionism to Monitoring, Transformational, and Servant Leadership Behavior. *Frontiers in Psychology*, 12, 657394. doi:10.3389/fpsyg.2021.657394.

Parker, W. D., & Adkins, K. K. (1995). Perfectionism and the gifted. *Roeper Review: A Journal on Gifted Education*, 17(3), 173–176. doi:10.1080/02783199509553653.

Richardson, M., Abraham, C., & Bond, R. (2012). Psychological correlates of university students' academic performance: A systemic review and meta-analysis. *Psychological Bulletin*, 138(2), 353–387. doi:10.1037/a0026838.

Robertson, I., & Cooper, C. (2011). *Well-Being: Productivity and Happiness at Work*. Palgrave Macmillan.

Schaufeli, W. B., & Bakker, A. B. (2004). Job demands, job resources and their relationship with burnout and engagement: A multi-sample study. *Journal of Organizational Behavior, 25*, 293–315. https://doi.org/10.1002/job.248.

Schaufeli, W. B., Bakker, A. B., & Salanova, M. (2006). The measurement of work engagement with a short questionnaire: A cross-national study. *Educational and Psychological Measurement, 66*, 701–716.

Schwenke, T. J., Ashby, J. S., & Gnilka, P. B. (2014). Sign language interpreters and burnout: The effects of perfectionism, perceived stress, and coping resources. *Interpreting, 16*(2), 209–232. https://doi.org/10.1075/intp.16.2.04sch.

Shanmugasegaram S., Flett G. L., Madan M., et al. (2014). Perfectionism, Type D personality, and illness-related coping styles in cardiac rehabilitation patients. *Journal of Health Psychology, 19*(3), 417–426. https://doi.org/10.1177/1359105312471571.

Sherry, S. B., Hewitt, P. L., Sherry, D. L., Flett, G. L., & Graham, A. R. (2010). Perfectionism dimensions and research productivity in psychology professors: Implications for understanding the (mal)adaptiveness of perfectionism. *Canadian Journal of Behavioural Science / Revue canadienne des sciences du comportement, 42*(4), 273–283. https://doi.org/10.1037/a0020466.

Sirois, F. M. (2016). Perfectionism and health behaviors: A self-regulation perspective. In F. M. Sirois & D. S. Molnar (Eds.), *Perfectionism, health, and well-being* (pp. 45–67). Springer.

Smith, M. M., Saklofske, D. H., Stoeber, D. H., & Sherry, S. B. (2016). The Big Three Perfectionism Scale: A New Measure of Perfectionism. *Journal of Psychoeducational Assessment, 34*(7), 670–687. https://doi.org/10.1177/0734282916651.

Smith, M. M., Sherry, S. B., Chen, S., Saklofske, D. H., Mushquash, C., Flett, G. L., & Hewitt, P. L. (2018). The perniciousness of perfectionism: A meta-analytic review of the perfectionism-suicide relationship. *Journal of Personality, 86*(3), 522–542. https://doi.org/10.1111/jopy.12333.

Smith, M. M., Sherry, S. B., Ge, S. Y. J., Hewitt, P. L., Flett, G. L., & Baggley, D. L. (2022). Multidimensional Perfectionism Turns 30: A Review of Known Knowns and Known Unknowns. *Canadian Psychology, 63*(1), 16–31. https://doi.org/10.1037/cap0000288.

Smith, M. M., Sherry, S. B., Vidovic, V., Saklofske, D. H., Stoeber, J., & Benoit, A. (2019). Perfectionism and the Five-Factor Model of Personality: A Meta-Analytic Review. *Personality and Social Psychology Review, 23*(4), 367–390. https://doi.org/10.1177/1088868318814973.

Spagnoli, P., Kovalchuk, L. S., Aiello, M. S., & Rice, K. G. (2021). The predictive role of perfectionism on heavy work investment: A two-waves cross-lagged panel study. *Personality and Individual Differences, 173*, 110632.

Spagnoli, P., Rice, K., Scafuri Kovalchuk, L., Rice, F., Molinaro, D., & Carpentieri, S. (2022). The Two-Factor Perfectionism Model and Heavy Work Investment in Italy and the U.S. *Journal of Personality Assessment, 104*(5), 680–691. https://doi.org/10.1080/00223891.2021.1975724.

Spence, J. T., & Robbins, A. S. (1992). Workaholism: Definition, measurement, and preliminary results. *Journal of Personality Assessment, 58*, 160–178. http://dx.doi.org/10.1207/s15327752jpa5801_15.

Stairs, A. M., Smith, G. T., Zapolski, T. C. B., Combs, J. L., & Settles, R. E. (2012). Clarifying the Construct of Perfectionism. *Assessment, 19*(2), 146–166. https://doi.org/10.1177/1073191111411663.

Stoeber, J. (2012). Perfectionism and performance. In S. M. Murphy (Ed.), *The Oxford handbook of sport and performance psychology* (pp. 294–306). Oxford University Press. https://doi.org/10.1093/oxfordhb/9780199731763.013.0015.

Stoeber, J. (2018). The psychology of perfectionism: An introduction. In J.Stoeber(Ed.), *The psychology of perfectionism: Theory, research, applications* (pp.3–16). Routledge/Taylor & Francis Group.

Stoeber, J., & Damian, L. E. (2014). The Clinical Perfectionism Questionnaire: Further evidence for two factors capturing perfectionistic strivings and concerns. *Personality and Individual Differences*, 61–62, 38–42. https://doi.org/10.1016/j.paid.2014.01.003.

Stoeber, J., & Damian, L. E. (2016). Perfectionism in employees: Work engagement, workaholism, and burnout. In F. M.Sirois D. S.& Molnar(Eds.), *Perfectionism, health, and well-being* (pp.265–283). Springer International Publishing/Springer Nature. https://doi.org/10.1007/978-3-319-18582-8_12.

Stoeber, J., Damian, L. E., & Madigan, D. J. (2018). Perfectionism: A motivational perspective. In J. Stoeber (Ed.), *The psychology of perfectionism: Theory, research, applications* (pp. 19–43). Routledge/Taylor & Francis Group.

Stoeber, J., Davis, C. R., & Townley, J. (2013). Perfectionism and workaholism in employees: The role of work motivation. *Personality and Individual Differences*, 55 (7), 733–738. https://doi.org/10.1016/j.paid.2013.06.001.

Stoeber, J., & Otto, K. (2006). Positive Conceptions of Perfectionism: Approaches, Evidence, Challenges. *Personality and Social Psychology Review*, 10(4), 295–319. https://doi.org/10.1207/s15327957pspr1004_2.

Stoeber, J., Smith, M. M., Saklofske, D. H., & Sherry, S. B. (2021). Perfectionism and interpersonal problems revisited. *Personality and Individual Differences*, 169, 110106. https://doi.org/10.1016/j.paid.2020.110106.

Sullivan, H. S. (1953). *The interpersonal theory of psychiatry*. W. W. Norton & Co.

Tetrick, L. E., & Peiró, J. M. (2012). Occupational safety and health. In S. W. J. Kozlowski (Ed.), *The Oxford Handbook of Organizational Psychology*, Vol. 2 (pp. 209–217). Oxford University Press. https://doi.org/10.1093/oxfordhb/9780199928286.013.0036.

Whiston, S. C. (2001). Selecting career outcome assessments: An organizational scheme. *Journal of Career Assessment*, 9(3), 215–228. https://doi.org/10.1177/106907270100900301.

Whiston, S. C. (2008). *Principles and applications of assessment in counseling*, 3rd edition. Brooks/Cole.

Zwaan, K., ter Bogt, T. F. M., & Raaijmakers, Q. (2009). So you want to be a rock "n" roll star? Career success of pop musicians in the Netherlands. *Poetics*, 37, 250–266. http://dx.doi.org/10.1016/j.poetic.2009.03.004.

13 Job Crafting for Sustainable Career Development

Ana Laguía, Juan A. Moriano and Gabriela Topa

Introduction

The focus of the psychology of sustainability and sustainable development on well-being in organizations relates to improving employees' quality of life (Di Fabio & Rosen, 2018; Di Fabio & Tsuda, 2018). Job satisfaction, job crafting, job design, and job redesign are all relevant for building sustainable life-work projects (Di Fabio, 2017a). Moreover, variables involved in sustainable development, such as reflexivity, meaningfulness, connectedness, authentic self, self-attunement, and harmonization (Di Fabio & Svicher, 2021), are also associated with job crafting. Thus, job-crafting behaviors are considered potential ways for realizing career sustainable development (e.g., Wang, 2022).

In its original formulation, the term "job crafting" was used to designate a type of proactive work behavior that prompts employees to engage in attempts to change their jobs (or their perception of their jobs) and to see more clearly what their job means and how they can relate it to their abilities, skills, and interests (Wrzesniewski & Dutton, 2001; Berg et al., 2013). According to Wrzesniewski and Dutton, job crafting occurs when employees are free to change the frequency or type of tasks they perform at work (e.g., by changing the amount of time they spend on a task or by trying out new activities), the relationships they experience in that environment (e.g., by trying to interact with people from different backgrounds or with more colleagues within their own department), or the way they think about their work (e.g., by considering the impact their work may have on other colleagues or visualizing how their position contributes to achieving the overall mission of the organization). These psychological, social, and physical actions affect work meaning and identity. Meaningfulness is integral to sustainability and promotes sustainability for employees (Di Fabio, 2017a, 2017b). Early work on job crafting was mainly qualitative in nature and focused on describing how different types of employees managed to make changes in their jobs through crafting in order to enhance their motivations, strengths, and passions.

More specifically, job crafting refers to the changes (both physical and cognitive) employees make to their tasks or their relationships at work in a bottom-up redesign process. Physical changes consist of modifications to the number of tasks performed, their scope, or their format; and cognitive

DOI: 10.4324/9781003212157-16

> anization.d.

changes affect employees' perception of their job. According to Wrzesniewski and Dutton (2001), employees would be motivated to apply job crafting when seeking to satisfy certain individual needs, such as controlling certain aspects of their work to avoid negative consequences. They may also be motivated to seek a more positive self-image or to satisfy their basic human need to connect with others. These needs are in line with those proposed for decent work, i.e., survival and power, social connections/contributions, and self-determination, as well as the core principles of sustainability from a psychological perspective (Di Fabio & Svicher, 2021; Svicher & Di Fabio, 2021). Petrou et al. (2012) also note that people try to modify aspects of their job to create conditions in which they can work in a healthy and motivated way. Moreover, job crafting is a process, not a one-time behavior (Berg et al., 2013).

Tims and Bakker (2010) transfer the concept of job crafting to the job demands-resources (JD-R) theory, arguing that employees can change their level of job demands and job resources to better match their own abilities and needs. Within this line of research, several empirical studies have shown that employees with higher engagement levels tend to exhibit job-crafting behaviors (e.g., Robledo et al., 2019). Moreover, these behaviors increase their work and personal resources and, in the long run, generate even more engagement. This leads to a virtuous cycle (a motivational gain spiral), whereby engagement leads to job crafting, which, in turn, increases employees' tendency towards greater engagement. The psychology of sustainability and sustainable development pays particular attention to the use of resources and regenerating resources (Di Fabio & Rosen, 2018).

Currently, empirical research on job crafting is developing rapidly, as recently published meta-analyses (e.g., Lichtenthaler & Fischbach, 2019; Rudolph et al., 2017; Wang et al., 2020), reviews (e.g., Dash & Vohra, 2020; Tims et al., 2022), and meta-syntheses of qualitative studies (e.g., Lazazzara et al., 2020) show. For instance, the scientometric analysis conducted by Gemmano et al. (2020) found that 375 papers related to job crafting had been published between January 2001 and December 2019. This analysis notes the relationships between job crafting and other related constructs in the literature, such as work engagement, burnout, job resources, job satisfaction, and job performance. According to Dash and Vohra (2020), the growing body of research on job crafting can be grouped into three periods. The first period (2001–2012) is characterized by qualitative and mixed-method studies seeking to delineate the concept. The second period (2012 onwards) starts with the development of a quantitative scale based on the JD-R model, which has been the tool most commonly used to examine the relationship between job crafting and other variables, particularly work engagement and burnout. Finally, the last period (2016 onwards) is more ambiguous and heterogeneous, and it is characterized by the emergence of new approaches.

This chapter begins by discussing the different conceptualizations of job crafting and the corresponding measurement scales. This is followed by a summary of the most widely studied antecedents and outcomes as well as the different moderating and mediating variables. The next section explores new approaches to the study of job crafting and includes an empirical work analyzing three dimensions of this construct: strengths, interests, and development. Next, we focus on changes in the object of study, from task-related to cognitive job crafting and from individual to collaborative job crafting. The chapter ends with some suggestions for future research, implications for Work and Organizational Psychology, and conclusions.

Conceptualization and Measurement of Job Crafting

Job crafting is a novel construct that holds promise for the design of interventions. However, there is still no solid consensus regarding its various dimensions. Authors have proposed different dimensions, each focusing on different aspects of this daily behavior. For example, in their role-based conceptualization, Wrzesniewski and Dutton (2001) differentiate between three types of job crafting: task crafting, relational crafting, and cognitive crafting. Task crafting involves employees actively shaping the tasks they must accomplish at work by taking on more or fewer tasks, altering the scope of said tasks, and/or changing the means of task accomplishment. Relationship crafting involves changing the quality and/or quantity of interactions with others at work. Finally, cognitive crafting refers to employees reframing the way they perceive their work and altering their cognitive representation of it (e.g., viewing work as either an integrated whole or discrete parts). This conceptualization of job crafting focuses on motivational aspects and comprises changes in tangible work-role boundaries as well as in intangible work role perceptions (Lichtenthaler & Fischbach, 2019).

Based on the model developed by Tims and Bakker (2010), who integrated the JD-R theory and job crafting into a resource-based perspective, Tims et al. (2012) suggest that job crafting is made up of four independent dimensions: (1) increasing challenging job demands so that employees experience an adequate level of job demand and are not under-stimulated (this involves behaviors such as asking for more responsibility); (2) decreasing hindering demands, which alludes to behaviors that aim to minimize different types of overwhelming job demands (e.g., physical, cognitive, and emotional) – for instance, reducing workload and work-family conflicts; (3) increasing structural resources, which includes behaviors designed to increase motivational job characteristics, such as variety, opportunity for development, and autonomy – this dimension is related to assuming more responsibility and/or gaining greater knowledge about the job; and (4) increasing social resources, which refers to soliciting feedback, advice, or support from supervisors and colleagues. This conceptualization takes both motivational and occupational health aspects into account, but it comprises of only changes in tangible work-role boundaries (Lichtenthaler & Fischbach, 2019). As such, it does not contemplate a cognitive dimension and focuses exclusively on actual or tangible changes that employees can make in their jobs. In the literature, these four dimensions are often considered independently. However, several studies have also summed up or averaged the scores across dimensions to represent an overall measure of job crafting (e.g., Akkermans & Tims, 2017). Although this suggests that the different crafting dimensions reflect a latent, composite, or higher-order concept, some concerns and criticisms have arisen regarding the operationalization of a single second-order construct (e.g., Dash & Vohra, 2020).

The two conceptualizations of job crafting outlined above, which are also known as the North American school and the European school due to their respective origins (Tian et al., 2022), are the most widespread and empirically analyzed. They differ in their definition of the content, motivation, and purpose of crafting (de Devotto & Wechsler, 2019; Zhang & Parker, 2019). Whereas the former focuses on changes in task, relational, and/or cognitive boundaries aimed at improving work meaning and identity, the latter encompasses changes in job characteristics aimed at balancing job resources and demands to increase person-job fit and deal with stress at work. Job crafting can be viewed as a process by which employees create change over time or as a behavior in which employees engage with greater or lesser frequency. These two conceptualizations have encouraged the design of mainly qualitative or quantitative studies, respectively (Lazazzara et al., 2020).

Measuring Job Crafting

In line with the different theoretical models, various measurement scales have been developed. Within the role-based approach, Slemp and Vella-Brodrick's (2013) Job Crafting Questionnaire (JCQ) measures all three dimensions (i.e., task, relational, and cognitive crafting) originally conceptualized by Wrzesniewski and Dutton (2001). The JCQ consists of 15 items distributed across three subscales, each containing five items (e.g., "Choose to take on additional tasks at work"; "Think about how your job gives your life purpose"; "Organise or attend work-related social functions"). Participants are instructed to indicate the frequency with which they have engaged in each job-crafting activity (1 = *hardly ever* to 6 = *very often*). From the resource-based perspective, Tims et al. (2012) have developed a 21-item instrument called the Job Crafting Scale (JCS). This four-dimensional scale is distributed across four subscales: increasing structural job resources (five items; e.g., "I decide on my own how I do things"), increasing social job resources (five items; e.g., "I look to my supervisor for inspiration"), increasing challenging job demands (five items; e.g., "I regularly take on extra tasks even though I do not receive extra salary for them"), and decreasing hindering job demands (six items; e.g., "I make sure that my work is mentally less intense"). Items are rated on a five-point frequency scale ranging from 1 (*never*) to 5 (*often*). Petrou et al. (2012) have modified the JCS to measure general-level and day-level job crafting, and Nielsen and Abildgaard (2012) have adapted the same scale to blue-collar workers. Studies support the reliability and validity (factorial, criterion, and convergent) of these scales. Furthermore, several scales have been adapted to non-English-speaking populations and validated in different countries (e.g., Bakker et al., 2018). However, the cross-cultural consistency of some measures and several aspects have been challenged (Dash & Vohra, 2020). Other scales have also been developed, although their use to date is not so widespread (for further information, see Dash & Vohra, 2020; de Devotto & Wechsler, 2019; Wang et al., 2020). Indeed, the creation of ad hoc measures for each study, unsupported by subsequent studies, constitutes an important limitation for the development of research and comparisons between approaches.

Job Crafting Process: From Antecedents to Outcomes

The antecedents of job crafting may be grouped into personal attributes (the determinants of job crafting) and organizational factors (the stimulators of job crafting) (Dash & Vohra, 2020; Park & Park, 2023; Rudolph et al., 2017; Wang et al., 2017). The former includes antecedents such as individual temperament (e.g., approach/avoidance), proactive personality, big-five traits, individual competitiveness, work orientation, entrepreneurial orientation, work locus of control, general self-efficacy, adaptability, autonomy, regulatory focus (promotion/prevention), empowerment, basic psychological needs fulfillment, or personal resources. The latter encompasses a combination of job-related (job demands and resources at work, such as daily working conditions, work pressure, workload, autonomy, and feedback), group (e.g., friendship among employees, internal social capital), leadership, and organizational (e.g., employee rank, organizational embeddedness) antecedents. The mismatch between personal characteristics and task characteristics can promote job crafting. Wang et al. (2017, p. 84) suggest that "job crafting is a self-initiated process of changing job characteristics in order to adaptively and proactively achieve greater compatibility between personal attributes and dynamic work environments," either in the present or in anticipation of future job changes. The meta-analytic review conducted by Wang et al. (2020) focuses specifically on the relationship between social factors and job crafting. These authors distinguish between organizational insiders (leadership and colleagues) and organizational outsiders (family, customers, patients, etc.). Different leadership styles (e.g., transformational leadership, empowering leadership, servant leadership, leader-member exchange) have an impact on job crafting (Dash & Vohra, 2020; Park & Park, 2023; Wang et al., 2020), although this effect depends on several moderators, such as, for instance, employee personality (e.g., proactive personality) and temperament, power distance, job autonomy, job uncertainty, or workload (Wang et al., 2017). Demographics and employment characteristics usually include age, gender, education, tenure, and working hours (Rudolph et al., 2017). Being female, being more highly educated, and working longer hours are positively associated with job crafting, whereas age and tenure are negatively associated with this construct.

The main outcomes identified in previous reviews and meta-analytical analyses include both individual and organizational outcomes as well as immediate and long-term outcomes (Dash & Vohra, 2020; Rudolph et al., 2017; Wang et al., 2017; Wang et al., 2020). The most widely studied outcomes include occupational well-being, job attitudes, and performance indicators. Some individual outcomes are work engagement, work enjoyment, need fulfillment, meaning, identity, flourishing, flow, eudemonic/psychological and hedonic/subjective well-being, work-related affect, work-life balance, job satisfaction, organizational commitment, employability, and person-job fit. Organizational outcomes include job performance, team efficacy, innovation, creativity, design, and organizational citizenship behavior. Interestingly, as job crafting is aimed at improving person-job fit, the result is not necessarily an organizationally beneficial outcome (e.g., it may have a detrimental effect on the achievement of organizational goals and performance), nor is it even one that is compatible with the needs of supervisors or colleagues (e.g., job crafting may result in dysfunctional consequences linked to job stress, strain, burnout, emotional exhaustion, frustration, counterproductive work behavior, increased workplace conflict and workload, and turnover intention). If each employee crafts their job to their own needs and personal characteristics, teamwork can suffer. In tasks subject to strict regulations, changes can even be counterproductive. Thus, more research is required in relation to destructive social factors, such as conflicts with clients and families (Wang et al., 2020). This ties in with the objective of pursuing harmony with others and workplace relational civility, which is so relevant to achieving sustainability (Di Fabio & Tsuda, 2018).

Work engagement is often considered a mediator between job-crafting dimensions and other organizational outcomes. However, work engagement can also be considered an antecedent of job crafting (e.g., Robledo et al., 2019; Topa & Aranda-Carmena, 2022a), and a gain cycle over time may explain the relationship between these two constructs (e.g., Topa & Aranda-Carmena, 2022b).

Following Bruning and Campion's (2018) taxonomy, Lazazzara et al. (2020) organized their meta-synthesis of qualitative research on job crafting into approach and avoidance forms of job crafting. Approach crafting deals with the enrichment and expansion of job boundaries, and in their meta-synthesis, examples include caring moves (responding to requests, practicing care), maintenance and upgrading of qualifications, one's own professional development, task prioritization, innovation practices, proactive use of technology, active changing of relationships at work, creation of additional relationships, persuading others to take over tasks, project coordination, reframing one's job purpose, stakeholder prioritization, and emphasis on the positive qualities of work. In contrast, avoidance crafting aims to reduce and limit certain aspects of the job and includes, among others, reducing the number of tasks, responsibilities and requirements; minimizing effort expenditure, task scope, and/or workload; reducing the number of meetings and the time devoted to socializing with colleagues and interacting with supervisors, colleagues, and/or customers; reducing cognitive demands; withdrawal crafting; and offloading responsibility for incidents or critical situations onto colleagues. Crafting may also be observed in other domains, such as work-life crafting (e.g., locational crafting, travel-time reduction, meeting colleagues during free time) and leisure crafting (e.g., sports, hobbies). Lazazzara et al. (2020) have also identified the most widely studied antecedents of job crafting (proactive and reactive motives [e.g., additional callings, pro-social motivation, improving performance, work-life balance, career aspiration, coping with hardship/extremely high competition/re-organization threats/shaming/dirty jobs, lack of resources, work overload and pressure, time pressure, context] grouped into supportive/constraining climate and supportive/constraining design; as well as personal factors [e.g., personality traits or personal characteristics, influence or self-confidence vs. lack of personal resources, difficulties in managing overload]), along with its consequences (positive [e.g., meaningfulness, well-being, better performance and relationships, work–life balance, satisfaction, engagement] and negative [e.g., strain, sleep problems, health issues, stress, conflicts, turnover, work withdrawal, low customer satisfaction]). Proactive and reactive job-crafting motives are related to both approach and avoidance forms of job crafting. Supportive and constraining contextual factors moderate these relationships, determining which job-crafting form is activated. In turn, job-crafting forms are associated with both positive and negative consequences. The consequences derived from avoidance crafting are always negative, whereas those derived from approach crafting may be positive or negative, depending on the supportive or constraining personal factors involved. The proposed process model covers from the initial motivation and the crafting process itself to the results obtained, and it helps further our understanding of when and how employees engage in certain forms of job crafting.

New Approaches to Job Crafting

Other authors differentiate between expansion-oriented (i.e., increasing the number or complexity of tasks and relationships at work – for instance, seeking challenges and resources) and contraction-oriented job crafting (i.e., reducing task complexity or the number of interactions with others – for instance, decreasing demands) (see Wang et al., 2017). Bindl et al. (2019) incorporated individuals' needs and the regulatory focus into the study of job crafting, developing a novel measure of the construct based on their theoretical model, which distinguishes between the promotion- and prevention-oriented forms of each different type of job crafting (task, relationship, skill, and cognitive). In their meta-analysis, Lichtenthaler and Fischbach (2019) integrated both the role-based (Wrzesniewski & Dutton, 2001) and the resource-based conceptualizations (Tims et al., 2012), adopting the regulatory perspective applied to job crafting by Bindl et al. (2019). This new model comprises promotion-focused job crafting (increasing job resources and challenging job demands, expansion-oriented tasks, and relational and cognitive crafting) and prevention-focused job crafting (decreasing hindering job demands, contraction-oriented tasks, and relational crafting). The cross-sectional meta-analysis shows that promotion-focused job crafting is positively associated with work engagement and negatively associated with burnout. For its part, prevention-focused job crafting is negatively associated with work engagement and positively associated with burnout. Moreover, work engagement and burnout mediate the relationship between both dimensions of job crafting and performance (positively in the case of promotion-focused job-crafting performance and negatively in the case of prevention-focused job-crafting performance). The longitudinal meta-analysis reveals reciprocal, positive relationships between promotion-focused job crafting and work engagement as well as between prevention-focused job crafting and burnout over time. The meta-analytic review conducted by Wang et al. (2020) also distinguishes between promotion- and prevention-focused job crafting when analyzing the associations between social factors and work outcomes mediated by job crafting.

Zhang and Parker (2019) also synthesized the role-based (Wrzesniewski & Dutton, 2001) and the resource-based conceptualizations (Tims et al., 2012) and proposed a three-level hierarchical structure of job crafting: (1) crafting orientation (approach versus avoidance crafting), (2) crafting form (behavioral versus cognitive crafting), and (3) crafting content (job resources versus job demands). Rather than understanding the construct as multidimensional, as assumed by previous conceptualizations, this structure defines eight types of job crafting, which allows research to advance along new avenues. Tian et al. (2022) proposed a new taxonomy of job crafting that includes two perspectives, the rational and the emotional, emphasizing the relevance of emotional needs and the realization of values in work settings. Rationality has attracted the attention of much of the research community and is related to person-job fit, efficiency, external goals, and a decrease in work demands; whereas emotional crafting is related to the pursuit of unanswered callings or a decrease in career regret and is very common, for instance, among older employees.

Other researchers have developed proposals to capture other dimensions of job crafting. For instance, Kuijpers et al. (2020) focused on three dimensions of job crafting that can be fostered by organizational interventions: crafting towards strengths, crafting towards interests, and crafting towards development. Crafting towards strengths refers to self-initiated changes that individuals make by modifying the boundaries of their job tasks to make better use of their strengths (e.g., "I make sure that I take on tasks that I am good at"). Personal strengths are the characteristics of a person that enable them to perform better and, as such, constitute important personal resources. Crafting towards interests aims to change the job in such a way that it matches the employee's interests, which are powerful personal resources, as they are perceived as motivational factors that make it possible for employees to invest their time and energy in what interests them (e.g., "I make sure that I take on tasks that I like"). Lastly, developmental crafting refers to initiatives that employees take to activate their potential by creating opportunities, for instance, to apply unused knowledge and skills (e.g., "I look for tasks through which I can develop myself"). Employees can only benefit from learning opportunities if they are aware of their own developmental potential, so this is also a valuable personal resource.

Following this model, the authors of this chapter empirically analyzed the relationship between these three dimensions of job crafting (i.e., strengths, interests, and development) and three individual outcomes: emotional exhaustion, job satisfaction, and person-job fit. In previous research, these outcomes have generally been analyzed in relation to other conceptualizations of job crafting. Additionally, we explored two antecedents of job crafting: proactive personality and core self-evaluations. As far as proactive personality is concerned (Topa & Morales Domínguez, 2006), more proactive employees are generally more likely to engage in all forms of job crafting because they have high levels of initiative, identify opportunities, overcome barriers, and persevere until they achieve their goals (Bakker et al., 2012). Core self-evaluations include four interrelated core traits – namely, self-esteem, general self-efficacy, locus of control, and (low) neuroticism (Beléndez et al., 2018) – that are positively related to job satisfaction.

Our sample comprised a total of 646 participants (58.7% females; Mage = 38.9 years, SD = 11.5, 18–78 years) who had been working for at least one year (M = 10.5 years, SD = 10.4, 1–60 years). In terms of education level, most participants had university (52.2%) or vocational training qualifications (19.2%) and, to a lesser extent, high school (18.2%) or primary qualifications (10.4%). We carried out a back-translation of Kuijpers et al.'s (2020) nine-item job crafting scale and used scales validated in Spain for the rest of the measurements. The instruments used were the Spanish version (Beléndez et al., 2018) of the Core Self-Evaluation Scale (CSES-SP) developed by Judge et al. (2003), which consists of 12 items and comprises two dimensions (positive and negative core self-evaluations); the Proactive Personality Scale (Bateman & Crant, 1993); the emotional exhaustion subscale of the Maslach Burnout Inventory – General Survey (Schaufeli et al., 1996); the Spanish version of the Brief Index of Affective Job Satisfaction (Fernández-Muñoz & Topa, 2018), and the Person-Job Fit Scale (P-J Fit; Brkich et al., 2002). In order to gain a better understanding of the associations that exist between the study variables, we used partial least squares structural modeling (PLS-SEM; Ringle et al., 2015). All items were rated on a five-point response scale.

The mean scores were moderate to high for most of the variables (between 3.39 and 3.82), except for negative core self-evaluations and emotional exhaustion, for which scores below 3 were obtained (Table 13.1). The correlations were significant and in the expected direction, except for the interests

Table 13.1 Empirical study on job crafting: Descriptive statistics and correlations

	α	Overall (n = 646) M (SD)	Female (n = 379) M (SD)	Male (n = 267) M (SD)	1	2	3	4	5	6	7	8	9
1. Job crafting – strengths	.72	3.82 (0.70)	3.83 (0.72)	3.80 (0.67)	-								
2. Job crafting – interests	.74	3.44 (0.78)	3.46 (0.80)	3.41 (0.74)	.69***	-							
3. Job crafting – development	.81	3.79 (0.77)	3.82 (0.77)	3.75 (0.76)	.74***	.54***	-						
4. Proactive personality	.80	3.63 (0.74)	3.59 (0.76)	3.68 (0.71)	.55***	.44***	.52***	-					
5. Positive self-evaluations	.84	3.79 (0.65)	3.78 (0.65)	3.82 (0.65)	.55***	.42***	.55***	.67***	-				
6. Negative self-evaluations	.82	2.60 (0.82)	**2.69 (0.86)**	**2.46 (0.75)**	-.22***	-.14***	-.25***	-.27***	-.51***	-			
7. Emotional exhaustion	.92	2.51 (1.05)	2.53 (1.09)	2.47 (0.98)	-.18***	-.06	-.22***	-.18***	-.38***	.55***	-		
8. Job satisfaction	.94	3.39 (1.06)	3.39 (1.09)	3.38 (1.03)	.42***	.30***	.43***	.36***	.54***	-.42***	-.58***	-	
9. Person-job fit	.93	3.39 (0.96)	3.33 (0.99)	3.48 (0.92)	.30***	.19***	.30***	.23***	.43***	-.48***	-.52***	.81***	-

Note. Means in bold denote significant differences between female and male participants at $p < .05$. $*p < .05$. $**p < .01$. $***p < .001$. α = Cronbach's alpha.

dimension of job crafting and emotional exhaustion. Proactive personality and positive core self-evaluations were positively associated with the three dimensions of job crafting, whereas negative self-evaluations correlated negatively with all the variables. The three dimensions of job crafting correlated positively with job satisfaction and person-job fit, they correlated negatively with emotional exhaustion, and a nonsignificant relationship was found between the interests dimension of job crafting and emotional exhaustion.

Figure 13.1 illustrates the associations observed between the different study variables. Proactive personality and positive core self-evaluations (although not negative core self-evaluations) were found to be significant antecedents of all three job-crafting dimensions. The results also revealed that interests and developmental job crafting were significantly associated with emotional exhaustion (positively in the case of interests: β =.13, p =.023; negatively in the case of developmental crafting: β = −.23, p <.001; and the association between strengths and emotional exhaustion was nonsignificant: β = −.12, p =.12), whereas both strengths and developmental job crafting were positively associated with job satisfaction (β =.20, p =.003 and β =.28, p <.001, respectively; the association between interests and job satisfaction was nonsignificant: β =.01, p =.868) and person-job fit (β =.23, p =.001 and β =.21, p <.001, respectively; the association between interests and person-job fit was nonsignificant: β = −.03, p =.544). The interests dimension was observed to have a complex pattern of associations with other variables, something that was remarked upon also in the study by Kuijpers et al. (2020), in which job crafting interests at Time 1 were found to negatively predict dedication and absorption at Time 2. This conceptualization of job crafting is promising, although more research is needed to establish a pattern of consistent relationships between the different dimensions proposed and the antecedents and consequences traditionally analyzed in Work and Organizational Psychology.

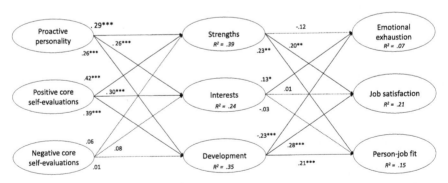

Figure 13.1 Empirical study on job crafting: Structural model
Note. *p <.05. **p <.01. ***p <.001. Nonsignificant pathways are represented by dotted lines.

From Task-related to Cognitive Job Crafting

Task crafting refers to taking control of job tasks and adjusting their quantity (i.e., amount) or content (Wrzesniewski & Dutton, 2001). It involves modifying the scope or types of tasks accomplished at work (Slemp & Vella-Brodrick, 2013). Expansion-oriented task crafting refers to taking on additional tasks, whereas contraction-oriented task crafting refers to avoiding certain tasks (Lichtenthaler & Fischbach, 2019). According to Geldenhuys et al. (2021), this involves employees personally taking the initiative to change the tasks they perform (e.g., doing different tasks), modify their approach to work (e.g., adjusting their work process), or change the timing of their tasks (e.g., performing complex tasks in the morning, when they have high energy levels, and leaving routine tasks for the afternoon, when they have less energy).

Several job-crafting dimensions have attracted relatively little attention, one example being cognitive crafting (Tims et al., 2022). Cognitive crafting is related to psychological redefinitions and reinterpretations of work characteristics (Wrzesniewski & Dutton, 2001) as well as the belief that work is meaningful and important and that work outcomes can significantly affect other people's lives or well-being. In other words, it refers to thoughts about how work gives people purpose, and how the tasks and duties one has at work have a profounder meaning than is initially evident. The study of how "dirty workers" change the way they view their tasks and work roles is a good example of cognitive crafting (e.g., a hospital cleaner who considers their job to be a means of helping patients recover, rather than just a matter of cleaning up).

Nevertheless, authors subscribing to the JD-R approach argue that cognitive crafting is more likely a form of passive adaptation to work that does not lead to any real change in job content and, therefore, is not actually crafting (Bakker et al., 2012; Tims & Bakker, 2010). Zhang and Parker (2019) attempt to overcome this dispute among scholars by proposing a hierarchical structure of job crafting, conceptualizing the form of crafting (behavioral vs. cognitive) as a hierarchical set of constructs. The cognitive approach to crafting can be resource-focused or demand-focused. Resource-focused crafting involves reframing one's work in such a way as to perceive more positive aspects of the job (e.g., actively remembering the broader meaning of one's work), whereas demand-focused crafting involves a positive reappraisal of one's own demands (e.g., seeing demands as opportunities to learn and develop). Cognitive crafting may be most beneficial in very fixed and restricted jobs, where there are relatively few opportunities for behavioral crafting. Furthermore, some job characteristics, such as task significance and identity, are probably much easier to modify through cognitive crafting than other job characteristics, such as task variety. All these forms of cognitive crafting are active and positive (Zhang & Parker, 2019).

Research into cognitive crafting is scarce, but it appears that this type of crafting may benefit attitudes, probably because it changes employees' perceptions of their own work, and it also relates specifically to meaningfulness by enabling them to control how they understand and align their work with their self-concept. Geldenhuys et al. (2021) argue that cognitive crafting allows employees to achieve a better job fit, thereby enabling them to invest the necessary energy and effort. Experiencing meaning helps employees understand why they should go the extra mile in relation to difficult work problems and why they need to persist in the face of job demands.

As cognitive crafting is a process that arises predominantly within the individual, changes in cognitions may not always be expressed in behavior. Consequently, greater effort will not necessarily translate into better performance since, in order to do so, cognitive crafting must first translate into actual behavior (Weseler & Niessen, 2016). However, Geldenhuys et al. (2021) point out that employees will help their colleagues achieve their job performance goals if they have created meaning through cognitive crafting (e.g., perhaps by thinking about the importance of their contribution to other people's tasks). Consistently with this, the process of cognitive crafting also involves thinking about job tasks as part of the collective whole, which implies that employees may be more willing to invest time in extra-role performance, e.g., helping colleagues with their tasks.

From an Individual-level Activity to Collaborative Job Crafting

Job crafting was initially considered an individual-level activity. Employees can gain sustainable competitive advantages through crafting their jobs (Wang, 2022). However, Leana et al. (2009) later expanded Wrzesniewski and Dutton's (2001) theory to include the concept of collaborative job crafting. Focusing on task crafting, these authors tried to overcome the limitation that many jobs impose on individual job crafting, since in some cases, employee interdependence in the execution of tasks makes it impossible to propose or execute changes without taking other colleagues into consideration. Leana et al. also argued that employees involved in similar work processes relate to each other and experience common events, meaning that they can jointly determine how to modify their work to meet their shared goals. Furthermore, these authors noted that job crafting applied to collaboration with others had much more powerful effects than individual job crafting. Leana et al. developed a new scale composed of two subscales, each containing six items. Both subscales contain the same items but differ in their focus: employees' engagement in crafting behaviors "on their own" or "in collaboration with" colleagues (e.g., How often do you do any of the following?: "On your own, change the way you do your job to make it easier to yourself" vs. "Decide together with your coworkers to change the way you do your job to make it easier to yourself"). Their study demonstrated that job crafting is, indeed, composed of two different constructs, individual crafting and collaborative crafting, which are two independent yet closely related dimensions with different antecedents. The two dimensions are not mutually exclusive, and employees can engage in individual and collective crafting at the same time. The incidence and strength of one form or the other depends on how the work environment is perceived, the characteristics of the job, and individuals' work preferences and orientation. Leana et al.'s (2009) study hypothesizes both common and differentiated predictors for individual and collective crafting. For example, discretion at work may be an antecedent of both forms of crafting; specific predictors of individual crafting would be aspects, such as a career orientation toward work and a higher-status position; and predictors of collective crafting would include interdependence, supportive supervision, and social ties with colleagues.

More recently, Cheng et al. (2016) pointed out that through individual crafting, employees actively alter their task boundaries, whereas in collaborative crafting, employees work collaboratively to revise the work process. Depending on the interdependency of the jobs within a team, employees can embark on individual or collaborative job crafting (Wang et al., 2017). Leana et al. (2009) also examined the associations between job crafting and organizational outcomes. According to their theoretical model, collaborative crafting predicts higher levels of job performance and organizational commitment, whereas individual crafting does not predict such outcomes. Moreover, collaborative crafting is positively related to job satisfaction, whereas individual crafting is negatively associated with this variable. In their study with teachers, they found that teaching experience moderated the association between collaborative crafting and performance, with this relationship being stronger among less experienced teachers than among more experienced ones. In the same vein, Chen et al. (2014) found that both types (individual and collaborative crafting) strengthened engagement. Cheng and O-Yang (2018) also suggest that job crafting is related to job satisfaction, insofar as employees who construct and develop their work feel more committed to their job tasks and decisions and, consequently, experience higher levels of job satisfaction.

In Spain, Llorente-Alonso and Topa (2019) provided evidence of the validity and reliability of the Spanish version of Leana et al.'s (2009) job-crafting scale with a sample of 301 Spanish employees. Their study identified a similar factor structure to that of the original scale, composed of two factors (individual crafting and collaborative crafting). Moreover, in an attempt to provide theoretical evidence of individual and collaborative crafting as different constructs, they found that work engagement mediates the relationship between both individual and collaborative crafting and job satisfaction. Consistently with Leana et al.'s perspective, Alonso et al. (2019) applied this approach to an empirical study with a sample of 146 teachers. As teaching work is performed in the school environment, where many activities and processes are shared with colleagues, job-crafting behaviors engaged in by teachers are often limited by coworker collaboration (or lack thereof). Therefore, distinguishing between individual and collaborative job crafting seems to be the most appropriate option for analyzing teachers' proactive behaviors.

These authors analyzed the effect of both types of job crafting in relation to job satisfaction, work engagement, and teaching job performance.

Topa and Aranda-Carmena (2022a) analyzed the three most prominent conceptualizations of job crafting (i.e., resource-based, role-based, and individual/collective crafting) in three independent samples of nurses ($n_1 = 699$, $n_2 = 498$, and $n_3 = 308$). Nursing is a health-related working environment of interest due to its high levels of stress and burnout. The results of the study revealed that nurses' engagement can affect their performance at work, with job crafting dimensions acting as mediators in this relationship. The results also enable comparisons between different conceptualizations. The effectiveness of diverse job-crafting behaviors may vary depending on different job-crafting conceptualizations and measures. Drawing on the resource-based model, the results reveal a positive total effect of work engagement on job performance, a nonsignificant direct effect, and a mediating effect for only one of the four dimensions, namely increase in structural resources. In relation to the role-based approach, the results indicate a positive total effect of work engagement on job performance, a nonsignificant direct effect, and a mediating effect for only one of the three dimensions, namely task-related crafting. Finally, in relation to individual and collective crafting, the results indicate positive total and direct effects of work engagement on job performance, as well as a mediating effect only for individual crafting.

Avenues for Future Research

The growing number of empirical studies in this area makes it advisable to conduct systematic reviews, meta-analyses, and meta-syntheses to integrate the results and advance the literature on job crafting from the lens of the psychology of sustainability and sustainable development. Specifically, umbrella revisions are needed in order to highlight the caveats and the advancements made in the field. Moreover, a nomological network of job-crafting dimensions should be proposed in order to differentiate between the specific antecedents and consequences of each one. For instance, task-related crafting may trigger a process that, in turn, leads to developmental crafting (Kuijpers et al., 2020). Although the number of meta-analyses has grown in recent years, the lack of studies that simultaneously employ the different conceptualizations makes it difficult to compare models. Moreover, some previous studies view job crafting in a unidimensional way, whereas others take into account its different dimensions. In general, however, the recommendation is to consider the different dimensions of job crafting separately, avoiding a global aggregate score (Rudolph et al., 2017; Topa & Aranda-Carmena, 2022a). Not all types of crafting would be advisable for all types of jobs, and not all forms of job crafting would be equally adequate in all work settings, due to specific organizational characteristics.

From an individual perspective, more studies should focus on boundary conditions and the mechanisms that link job crafting to its outcomes. For instance, job crafting has been proposed as a promising way to develop decent work (Svicher & Di Fabio, 2021). From a team perspective, consideration should be given to how individual job crafting combines with collective job crafting. In particular, individual preferences or orientations can interact in complex ways with group processes. One example would be leadership and the relative power position and prototypicality of group members. Future research should clarify whether job-crafting proposals are more widely accepted by all members when they stem from the leader, in which case the job-crafting phenomenon would be subsumed under the influence of said figure, or whether they are also accepted when the job-crafter is a non-prototypical and powerless member of the group, in which case it would be necessary to establish the possible interaction between prototypicality and job crafting. Furthermore, empirical research to date seems to have explored the application of job crafting in the group context, but it is still necessary to ascertain whether group decision-making, communication, and information-sharing processes interact with job-crafting initiatives. In sum, we have yet to determine how crafting plans are proposed, how social influences can affect their acceptance, what role is played by each group member during the job-crafting process itself, and how potential job-crafting-related consequences (both negative and positive) are acknowledged and accepted.

From a social perspective, the potential impact of job crafting on others should be considered from a multi-stakeholder perspective. First, job crafting at work may impact employees' families (due to an increase in employee duties and the consequent work-family conflict), and avoidance crafting may be inversely related to a decrease in work-family conflict, although these linear relationships may also be affected by a plethora of other variables, including attributional processes and career-development expectancies, among others. Second, colleagues, and specifically supervisors, may also be affected by the job-crafting intentions and actions of a focal employee. Since they modify the distribution of tasks and responsibilities, job-crafting proposals may be viewed as a threat, due to their potential for reducing group or organizational performance and increasing the focal employee's benefits. Third, the norms and values of the organization's culture may be considered potential moderators of the associations between job-crafting initiatives and their consequences. A collaborative and trusting culture, where mistakes are viewed as opportunities rather than failures, may promote and encourage job-crafting initiatives. Finally, some specific and strictly regulated work environments, such as nursing, banking, and others, would be differently oriented to accepting job-crafting initiatives; moreover, the job-crafting process itself would result in different outcomes, depending on the type of work environment in question.

As set out in the extant literature, interventions in the work context should have a theoretical basis and incorporate the various phases and elements involved. They should also be adequately prepared and evaluated in a rigorous manner, using a treatment group and a control group, with random assignment of participants to each one. Only in this way will it be possible to advance in the practical application of job crafting in organizations, expanding on the contributions made by authors such as Kuijpers et al. (2020), who analyzed the relationship between a job-crafting intervention and work engagement. Although no direct association was observed in this study, significant results were found in relation to some of the dimensions of job crafting, particularly when the workload was high. Specific training can enhance important resources useful for the well-being of employees in their work environments; for instance, positive outcomes may be achieved through sustainability measures (Di Fabio & Rosen, 2018). Furthermore, in addition to randomized, controlled trials, realistic evaluations in organizational settings may help determine "what works for whom in which circumstances" (Nielsen & Miraglia, 2017), taking context, intervention mechanisms, and outcomes into account from an integrated perspective. From a psychology of sustainability perspective, the application of sustainable career-management and self-management processes allows gaining psychological strengths, personal resources, and growth of employees (Di Fabio & Svicher, 2021). To be successful, interventions should consider the sustainability of the work-life project (Di Fabio, 2017a, 2017b).

The underlying mechanisms of job crafting are still unclear. Several studies have analyzed the mediating role of some constructs (e.g., work engagement) in the relationship between job crafting and its outcomes, and others have explored the moderating role of other variables, such as leadership and perceived organizational support. However, the study of the mechanisms involved is still less developed than the analysis of antecedents and outcomes. For instance, leaders are acknowledged as playing a relevant role in promoting organizational identification and creating climates that support job crafting (Wang et al., 2017). The psychology of sustainability and sustainable development calls for leadership styles that recognize and respect the importance of relationships in organizational contexts for the well-being of workers (Di Fabio, 2017a). Since leadership has been found to be associated with job crafting (e.g., transformational leadership), future research should examine the individual contribution of various leadership styles, including sustainable leadership (Di Fabio & Peiró, 2018; Hallinger & Suriyankietkaew, 2018) and recent proposals, such as security providing leadership (e.g., Moriano et al., 2021) and identity leadership (e.g., Laguía et al., 2021). Moreover, the majority of studies to date have focused on the positive consequences of leadership, and more research is required into destructive leaders (Wang et al., 2020).

In terms of the methodological features of the empirical studies conducted to date, most have relied on self-report questionnaires, without efficiently managing the common method bias. Future research should include hetero-reported measures (e.g., colleagues, supervisors, clients) as well as objective indicators of performance (e.g., individual or team level sales ratings) or well-being (e.g., salivary biochemical stress indicators), with the aim of providing greater insight into the process. The quantitative study of job crafting has largely been limited to salaried employees, under the assumption that this behavior occurs only in prescribed jobs. However, some qualitative studies have begun to consider job crafting in self-employment, mostly in well-defined contexts characterized by restrictive legislation (see the meta-synthesis by Lazazzara et al., 2020). Likewise, reemployment crafting (i.e., job crafting in the unemployed) may be of interest for the study of job crafting in vulnerable populations and in relation to decent work (Svicher & Di Fabio, 2021). The emergence of different work arrangements may also render an in-depth study of non-traditional salaried jobs advisable. Furthermore, cultural influences should be analyzed in broad cross-cultural studies. Although calls for more longitudinal studies are a common element of all reviews, empirical research on job crafting would benefit greatly from these designs, enabling an analysis of not only the short-term but also the long-term effects of job crafting and its different dimensions on both individual and organizational outcomes. Future studies should strive to develop a valid inventory, including fewer items for each dimension, while simultaneously assessing all the crafting dimensions proposed by several theoretical models. This empirical evidence could help clarify how the dimensions themselves are associated with each other as well as their potential mediator role between antecedents and work-related outcomes. Given that job crafting entails some degree of expertise at work, future studies should seek to determine how job crafting initiatives develop throughout the organizational socialization process and to explore the differences between newcomers and experts in terms of job-crafting motivations and behaviors. Finally, both qualitative and quantitative research is necessary to deepen our comprehension of the job-crafting process. A quali + quanti approach is also important in the study of meaning and details of meaning (Di Fabio, 2017b).

Implications for Applications in Work and Organizational Psychology

By promoting employees' job crafting, organizations can advance towards sustainability. Job crafting can contribute to both organizational and employee sustainability in different ways (Le Blanc et al., 2017): as a supplement to traditional top-down redesign approaches creating sustainable changes, as a means encouraged by organizations to motivate employees' engagement (thus attracting and retaining employees), as a means to adjust jobs to the needs of specific populations (particularly, vulnerable employees), and as a means to deal with tasks and roles that are in flux.

Existing knowledge of the different dimensions of job crafting (predictors, outcomes, and underlying processes), including individual and collaborative job crafting, is useful for identifying best practices and designing interventions and training. As a type of employee-driven job redesign behavior, job-crafting interventions and training can be combined with and complement management-driven redesign efforts. Both individual and collective approaches are needed to achieve sustainability and sustainable development (Di

Fabio, 2017a). Moreover, this in-depth knowledge of job crafting is not only useful for employees and organizations, it can also be used to design better public policies.

The literature on job-crafting interventions is still incipient, although research can also be part of more comprehensive organizational interventions. These interventions mainly include training or exercises designed to stimulate job-crafting behaviors, the use of the JD-R model, and personal development (see Tian et al., 2022). Berg et al. (2013) propose different strategies to enhance job meaning through task crafting (e.g., by emphasizing meaningful tasks – more time, energy, attention), relationship crafting (e.g., adapting existing relationships to higher-quality connections by providing help and support), and cognitive crafting (e.g., linking perceptions to meaningful personal aspects). A recent systematic review by de Devotto and Wechsler (2019) on the effects of job-crafting interventions in work environments identified only eight experimental or quasi-experimental studies published between 2007 and 2017. Of these, seven were based on the JD-R approach, whereas only one was grounded in the role-based approach. Job-crafting interventions were found to lead to an increase in at least one type of job-crafting behavior. Moreover, after said interventions, significant increases were observed in personal resources (psychological capital, openness to change, work-related basic need satisfaction, and self-efficacy), job resources (performance feedback), occupational well-being (decreased psychological distress), and job performance (adaptive performance). Inconsistencies – or, in other words, mixed significant and nonsignificant results – were found regarding job resources (opportunities for development), occupational well-being (work engagement and positive affect), and job performance (in-role performance). Nonsignificant results were obtained for other outcomes (e.g., person-job fit, leader-member exchange). De Devotto and Wechsler conclude that not all types of job crafting are equally developed through interventions. More longitudinal and long-term-effects studies will allow for greater knowledge in the future.

Since not all outcomes of job crafting are positive for the organization, supervisors, and/or colleagues, it is important to inform employees of the possible negative consequences of their behavior. As Tian et al. (2022) suggest, it is necessary to help employees craft their jobs to make them more meaningful and to meet their needs in a way that is beneficial, or at least not harmful, to others. According to Le Blanc et al. (2017), when organizations successfully avoid costly or dysfunctional job-crafting behaviors and encourage beneficial ones, employees become more adaptive to change and responsive. This, in turn, will contribute to employees' sustainable employability and the sustainability of the organization.

Conclusions

Job crafting is considered a proactive behavior whereby employees actively change the characteristics of their jobs, whether actual or perceived, to attain meaning and achieve a better person-job fit. These changes can be incremental or radical. Job crafting can occur in all types of industries and organizational sizes, and at all levels, which is what makes its study so appealing to researchers and practitioners. In the current work context, both in stable and, particularly, in changing environments, job crafting constitutes an attractive job redesign alternative that contributes to the sustainability of employees together with the organization they work for. The existence of valid and reliable measurement instruments facilitates research and helps guide intervention and training, without forgetting the importance of continuing in-depth qualitative research.

Moreover, job crafting is a good complement for other traditional top-down management-driven strategies. According to Wrzesniewski and Dutton (2001), those employees whose jobs fulfill their basic needs for control, positive self-image, and connection with others may not be motivated to become job crafters. Those employees whose jobs do not fulfill their needs, however, may seek to craft their jobs or look for opportunities to meet their needs outside of work. In either case, if there are no opportunities within the organization to make changes at work, or if the employee does not perceive them, job crafting cannot be carried out effectively. Through job crafting, organizations can strengthen their sustainability and that of their employees by creating environments conducive to healthy organizations.

References

Akkermans, J., & Tims, M. (2017). Crafting your career: How career competencies relate to career success via job crafting. *Applied Psychology*, 66(1), 168–195. https://doi.org/10.1111/apps.12082.

Alonso, C., Fernández-Salinero, S., & Topa, G. (2019). The impact of both individual and collaborative job crafting on Spanish teachers' well-being. *Education Sciences*, 9(2), 74. http://doi.org/10.3390/educsci9020074.

Bakker, A. B., Ficapal-Cusí, P., Torrent-Sellens, J., Boada-Grau, J., & Hontangas-Beltrán, P. M. (2018). The Spanish version of the job crafting scale. *Psicothema*, 30(1), 136–142. https://doi.org/10.7334/psicothema2016.293.

Bakker, A. B., Tims, M., & Derks, D. (2012). Proactive personality and job performance: The role of job crafting and work engagement. *Human Relations*, 65(10), 1359–1378. https://doi.org/10.1177/0018726712453471.

Bateman, T. S., & Crant, J. M. (1993). The proactive component of organizational behavior. *Journal of Organizational Behavior*, 14, 103–118.

Beléndez, M., Gómez, A., López, S., & Topa, G. (2018). Psychometric properties of the Spanish version of the Core Self-Evaluations Scale (CSES-SP). *Personality and Individual Differences*, 122, 195–197. http://doi.org/10.1016/j.paid.2017.10.034.

Berg, J. M., Dutton, J. E., & Wrzesniewski, A. (2013). Job crafting and meaningful work. In B. J. Dik, Z. S. Byrne, & M. F. Steger (Eds.), *Purpose and meaning in the workplace* (pp. 81–104). American Psychological Association.

Bindl, U. K., Unsworth, K. L., Gibson, C. B., & Stride, C. B. (2019). Job crafting revisited: Implications of an extended framework for active changes at work. *Journal of Applied Psychology*, 104(5), 605–628. http://doi.org/10.1037/apl0000362.

Brkich, M., Jeffs, D., & Carless, S. A. (2002). A global self-report measure of person-job fit. *European Journal of Psychological Assessment*, 18(1), 43–51. http://doi.org/10.1027//1015-5759.18.1.43.

Bruning, P. F., & Campion, M. A. (2018). A role-resource approach-avoidance model of job crafting: A multimethod integration and extension of job crafting theory. *Academy of Management Journal*, 61(2), 499–522. https://doi.org/10.5465/amj.2015.0604.

Chen, C. Y., Yen, C. H., & Tsai, F. C. (2014). Job crafting and job engagement: The mediating role of person-job fit. *International Journal of Hospitality Management*, 37, 21–28. https://doi.org/10.1016/j.ijhm.2013.10.006.

Cheng, J.-C., Chen, C. Y., Teng, H. Y., & Yen, C. H. (2016). Tour leaders' job crafting and job outcomes: The moderating role of perceived organizational support. *Tourism Management Perspectives*, 20, 19–29. https://doi.org/10.1016/j.tmp.2016.06.001.

Cheng, J.-C., & O-Yang, Y. (2018). Hotel employee job crafting, burnout, and satisfaction: The moderating role of perceived organizational support. *International Journal of Hospitality Management*, 72, 78–85. https://doi.org/10.1016/j.ijhm.2018.01.005.

Dash, S. S., & Vohra, N. (2020). Job crafting: A critical review. *South Asian Journal of Management*, 27(1), 122–149. https://www.proquest.com/scholarly-journals/job-crafting-critical-review/docview/2410492471/se-2?accountid=14609.

de Devotto, R. P., & Wechsler, S. M. (2019). Job crafting interventions: Systematic review. *Trends in Psychology*, 27(2), 371–383. https://doi.org/10.9788/TP2019.2-06.

Di Fabio, A. (2017a). The psychology of sustainability and sustainable development for well-being in organizations. *Frontiers in Psychology*, 8, 1534. https://doi.org/10.3389/fpsyg.2017.01534.

Di Fabio, A. (2017b). Positive healthy organizations: Promoting well-being, meaningfulness, and sustainability in organizations. *Frontiers in Psychology*, 8, 1938. https://doi.org/10.3389/fpsyg.2017.01938.

Di Fabio, A., & Peiró, J. M. (2018). Human capital sustainability leadership to promote sustainable development and healthy organizations: A new scale. *Sustainability*, 10(7), 2413. https://doi.org/10.3390/su10072413.

Di Fabio, A., & Rosen, M. A. (2018). Opening the black box of psychological processes in the science of sustainable development: A new frontier. *European Journal of Sustainable Development Research*, 2(4), 47. https://doi.org/10.20897/ejosdr/3933.

Di Fabio, A., & Svicher, A. (2021). The psychology of sustainability and sustainable development: Advancing decent work, inclusivity, and positive strengths-based primary preventive interventions for vulnerable workers. *Frontiers in Psychology*, 12, 2946. https://doi.org/10.3389/fpsyg.2021.718354.

Di Fabio, A., & Tsuda, A. (2018). The psychology of harmony and harmonization: Advancing the perspectives for the psychology of sustainability and sustainable development. *Sustainability*, 10(12), 4726. https://doi.org/10.3390/su10124726.

Fernández-Muñoz, J., & Topa, G. (2018). Older workers and affective job satisfaction: Gender invariance in Spain. *Frontiers in Psychology*, 9, 930. https://doi.org/10.3389/fpsyg.2018.00930.

Geldenhuys, M., Bakker, A. B., & Demerouti, E. (2021). How task, relational and cognitive crafting relate to job performance: A weekly diary study on the role of meaningfulness. *European Journal of Work and Organizational Psychology*, 30(1), 83–94. https://doi.org/10.1080/1359432X.2020.1825378.

Gemmano, C., Signore, F., Caffò, A., Palmisano, G., Bosco, A., & Manuti, A. (2020). What a difference a workplace makes. A scientometric analysis on the relationship between job crafting and healthy organizations' factors. *Electronic Journal of Applied Statistical Analysis*, 13(3), 652–681. http://doi.org/10.1285/i20705948v13n3p652.

Hallinger, P., & Suriyankietkaew, S. (2018). Science mapping of the knowledge base on sustainable leadership, 1990–2018. *Sustainability*, 10(12), 4846. http://doi.org/10.3390/su10124846.

Judge, T. A., Erez, A., Bono, J. E., & Thoresen, C. J. (2003). The core self–evaluations scale: Development of a measure. *Personnel Psychology*, 56(2), 303–331. http://doi.org/10.1111/j.1744-6570.2003.tb00152.x.

Kuijpers, E., Kooij, D. T., & van Woerkom, M. (2020). Align your job with yourself: The relationship between a job crafting intervention and work engagement, and the role of workload. *Journal of Occupational Health Psychology*, 25(1), 1–16. http://doi.org/10.1037/ocp0000175.

Laguía, A., Moriano, J. A., Molero, F., García-Ael, C., & van Dick, R. (2021). Identity leadership and work engagement in Spain: A cross-cultural adaptation of the Identity Leadership Inventory. *Universitas Psychologica*, 20, 1–13. https://doi.org/10.11144/Javeriana.upsy20.ilwe.

Lazazzara, A., Tims, M., & De Gennaro, D. (2020). The process of reinventing a job: A meta–synthesis of qualitative job crafting research. *Journal of Vocational Behavior*, 116, 103267. https://doi.org/10.1016/j.jvb.2019.01.001.

Leana, C., Appelbaum, E., & Shevchuk, I. (2009). Work process and quality of care in early childhood education: The role of job crafting. *Academy of Management Journal*, 52, 1169–1192. https://www.jstor.org/stable/40390365.

Le Blanc, P. M., Demerouti, E., & Bakker, A. B. (2017). How can I shape my job to suit me better? Job crafting for sustainable employees and organizations. In N. Chmiel, F. Fraccaroli, and M. Sverke (Eds.), *An introduction to work and organizational psychology: An international perspective* (3rd ed., pp. 48–63). Wiley Blackwell.

Lichtenthaler, P. W., & Fischbach, A. (2019). A meta-analysis on promotion-and prevention-focused job crafting. *European Journal of Work and Organizational Psychology*, 28(1), 30–50. https://doi.org/10.1080/1359432X.2018.1527767.

Llorente-Alonso, M., & Topa, G. (2019). Individual crafting, collaborative crafting, and job satisfaction: The mediator role of engagement. *Journal of Work and Organizational Psychology*, 35(3), 217–226. https://doi.org/10.5093/jwop2019a23.

Moriano, J. A., Molero, F., Laguía, A., Mikulincer, M., & Shaver, P. R. (2021). Security providing leadership: A job resource to prevent employees' burnout. *International Journal of Environmental Research and Public Health*, 18(23), 12551. https://doi.org/10.3390/ijerph182312551.

Nielsen, K., & Abildgaard, J. S. (2012). The development and validation of a job crafting measure for use with blue-collar workers. *Work & Stress*, 26(4), 365–384. https://doi.org/10.1080/02678373.2012.733543.

Nielsen, K., & Miraglia, M. (2017). What works for whom in which circumstances? On the need to move beyond the "what works?" question in organizational intervention research. *Human Relations*, 70(1), 40–62. https://doi.org/10.1177/0018726716670226.

Park, S., & Park, S. (2023). Contextual antecedents of job crafting: Review and future research agenda. *European Journal of Training and Development*, 42(1/2), 141–155. https://doi.org/10.1108/EJTD-06-2021-0071.

Petrou, P., Demerouti, E., Peeters, M. C., Schaufeli, W. B., & Hetland, J. (2012). Crafting a job on a daily basis: Contextual correlates and the link to work engagement. *Journal of Organizational Behavior*, 33(8), 1120–1141. https://doi.org/10.1002/job.1783.

Ringle, C., Wende, S., & Becker, J. (2015). *SmartPLS* 3 [Computer software]. https://www.smartpls.com.

Robledo, E., Zappalà, S., & Topa, G. (2019). Job crafting as a mediator between work engagement and wellbeing outcomes: A time-lagged study. *International Journal of Environmental Research and Public Health*, 16(8), 1376. http://doi.org/10.3390/ijerph16081376.

Rudolph, C. W., Katz, I. M., Lavigne, K. N., & Zacher, H. (2017). Job crafting: A meta-analysis of relationships with individual differences, job characteristics, and work outcomes. *Journal of Vocational Behavior*, 102, 112–138. https://doi.org/10.1016/j.jvb.2017.05.008.

Schaufeli, W. B., Leiter, M. P., Maslach, C., & Jackson, S. E. (1996). The Maslach Burnout Inventory – General survey. In C. Maslach, S. E. Jackson, & M. P. Leiter (Eds.), *Maslach Burnout Inventory* (pp. 19–26). Consulting Psychologists Press.

Slemp, G. R., & Vella-Brodrick, D. A. (2013). The job crafting questionnaire: A new scale to measure the extent to which employees engage in job crafting. *International Journal of Wellbeing*, 3(2), 126–146. https://doi.org/10.5502/ijw.v3i2.1.

Svicher, A., & Di Fabio, A. (2021). Job crafting: A challenge to promoting decent work for vulnerable workers. *Frontiers in Psychology*, 12, 1827. https://doi.org/10.3389/fpsyg.2021.681022.

Tian, X., Liu, M., Jiao, Q., Wei, X., & Huang, R. (2022). Job crafting: A review of theoretical integration and application extension. *Journal of Human Resource Management*, 10(2), 38–48. http://doi.org/10.11648/j.jhrm.20221002.11.

Tims, M., & Bakker, A. B. (2010). Job crafting: Towards a new model of individual job redesign. *SA Journal of Industrial Psychology*, 36(2), 841. https://doi.org/10.4102/sajip.v36i2.841.

Tims, M., Bakker, A. B., & Derks, D. (2012). Development and validation of the job crafting scale. *Journal of Vocational Behavior*, 80(1), 173–186. http://doi.org/10.1016/j.jvb.2011.05.009.

Tims, M., Twemlow, M., & Fong, C. Y. M. (2022). A state-of-the-art overview of job-crafting research: Current trends and future research directions. *Career Development International*, 27(1), 54–78. http://doi.org/10.1108/CDI-08-2021-0216.

Topa, G., & Aranda-Carmena, M. (2022a). Job crafting in nursing: Mediation between work engagement and job performance in a multisample study. *International Journal of Environmental Research and Public Health*, 19(19), 12711. https://doi.org/10.3390/ijerph191912711.

Topa, G., & Aranda-Carmena, M. (2022b). It is better for younger workers: The gain cycle between job crafting and work engagement. *International Journal of Environmental Research and Public Health*, 19(21), 14378. https://doi.org/10.3390/ijerph192114378.

Topa, G., & Morales Domínguez, F. (2006). Identificación organizacional y proactividad personal en grupos de trabajo: un modelo de ecuaciones estructurales. *Anales de Psicología/Annals of Psychology*, 22(2), 234–242.

Wang, H., Li, P., & Chen, S. (2020). The impact of social factors on job crafting: A meta-analysis and review. *International Journal of Environmental Research and Public Health*, 17(21), 8016. http://doi.org/10.3390/ijerph17218016.

Wang, H. J., Demerouti, E., & Bakker, A. B. (2017). A review of job crafting research: The role of leader behaviors in cultivating successful job crafters. In S. K. Parker & U. K. Bindl (Eds.), *Proactivity at work: Making things happen in organizations* (pp. 77–104). Routledge.

Wang, Q. (2022). Research on job crafting from the perspective of sustainable career: Motivation, paths and intervention mechanisms. *Advances in Psychological Science*, 30(3), 499. https://doi.org/10.3724/SP.J.1042.2022.00499.

Weseler, D., & Niessen, C. (2016). How job crafting relates to task performance. *Journal of Managerial Psychology*, 31(3), 672–685. https://doi.org/10.1108/JMP-09-2014-0269.

Wrzesniewski, A., & Dutton, J. E. (2001). Crafting a job: Revisioning employees as active crafters of their work. *Academy of Management Review*, 26(2), 179–201. https://doi.org/10.2307/259118.

Zhang, F., & Parker, S. K. (2019). Reorienting job crafting research: A hierarchical structure of job crafting concepts and integrative review. *Journal of Organizational Behavior*, 40(2), 126–146. https://doi.org/10.1002/job.2332.

Index

Page numbers in **bold** refer to figures, page numbers in *italic* refer to tables.

Printed in the United States
by Baker & Taylor Publisher Services